Japan
& China
In East Asian
Integration

The **Institute of Southeast Asian Studies (ISEAS)** was established as an autonomous organization in 1968. It is a regional centre dedicated to the study of socio-political, security and economic trends and developments in Southeast Asia and its wider geostrategic and economic environment. The Institute's research programmes are the Regional Economic Studies (RES, including ASEAN and APEC), Regional Strategic and Political Studies (RSPS), and Regional Social and Cultural Studies (RSCS).

ISEAS Publishing, an established academic press, has issued almost 2,000 books and journals. It is the largest scholarly publisher of research about Southeast Asia from within the region. ISEAS Publishing works with many other academic and trade publishers and distributors to disseminate important research and analyses from and about Southeast Asia to the rest of the world.

Japan
& China

In East Asian Integration

LIM HUA SING

ISEAS

INSTITUTE OF SOUTHEAST ASIAN STUDIES

Singapore

Fifth edition published in Singapore in 2008 by
Institute of Southeast Asian Studies
30 Heng Mui Keng Terrace
Pasir Panjang
Singapore 119614

E-mail: publish@iseas.edu.sg
Website: <http://bookshop.iseas.edu.sg>

First edition 1995 (Times Academic Press)

*The responsibility for facts and opinions in this publication rests exclusively with the author
and his interpretations do not necessarily reflect the views or the policy of the publisher or its
supporters.*

ISEAS Library Cataloguing-in-Publication Data

Lim Hua Sing.
    Japan and China in East Asian integration.
    (Japan and the Asia-Pacific)
1. Asian cooperation.
2. Asia—Foreign economic relations—Japan.
3. Japan—Foreign economic relations—Asia.
4. Japan—Foreign economic relation—China.
5. China—Foreign economic relations—Japan.
6. China—Foreign economic relations—Asia.
7. Asia—Foreign economic relations—China.
8. ASEAN.
9. Financial crises—Asia.
I. Title
II. Series
HF1583 Z4J3L73   2008

ISBN 978-981-230-744-6 (soft cover)
ISBN 978-981-230-748-4 (PDF)

Typeset by Superskill Graphics Pte Ltd
Printed in Singapore by Seng Lee Press Pte Ltd

This book is dedicated to my parents,
Lim Chong Leng and Yap Ah Chuan

Contents

ABOUT THE AUTHOR

Lim Hua Sing, PhD, is Professor at the Institute of Asia-Pacific Studies and the Graduate School of Asia-Pacific Studies at Waseda University, Tokyo, Japan. He is also Director of the Institute of Chinese Economies, Waseda University. He has published extensively in the fields of Asian and Japanese economics, the modern economic history of Japan, and Japan-Asian as well as China-Asian economic relations, which are his special interests. Recently, he has also paid attention to the economic development in China, ethnic Chinese economies and China-ethnic Chinese economic relations in Asia.

List of Tables

List of Charts

Abbreviations

AA	Asia-Africa Linguistic Institute
AFTA	ASEAN Free Trade Area
AICO	ASEAN Industrial Cooperation Scheme
AIDS	acquired immunodeficiency syndrome
AMF	Asian Monetary Fund
APEC	Asia Pacific Economic Cooperation
ASEAN	Association of Southeast Asian Nations
CAFTA	China-ASEAN Free Trade Area
CEC	Chinese Economic Community
CEPT	Common Effective Preferential Tariffs
CER	Closer Economic Relations
CIS	Commonwealth of Independent States
CPF	Central Provident Fund
DAC	Development Assistance Committee (of OECD)
EA	East Asia
EAEC	East Asian Economic Caucus
EAEC	East Asian Economic Circle
EAEC	East Asian Economic Community
EAEG	East Asian Economic Grouping
EAEI	East Asian Economic Integration
EAMF	East Asian Monetary Fund
EC	European Community
ECEC	Ethnic Chinese Economic Community
EDB	Economic Development Board
EPA	Economic Partnership Agreement
EU	European Union (as of 1 November 1993)

FDI	Foreign Direct Investment
FTA	Free Trade Agreement
	Free Trade Area
FTAAP	Free Trade Agreement of the Asia Pacific
FTAs	Free Trade Agreements
FMP	Fourth Malaysia Plan
GATT	General Agreement on Tariffs and Trade
GDP	gross domestic product
GNP	Gross National Product
GPS	Global Positioning System
GSP	Generalized Scheme of Preferences
HICOM	Heavy Industries Corporation
IAFTA	India-ASEAN Free Trade Agreement
IDE	Institute of Developing Economies
IDEA	the Initiative for the Development in East Asia
IMF	International Monetary Fund
JAFTA	Japan-ASEAN Free Trade Agreement
JCCI	Japanese Chamber of Commerce and Industry
JE	Japan Embassy
JETRO	Japanese External Trade Organization
JICA	Japan International Co-operation Agency
JIS	Japanese Industry Standard
JOFTA	Japan-Oceania Free Trade Agreement
JSE	Japan Singapore Association
JSEPA	Japan-Singapore Economic Partnership Agreement
JTC	Japan Trade Centre
KAFTA	Korea-ASEAN Free Trade Agreement
LDP	Liberal Democratic Party
M&A	merger and acquisition
MD	Missile Defense
MIPRO	Manufacturers Import Promotion Organization
MITI	Ministry of International Trade and Industry
MNCs	Multinational Corporations
MSC	Multimedia Super Corridor
NAFTA	North America Free Trade Area
NAFTA	North America Free Trade Agreement

NIEs	Newly Industrializing Economies
NGO	Non-governmental Organization
NPB	National Productivity Board
NTB	non-tariff barrier
NTUC	National Trades Union Congress
NWC	National Wages Council
ODA	Official Development Assistance
OECD	Organization for Economic Cooperation and Development
OEM	Original Equipment Manufacturing
OPEC	Organization of Petroleum Exporting Countries
PAS	Parti Islam
PNOC	Philippine National Oil Company
R&D	research and development
ROC	Registrar of Companies
SCCCI	Singapore Chinese Chamber of Commerce and Industry
SFCCI	Singapore Federation of Chambers of Commerce and Industry
SIJORI	Growth Triangle (Singapore-Johor-Riau Growth Triangle)
SISIR	Singapore Institute of Standards and Industrial Research
SJEZ	Sea of Japan Economic Zone
SMA	Singapore Manufacturers' Association
SMB	small and medium-sized businesses
SPC	Singapore Petroleum Company
TDB	Trade Development Board
UNCTAD	United Nations Conference on Trade and Development
UK	United Kingdom
US	United States of America
WB	The World Bank
WTO	World Trade Organization

Acknowledgements

The author is grateful to Professor Okushima Takayasu, former President of Waseda University, Professor Shiraishi Katsuhiko, current President of Waseda University and Professor Enatsu Ken'ichi, Vice-President of Waseda University. To friends and colleagues of the Graduate School of Asia-Pacific Studies, Professors Nishikawa Jun, Taniguchi Makoto, Goto Ken'ichi, Nakane Jin'ichiro and Takahashi Teruo. Acknowledgement also goes to Professor Tsuru Shigeto (former President of Hitotsubashi University, Japan), Professor Nagahara Keiji (Emeritius Professor of Hitotsubashi University, Japan), Professor Huang Chihlien (Chairman of Hong Kong Society of Asia & Pacific 21), Professor Pang Jin Ju (Vice-President of Nankai University, China), Professor He Fang Chuan (former Vice-President of Beijing University, China), Dr. Harold H.C. Han (Chairman of Himalaya Foundation, Taiwan), Professor Ian Brown (London University, UK), Professor Chew Soon Beng (Nanyang Technological University, Singapore) and Professor Hans Blomqvist (Swedish School of Economics and Business Administration, Finland). To Professors Kojima Rei'itsu and Uchida Tomoyuki (both from Daito Bunka University, Japan), Mr. Eric Loewe (Executive Director, Ouachita Enterprise Community, USA) and Mr. Anthony Thomas (Managing Editor, Times Media (Academic Publishing)) for displaying an interest in and extending moral support to the author's work.

On a personal level, the author wishes to thank his parents for their enthusiastic support, and to his wife, Shuat Chiu and his three children, Hong Jing, Hong Yi and Ting Hui, for their understanding, co-operation and cheerful support. Without the foregoing, this 4th edition would not have been published.

June 2003

Preface to the Fifth Edition

Asia is Moving Towards Closer Economic Cooperation and Integration

Since the Asian financial crisis erupted in 1997, most of the affected countries in Asia have, to some degree, miraculously recovered from the hard-hitting crisis within a year or two. Asia, as a dynamic region, has once again attracted the world's attention. Over the last few years, economic cooperation and integration have been further promoted and stimulated in the region through the signing of Free Trade Agreements (FTAs) and Economic Partnership Agreements (EPAs) among the Asian countries. The Newly Industrializing Economies (NIEs) and the Association of Southeast Asian Nations (ASEAN), together with China and India, have succeeded in a promising and sustainable economic development path. This is despite the fact that some countries, such as Thailand and Myanmar and to a lesser extent Indonesia and the Philippines, have encountered some form of social and political instabilities, which has somehow adversely affected the economic performances of these countries. Certainly, these instabilities have affected but not prevented the Asian countries from moving forward towards economic development. Asia has again, by and large, become the centre of economic development in the world.

Japan and China in Asia

Japan is a highly regulated, rigid and systematic society without much flexibility and tolerance. Japanese prefer thorough and long-term results when they conduct political, economic and social changes. It may be one of the reasons to explain why Japan takes a longer time to conduct structural reforms. Japan has to-date not completely recovered from the implosion of the bubble economy starting 1991. It has however, over the last 16 years, conducted numerous reforms (political, economic, industrial, social and structural) with eagerness and seriousness. It is said that once Japan has returned to the right developmental tracks, economic development will be fast and impressive, compared to most of the other Western nations. Besides, economic fundamentals in Japan have been sound and have not worsened much over the last one-and-a-half decades. In the long run, however, the ageing and decreasing population problems, the reluctance of taking foreign professionals, huge fiscal deficits, and the closed agricultural and fishery market issues, will either leave Japan out from the rest of Asia, or cause Japan to develop without substance.

China, on the other hand, has developed rapidly and consistently over the last 29 years. She has become a regional as well as an international power. Within the next few decades, China will likely, together with the United States, become one of the two megapowers in the world. China, of course, is not without its difficulties. Commonly cited problems include environmental pollution, income disparity, corruption, uneven development between rural and coastal areas etc. These difficulties are likely to be solved gradually together with economic development, as the central government has implemented forceful policies to tackle them.

It is said that China's economic development is lagging behind Japan's, in terms of per capita GDP, by at least forty to fifty years. China's present economic developmental level is about that of Japan's in the 1960s or late 1950s. However, the pace of China's economic development has been much faster than that of Japan. It is possible for China to catch up with Japan and the Western nations in a shorter period. At present, as the largest developing country, China's foreign currency reserves have reached US\$1 trillion 66.3 billion (2006) and is ranked the number one country in the world. Foreign direct investments and international trade surpluses (US\$177.5 billion in 2006), together with the inflow of billions of "hot-money" due to the expectation of the appreciation of the Renminbi, have contributed to China's impressive domestic savings and capital formation. The speedy accumulation of capital and savings in Chinese banks and in central government treasury has annoyed even the Government as to how to utilize the funds for economic development purposes. Some of the measures, for instance, to increase social and industrial infrastructure spending, to increase foreign investments and foreign aids, to increase investments in education, to assist and nurture domestic small and medium-sized enterprises, and to improve and upgrade welfare system etc., have to be taken vigorously. By doing so, it will help China upgrade its economic level and international status, and to get rid of her developing country status and at a faster pace, to become one of the newly industrializing countries (NIEs).

As an NIE, China will then, together with Japan, play a bigger role in East Asian economic cooperation and integration advancement.

From ASEAN 10+3 to ASEAN 10+3+3

China, together with Malaysia under the Mahathir administration, and to a lesser extent, Korea, were strong advocates of the ASEAN 10+3 grouping towards East Asian economic cooperation and integration. On the other hand, Japan was a strong advocate of ASEAN 10+3+3 or even ASEAN 10+3+3+1, as shown in previous Prime Minister Koizumi Zunichiro's speech on the concept of "Comprehensive Economic Partnership" in Singapore in January 2002. When Dr. Mahathir proposed the concept of East Asian Economic Community (EAEC, later changed to East Asian Economic Caucus) in December 1990, obviously the countries involved were limited to ASEAN 10+3. Together with the United States, Oceania (Australia and New Zealand) was also excluded from the grouping, but the status of India was then not specifically mentioned. It seemed that the members of EAEC did not exclude India. In other words, Dr. Mahathir's EAEC concept did not have any intention to exclude India from the beginning. In that case, members of EAEC would have been ASEAN 10+3+1 (India).

In December 2005, the first East Asian Summit Meeting in Malaysia eventually agreed with the concept of ASEAN 10+3+3, despite some disagreements from the member countries. Russia was also invited to the meeting since it is a big power in Asia Pacific and also a resource rich country. Presently, East Asian economic integration has moved towards ASEAN 10+3+3, and the status of Pakistan and Bangladesh will sooner or later be put on the discussion table during the subsequent East Asian Summit Meetings. Maybe, at a later stage, some more island countries in the Pacific may wish to apply for membership. Will the EAEC then not become an entity even bigger than APEC?

The second East Asian Summit Meeting was held in the Philippines in January 2007. The ASEAN 10+3 summit meeting was held only one day before the ASEAN 10+3+3 summit meeting. Did it imply anything substantial and crucial? Did it mean the former was the core entity of the latter? Or the latter must be accomplished on the foundation of the former? Was it a temporary arrangement or was it going to be a permanent setting? So far, it has remained uncertain.

The Meaning of ASEAN 10+3+3+1 and FTAAP

The President of the United States, Mr. George Bush, had suggested the idea of FTAAP (Free Trade Agreement of the Asia Pacific), just before the APEC meeting which was held in Vietnam in November 2006. No country opposed the idea openly or officially, although some countries were skeptical and suspicious about the US's motive behind the idea. The APEC meeting in Vietnam did not discuss the idea at the meeting but had however taken the idea seriously, and it is likely that the next APEC meeting in Australia at the end of this year, will discuss the issue seriously in USA's favour.

The United States had been left out from the concept of the EAEC from the beginning, as early as in 1990. Over the last 17 years, the USA has been concerned about the development of regional cooperation and integration in the Asia Pacific region. She has so far signed or is in the process of signing FTAs with some of the Asian countries. However, unlike the China–ASEAN FTA (CAFTA), the India–ASEAN FTA (IAFTA), the Japan–ASEAN FTA (JAFTA) and the Korea–ASEAN FTA (KAFTA), the USA has not signed an FTA with the ASEAN10 as a group. Moreover, besides APEC, of which the USA has been playing a leading role, the USA does not have any formal economic relationship with the Asia Pacific region as a group. It has therefore been a main concern of the policy-makers in the USA to link with the Asia Pacific region as a group. The idea of the FTAAP has just reflected the USA's long-term concern.

East Asian Economic Community Has Become Unpredictable

The evolution of EAEC — ASEAN 10+3 — ASEAN 10+3+3 — ASEAN 10+3+3+1

(FTAAP) has been a long process. Throughout this process, despite so many negotiations, disagreements and conflict of interests, East Asian countries have signed numerous FTAs or EPAs bilaterally and multilaterally, and economic cooperation and integration have been pushed forward steadily. The new framework of ASEAN 10+3+3, however, has created a new challenge to the region. It was against the wishes of China and Malaysia, but reflected the strong wish and intention of Japan. How the three new members, namely India, Australia and New Zealand, play a constructive role towards East Asian economic integration will remain one of our main concerns. Is it necessary for the new three, India in particular, to be manipulated politically to counter balance or to dilute the increasing influence of China? As an international strategy, do the USA and Japan really need to make use of the new three to counterbalance China?

When it comes to the concept of the FTAAP, the situation in the Asia Pacific region has already become more complex. The FTAAP is no more than APEC. Is FTAAP an institutionalized and functional APEC? How can the FTAAP develop in parallel with APEC? Should the FTAAP replace APEC in the end? These are some questions which are not easy to answer now.

In any case, the fact is that East Asian economic cooperation and integration have become more complex. If the APEC members at the 2007 APEC summit meeting in Australia agree with the FTAAP, the USA, judging from her political and economic powers, will be playing an increasingly more important role in the East Asian economic integration process. Would not the USA's interest contradict with the interests of China, Japan, Korea and India? Will the America–ASEAN FTA develop with the Four ASEAN 10+1? These are some questions to be faced by countries in the Asia Pacific region, once the idea of the FTAAP has been accepted by the APEC meeting in Australia.

This is a new book based on "Japan's Role in Asia — Mutual Development or Ruthless Competition" (4th Edition), published by Eastern Universities Press, Singapore, 2003. In this new book, "Part 8 Japan and China in Asia-Pacific" has been added. Under Part 8, nine new articles are included to analyse the current economic development of the Asia-Pacific region. Special attention is particularly paid to the domestic economic development of Japan, China and India. Besides, analyses on the politico-economic relationship between Japan and China, and a comparison of economic strengths between China and India in East Asian economic integration, are examined. Finally, an overall analysis on East Asian economic integration, including some observations on the recent development and future prospects of the region, are provided.

In carrying out country research, attending international conferences and collecting data for writing these articles, the author is grateful for the generous financial support of the Ting Hsin International Group, without which this new book would not have been completed and published.

Lim Hua Sing
Waseda University
Tokyo, Japan

26 September 2007

Preface to the Fourth Edition

Forceful measures have not been taken despite favourable economic fundamentals

Japan's economic role in the world and Asia in particular, has been diminishing since the collapse of the bubble economy in 1991. Over the last 12 years, the Japanese economy has not managed to recover and her contribution to Asia (in terms of foreign direct investment, international trade, Official Development Assistance and technology transfer) is becoming less and less important.

Needless to say, the Japanese and Asian economies are interdependent as well as complementary. Japan can contribute more to Asia only when she has recovered economically. Similarly, Japan can benefit more from Asia only when Asia's economic development is on the right track. On Japan's side, despite a long period of economic sluggishness, some economic strengths have surprisingly remained unchanged. Japan is considered as number one in the following categories.

First, foreign currency reserves have amounted to US$485.3 billion as of March 2003 (China ranks second in the world with US$212.2 billion in year 2001). It is due in large part to Japan's international trade drive and more recently, the government's currency interference through selling Japanese yen in exchange for the greenback, in order to fulfill a weak yen policy.

Second, Japan's total net overseas assets amount to 133 trillion yen as of December 2000. Overseas assets held by Japanese banking corporations alone have amounted to 45 trillion yen as of December 2002. It indicates that Japan has accumulated a substantial amount of long term overseas capital investments as well as foreign national bonds and equities, especially in the United States.

Third, Japan's ODA during the 1991–2001 period was the largest among the DAC countries. It became the second largest since 2002 but still accounted for US$9.7 billion (1 trillion 250 billion yen) in May 2002. The ODA budget reflects the economic strengths of a country and it has also been used to stimulate the advancement of a country's foreign business activities.

Fourth, Japanese national assets (cash, deposits, bonds, investment securities, shares, insurance and pension) amounted to 1386 trillion yen by March 2001. It reached 8275 trillion yen in December 2002, if real estate and buildings are included. The main task of the Japanese government now is to mobilize these national assets in order to expand the domestic market and to activate the economy.

Besides these economic strengths, both big and medium-small sized Japanese enterprises have accumulated world-class technologies, which guarantee Japan's industrial development despite the economic recession. Furthermore, the economic downturn over the last 12 years has created a 5.6% unemployment rate in Japan, which is still rather healthy compared to the double digits we see in some European countries. And this is the reason why Japan is not in a chaotic situation.

Very few people could have predicted that Japan's economic downturn would drag on for 12 years, with no sign of recovery. Many Japan watchers are puzzled and cannot pinpoint what exactly is wrong with the Japanese economy. Policy-makers in Japan have so far managed to identify some basic ailments of the Japanese economy: non-performing loans, deregulation, deflation, strong Japanese currency and privatization etc. However, forceful measures still need to be taken to counteract these problems and fulfill economic goals.

Asia sees Japan's economic deterioration as a burden to Asian economic development. Now, Asia is expecting Japan to emerge from the economic doldrums, hopefully in 2–3 years time, and contribute to Asia's economic development in accordance with her economic strengths.

Can Japan's Role be Replaced by China?

China has been Japan's rival in Asia, in the economic, political, military and diplomatic arena. China's role in Asia, even if we restrict it to the economic front, has been increasing and to a certain extent, has replaced Japan. In the long run, China's role will become significantly more important at the expense of Japan.

Over the last 25 years, since she started implementing a 'reforms and open-door policy' in 1978, China has become the first country in the world to succeed in rapid and continuous economic development. Economic development in special economic zones and coastal areas has been particularly remarkable. The per capita GNP of Guangzhou, Shenzhen, Shanghai and Beijing have already exceeded most of the developing countries in Asia. As a developing country with a 1.3 billion population, China's economic development will continue to attract much attention.

However, together with economic development, China has encountered many serious problems — a drastic increase in income disparity between coastal and rural areas (in the year 2002, the ratio was 6:1), unemployment, expanding social gap between the poor and the rich, the 3Cs (corruption, collusion and cronyism), environmental pollution, non-performing loans and the privatization of state enterprises etc. Of course, it is unrealistic to expect China to have rapid economic development for such a long period without experiencing some serious economic distortions. The issue is whether China can solve these problems efficiently before they deteriorate farther to create political, economic and social instabilities in the country.

At current levels, the rate of economic development in China is said to be about that of Japan in the 1960s. In other words, if we assume that Japan's economy is standing still, China will have to develop for another forty years to reach Japan's present standard. China's per capita GNP is US$854 (year 2000) compared to US$32,585 (year 2001) of Japan. The former is merely 2.6% of the latter.

China has become a "factory of the world". Chinese manufacturing goods have penetrated into international markets and Japan, together with the Western nations, have considered China as an economic threat. However, China's economic strengths should not be over exaggerated. Over the last two-and-a-half decades, how much technology has been accumulated by Chinese enterprises in China? How many local enterprises have been nurtured to become big enterprises or multinational corporations? How many local enterprises in China are run based on world level managerial practices? In other words, China's economic development has been relying heavily on foreign direct investment, technology and managerial know-how.

Also, some critics claim that China's legal system has not been developed to match domestic economic development processes, nor serve a highly developing nation such as China.

China still has a long way to go. The GDPs of China, Japan and the USA are US$1.08 trillion (year 2000), US$4.14 trillion (year 2001) and

US$8.35 trillion (year 1999) respectively. The ratios are 1: 3.8: 7.7. China pledges to increase her GDP to around US$5 trillion in twenty years, as is the Japanese standard today. Obviously, it is a very difficult task for China, but the Chinese people seem to have the confidence to fulfill it.

Some China watchers have even warned that the present bubble economy would burst sooner or later. They also claim that the "socialist market economy" (politically, it is a centrally controlled socialist system but economically, it is a western way of free competition capitalist economy) would not last very long. However, as the Chinese like to say, China has pledged to develop her economy with Chinese socialist characteristics.

Frankly, I am also rather optimistic about China's economic development. Despite various economic distortions and contradictory economic development strategies, by the year 2008 when China hosts the Olympic Games, and by the year 2010 when China holds the World Exhibitions, China would by all means be able to develop without drastic setbacks. Even after the year 2010, say for another farther 10–15 years, it is unlikely that economic development in China will have major retrogressions caused by serious macro-economic mismanagement. In China, the following factors are contributory reasons to economic development: approximately 900 million peasants are potential industrial labourers, cheap agricultural and industrial raw materials, big domestic market with a 1.3 billion population of which the middle class population has been increasing rapidly, political and social stability, and a mechanism set in place to proceed with economic reforms and an open-door policy.

Regional Economic Integration is An Engine for Asian Economic Development Japan and China are two important players in Asia, a declining player and an emerging player (although Korea can be considered as a recovering player with economic potential). Other than the USA and the EU, Japan and China have had the most profound influence in Asia.

ASEAN 10 is a well-organized entity to which Japan and China have established increasingly important cooperation links with. In November 2001, China proposed the concept of a FTA (Free Trade Area) with ASEAN to be set up within 10 years. This concept, termed as CAFTA (China-ASEAN Free Trade Area) or ASEAN 10-plus-1, is being materialized faster than expected. Meetings and feasibility negotiations at governmental levels have been carried out frequently to expedite the process of regional economic cooperation and integration.

On the other hand, stimulated by China's initiative, Japan has also proposed "comprehensive economic cooperation" with ASEAN in January

2002. This proposal was later termed as JAFTA (Japan-ASEAN Free Trade Agreement) or another ASEAN 10-plus-1. At the beginning, it was criticized as being without a definitive timeframe. How long was it going to take to set up? But recent sources indicate that Japan intends to realize the JAFTA within a period, which is even shorter than that of China.

Obviously, economic cooperation and integration endeavors in Asia are basically prompted by two factors. First, the formation of the EU and the NAFTA, with strong exclusive undertones, has restricted economic growth and cooperation of the Asian countries with these 2 blocs. Hence, the need exists to setup their own trading entities. Second, economic development within Asia has necessitated intra-Asia regional economic cooperation and integration, with an eye to expand into each other's trading markets.

With the initiatives of China and Japan, and most probably Korea in future, economic cooperation and integration among the Asian countries will be strengthened. Although China and Japan are rivals, they need to work closely for the benefit of Asia's economic development and infra-regional integration. Both CAFTA and JAFTA should be promoted accordingly, and eventually ASEAN 10-plus-3 (China, Japan and Korea) should be materialized under the concept of a pan-Asia regional economic integration outfit.

As an important economic power, it is hoped that Japan will move to implement economic policies more resolutely and consistently, in order to recover from her current economic downturn as quickly as possible, before its leading role in Asia is overtaken by China.

Lim Hua Sing
Waseda University
Tokyo, Japan

June 2003

Preface to the Third Edition

Japan is at the crossroads of Asia. She is expected to contribute more towards Asia's economic revitalization and development, but encounters two problems. One, the Japanese economy has not bottomed out since the collapse of the bubble economy in 1991. The prolonged stagnant economy of Japan Inc. has forced her to pay more attention to domestic issues, such as deregulation, opening up of the domestic market, Big Bang programs and industrial restructuring etc. All these policies and measures are aimed at resuscitating Japanese economy but have so far not reaped any concrete results.

Two, Japan's role and initiatives in Asia have always been suspect and questioned by the Asian countries, especially by China and the two Koreas. Japan's military expansions in Asia in the 1930s and 1940s, together with her non-thorough 'war liquidation' after World War II, have always created suspicions about her motives and intentions in Asia. Japan should act collectively rather than individually, should she want to play a more active and positive role in Asia. In principal, Japan should invite China and Korea, and cooperate closely with the ASEANF 10, to find ways and solutions for Asia to achieve a stable and conducive environment for better economic development.

The economic relationship between Japan and Asia is supplementary as well as complementary. In retrospect, the stagnant economy of Japan during the 1991–1996 period can be considered as one of the important factors contributing to the Asian financial crisis. Japan's Foreign Direct Investment (FDI) in Asia decreased, exports from Asia to Japan diminished and the strong Japanese currency left Asia with highly indebted countries. All these have affected Asia's overall economic performance and have eventually led to the eruption of the Asian financial crisis. On the other hand, during the 1985–1990 period of the bubble economy, Japan invested heavily in Asia and Asia's exports to Japan as well as to other international markets recorded phenomenal growth. The Japanese government, banking corporations and industrial enterprises extended substantial capital and loans to Asia. When the Asian countries suffered from crippling bad debts during the Asian financial crisis period, Japan suffered the most among the creditor nations. Japan will continue to suffer if the bad debt issues among the Asian countries cannot be resolved. In fact, these bad debt issues have not been resolved for many years. Needless to say, Japan will feel the impact if the debtor countries push for debt write-offs in place of good faith. One of the aims of the New Miyazawa Plan is designed to help the Asian countries settle their bad debts.

In the meantime, there is a consensus that economic cooperation among the Asian countries should be strengthened. One point in mind is to implement the New Miyazawa Plan, leading to the setting up of the Asian Monetary Fund (AMF). China and Korea had reservations about this but have become more supportive in recent months. Japan should not move as a distinct entity but should invite China and Korea to participate more actively. At the same time, close cooperation from the ASEAN 10 is also critical. In this way, Japan is expected to assist the Asian countries to recover from the Asian financial crisis and to revitalize and move forward to rapid economic development in the 21st century.

Lim Hua Sing
Waseda University
Tokyo, Japan

September 2000

Preface to the Second Edition

For about two months before Lee Teng Hui made the sudden "state-to-state" announcement on 9 July 1999, most of the countries in the Asia-Pacific region had started experiencing some kind of economic recovery from the recent crisis. With relatively stable currency exchange rates installed, stock and property markets improved, foreign currency reserves increased and confidence in market economy was restored — almost two years after the Asian financial crisis erupted on 2 July 1997.

On analysis, Asian countries used various policies to tackle the financial crisis. These countries can be divided into three groups. The first group, such as Korea and Thailand, resorted to the prescription proposed by the International Monetary Fund (IMF): deflationary fiscal policies, higher interest rates and thorough industrial restructuring. The second group, such as Malaysia and China (including Taiwan and Hong Kong), refused the IMF prescription and undertook expansionary fiscal policies, lower interest rates, gradual industrial restructuring and foreign exchange and capital controls. The third group, for example Indonesia, rejected the IMF prescription initially but later adopted it. The present situation in Indonesia is rather unpredictable, as the country has just held its general elections and the ruling Golkar party (which has governed Indonesia for 34 years), as generally predicted, lost ground to opposition parties. Both political and economic development in Indonesia have remained unstable, as the president in the country has yet to be elected and the country's overall reconstruction has yet to be carried out smoothly and speedily.

Incidentally, the Asian stock markets picked up again, soon after Lee Teng Hui made his "state-to-state" statement on 9 July. Taiwan's stock market dropped but experienced some recovery when the central bank in Taiwan interfered. The Asian stock markets have not been further jeopardized as the US, the EU, Japan and ASEAN 10 were quick to reconfirm their "One-China" policy. The cross-strait relations are tense, but at the present time, Taiwan is totally isolated. Pressures from the People's Republic of China (PRC) on Taiwan have been increasing but it is unlikely that the PRC will unify Taiwan by military means in the near future. The PRC prefers peaceful reunification as long as Taiwan does not proclaim "independence".

After 21 years of rapid economic development since it first implemented the open-door policy in 1978, China requires a peaceful environment in the Asia-Pacific region to ensure the success of its "socialist market economy". Besides, under such a severe economic environment in Asia, China has had her hands fall tackling the following problems: diminishing foreign direct investment, decreasing international trade surpluses, restructuring state enterprises, rapid increase of the unemployment rate, income disparity, developmental gap between coastal and inland areas, worsening deflationary tendency and so forth. China has to solve these problems speedily and recover the 7–8% economic growth rate this year before its unemployment issues worsen. In the meantime, China not only has to strengthen its economic relationship with the West (in terms of expanding international trade and luring foreign direct investment and technology), but also with her neighbouring countries in Asia, particularly those with a significant overseas Chinese presence. Chinese economic communities in Asia will, in the long run, make a notable impact on China's economic development in terms of capital, technology and managerial know-how.

It is fair to say that China can claim to be a stabiliser since the financial crisis erupted on 2 July 1997. On many occasions, China was under great pressure to surrender to Renminbi depreciation but managed to maintain a considerably stable exchange rate level with the US dollar throughout the period of the Asian economic crisis. China has, therefore, contributed greatly both to the stability of the Asian currencies and to the recovery of the Asian economies.

Obviously, China is a big player in the Asia-Pacific arena. However, Japan's economic impact and influence on Asia should, without doubt, be considered with special attention. Japan's role in Asia should be properly assessed, both as an economic superpower and the world's second largest economy. As early as in September 1985, due to the phenomenal appreciation of the Japanese currency, Japanese companies started investing heavily in Asia, and this greatly stimulated economic development of the Asian countries. Both the supply and demand sides among the industries in

Asia were prompted by Japanese heavy investment, which had undoubtedly contributed to the creation of the Asian "economic miracle".

However, the bubble economy in Japan burst in early 1991. Despite efforts (such as deregulation, opening up of domestic markets, financial restructuring, economic stimulus and rescue packages) made by Japan over the period 1991 till today, the Japanese economy has so far not shown any promising signs of bottoming out. The Japanese economy has been stagnant and the unemployment rate has reached approximately 5%, which is the highest since World War II.

Asia has long been expecting Japan to recover from its economic woes. Its prompt recovery would mean that Asian economies would be pulled along with Japan's due to Japan's substantial foreign direct investments in the region and Japan's importation of manufactured products from Asia. Japan should have invested heavily in Asia during the 1991–1995 period as the Japanese currency continued to appreciate, reaching its unprecedented level of 78 yen per US dollar in April 1995. However, Japan's capital investment in Asia was stagnant during this period when the yen was strong. Surprisingly, the strong yen did not stimulate exports of manufactured products from Asia to Japan. Just before the Asian financial crisis in July 1997, exports of manufactured products (machinery in particular) from Asia to Japan had in fact decreased abruptly. Japan's poor economic performance in helping Asia was basically due to her domestic economic sluggishness. To a large extent, the sluggish Japanese economy contributed adversely to the slowdown of many Asian economies, which eventually resulted in the eruption of the Asian economic crisis. Asia would not have experienced the worst of the economic crisis had Japan's economy not been in the doldrums then, as it is today.

Japan has also been seriously affected by the Asian economic crisis. As Asia imports less manufactured products from Japan, Japanese manufacturing industries in Asia are forced to reduce or to stop production; bad debts accumulate and are not recoverable due to companies' going bankrupt; and foreign debts and loans are not paid due to lack of foreign currency reserves. Moreover, Japan has been the largest official development assistance donor to the world and to Asia in particular. Japanese banks, financial institutions and private companies have extended the most loans to the Asian countries, Thailand and Indonesia in particular. Among the highly industrialized countries in the world, Japan suffered the most from Asia during the Asian economic crisis period. The crisis has in fact postponed Japan's economic recovery.

Economic relations between Asia and Japan are complementary. The New Miyazawa Plan (Shin Miyazawa Koso) planned to distribute some US$30 billion (which has been increased to US$80 billion to-date) to the Asian countries to help their economies recover. Loans have been extended to some of the Asian countries to develop industrial infrastructure and to nurture supporting industries; to purchase national bonds issued by cash scarce countries in Asia; and to settle bad debts incurred by banks and financial institutions in Asia. Increasingly more feasibility studies have been carried out and more useful and insightful results are expected. As a substitute to the IMF, the idea that the New Miyazawa Plan should develop into the Asian Monetary Fund (AMF) has yet to be explored. The AMF concept should, in principle, be based on the consensus involving all the Asian countries. It is advisable to set up an international institution or organization in the Asia-Pacific region to supervise capital flows and overall macroeconomic policies among member countries. Furthermore, economic co-operation among member countries in the region should be farther encouraged and strengthened in the 21st century. Japan will then be expected to play a more constructive and decisive role in this context in the Asia-Pacific region.

Lim Hua Sing
Singapore

August 1999

Preface to the First Edition

The increasing trauma of worldwide economic recession has generated a disconcerting tendency: short-sighted protectionist policies are being established in some major industrialized countries, at the serious expense of fruitful international co-operation, to increase world trade and development. Protectionist policies have been rationalized as important and necessary measures to protect domestic industries, to remedy chronic trade imbalances and fiscal deficit, and also to reverse the worsening dde of unemployment. But notable authorities have agreed that the global economic depression of the 1930s, which later led to the outbreak of World War II, is attributable essentially to the protectionism embraced by different countries in the world at that time. The Newly Industrializing Economies (NIEs) and the Association of Southeast Asian Nations (ASEAN) could continue to demonstrate, as they have been doing, the fruitfalness of a co-operative and open partnership in achieving economic affluence and progress. Other countries too can benefit from this tie, based on an open economic interdependence among the countries in the Asia-Pacific region.

Most of the countries in Asia, especially the NIEs and ASEAN, have taken a common stand strongly critical of protectionist policies and practices. Both the NIEs and the economies of ASEAN are basically outward-looking. The NIEs have succeeded in shifting the emphasis from import-substitution to export-orientation activities. The ASEAN countries are now moving towards export-orientation activities. Likewise, both the NIEs and ASEAN require an open economic environment to promote international trade and economic co-operation.

Nevertheless, among the industrialized nations, trade frictions between Japan and the Western nations (the United States in particular) have not been resolved, despite numerous negotiations at government level and between economic circles. Exports into the Western markets of Japanese manufactured goods, particularly semiconductors, automobiles, and electronics and electrical products, have been seriously curtailed; exports of American and European goods — automobiles, machinery and equipment, electronics and electrical products, agricultural products (for example, rice, beef and oranges), and light manufactured goods (such as chocolates and cigarettes) — into the Japanese market have been alleviated. But such moves notwithstanding, the Western world continues to exert pressure upon Japan as the trade deficit, favourable always to Japan, fails to recede to an "acceptable" level.* Japan is still considered a "closed market" by the West. Trade conflicts between Japan and Western countries are likely to continue for some time.

The trade balance between Japan and the developing countries, particularly the NIEs and ASEAN, cannot be ignored either. The NIEs and ASEAN have been important customers of Japan for machinery and equipment, electronics and electrical products, base metals and various types of vehicles. At the same time, the NIEs have been important suppliers of light manufactured products and an increasing amount of industrial products (both intermediate and capital goods) to Japan. On the other hand, ASEAN has been an important supplier of mineral products and raw materials to Japan.

The NIEs have been very much geared to Japan. Their rapid economic development has been primarily reliant on the introduction of capital, technology and managerial know-how from the developed countries, and from Japan in particular. The more the NIEs develop economically, the more they have to import from Japan. Likewise, the NIEs have long been suffering trade deficits with Japan. Despite the fact that the trade relationship between the NIEs and Japan has, in recent years, been shifting significantly from "vertical" to "horizontal", it still has not been satisfactorily rectified. This is partly due to Japan's non-tariff barriers and "closed market", and partly due to the fact that the NIEs' industrial products are less competitive (in terms of quality, design and packaging).

Through most of the 1970s, excepting the years 1970, 1972 and 1974, Japan–ASEAN trade was favourable to the ASEAN countries, mainly because of the massive consumption of ASEAN natural resources and raw materials by Japan. In the 1980s, this basic trade pattern remained unchanged. In the 1990s, ASEAN's exports of manufactured goods to Japan will probably increase substantially, but the Japan–ASEAN trade relationship will presumably remain as "vertical". Japan is expected to open its market wider in order to reduce its trade surpluses with ASEAN.

In the 1960s, the strategy for industrial development in different ASEAN countries was based primarily on policies advocating import substitution. But in the 1970s, a general shift to export-oriented policies occurred, triggered by two trends: import-substituting industries were becoming unattractive as they are restricted to products merely involving assembly; and some ASEAN countries were incurring serious trade deficits as a result of excessive imports of materials and accessories flooding in from industrialized nations, Japan in particular. During the first half of the 1980s, the ASEAN economies were either stagnated or recessed. ASEAN recovered only after the second half of the 1980s, when resource-based and export-oriented industries were launched, mainly to promote primary and related industries. In recent years, the ASEAN economies have been shifting gradually from labour-intensive to capital- and technology-intensive activities. ASEAN's exports of industrial products have gained momentum. Nevertheless, export-oriented industries in the ASEAN countries experienced varying difficulties in obtaining access for their products to the Japanese market. The quality and design, relatively inferior to those of Japanese products, were partly responsible. But responsible also were the Japanese non-tariff barriers and "closed market" which restricted exports of the NIEs and ASEAN manufactured goods into the Japanese market.

In general, the Japan–NIEs/ASEAN trade relationship has remained vertical and asymmetrical. The NIEs and ASEAN are likely to increase imports of intermediate and capital goods from Japan owing to their rapid industrialization and close relationships with Japan. But the Japan–NIEs/ASEAN trade relationships will be jeopardized should Japan not increase its import of manufactured goods from the NIEs and ASEAN. The phenomenal yen appreciation after September 1985 and the increase in Japanese foreign direct investment (FDI) in Asia are seen as stimulants of imports of manufactured goods, especially from the NIEs and ASEAN.

The economic performance of the NIEs and ASEAN is greatly reliant on the Asia-Pacific region. As the major economic player in this region, Japan can largely determine whether its relationship with its neighbours in the Asia-Pacific region is either (1) one of mutual development and prosperity, a symbiotic relationship, resulting in the region's countries affecting the transition from underdeveloped and developing to a developed, economically cohesive bloc or (2) one of ruthless competition, systematic underdevelopment by Japan of its neighbours and distrust of Japan by its neighbours, resulting in an economically balkanized Asia-Pacific region.

This book was published under the title *Japan's Role in ASEAN: Issues and Prospects* in 1994. The title of this edition has been altered to *Japan's Role in Asia: Issues and Prospects* as two new chapters, "Japan's Economic Involvement in Asia and Chinese Partnerships" and "Economic Superpower and International Roles" have been incorporated as Part 4. In addition, statistical data has been updated to reflect the latest economic development between Japan and Asia.

The author is grateful to Mr Umemura Kiyohiro, Chairman of Chukyo University, to Mr Mew Yew Hwa, vice-president and general manager of Education Division, Times Media Private Limited, for displaying an interest in the author's work, and to Mr Eric Loewe, a long-time friend of the author, for his encouragement and enthusiasm about this publication.

The author is obliged to the Institute of Southeast Asian Studies for allowing him to utilize three articles for this publication: "Japanese Perspectives on Malaysia's 'Look East' Policy" (*Southeast Asian Affairs*, 1984); "Singapore–Japan Trade Frictions: A Study of Japanese Non-Tariff Barriers" (*ASEAN Economic Bulletin*, vol. 4, no. 1, July 1987) and "Japan in ASEAN: Potential Trade Frictions" (*ASEAN Economic Bulletin*, vol. 1, no. 2, November 1984). The first and third articles, with minor modifications, provide background understanding of the economic relationship between Japan and Malaysia, as well as between Japan and ASEAN. The second article, with substantial revision and updating (besides the questionnaire survey results) to incorporate the latest data on the Japan-Singapore trade relationship, analyses Singapore's lopsided trade relationship with Japan, and the substance of Japan's non-tariff barriers encountered by Singapore's manufacturers and exporters. The author is also indebted to the University of Tokyo Press, for permission to republish his article entitled "Features of Japanese Direct Investment and Japanese-Style Management in Singapore" (1991), with modifications and updating, in the form contained in this book.

Lim Hua Sing
Nagoya, Japan

December 1994

---

* In 1991, the major Western countries "which suffered trade deficits with Japan were as follows: the United States US$43.4 billion, UK £4.5 billion, Germany DM 23.2 billion and France F24.6 billion. In 1992, the United States and the EC suffered US$43.6 billion and US$31.2 billion trade deficits respectively with Japan. In 1993, the United States and the EU suffered US$50.2 billion and US$26.3 billion trade deficits respectively with Japan.

CHAPTER 1

Japanese Perspectives on Malaysia's "Look East" Policy

Introduction

The "Look East" policy was publicly announced by the Malaysian Prime Minister, Datuk Seri Dr Mahathir Mohamad, in December 1981. This policy has gained momentum and has become an important part of Malaysia's national policy. However, it has also probably created some misunderstanding, controversy, and disarray in policy-making in Malaysia as well as in Japan. The policy seems to aim at introducing Japanese work ethics and managerial systems in order to improve the economic performance and productivity of Malaysia. It is argued, for example, that the "Look East" policy, which proposes to combine Malaysia's resource-based industrialization with Japanese technology and capital, might eventually form an important part of Malaysia's New Economic Policy. Some people, however, also argue that this policy is ultimately unrealistic due to Malaysia being a heterogeneous society and Japan, a homogeneous society. They further argue that these two countries are totally different in culture, social values, and historical background which will undoubtedly create serious impediments for Malaysia to "Look East".

This chapter examines the reactions to this policy from the Japanese government, the business community, academic circles, and the mass media.

Government and Diplomats

The Japanese government has shown special concern towards the Association of Southeast Asian Nations (ASEAN) following its formation in 1967. This was basically due to its immense increase in capital investment and trade in the region. ASEAN's criticisms of Japan began to emerge gradually because of fears of possible economic domination by Japan. This anxiety was escalated by a tendency for a revival of Japanese militarism. In July 1972, the third Sato administration was taken over by Tanaka Kakuei after a decisive battle with Fukuda Takeo. Tanaka was aware that his predecessor, Sato Eisaku, had created a "hawkish image" in the ASEAN countries and he decided to improve the relationship between ASEAN and Japan. However, his good intentions were met with ASEAN's anti-Japanese campaigns when he toured the region in January 1974. He was unable to devote himself to promoting Japan-ASEAN friendship partly because he was soon involved in the "Lockheed Scandal" and partly because he concentrated his attention on making his faction the most influential representative in the Liberal Democratic Party (LDP) of Japan. He was thus too occupied with domestic issues to pay much attention to Malaysia and the ASEAN region.

In December 1974, a compromise cabinet led by Miki Takeo emerged when he dissolved the Tanaka Cabinet with the indispensable support of Tanaka's old rival, Fukuda Takeo. Miki did not even have an opportunity to tour the ASEAN countries simply because during his two-year premiership, domestic structural reforms and the "Tanaka Lockheed Scandal" consumed a great part of his energy. He was an enthusiastic reformist in Japan's internal affairs but not much concerned with ASEAN.

Fukuda Takeo succeeded Miki Takeo in December 1976 after a fierce power struggle among LDP factions. During his two-year premiership, which was shorter than he had expected, he toured ASEAN in August 1977. He proclaimed his "heart-to-heart doctrine" (or the so-called Fukuda Doctrine) in the Philippines at the end of his ASEAN tour. His "heart-to-heart" efforts have, to some extent, eased ASEAN's criticisms of Japanese economic domination in the region. However, in December 1978, his intention to remain in power was foiled by Ohira Masayoshi. Ohira managed to attend the United Nations Conference on Trade and Development (UNCTAD) in the Philippines in May

1979 but did not get to tour ASEAN before his death in June 1980. A compromise administration, led by Suzuki Zenko, succeeded Ohira Masayoshi in July 1980. Suzuki's tour of ASEAN in January 1981 attracted world-wide attention as he was the first Japanese premier to travel to this region before paying a courtesy visit to the United States of America (US). His extraordinary decision, however, did not create any widespread repercussions among the ASEAN countries. He seldom commented on ASEAN due partly to his reticent character. He was a comparatively less ambitious Japanese politician in his efforts to solve the numerous problems, both external and internal, which had piled up during the period of his administration. He was supposed to be re-elected as premier, with strong support from "Tanakasone" factions, but handed over power to Nakasone Yasuhiro in November 1982. Nakasone made unprecedented telephone calls to Reagan and leaders in the ASEAN countries, expressing his strong intention to improve relations with the US and ASEAN. Nakasone then toured ASEAN and Brunei in April-May 1983. He ended his tour on 9 May 1983 in Malaysia, as many observers had predicted he would, because of Malaysia's officially proclaimed "Look East" policy.

Over the last ten years, six Japanese premiers, from Tanaka to Nakasone, have alternated in power. Apart from Miki and Ohira, four other Japanese premiers have visited ASEAN. They have all expressed great concern for improving economic co-operation, political harmony, and cultural exchange with ASEAN. They have also emphasized the need for both bilateral and multilateral relations with the region. Apart from Fukuda and Nakasone, however, the other former leaders who are still in parliament have not expressed any views on Malaysia's "Look East" policy. The Japanese government's reaction to Malaysia's "Look East" policy has been deliberately dispassionate. It has tried not to be overly eager although it has welcomed Malaysia's decision to "Look East". It is generally acknowledged that under the LDP's administration, Japan has accomplished rapid economic growth since World War II and the Japanese government welcomes appraisals of its economic miracle.

According to Fukuda:

[the] "Look East" policy ... deserves serious great attention in the context of the Japan-ASEAN relationship. ...

Japan has voluntarily and actively adopted Western technology and knowledge, on the basis of its historical and traditional social system and work ethics. While the life style of the Japanese people has gone through rather drastic changes by the introduction of new technology, their traditional social system and work ethics have been preserved to date without impairment.

I am extremely happy that Japan is able to co-operate with Malaysia in its nation-building and human resource development efforts. But at the same time, it is my belief that Malaysia should make its own independent judgement on what should be learnt from the Japanese experience and that Japan should never meddle in that judgement. ... It is my great pleasure to see Japan help Malaysia in such a way in one of its major national programmes. Considering the epoch-making significance of this programme, I believe that we should watchfully wait for its success from a long-term perspective, regardless of its short-term results. As the "Look East" policy is something that will cause a fundamental effect upon the course of Malaysia's economic development, I sincerely hope for its success and progress.[1]

From the above statement we understand that Fukuda considered the "Look East" policy as one of Malaysia's major national programmes which deserved serious attention in the context of the Japan-ASEAN relationship. He stressed the willingness of Japan to help Malaysia in its nation-building but left the initiative and independent judgement to the host country.

This appears to be a cautious approach to the "Look East" policy by a Japanese politician, or at least a statement in principle. It was argued that the Malaysian government did not at the time provide Japan with a clear picture regarding concrete plans and measures for actualizing the policy. The Japanese side also did not work out any concrete measures to respond to the policy, although the Suzuki administration did not deny the importance of the trade relationship with Malaysia and of Japan's investment potential in the country. However, externally, Japan faced economic and trade frictions with the US and European Community (EC); and internally, Japan was plagued by stagflation and financial crisis. Thus, Suzuki was unable to react positively to the "Look East" policy or to provide any substantial assistance, either financially or materially, to Malaysia. The Mahathir administration was supposed to meet the Japanese government but the plan was postponed due to Suzuki's resignation from the LDP's presidency in October 1982.

Dr Mahathir visited Japan two months after the formation of the Nakasone administration. When Mahathir invited Japan to react positively on the "Look East" policy, Nakasone, in the joint press statement issued on 25 January 1983, expressed his views by stressing that he

> hoped that this "Look East" policy will contribute to a further broadening of relations between the two countries [Japan and Malaysia], particularly in the field of industrial and technical training, academic and technical studies and the transfer of technology, in addition to the existing close co-operation in the economic field.[2]

He also added that the Japanese government

> intends to co-operate to the extent possible on this matter, recognizing that the implementation of the policy will be very important for the development of Malaysia and that the policy is in line with Japan's policy of developing human resources in Malaysia.[3]

Nakasone promised Malaysia:

> Firstly, to invite more Malaysians to be trained and educated in Japan. Secondly, to extend grant aid in order to construct a Japanese language school attached to the University of Malaya. Thirdly, to extend a loan of up to ¥21 billion to the Paka Power

Station Project and Sabah Gas Grid Project; to extend direct loans of up to ¥50 billion inclusive of the yen loan from the Overseas Economic Co-operation Fund and up to ¥40 billion to the Port Kelang Power Station (Phase II) Project.[4]

At a meeting with ASEAN journalists in Tokyo, in April 1983, two weeks before he came to Malaysia, Nakasone re-emphasized that Japan would co-operate on the development of human resources, extend economic co-operation through yen loans and also provide co-operation in science and technology in response to Malaysia's "Look East" policy. On 9 May 1983, when Mahathir voiced that there were some people in Europe, America, and Malaysia who were criticizing Malaysia's "Look East" policy, Nakasone emphasized that he had been deeply moved by Mahathir's profound wisdom in encouraging Malaysians to learn not only from Western experience but also from Asian heritage.[5]

The Japanese government under Nakasone has also been trying to react positively to Malaysia's "Look East" policy. Esaki Masumi, a powerful LDP politician and a former International Trade and Industry Minister, promised Mahathir that "Japan would further assist Malaysia in such fields as technology transfer, human resource development and small-and-medium size industries", when he visited Malaysia on 1 August 1982.[6] He further stressed that the "Japanese as a race have traits of responsibility. Since Malaysia is looking to Japan, we have to think seriously and respond positively to it. ... Japan should play an important role in helping Malaysia to construct infrastructure and to succeed in its Fourth Five-Year Plan".[7]

According to the Japan Trade Centre in Kuala Lumpur, Japan has been the largest contributor of project loans to Malaysia for the past three years. In 1982, Malaysia obtained a total of M$3.5 billion project loans of which 33.5 per cent (or M$1.2 billion) was contributed by Japan. The amount disbursed by Japan to Malaysia was apparently even more than that by the World Bank (M$971 million). Japan also topped the list in 1980 and 1981 with project loans amounting to M$845 million and M$1.03 billion respectively. As for official yen loans, Japan had provided ¥216,000 million (M$2.16 billion) through nine loans.[8] The data in Table 1.1 also indicate that yen credit co-operation extended by Japan to many Malaysian projects, centring on development of electric power, communications, and railways, has been increased substantially since 1981. Japan would not have extended this huge amount of project loans to Malaysia without special consideration, said a Japanese diplomat.[9] He said Japan was not as rich as was seen by people from outside. More importantly, he argued that Japan was badly affected by the world-wide economic recession. He seemed to be quite confident that if there had not been a "Look East" policy campaign in Malaysia, the Japanese government would not have extended the huge project loans to Malaysia while Japan was plagued by severe stagnation and financial crisis.[10] In fact, as early as October 1982, when Malaysia asked for large project loans, the Japanese Ministry of Finance expressed its unwillingness to help due to its own financial difficulties. However, the Ministry of Foreign Affairs and the Ministry of International Trade and Industry were more inclined to respond positively as they realized that Malaysia was implementing the "pro-Japanese 'Look East' policy".[11] The Ministry

Table 1.1

Annual Provision of Yen Credits to Malaysia

FY	Yen Credit Program	Amount (¥1 billion)
1966	1st	18
1972	2nd	36
1974	3rd	36
1978	4th	21
1978	5th	21
1979	6th	21
1981	7th	21
1982	Special	33.6
1982	8th	21
1983	Special	40
1983	9th	21

Source: Look Japan 29, *no. 333 (Tokyo, 10 December 1983): p. 14.*

of Finance's reluctant response might be understandable in terms of the relatively slow rate of growth of the Japanese economy — 2.7 per cent in the 1981 fiscal year, the lowest growth rate since 1974 and well below the official government projection of 4.1 per cent.[12] The then Prime Minister, Suzuki Zenko, declared that Japan's national finances were in a state of emergency, estimating that revenue shortfalls would amount to ¥5–6 trillion (about US$20–24 billion) in that fiscal year.[13] Even in these difficult circumstances, the Japanese government (as expressed by Premier Nakasone on 25 January 1983) nevertheless extended ¥50 billion in direct loans to Malaysia because it wanted Malaysia's "Look East" policy to be a success.[14]

The Japanese government and Japanese diplomats in this region seem to project a kind of "moral responsibility". This point was particularly emphasized by Japanese diplomats interviewed recently.[15] One felt that the "Look East" policy had created an extra "mental burden" (*seishin teki futan*), although he tried to avoid the word "annoyance" (*meiwaku*). They suggested that Malaysia was expecting too much from Japan, and if Japan could not meet their expectations to their satisfaction, the "learn from Japan" campaign might change to an "anti-Japan campaign", as had happened in 1974.[16]

To sum up the views on Malaysia's "Look East" policy as expressed by Japanese government officials and diplomats, the following are a few main points:

Firstly, the Japanese government welcomes Malaysia's "Look East" policy and has decided to extend various forms of assistance. However, the Japanese seem to grow more worried day by day as they do not have any concrete policy in response to it.[17]

Secondly, the "Look East" policy forms a very important part of Malaysia's New Economic Policy which basically aims at improving the economic well-being of the *bumiputras* (indigenous community). Mahathir has regarded the "Look East" campaign as a kind of spiritual revolution aimed at introducing Japanese experience to Malaysia in order to improve the country's productivity and work ethics. Some of the Japanese officials felt that this was a challenging policy and Mahathir could be risking his political career. He has been criticized not only within the National Front Party, but also inside and outside Malaysia.[18] The continuance of the "Look East" policy may be a problem.

Thirdly, the policy seems to have limitations. This is because (i) although it aims at upgrading work ethics and skills improvement, only the Malays seem to have been purposely mobilized (in terms of sending Malaysian students and trainees to Japan);[19] (ii) the government has tried to achieve great results in a short time; and (iii) Malaysia is a heterogeneous society with different cultures, languages, and customs, while Japan is a homogeneous society.

Fourthly, Japan's development process had been one of learning and improving on Western technology and experience. This process has taken almost 130 years since the Tokugawa Shogunate was forced to open its ports to the Western powers in 1854. Undoubtedly, Japan has accumulated valuable experience which would definitely contribute to Malaysia's economic and social development. However, there are some shortcomings and weaknesses which should not be imitated by Malaysia.

Business Community

According to the Japan Trade Centre in Kuala Lumpur, as of March 1983, there were 720 cases of Japanese investments totalling M$1.76 billion in Malaysia. Its investments in the manufacturing and hotel sectors, amounted to M$595 million or 20 per cent of the total. In 1982, Japan's exports to Malaysia amounted to M$5.75 billion while its imports from Malaysia totalled M$6.9 billion. From Japan's point of view, its export and import trade with that country represented 1.8 per cent and 2.3 per cent respectively of its overall trade. From Malaysia's point of view, these accounted for 21.1 per cent and 24.3 per cent respectively.[20] On the other hand, by June 1983, it had been reported that there were more than 25 Japanese construction companies and 12 Japanese banks in Malaysia. As a result of Malaysia's "Look East" policy, Japanese investment and trade have increased markedly, and the Japanese companies in Malaysia totalled 350 in June 1983.[21] On 9 May 1983, Mahathir told Nakasone that Malaysia was trying to transfer some public sector corporations (for instance, railways, the television broadcasting corporation, and communication companies) into the private sector and invited Japanese participation. Mahathir invited particularly the Japan International Corporation Agency (JICA) to conduct surveys on the feasibility of modernizing the railway line between Penang and Johore (750 km) and of building a new railway line between Kuala Lumpur and the East Coast of Malaysia.[22] Understandably, Japanese businessmen in Kuala Lumpur are happy with the implementation of the "Look East" policy as they feel that it would be relatively easier to do business in Malaysia.[23] However, the Japanese have also expressed their cautious approach to the policy. From my interviews with Japanese business representatives in Malaysia, their viewpoints on the policy can be summarized as follows:

Firstly, the business community has perceived and reacted to the policy more quickly than the diplomats. The businessmen have opportunities to communicate with numerous local staff in their day-to-day activities. Therefore, although the Japanese government might be able to provide some guidelines or instructions to Japanese firms, it is the businessmen who must take action in order to better contribute to the economic development of Malaysia. In short, the Japanese government should avoid over-interference and allow the Japanese enterprises to play a more important role in Malaysia's "Look East" policy.

Secondly, Japanese firms should not "exploit" or be involved in purely "profit-seeking" (*rieki tsuikyu*) activities under the guise of promoting Malaysia's "Look East" policy. British colonialism has been severely criticized by Malaysia because of its exploitative policy and activities. Malaysia had an unhappy experience under Japan during World War II. Therefore, Japan should be cautious and must not be "overheated" (*kanetsu*) over the policy.

Thirdly, the Japanese business community stress that this policy should be carried out consistently over a long period. However, they suspect that the next Malaysian government might not pursue the same policy. They perceive that the Deputy Prime Minister, Datuk Musa Hitam, has a different approach to the policy. Musa is also regarded as being less enthusiastic than Mahathir. It is said that Mahathir has met with resistance to the "Look East" policy from British-educated politicians in his government.

Fourthly, the "Look East" policy will encourage Japanese investors to co-operate with the *bumiputras* in the implementation of the New Economic Policy. This will possibly alter the existing structure of ownership and control of certain sectors of the Malaysian economy. For instance, in the construction sector, big construction companies especially are overwhelmingly controlled by Malaysian Chinese but they would be rapidly replaced by the Japanese. Therefore, it is understandable that the Malaysian Chinese community does not support the policy.[24] According to the view of a Japanese writer, the "brain drain" of some of the Malaysian citizens of Chinese descent might be a reflection of their non-co-operative attitude towards this national policy.[25]

The Japanese businessmen foresee, with mixed anticipation and anxiety, that Japanese investment and economic expansion in Malaysia will be stimulated by the enthusiastic implementation of the policy. They perceive the Malaysian government as being "generous in giving special consideration" to them. For instance, a Japanese construction company has been assigned to construct the Dayabumi Building by the Malaysian government. The Japanese tender was ¥70 billion higher than a local tender, but owing to the shorter completion period and the expectation of the transfer of modern construction technology to Malaysia, the Japanese construction company was chosen.[26]

Some Japanese businessmen in Japan, especially those who do not have any economic interests in Malaysia, have tried to sound a warning note to their counterparts in Malaysia by saying "do not take advantage of the policy and violate the commercial practices in the host country". Japanese "over presence" in Malaysia has long been criticized by the various local communities. This has created several economic and trade frictions between the two parties, that is, the Malaysian and Japanese. For instance, at the end of April 1983, about two weeks before the Japanese Premier Nakasone visited Malaysia, the mass media in Malaysia criticized Japanese commercial practices and business behaviour in the country. The Malay Chamber of Commerce accused Japanese companies of refusing to appoint local dealers for their exports. It said that "since the start of the 'Look East' policy, Japanese companies had won over M$3 billion worth of contracts in Malaysia but Malaysians had gained 'practically nothing' in terms of invisible trade with Japanese contractors. All shipping, insurance, and other invisibles were exclusively handled by the Japanese companies themselves, shutting out the opportunities for local companies".[27]

Obviously, the local organization raised these issues on the eve of Nakasone's visit to Malaysia in the hope that the two governments would discuss them seriously and improve the situation.[28] However, Mahathir rapped out at the critics of Japanese firms by saying that it was unfair to single out Japanese businessmen for criticism when other businessmen had also not given *bumiputra* (contractors) a chance.[29]

Mahathir's sympathetic consideration towards the Japanese companies created both excitement and anxiety in the Japanese business community in Malaysia. Some Japanese businessmen suggested that "it is almost impossible to say no if we are passionately loved"; "this policy will be a success if we can enlarge the pie for distribution".[30] Some other businessmen, however, revealed that their "mental burden has increased" and suggested a "cautious approach" to the "Look East" policy.[31]

Academics

Compared with the Japanese government and the business community, the academics in Japan have shown the least interest in Malaysia's "Look East" policy. This is partly because they do not have any pragmatic or direct interest, compared with the business community in particular, in doing research on the "Look East" policy. There are also few Japanese scholars specializing in contemporary Southeast Asian studies and fewer studying specifically Malaysia. More importantly, in real terms, academics may find it difficult to obtain substantial information or facts to carry out research on this specific topic, since the policy was implemented in December 1981.

Nevertheless, at least three research studies were conducted by Japanese academics in 1982–1983. The first was published by the *Kokusai Kaihatsu Jyanaru* [International Development Journal],[32] the second was by Suzuki Yuzi of Kanagawa University,[33] and the third, by Kimura Michio of the Institute of Developing Economies.[34] The following is a summary of their findings:

1. *Kokusai Kaihatsu Jyanaru's View*

(a) **The editorial staffs view**:[35] The editorial staff frankly expresses its "embarrassment" (*konwaku*) that Malaysians are learning from the Japanese and regards the "Look East" campaign as "a little unexpected" (*isasaka tototsu*) by the Japanese in general. The aims of this policy are firstly, to fundamentally change the work ethics of the Malays in order to encourage them to participate more productively in the economic activities of Malaysia; and secondly, to foster a high economic growth modelled on Japanese development experience. This is regarded as an extension of the New Economic Policy. Economic frictions with Britain, and domestic economic difficulties and the unfavourable trade balance have also prompted Malaysia to "Look East". However, the Japanese government has not formulated any concrete policy to co-operate with Malaysia in this campaign, especially in terms of receiving students and trainees sent by the Malaysian government.

(b) **Hanada Mitsuyo's view**:[36] The "Look East" policy is seen as a plan to "look less to the West and more to Japan" in Malaysia's effort to learn from Japanese industrial technology, education system, business management and work ethics. It cannot be regarded as having been influenced by Singapore's "Learn from Japan" campaign, as Malaysia has had a tendency to have a cool attitude towards those policies carried out enthusiastically by Singapore. Malaysia is a typical heterogeneous society in which the government is forcefully introducing the New Economic Policy to help the *bumiputras*. It

seems very difficult, if not impossible, for Malaysia to adopt the Japanese managerial system, although it would be easier in Singapore. *(c)* **Araki Mitsuya's view**:[37] The "Look East" policy, as a "tactic" (*senjyutsu*), has been used to strengthen the Mahathir administration. This tactic is derived from Mahathir's overall strategy based on the ideas expressed in his book, *The Malay Dilemma*. Mahathir is trying to improve the economic and social status of the Malays so that the Malaysian economy and politics will not be controlled by other races or foreigners (mainly British). In order to do this, Japan is seen as a model since it has achieved remarkable economic growth even when other economic powers are in stagnation. Malaysia has not, however, formulated any concrete measures to learn from Japan. Nevertheless, in reaction to Malaysia's "Look East" policy, Japan has firstly to avoid seeking hegemony in Asia since people in this region are still aware of the "Greater East Asia Co-prosperity Sphere" which Japan tried to create during World War II; secondly, since the developing countries are expecting Japan to react positively to Malaysia's "Look East" policy, Japan should help to create more "stable and peaceful countries" in the region through contributing to Malaysia's economic development and social stability.

2. *Suzuki Yuzi's View*

The "Look East" policy forms an essential part of Malaysia's New Economic Policy which was launched in 1970, aimed at increasing the *bumiputras'* participation in managerial levels, ownership, and employment to represent a share of 30 per cent of Malaysia's national economy. Under the new leadership of the Mahathir administration, Malaysia is trying to do three things to fulfil this task: firstly, in order to reduce British and non-Malay control over Malaysia's economy (for instance, control predominantly over rubber plantations and tin mines), Malaysia has to strengthen economic relations with Japan. This is based on the idea that Malaysia's economic relationship with Britain is "unequal or dependent" while that with Japan is "equal or independent"; secondly, in order to change Malaysia's industrial structure, that is, from producing raw material centred around rubber and tin, to a more diversified and larger manufacturing sector, Malaysia has to improve its relationship with Japan since the latter has capital, technology, and a big domestic market; thirdly, it is easier for Malaysia to emulate Japan since the Japanese experience of industrialization is not tied with political ambition and military expansion. Besides, as a nation blessed with many natural resources, Malaysia will be able to reject Japan if any irrational demands are imposed on it. The "Look East" policy is being used to accomplish the New Economic Policy goal, and also, as a tactic, was used to stabilize the Mahathir administration during the general election in March 1982. Japan should respond positively to the policy from a broader viewpoint of North-South problems.

3. *Kimura Michio's View*

Kimura concludes that the background and aims of the policy are as follows: Malaysia succeeded in carrying out its industrial policy in developing labour-intensive and export-oriented industries in the 1970s. In Peninsular Malaysia, the unemployment rate decreased from 8 per cent in 1970 to 5.6 per cent in 1980. This created a new situation: the attraction of high wages has increased the outflow of young labour from the rural to the urban areas. Malaysia worked out a new industrial strategy in the Fourth Malaysia Plan (1981–1985), by shifting from labour-intensive to capital-intensive industries. But in order to do so, Malaysia had to acquire experience and technology from the East. Secondly, since 1979, Singapore has been learning from Japan in order to improve its industrial structure. Obviously, Malaysia's "Look East" policy has been stimulated by Singapore's "Learn from Japan" campaign. Thirdly, as a nationalist, Mahathir is trying to improve the *bumiputras'* discipline and work ethics so as to narrow the economic gap between the Malays and other races in Malaysia. Fourthly, Mahathir is devoting every effort to combine the "Look East" policy with Islamic doctrine. He is suggesting that Islamic doctrine teaches diligence and the pursuit of knowledge, which are also the aims of the "Look East" policy. The implementation of the policy is therefore expected to strengthen Islamic ideology and help to isolate Islamic extremists in Malaysia.

Japanese academics, especially economists and political scientists, try to explain the "Look East" policy based on Malaysia's economic and social structure, its attitude towards British interests in Malaysia, the country's unfavourable trade balance, and continuing economic slowdown. They are not optimistic about the implementation of the policy. This is partly because Japan is a homogeneous society and Malaysia a heterogeneous nation, and partly because the concept of the "Look East" policy is rather abstract and Japan has not worked out any plans to support it. Japan has been learning from Western countries but not from Southeast Asia.[38] The Japanese are also very good at learning from others but not at introducing their own experiences to others. Japan does not have a "social equipment or policy" to transfer knowledge and technology to other countries.[39] Therefore, Malaysia has to "rob" (*ubaitoru*) if it wants to get something from Japan.[40] However, Malaysia should not learn "evil things" from Japan.[41] Environmental pollution, housing shortages, a closed policy, an anti-foreign attitude, and exoticism must be avoided.[42] A Japanese official reminded Malaysia that economic development in his country had been accompanied by military expansion (as had happened during World War II) and implied that Malaysia should not follow its example.[43]

Mass Media

There are many Japanese correspondents based in this region who write on Southeast Asia. Almost all major Japanese newspapers such as *Asahi Shimbun, Yomiuri Shimbun, Mainichi Shimbun,* and *Nihon Keizai Shimbun* have their offices in Singapore staffed with experienced correspondents, and reports on Malaysia have long been covered by correspondents stationed outside the country. Japanese reporters visit Malaysia only when they want to gather data or to cover certain events in the country. The *Asahi Shimbun* recently appointed a correspondent who was based in Singapore to cover Malaysia. He travels to Kuala

Lumpur regularly and presents his observations and interpretations mainly on Malaysia's "Look East" policy and Japanese economic activities to the Japanese readers. Apart from this, it is difficult for the Japanese to obtain regular information on Malaysia in Japan.

The Japanese mass media only focused on Malaysia when the Japanese Premier toured the country. Some documentaries have also featured Malaysia but do not seem to have provided a comprehensive understanding of the country. So it is rather unrealistic to expect the Japanese mass media to comment on the "Look East" policy on a more regular basis. Thus, the Japanese public have a very limited knowledge of Malaysia's "Look East" policy. Surveys conducted in Tokyo recently revealed that Japanese students also have very little knowledge of Malaysia's "Look East" policy (see Tables 1.2 and 1.3).[44] Most of them either have not heard of the policy or, if they have heard about it, do not know the details. About one-quarter of the students interviewed expressed their limited knowledge of the policy which they acquired from local television and newspapers. Nevertheless, 52 per cent of the interviewees approved of Malaysia's intention to learn from Japan. They suggested that Malaysia could learn from Japan's experience in post-war economic and technical development, and also the effective and rapid modernization of its educational system. About a quarter of interviewees stressed it was "not necessary", while 18 per cent suggested that "it is impossible" for Malaysia to learn from Japan. The former were critics of Japan's "industrialization and modernization" and suggested that Malaysia should not follow Japan's development process which did entail less-publicized but very substantial social costs. The latter emphasized the sharp differences between Malaysia and Japan in basic characteristics like religion, culture, and work ethics, which might not make Japan a suitable model for Malaysia.

In general, therefore, it could be argued that the Japanese might have heard this policy been mentioned but do not know the details. They might be impressed that there are more and more Malaysian students and trainees coming to Japan, and more and more project loans requested by Malaysia. However, the Japanese mass media

Table 1.2

Level of Understanding of Malaysia's "Look East" Policy

	Never heard of it	Have heard of it but do not know the details	To a certain extent do know the details	Total No. of Interviewees*
Seijo Univ.	5(25%)	10(50%)	5(25%)	20(100%)
AA	24(33.3%)	28(38.9%)	20(27.8%)	72(100%)

Table 1.3

Japanese Students' Reactions to Malaysia's Learning from Japan

	Not necessary	Worth learning	Impossible to learn	Others	Total No. of Interviewees*
Seijo Univ.	6(30.0%)	9(45.0%)	5(25.0%)	0(0%)	20(100%)
AA	14(19.4%)	43(59.7%)	8(11.1%)	7(9.7%)	72(100%)

Note: * *(a) Students aged between 19 and 21.*

(b) Students of Seijo University do not have a basic interest in or knowledge of Southeast Asia or Malaysia.

(c) Students of AA do have an interest in and knowledge of developing countries and some are learning Southeast Asian languages.

AA = Asia-Africa Linguistic Institute

makes no effort to explain why Japan must train more Malaysians, extend more project loans, and play a more important role in the "Look East" policy.

Some Japanese newspapers (for instance, *Nihon Keizai Shimbun*) have foreseen difficulties for Malaysia in its efforts to "Look East". They have suggested that Malaysia's universities, businesses, and the people in general have already been overly geared to the West which would make it very difficult for Malaysia to follow effectively the Japanese model.[45] Another article explicitly suggests that the "Look

East" policy is aimed at "revolting" (*hanran*) against Europe in order to "restore power" (*fukken*) to the *bumiputra* by implementing the New Economic Policy. It is also regarded as an attempt to search for "spiritual independence" (*seishin teki dokuritsu*) after gaining political and economic independence.[46] On the other hand, the "Look East" policy is also regarded as "a racial policy closely related to a pro-*bumiputra* policy which is unlikely to gain full co-operation from the Malaysian Chinese".[47] The Japanese are also warned not to interpret the "Look East" policy as "Japanization". *Toyo Keizai* further argues that Malaysia is a "tough fellow" (*shitataka-mono*) with strong pragmatism like other Asian countries. These countries maintain economic and political grievances and criticism against Japan. The Japanese military occupation during World War II is particularly regarded as the "potential mainstream" of the anti-Japan movement. It is therefore advisable, it is argued, to promote cultural exchange, to extend technological assistance, and owing to Malaysia's current difficult economic situation, to open the Japanese market to Malaysia.[48]

When Mahathir visited Japan in January 1983 and Nakasone in turn visited Malaysia in May 1983, reports on Malaysia increased. Between 21 and 30 January 1983, the *Nihon Keizai Shimbun*, the most influential Japanese newspaper on economic issues, published at least eight news items on Malaysia. The news was mainly on Malaysia's requests for loans and Japan's positive responses.[49] Between 2 and 10 May 1983, reports on Japanese capital investment in Malaysia and technology co-operation between Malaysia and Japan occupied the major part of the *Shimbun*.[50] This was also evident in the other newspapers, particular the *Mainichi Shimbun*, during that time. To a lesser extent, the *Nikkei Sangyo Shimbun*, the *Jyukagaku Kogyo Shimpo*, the *Nikkan Kogyo Shimbun*, and the *Asahi Shimbun* also published similar news. Occasionally the *Asahi Shimbun*, through its correspondent in Singapore, also published a few comprehensive reports on the "Look East" policy and Japanese economic activities in Malaysia.

On 10 May 1983, the *Nihon Keizai Shimbun* published a relatively discreet editorial on "How Can Japan Survive in Asia". It suggested that Nakasone's speech towards the end of his ASEAN tour in Kuala Lumpur emphasizing mutual concern and interests between Japan and ASEAN was presumably stimulated by Mahathir's "Look East" policy. Secondly, it warned the Japanese government not to interpret Malaysia's "Look East" policy as purely an attempt to emulate Japan's identity or "indiscriminately adopt values from Japan". It advised Japan not to conjure up the "revival of Japanese militarism" image for ASEAN, but to increase economic co-operation and to transfer technology to the ASEAN region. More importantly, it also argued that Japan should open its market to ASEAN, including Malaysia, in order to reduce the serious trade deficits. This would be a more friendly and productive response to Malaysia's "Look East" policy. Therefore, it can be argued that, through the Japanese mass media, Malaysia's "Look East" policy seems to the Japanese to be basically focused on economic issues. They realize that through the implementation of the policy, more economic aid will be expected by Malaysia and more Japanese capital will be flown into Malaysia. Malaysia's business and government delegations sent to Japan can easily be regarded by the Japanese mass media as a practical way to promote economic co-operation through trade and investment, in order to implement the "Look East" policy.[51]

The mass media thus play a very limited role in introducing the background, aims, and impact of the policy. Furthermore, they hardly emphasize the need to encourage cultural exchange between the two countries for the purpose of better understanding which will definitely contribute to the implementation of the policy. Therefore, it is suggested that the Japanese should know more about Malaysia and its people at a time when Japan is actively trying to render substantive assistance as well as promote the Malaysian policy.[52]

Conclusion

The Japanese people are not much concerned about Malaysia's "Look East" policy. This is partly because they are not well-informed by the domestic mass media which has long been looking West and has paid less attention to this part of the world, and partly because the "Look East" policy has not had any direct impact on their daily lives. They thus leave politicians and businessmen to respond to the policy. The Japanese government, on the other hand, considers the policy to be a serious challenge from Malaysia, and it is expected that it will soon instruct and mobilize the Ministry of International Trade and Industry, the Ministry of Foreign Affairs, and the Ministry of Education to work out some concrete measures in response to the policy. Presently, the Japanese government, despite a reversing domestic financial situation, is increasing its economic aid to Malaysia as an immediate response to prove its favourable attitude towards the policy. Politicians and diplomats directly in charge of Malaysian affairs, although realizing that it is an "extra burden which is full of annoyance", will try to understand fully the development and implementation of the policy and, hopefully, make timely suggestions for its success. The Japanese business community, which will benefit most from the policy among the various groups, will, with the strong support of the Japanese government and its representatives (for instance, business organizations such as the Keidanren, the Keizai Doyu-Kai, and the Nihon Shoko Kaigi-sho), find opportunities to participate in the implementation of the "Look East" policy. Having given an adverse impression of its notorious ambition of a "Greater East Asia Co-prosperity Sphere" to Malaysians during World War II, the Japanese community has to be particularly careful that it does not replace the British colonialists, who are presently being criticized by the Malaysian government. Japanese academics — although there is only a small group of "Malaysia watchers" — have expressed concern that there are some serious impediments in the implementation of the "Look East" policy. In theory, they agree that it is possible for Malaysia to learn from Japan; in practice, they caution the necessity to look into social costs incurred by Japan in its "industrialization and modernization process". The "distortions" (*yugami*) emerging from the Japanese economic development process, for instance, environmental pollution, the neglect of human aspects (*ningen sogai*) in factories, housing shortages, and capitalistic expansion, must particularly be avoided, if Malaysia wants to learn from Japanese experience.

There is no evidence to suggest that the "Look East" policy concept was formulated by Japan and imposed on Malaysia. It is widely regarded that this policy was derived from Dr Mahathir's personal national development philosophy aimed at introducing Japanese values for the purpose of improving the economic performance and productivity of Malaysia. The "Look East" policy did, however, gain support and warm applause by Japan, or more precisely, by the Japanese government and business community, even at the very early stage when the Mahathir administration tried to introduce the concept to Malaysia.[53] Although Japan worries about its lack of a concrete policy to respond to Malaysia's "Look East" policy and about being criticized for taking advantage of the policy for its economic expansion, it welcomes the notion of being looked up to.

It is hard to predict to what extent or for how long the Mahathir administration will "Look East" or whether the next Malaysian government would continue to do so. However, the Japanese government will, regardless of who leads the Liberal Democratic Party in Japan, continue to co-operate with the implementation of Malaysia's "Look East" policy so long as Malaysia maintains this policy. For the long-term, the Japanese government or Japanese business organizations should provide some guidelines in order to supervise Japanese business activities in Malaysia. A close monitoring of Japanese firms operating in Malaysia would contribute to minimizing any Japanese firms' unacceptable commercial practices, thereby promoting cordial and productive relations between the local and Japanese business communities.

It is unwise to regard Malaysia as a pro-Japanese country. It would also be disastrous to formulate Japan's foreign and economic policy towards Malaysia based on this notion. Malaysia's "Look East" policy has undoubtedly created a better understanding and has enhanced more opportunities for economic co-operation between

Malaysia and Japan. Japan, however, should be cautious in taking advantage of this policy solely to further its economic expansion since its business activities and practices in Malaysia (or in Southeast Asia) have increasingly received serious criticisms. Malaysia should also avoid giving the impression to the Japanese that it is using the "Look East" policy as a means to wield bargaining power and gain more economic aid from Japan.

Learning from Japan — through the introduction of technology, managerial systems, work ethics, economic development experiences, and so forth — is understandably a painstaking task which needs years to formulate and implement. Presently, it appears that economic co-operation in trade and investment has received the most attention in Malaysia-Japan relations while cultural exchange seems to have been of lesser significance or given inadequate attention. Generally, although cultural exchange does not directly contribute to economic co-operation, it forms a necessary basis for the deeper understanding of a nation's overall developmental achievements. Indeed, it is most essential to have a thorough appreciation of the Japanese social and cultural values, institutions, and practices at a time when Malaysia is attempting to learn from Japanese business and economic performance.

The Japanese image will depend very much on how it responds to the South.

Notes

1 Commemorative speech by Mr Fukuda Takeo at the Fifth Japan-ASEAN Symposium, Kuala Lumpur, 24 August 1982.

2 Text of the joint press statement issued on the occasion of the official visit to Japan by the Prime Minister of Malaysia, Datuk Seri Dr Mahathir Mohamad, and released on 25 January 1983, in *Foreign Affairs Malaysia*, 16, no. 1 (Kuala Lumpur: Ministry of Foreign Affairs, March 1983), p. 23.

3 Ibid.

4 Ibid, pp. 24-25.

5 Address by Prime Minister Nakasone Yasuhiro in Kuala Lumpur on 9 May 1983. See also the *Nihon Keizai Shimbun* (Tokyo), 10 May 1983.

6 *Straits Times* (Singapore), 2 August 1982.

7 *APIC*, issue 54 (Tokyo: Kokusai Kyoryoku Suisin Kyokai [Association for the Promotion of International Co-operation], 25 September 1982).

8 *Straits Times*, 27 August 1983.

9   Interview with a Japanese diplomat in this region (Diplomat A) on 27 June 1983, but this argument was rejected by another Japanese diplomat (Diplomat B) whom I interviewed on 28 July 1983. Diplomat B made a general point that the Asian countries, particularly the ASEAN nations, are important recipients of Japan's project loans. Therefore, he tried to suggest that Japan had extended huge amounts of project loans to Malaysia through Japan's consistent policy to assist developing countries, and was not influenced by Malaysia's "Look East" policy.

10 View of Diplomat A (see note 9).

11 *Nihon Keizai Shimbun*, 20 October 1982. It was reported that Esaki Masumi was asked by the Malaysian government to extend further yen loans on 1 August 1982. Esaki, however, stated that it would be difficult for Japan to do so as Japan was facing its own financial difficulties. See *Straits Times*, 2 August 1982.

12 *Straits Times*, 7 August 1982.

13 *Straits Times*, 13 September 1982.

14 It was also suggested that the Japanese government should pay special consideration to Mahathir's loans request since Malaysia was "carrying out the 'Look East' policy campaign and also it is one of the most pro-Japanese countries". (See the *Jyukagaku Kogyo Simpo* [Tokyo], 3 September 1982.) However, Muto Ichiyo, Director of the Asia-Pacific Resources Centre of Tokyo, commented that this economic aid was given to get recipients to support Japan's rearmament ("The Sun Also Sets", *Far Eastern Economic Review*, 8 September 1983). Another criticism of Japan's loans is made by the former Malaysian Prime Minister, Tunku Abdul Rahman. He stated that "although Japan furnishes loans, it takes back with its other hand, as if by magic, almost twice the amount it provides". See Jomo Kwame Sundaram, ed., *The Sun Also Sets — Lessons in Looking East* (Kuala Lumpur: Institute for Social Analysis, 1983).

15 Interviews with Japanese Diplomat C on 4 August 1983 and Diplomat D on 27 July 1983.

16 See also Hayashi Risuke, "Ryoba no Ken-Maleisha no Toho Seisaku" [A Double-edged Sword — Malaysia's Look East Policy] in *Toyo Keizai* (Tokyo), 4 June 1983.

17 For instance, it was reported that Malaysia tried to send 140 trainees to Japan in Autumn 1982. The Japanese Embassy in Malaysia and the Kaigai Kensetsu Kyokai (Overseas Construction Association) in Japan were asked for co-operation. Since Nagano Shigeo was the President of the Japan-Malaysia Economic Congress and the Japanese Chamber of Commerce and Industry (JCCI), he had been appointed to the Secretariat of the trainee programme, but up to mid-April 1982, this Secretariat had not been set up by the JCCI. Furthermore, it was reported that the Ministry of International Trade and Industry (MITI), which had a close relationship with Japanese enterprises, had not been informed either by the Ministry of Foreign Affairs or the JCCI. Therefore, MITI was unable to instruct Kaigai Gijyutsusya Kensyu Kyokai (Association for Foreign Trainees) which was under the jurisdiction of MITI, to accept trainees from Malaysia. See "Minami Kara no Kurosen Look East to Nihon no Kaikoku" [A Black Ship called "Look East" from the South and the Opening of Japan] in *Kokusai Kaihatsu Jyanaru* [International Development Journal] no. 311 (Tokyo, May 1982), p. 24.

18 See also "Learning from Japan", Asiaweek, 8 July 1983. Hayashi Risuke suggested that Malaysia's "Look East" policy was opposed by some of the European, Chinese, Indian, and Malaysian entrepreneurs, and Malay politicians in PAS.

More importantly, it added that it was opposed by the "Malay conservative upper class". See Hayashi Risuke, op. cit., p. 54.

19   The Malaysian government started by sending 135 Malay technical trainees to Japan in September 1982 and 238 in April 1983. (*Malaysia*, no. 38 [Tokyo: Perbadanan Persatuan Jepun/Malaysia, April 1983]).
As an indicator of the "Look East" policy, the number of Malaysian students studying in Japan increased substantially. Take, for example, Malaysian students at the International Students Institute, the largest Japanese language school for foreign students in Japan, based in Tokyo, increased from only 5 in 1981 to 15 in 1982 and 50 (nearly 20 per cent of the total number) in 1983. (*Fiscal Bulletin of the International Students Institute*, Tokyo, 1982 and 1983.)

20   *Straits Times*, 27 August 1983.

21   *Asahi Shimbun*, 16 June 1983.

22   *Nihon Keizai Shimbun*, 10 May 1983.

23   *Asahi Shimbun*, 24 April 1982. When I interviewed a general manager of a *sogoshosha* (trading company) in Kuala Lumpur on 28 June 1983, he expressed the same view.

24   *Asahi Shimbun*, 16 April 1982.

25   *Asahi Shimbun*, 24 April 1982.

26   *Asahi Shimbun*, 3 January 1983. See also Hiramatsu Kenji, "Mareishia-Kindai-ka e Maishin" [Malaysia — Towards Modernization], *Nihon Keizai Shimbun*, 8 October 1982 and Hayashi Risuke, op. cit., p. 55. Some Japanese *sogoshoshas* I interviewed in Kuala Lumpur did not deny that the Malaysian government had paid "some special considerations" to Japanese companies in Malaysia. They, however, interpreted it as the Malaysian government's "trust and appreciation" towards Japanese enterprises. They argued that the Japanese could complete projects in a shorter period with satisfactory results, although their tenders might be higher than others. From the economic point of view, they continued to argue, these projects contributed to Malaysia's economic development since the Malaysian government could gain benefit more quickly from these projects. On 1 November 1983, when I raised this issue to a group of Japanese whom I interviewed in Tokyo, they suspected that there was "conglutination" (*yuchaku*) between Japanese businessmen and Malaysian technocrats, or at least, as they suggested that that would lead to a formation of "conglutination" between the two parties. This should be avoided, as they warned, if Malaysia's industrial programmes were expected to be carried out systematically.

27   *Straits Times*, 23 April 1983. See also *Asahi Shimbun*, 16 June 1983.

28   Dr Mahathir discussed this matter with Nakasone when he visited Malaysia on 8–9 May 1983. Mahathir declined to comment when asked whether Nakasone had made any promises on the matter (*Straits Times*, 11 May 1983).

29   *Straits Times*, 11 May 1983.

30   *Asahi Shimbun*, 16 June 1983.

31   Interview with Japanese businessmen in Malaysia on 28 June 1983.

32   "Look East — A Challenge from Malaysia", *Kokusai Kaihatsu Jyanaru*, A Special Edition [International Development Journal], no. 311 (Tokyo, May 1982).

33   Suzuki Yuzi, "Atarashii Kadai to Look East" [A New Task and "Look East"], in *Tonanajia no Kiki no Kozo* [The Critical Structure of Southeast Asia], (Tokyo: Keiso Shobo, 1982). See also Suzuki Yuzi, "Mahatiru Shusho no Kodo no Genten wo Saguru" [In Search of the Basis of Premier Mahathir's Policy], *Kokusai Kaihatsu Jyanaru*, op. cit., pp. 14–17.

34   Kimura Michio, "Sen Kyuhyaku Hachi-Jyu-Ni Nen no Mareishia" [Malaysia in

the Year 1982] in *Ajia Chuto Doko Nempo* [An Annual Report on the Trends in Asia and the Middle East], (Tokyo: Institute of Developing Economies, 31 March 1983), pp. 306–14.

35 The Editorial Staff, "Naze Ima Jyapan Fuiba Nanoka" [Why Is It Japan Fever Now?], *Kokusai Kaihatsu Jyanaru*, op. cit., pp. 10–13.

36 Hanada Mitsuyo, "Mareishia Fudo no Naka no Nikkei Kigyo" [Japanese Enterprises in Malaysia's Climate], *Kokusai Kaihatsu Jyanaru*, op. cit., pp. 18–21.

37 Araki Mitsuya, not cited, pp. 22–24.

38 Interview with Mori Takeshi of the Institute of Developing Economies by Loke Pooi-choon, *Lian He Zao Bao* (Singapore), 3 June 1983.

39 Araki Mitsuya, not cited, p. 22.

40 Interview with a Japanese businessman on 28 June 1983.

41 Frank opinions expressed by Japanese scholars through correspondence.

42 Interview with a Japanese academic on 17 August 1983 in Singapore.

43 Interview with Watanabe Takeshi, Japanese Chairman of Japan-America-Europe Committee, *by Loke Pooi-choon, Sin Chew Jit Poh (Singapore)*, 16 June 1982.

44 Questionnaire surveys conducted at the Seijo University and Asia-Africa Linguistic Institute (AA) on 2, 8, and 9 November 1983 in Tokyo.

45 *Nihon Keizai Shimbun*, 30 January 1983.

46 *Mainichi Shimbun*, January 1983. See also Hayashi Risuke, "Tonan-ajia no Shinjyosei to Nihon" [Japan and New Trends in Southeast Asia], *Keizai Kyoryoku* no. 144 (Tokyo, 25 September 1983).

47 "Toho wo Miyo", in *Asahi Shimbun* (evening issue), 24 April 1982.

48 Editorial of *Shukan Toyo-Keizai*, 21 May 1983.

49 See Nihon Keizai Shimbun, 21, 22, 24, 25, 26, 27, and 30 January 1983. In March 1983, there were also many reports on this topic in the *Shimbun*.

50 Ibid., 2, 9, 10 May 1983.

51 For example, see "Kokusai Keizai, Kaigai Gigyutsu", *Nikkan Kogyo Shimbun*, 21 August 1982.

52 *Kokusai Kyoryoku Tokubetsu Jyoho* 8 (Tokyo: Association for Promotion of International Co-operation, 15 October 1983).

53 See speech delivered by Nagano Shigeo, Chairman of the Japan Chamber of Commerce and Industry, at the Malaysia-Japan Economic Congress held in Kuala Lumpur on 8 February 1982; and speech delivered by Fukuda Takeo, former Prime Minister of Japan, at the Fifth Japan-ASEAN Symposium held in Kuala Lumpur on 24–26 August 1982. These two speeches were direct responses to the "Look East" policy when Mahathir elaborated on it at both meetings.

CHAPTER 2

The Japan-Malaysia Economic Relationship towards the Twenty-first Century

Introduction

The Japan-Malaysia economic relationship has developed rapidly especially after the "Look East" policy was publicly announced in December 1981. The Japan–Malaysia relationship has, however, become an important concern of the two countries, especially the latter, when they formulated their foreign and industrial development policies. This chapter attempts to examine the recent development of the Japan–Malaysia relationship (focusing on foreign trade, investment and development aid) and predicts their possible development towards the twenty-first century. This chapter also attempts to make some suggestions and recommendations towards the improvement and development of the economic relationship between the two countries.

Foreign Trade

Japan has been the most resource-poor nation of all industrialized countries. Most of its industrial and agricultural resources have had to be imported from abroad. Malaysia has been a resource-rich country and its exports of tin, petroleum (crude and partly refined), fixed vegetable oils (crude, refined, and purified), timber, and natural rubber and latex to Japan have been promising. Malaysia had a trade surplus with Japan in 1976-1980. In 1981–1983, however, Malaysia experienced a trade deficit with Japan. This was basically due to two reasons: (a) commodity prices dropped abruptly, which seriously affected Malaysia's exports to Japan; and (b) increased demand for Japanese imports, particularly for heavy industrial and chemical products.[1]

Table 2.1 reveals the commodity composition of Japan's trade with Malaysia in 1985–1993.[2] The following features can be identified:

Firstly, Malaysia had a trade deficit with Japan in 1990–1993. This was largely because of the substantial rise of the imports of heavy chemical and industrial products (particularly metal products, and machinery and equipment) from Japan. As a resource-rich country, Malaysia has long been experiencing trade surpluses with Japan. Over the 1976–1980 period and the 1984–1989 period, Malaysia had trade surpluses with Japan. Secondly, heavy chemical and industrial products have been predominant (88 to 91 per cent throughout the 1985–1993 period) in Japan's exports to Malaysia. Among heavy chemical and industrial products, exports of machinery and equipment have been particularly significant. Exports of machinery and equipment have maintained at 67 to 74 per cent of Japan's total exports to Malaysia throughout the 1985–1993 period. Thirdly, imports of raw materials and fossil fuels have been predominant in Japan's import trade with Malaysia. In 1993, they constituted 62 per cent of Japan's total imports from Malaysia. Timber has been the most important export item among raw materials, whereas crude oil and liquefied natural gas have been predominant among fossil fuels.

It can then be argued that the Japan–Malaysia trade relationship has been vertical, i.e. exports of manufactures (especially heavy chemical and industrial products) and imports of raw materials (timber and fossil fuels e.g., crude oil and liquefied natural gas). Despite the fact that trade relations between Japan and the NIEs have been shifting from vertical towards horizontal, Malaysia's exports of manufactured goods to Japan dropped from US$467.5 million in 1984 (10.6 per cent of Japan's total imports from Malaysia) to US$466.1 million (9.9 per cent) in 1988. Malaysia's exports of manufactured goods gained its upward momentum again only after 1989. Malaysia's exports of manufactured goods constituted 28 and 32 per cent of Malaysia's total exports to Japan in 1992 and 1993 respectively. Towards the twenty-first century, the Japan–Malaysia vertical trade relationship

Table 2.1

Commodity Composition of Japan's Trade with Malaysia

(US$ million)

	1985 Value	1985 %	1989 Value	1989 %	1990 Value	1990 %
Exports						
1. Foods	30.6	1.4	20.2	0.5	18.6	0.3
2. Cmde Material	9.3	0.4	17.7	0.4	20.7	0.4
3. Light Manufactures	214.3	9.9	284.7	6.9	390.0	7.1
4. Heavy Chemical & Industrial Products	1897.0	87.5	3758.2	91.1	4999.5	90.7
(Metal Products)	(330.9	15.3)	(569.4	13.8)	(680.9	12.4)
(Machinery & Equipment)	(1444.4	66.6)	(2908.6	70.5)	(3962.1	71.9)
5. Others	17.1	0.8	43.3	1.0	82.6	1.5
Total	2168.2	100.0	4124.0	100.0	5511.4	100.0
Imports						
1. Foods	62.2	1.4	92.3	1.8	102.4	1.9
2. Raw Materials	1501.5	34.7	2499.8	49.0	2201.1	40.7
(Timber)	(1179.2	27.2)	(2055.0	40.2)	(1804.4	33.4)
3. Fossil Fuels	2369.2	54.7	1746.7	34.2	2008.3	37.2
(Crude Oil)	(1156.6	26.7)	(517.1	10.1)	(752.4	13.9)
(Liquified Natural Gas)	(1122.3	25.9)	(1052.3	20.6)	(1082.4	20.0)
4. Manufactured Goods	322.6	7.5	615.0	12.0	896.6	16.6
5. Others	74.5	1.7	153.1	3.0	193.2	3.6
Total	4330.1	100.0	5106.9	100.0	5401.6	100.0
Bilateral Trade Balance	–2161.9		–1649.8		–982.9	

	1991 Value	1991 %	1992 Value	1992 %	1993 Value	1993 %
Exports						
1. Foods	25.3	0.3	32.2	0.4	36.8	0.4
2. Crude Material	28.4	0.4	59.9	0.7	52.1	0.5
3. Light Manufactures	531.3	7.0	619.2	7.6	698.4	7.2
4. Heavy Chemical & Industrial Products	6929.7	90.8	7283.3	89.7	8754.2	90.7
(Metal Products)	(870.2	11.4)	(962.8	11.9)	(1060.7	11.0)
(Machinery & Equipment)	(5623.2	73.7)	(5795.3	71.4)	(7075.3	73.3)
5. Others	119.9	1.6	120.9	1.5	107.6	1.1
Total	7634.6	100.0	8115.6	100.0	9649.1	100.0
Imports						
1. Foods	127.1	2.0	145.4	2.2	171.1	2.2
2. Raw Materials	2176.0	33.6	2292.2	34.9	2616.9	34.2
(Timber)	(1765.2	27.3)	(1853.3	28.2)	(2202.0	28.8)
3. Fossil Fuels	2345.1	36.2	2099.8	31.9	2142.7	28.0
(Crude Oil)	(719.8	26.7)	(643.5	9.8)	(664.1	8.7)
(Liquified Natural Gas)	(1506.2	23.3)	(1299.4	19.8)	(1344.9	17.6)
4. Manufactured Goods	1590.3	24.6	1824.7	27.8	2455.3	32.1
5. Others	232.8	3.6	211.1	3.2	256.0	3.4
Total	6471.3	100.0	6573.2	100.0	7642.0	100.0
Bilateral Trade Balance	1163.3		1542.4		2007.1	

Source: *Compiled and computed from Tsusan-sho [MITI], Tsusho Hakusho [White Paper on International Trade], various years.*

will be unlikely to change rapidly. Malaysia will continue to restructure towards capital and technology intensive activities which require both the influx of capital and technology intensive industries, and substantial imports of capital and intermediate products, from Japan. Certainly, because of the stronger yen and the influx of FDI from Japan and the NIEs, exports of manufactured goods, particularly machinery and equipment (especially electrical machinery), and chemicals to Japan are also expected to increase. However, the increase is unlikely to be significant, since the NIEs, which are more advanced in these fields, have to a certain extent also penetrated into the Japanese market. Malaysia not only has to compete with the NIEs but also with other ASEAN countries (Thailand in particular). In terms of social and industrial infrastructure, managerial know-how, capital, technology and human resources etc., the NIEs are in general in a better position than Malaysia. Economic development in the NIEs is going to gain in momentum. The NIEs will become even stronger competitors of Malaysia. The degree of Malaysia's exports of manufactured goods will, therefore, depend very much not only on the openness of the Japanese market, but also on the success of industrialization in Malaysia in the years ahead.

Investment

Japan has been one of the most important investors in Malaysia. Japan's investment in Malaysia was particularly prompted in the early 1980s by the introduction of the "Look East" policy in December 1981 and later by the Fourth Malaysia Plan (FMP) in July 1984, as analysed in the previous chapter. The "Look East" policy was regarded as part of Malaysia's national policy, which has attracted pursuit by the Japanese investors of business expansion in Malaysia. The FMP emphasized the development of heavy industrial projects which had particularly prompted Japanese big enterprises to rush to Malaysia.[3]

Japanese investment (based on paid-up capital) in Malaysia increased from M$32.6 million in 1980 to M$69.1 million in 1981 and then to M$139.9 million (approximately 26.5 per cent of total foreign direct investment in Malaysia) in 1982. However, there were 35, 45 and 36 Japanese investment cases in Malaysia during the same years. This indicates that Japanese investment in Malaysia's heavy industrial projects has continued its upward momentum. In other words, the total amount of each Japanese investment in Malaysia has increased substantially in the early 1980s.

Table 2.2 reveals Japanese investment in Malaysia during the 1985–1992 period. From Table 2.2, the following features can be identified. Firstly, Japanese investment in Malaysia increased eleven-fold from US$79.3 million in 1985 to US$879.8 million in 1991. Apart from the "Look East" policy and the FMP, the phenomenal yen appreciation after September 1985 and the relaxation policies introduced by the Malaysian government on FDI in October 1984[4] had also prompted Japanese FDI in Malaysia. Secondly, Japanese FDI in Malaysia's manufacturing sector has been predominant compared to that in the non-manufacturing sector during the 1989–1992 period. By the end of March 1987, foreign companies were allowed to have 100 per cent equity shares for five years provided that 20 per cent (it was 50 per cent in October 1986) of their manufactures are for export. After five years, 49 per cent or their equity shares (30 per cent should be owned by the Malaysian Malays) should be transferred to the Malaysians. The government also announced that from 1st January 1989, corporation tax will be reduced from 40 per cent to 35 per cent; from 1990, development tax will be reduced from 5 per cent to 4 per cent until it is totally abolished; from July 1988, foreigners were allowed to have 100 per cent equity shares in the non-manufacturing sector such as tourist and hotel industries. Japanese investment in Malaysia's manufacturing sector has been maintained at 41 to 91 per cent level throughout the 1985–1992 period. Japanese FDI in branch offices and real estate in Malaysia has totally been negligible.

Table 2.3 reveals Japanese investment in Malaysia's manufacturing industry by major industry groups during the 1985–1992 period. The following features can be identified. Firstly, Japanese FDI in Malaysia's manufacturing sector increased substantially and consistently during the 1985–1990 period. In relative terms, it increased 2.9 times from 32

Table 2.2

Japanese Investment in Malaysia (1985-1992)

(Unit: Cases; US$ million)

Sector	1985			1989			1990			1991			1992			1951-1992 (Total)		
	Cases	Amount	%	Cases	Amount	%	Cases	Amount	%	Cases	Amount	%	Cases	Amount	%	Cases	Amount	%
Manufacturing	32	32.8	41.4	111	470.6	69.9	119	582.3	80.3	92	612.7	69.6	73	465.4	66.2	1072	3481.0	72.3
Non-Manufacturing	27	44.9	56.6	48	202.5	30.1	50	141.1	19.5	44	267.1	30.4	38	238.1	33.8	647	1322.0	27.4
Branch Office	1	1.6	2.0	0	0	0	0	1.4	0.2	-	-	-	-	-	-	23	8.7	0.2
Real Estate	-	-	-	-	-	-	-	-	-	-	-	-	-	-	-	14	3.0	0.1
Total	60	79.3	100	159	673.1	100	169	724.8	100	136	879.8	100	111	703.5	100	1756	4814.7	100

Source: *Compiled and computed from Okura-sho [Ministry of Finance], Zaisei Kinyu Tokei Geppo [Statistics on Finance-Monthly Bulletin], Tokyo, various years.*

Table 2.3

Japanese Investment in Malaysia's Manufacturing Industry by Major Industry Groups, 1985–1992

(Unit: Cases; US$ million)

Industry	1985			1989			1990			1991			1992			1951–1992 (Total)		
	Cases	Amount	%	Cases	Amount	%	Cases	Amount	%	Cases	Amount	%	Cases	Amount	%	Cases	Amount	%
Foods	4	0.7	2.1	–	–	–	2	2.7	0.5	1	7.2	1.2	1	0.3	0.1	52	48.0	1.4
Textile	2	0.6	1.8	3	1.3	0.3	1	3.4	0.6	2	7.8	1.3	5	1.4	0.3	64	157.1	4.5
Wood & Pulp	–	–	–	7	7.6	1.6	15	22.9	3.9	8	15.6	2.5	10	21.8	4.7	123	127.9	3.7
Chemicals	4	3.4	10.4	10	49.5	10.5	6	96.1	16.5	8	41.3	6.7	6	38.7	8.3	95	439.7	12.6
Metal & Non-Metal	2	9.5	29.0	17	45.4	9.6	14	51.7	8.9	11	94.1	15.4	8	38.7	8.3	124	417.4	12.0
Machinery	2	1.8	5.5	10	25.9	5.5	7	80.8	13.9	4	26.1	4.3	5	53.6	11.5	59	238.4	6.8
Electronics & Electrical	7	2.3	7.0	40	272.7	57.9	39	261.0	44.8	27	283.8	46.3	21	106.9	23.0	285	1306.5	37.5
Transport Equipment	4	3.6	11.0	3	2.9	0.6	5	10.7	1.8	1	26.9	4.4	<	3.4	0.7	48	227.8	6.5
Others	7	10.9	33.2	21	65.4	13.9	30	53.1	9.1	30	109.9	17.9	15	200.5	43.1	222	518.2	14.9
Total	32	32.8	100	111	470.6	100	119	582.3	100	92	612.7	100	73	465.4	100	1072	3481.0	100

Source: *Compiled and computed from Okura-sho [Ministry of Finance], op. cit., various years.*

cases in 1985 to 92 cases in 1991. In absolute terms, it increased 18.7 times from US$32.8 million to US$612.7 million during the same period. Secondly, Japanese FDI in Malaysia's manufacturing sector has been concentrated in electronics and electrical products, and to a lesser extent, in chemicals, machinery, and metal and non-metal products. The above-mentioned industry groups constituted 73 per cent of Japan's total FDI in Malaysia's manufacturing sector in 1991, but dropped to 51 per cent in 1992. Thirdly, despite the fact that between March 1981 and March 1987 Japanese cumulative FDI in chemicals has been the largest industry group, in relative terms it has declined abruptly from 36.6 per cent to 22.1 per cent. The largest share of Japanese FDI in Malaysia's manufacturing sector has been shifted from chemicals to electronics and electrical products during the 1986–1992 period (except in 1987, Japanese FDI in transport equipment constituted 57 per cent of Japan's total investment in Malaysia's manufacturing sector). Fourthly, together with electronics and electrical products, Japanese FDI in machinery, and metal and non-metal industries (with the obvious decline in textile industry) has particularly gained its upward momentum. Japanese FDI in Malaysia is shifting steadily from labour-intensive to capital- and technology-intensive. Owing to higher operation costs, more and more Japanese entrepreneurs prefer Malaysia to the NIEs when they invest in Asia.

Japanese investment in Malaysia's non-manufacturing sector by major industry groups during the 1985–1992 period is shown in Table 2.4. The following features can be identified. Firstly, soon after the yen appreciation in September 1985, Japanese investment in Malaysia's non-manufacturing sector increased by two-fold from US$44.9 million in 1985 to US$93 million in 1986, due basically to heavy investment in Malaysia's finance and insurance sector. However, this trend did not continue long, as in 1987–1988, Japanese FDI in Malaysia's non-manufacturing sector dropped substantially. Japanese FDI gained significant upward momentum again in 1989, with a record high of US$202.5 million, compared to only US$44.9 million in 1985. However, Japanese investment dropped by 70 per cent in 1990, mainly because of the collapse of the bubble economy in Japan. Secondly, Japanese FDI in Malaysia's non-manufacturing sector

Table 2.4

Japanese Investment in Malaysia's Non-Manufacturing Industry, by Major Industry Groups, 1985–1992

(Unit: Cases; US$ million)

Industry	1985			1989			1990			1991			1992			1951–1992 (Total)		
	Cases	Amount	%	Cases	Amount	%	Cases	Amount	%	Cases	Amount	%	Cases	Amount	%	Cases	Amount	%
Agriculture & Forestry	–	0.3	0.7	9	4.4	2.2	4	2.5	2.0	2	1.6	0.6	2	0.8	0.3	59	38.6	2.9
Fishery	–	–	–	3	1.4	0.7	–	–	–	1	10.0	3.7	–	–	–	11	12.5	0.9
Mining	–	–	–	9	24.5	12.1	–	5.9	4.2	–	31.4	11.8	3	71.4	30.0	39	281.9	21.3
Construction	10	4.4	9.8	16	71.0	35.1	7	5.1	3.6	5	22.4	8.4	1	1.2	0.5	132	128.2	9.7
Commerce	10	37.1	82.6	8	25.1	12.4	8	10.6	7.5	3	5.2	1.9	8	25.4	10.7	168	193.6	14.6
Finance & Insurance	2	1.7	3.8	4	39.7	19.6	1	21.6	15.3	3	57.7	21.6	4	18.2	7.6	43	187.9	14.2
Services	1	0.7	1.6	5	10.4	5.1	11	32.7	23.2	19	71.5	26.8	14	50.9	21.4	85	●210.4	15.9
Transportation	2	0.4	0.9	–	–	–	4	6.3	4.4	1	11.4	4.3	–	0.5	0.2	15	25.8	2.0
Real Estate	–	–	–	8	25.9	12.8	15	50.9	36.1	10	55.9	20.9	6	69.8	29.3	49	214.6	16.2
Others	2	0.4	0.9	–	–	–	5.2	3.7	5.8	–	–	–	–	–	–	46	28.5	2.2
Total	27	44.9	100	48	202.5	100	50	141.1	100	44	267.1	100	38	238.1	100	647	1322.0	100

Source: *Compiled and computed from Okura-sho [Ministry of Finance], op. cit., various years.*

was concentrated in mining in the early 1980s. In absolute terms, Japanese cumulative investment in the mining sector increased from US$120 million by the end of March 1981 to US$148 million by the end of March 1987. Nevertheless, in relative terms, it decreased abruptly from 63.5 per cent to 35.5 per cent during the same period. Over the 1987–1991 period, Japanese investment in mining has been taken by commerce, services, construction, and finance and insurance. Thirdly, in recent years, Japanese companies have shown more and more interest in Malaysia's construction and real estate sectors. Japanese FDI in construction in 1989, and real estate in 1990 constituted 35 per cent and 36 per cent respectively in Japan's total investment in Malaysia's non-manufacturing sector.

Despite some interruptions, Japanese FDI in Malaysia's non-manufacturing sector increased by fivefold from US$44.9 million in 1985 to US$238.1 million in 1992. In the next decade or two, Japanese FDI in Malaysia is likely to have the following noticeable changes. Firstly, Japanese FDI will continue to gain momentum in its investment drive in Malaysia. From the Malaysian side, improved social and industrial infrastructure, expanded domestic markets due to higher consumption power, labour resources improvement and development, abundant industrial and agricultural raw materials, and the government's supportive policies for faster industrial development, etc., are important pull-factors. From the Japanese side, however, phenomenal yen appreciation, high operation costs, trade frictions and economic conflicts with the West, and increased competition from the NIEs, etc., are important push-factors for Japan to invest in Malaysia. Secondly, compared to the NIEs, Malaysia will be much more attractive especially for Japanese labour-intensive industries. Operation costs in the NIEs are becoming more and more expensive due to labour disputes and wage increases, further currency readjustment and industrial restructuring. More and more Japanese industries in the NIEs and particularly in Singapore, are forced to shift their operation bases to Malaysia. Besides, the US 'graduated' the NIEs from the general system of preferences (GSP) in January 1989 and Japanese investors will find the NIEs less attractive if their manufactures are for markets in the West, especially the US. Likewise, Japanese FDI in Malaysia is likely to gain further upward momentum in the next decade. Thirdly, Japanese FDI in Malaysia's non-manufacturing sector is likely to increase at a faster rate than in the manufacturing sector towards the twenty-first century, despite the fact that by the end of March 1989, Japanese cumulative investment in Malaysia's manufacturing sector was twice that of the non-manufacturing sector. Even in 1990, Japanese FDI in Malaysia's manufacturing and non-manufacturing sectors was 80 per cent and 20 per cent respectively. It dropped to 66 and 34 per cent respectively in 1992. However, towards the twenty-first century, without any doubt, the proportion of Japanese FDI in Malaysia's manufacturing sector will continue to be larger than that in the non-manufacturing sector. Nevertheless, Japanese FDI in the non-manufacturing sector especially commerce, finance and insurance, and to a lesser extent, services, is likely to gain momentum at a faster speed. This is the result of the immense increase of the Japanese FDI in the manufacturing sector which required strong back-up from investments in the non-manufacturing sector. Fourthly, Japanese FDI in Malaysia will be moving toward capital-and technology-intensive sectors in the next decade in parallel with Malaysia's efforts to become a NIE by the twenty-first century and an industrialized nation by the year 2020. Operation costs in Malaysia are higher than in Thailand, the Philippines, and, of course, China. Japanese and the NIE's investors will, therefore, find Malaysia less attractive for their labour-intensive industries. Likewise, Malaysia will be increasingly receiving higher capital-intensive investments from Japan, as well as from the NIEs, compared to the countries just mentioned. Recently, the Malaysian government has shown keen interest to attract more high technology industries and foreign labour intensive industries will be scrutinized before being allowed to invest in Malaysia.

Development Aid

Economic assistance from overseas, especially from Japan, has become an important source to finance industrial projects and to develop human resources in Malaysia. The latest statistics available here suggest that in 1990, total bilateral official development assistance (ODA) from the Organisation for Economic Co-operation and Development (OECD) received by Malaysia amounted to as much as US$468.8 million. The breakdowns were, Japan US$372.6 million (79.5 per cent), UK US$29.8 million (6.4 per cent), Australia US$26.9 million (5.7 per cent) and others US$39.5 million (8.4 per cent). Over the 1986–1991 period, Japan, Australia and UK were Malaysia's top three ODA suppliers among the OECD members. Moreover, during the same period (except 1986 and 1988) Malaysia's bilateral ODA from Japan appeared to be particularly significant (see Table 2.5).

Table 2.6 reveals Japan's ODA disbursements in Malaysia over the 1982–1991 period. The ODA disbursements are divided into grants (grant aid and technical co-operation) and loan aid. In general, the total amount of grants is much smaller than loan aid. Among grants, technical co-operation appears to be more significant than grant aid. On the other hand, the total amount of grants is overwhelmed by loan aid. Table 2.6 shows that in 1990, grants on

Table 2.5

Share of DAC Countries in Total Bilateral ODA Received by Malaysia (1986–1991)

US$ million

	1986		1988		1989		1990		1991	
		%		%		%		%		%
Japan	37.8	(19.7)	24.8	(23.9)	79.6	(56.8)	372.6	(79.5)	199.8	(69.1)
Australia	40.8	(21.3)	37.1	(35.8)	21.4	(15.3)	26.9	(5.7)	24.1	(8.3)
UK	75.4	(39.3)	12.2	(11.8)	10.6	(7.6)	29.8	(6.4)	17.6	(6.1)
Others	38.0	(19.7)	29.6	(28.5)	28.6	(20.4)	39.5	(8.4)	47.5	(16.5)
Total	192.0	(100.0)	103.7	(100.0)	140.2	(100.0)	468.8	(100.0)	289.0	(100.0)

Note: *DAC = The Development Assistance Committee of the OECD.*
Source: *Ministry of Foreign Affairs, Japan's Official Development Assistance, Annual Report 1987, Tokyo, Japan, March 1988, p. 147.*

Kaigai Keizai Kyoryoku Kikin, Kaigai Keizai Kyoryoku Binran, Tokyo, various years.

Table 2.6

Japan's ODA Disbursements to Malaysia (1982–1991)

(US$ Million)

Year	Grants			Loan Aid	Total	(%)
	Grant Aid	Technical Co-operation	Total			
1982	1.1	15.5	16.6	58.7	75.3	(3.2)
1983	6.7	22.6	29.3	63.0	92.3	(3.8)
1984	11.0	24.8	35.8	209.3	245.1	(10.1)
1985	0.6	23.1	23.7	102.0	125.6	(4.9)
1986	7.1	36.4	43.5	5.7	37.8	(1.0)
1987	7.9	40.8	48.7	227.7	276.4	(5.3)
1988	2.9	54.7	57.6	32.8	24.8	(0.4)
1989	1.8	56.9	58.7	20.9	79.6	(1.2)
1990	1.8	58.5	60.3	312.3	372.6	(5.4)
1991	8.0	60.0	68.0	131.8	199.8	(2.3)

Note: *Figures in parentheses indicate the percentage within Japan's total bilateral ODA.*
Source: *Ministry of Foreign Affairs, Japan's Official Development Assistance, Annual Report 1987, Tokyo, Japan, March 1988.*

Gaimu-sho [Ministry of Foreign Affairs], Waga Kuni no Seifu Kaihatsu Enjyo [Japan's Official Development Assistance], Tokyo, Japan, 1988, and others.

technical co-operation were 32.5 times that of grant aid; loan aid (US$312.3 million) was 5.2 times that of grants (US$60.3 million) extended by Japan to Malaysia. It is, therefore, clear that loan aid has been of paramount importance in Japan's ODA disbursements to Malaysia in 1982–1991 (except in 1986, and 1988–1989). Take for example, in 1991, loan aid constituted 66.0 per cent of Japan's total ODA disbursements to Malaysia.

Table 2.7 reveals the distribution and utilization of Japan's ODA disbursements to Malaysia in 1982–1987. Firstly, loan aid is basically for two purposes: the improvement of infrastructure such as the Port Kelang power station project, the highway toll system project and the Perils Port construction project; and the development of big industrial projects such as the Sabah gas grid, ASEAN urea project in Malaysia and the polished rice plant construction. Secondly, grant aid basically

Table 2.7

Details of Japan's ODA Disbursements to Malaysia (1982–1987)

(¥100 Million)

Fiscal Year	Loan Aid	Grant Aid	Technical Co-operation*
1982		• Centre for Instructor and Advanced Skill Training (17.40) • Japanese Language Centre of the University of Malaya (3.90) • Cultural Grant Aid (0.45) (Total 21.75)	(Total 31.11)
1983	• Port Kelang Power Station Project (phase II) [the supporting equipment of the boiler portion and the turbine generator portion] (84.70) • Sabah Gas Grid Project (phase II) (125.30) • Port Kelang Power Station Project (phase II) (400.00) (Total 610.00)	• Centre for Instructor and Advanced Skill Training (20.60) • Cultural Grant Aid (3 projects) (0.89) (Total 21.49)	1. 357 persons 2. 44 persons 3. 223 persons 4. 39 persons 5. ¥246 million 6. 4 cases 7. 12 cases (Total 31.96)
1984	• Sabah Gas Grid Project (phase II) (173.60) • Malayan Railway Diesel Electric Locomotives Purchase Project and two other projects (36.40) (Total 210.00)	• Broadcasting equipment (0.50) • LL equipment (0.39) (Total 0.89)	1. 459 persons 2. 69 persons 3. 281 persons 4. 52 persons 5. ¥267 million 6. 5 cases 7. 12 cases (Total 34.52)
1985	• ASEAN Urea Project in Malaysia (47.97) (Total 47.97)	• The National Prawn Fry Production and Research Centre Project (1298) • Cultural Grant Aid (2 projects) (0.64) (Total 13.62)	1. 459 persons 2. 46 persons 3. 191 persons 4. 40 persons 5. ¥383 million 6. 6 cases 7. 14 cases (Total 36.21)

(*Continued on next page*)

Table 2.7 (*continued*)

(¥100 Million)

Fiscal Year	Loan Aid	Grant Aid	Technical Co-operation*
1986	• Highway Toll System Project (16.83) • Diesel Electronic Locomotives Projects (II) (16.18) • Engkili Sibu Transmission Line Construction Project (43.57) • Perils Port Construction Project (2.86) • Polished Rice Plant Construction Project (16.30) (Total 125.74)	• Audio-Visual Equipment to the National Cultural Complex (0.45) • Construction of the ASEAN Poultry Disease Research and Training Centre (8.73) • Robot for Educational Purposes (0.17) (Total 9.35)	1. 506 persons 2. 83 persons 3. 276 persons 4. 40 persons 5. ¥870 million 6. 6 cases 7. 13 cases (Total 44.19)
1987	Nil		1. 506 persons 2. 95 persons 3. 248 persons 4. 44 persons 5. ¥613 million 6. 7 cases 7. 15 cases
		(Total 4.41)	(Total 42.96)
Cumulative total by 1987			1. 4046 persons 2. 671 persons 3. 2629 persons 4. 704 persons 5. ¥4456 million 6. 14 cases 7. 58 cases
	(Total 3279.71)	(Total 82.99)	(Total 343.94)

Source: *Same as Table 2.6*

*Technical Co-operation:
1. *Acceptance of Trainees*
2. *Displacing of Experts*
3. *Development Survey*
4. *Dispatching Japan Overseas Co-operation Volunteers*
5. *Provision of Machinery & Equipment*
6. *Project-Type Technical Co-operation*
7. *Development Survey*

concentrates in the following two fields: providing advanced equipment such as broadcasting equipment, LL equipment and audio-visual equipment, and setting up institutions or centres for research or training such as the Centre for Instructor and Advanced Skill Training, Japanese Language Centre of the University of Malaya, and the National Prawn Fry Production and Research Centre. Thirdly, technical co-operation is widely diversified and in actual implementation it usually takes a form of acceptance of trainees, dispatching of experts, developing survey, dispatching Japan Overseas Co-operation volunteers, provision of machinery and equipment, project-type technical co-operation and development survey. An important point should be made here that the acceptance of trainees has been the main task of technical co-operation. By 1987, the cumulative number of Malaysian trainees accepted by Japan had amounted to 4,046 persons.

Table 2.8 shows Japan's loan aid to Malaysia over the 1966–1992 period. Japan had extended 14 loan aids to Malaysia by 1992, amounting to a total of ¥473.19 billion.[5]

In 1987, Malaysia was the seventh largest recipient country of Japan's ODA.[6] Japan also became the record largest ODA donor next only to the US in the same year.[7] Japan's main ODA recipient countries have been concentrated in Asia. In fiscal 1992, Japan offered a record ¥712 billion in ODA loans, a 22 per cent increase over the previous year. In terms of new commitments, Asia accounted for 77.9 per cent of the fiscal 1992 total.[8] Judging from Malaysia's financial situation and economic development drive, it is likely that Malaysia will continue to receive substantial Japanese ODA in the years ahead.

While grant aid and technical co-operation do not require repayment, Malaysia now faces serious problems repaying the loan aid received from Japan. She has received a double blow in recent years: sustained currency depreciation despite the fact that she has recovered from economic recession in the early 1980s; and phenomenal yen appreciation after September 1985.[9] The Malaysian government expected to have loan repayment reduced but was turned down by the previous Japanese Premier Takeshita Noboru during his last visit to

Table 2.8
Japan's Loan Aid to Malaysia, 1966–1992

Year		Amount (¥100 Million)
1966	1st Loan Aid	180.00
1971	2nd "	360.00
1974	3rd "	360.00
1977	4th "	210.00
1978	5th "	210.00
1979	6th "	210.00
1980	7th "	210.00
1981	8th "	336.00
1983	9th "	610.00
1984	10th "	210.00
1985	Additional Loan Aid	48.00
1986	llth Loan Aid	126.00
1988	12th "	420.00
1990	13th "	612.60
1992	14th "	629.30
Total	1st – 14th Loan Aid	4,731.9

Source: *Compiled from Gaimu-sho [Ministry of Foreign Affairs], op. cit., pp. 10, 100–103 and others.*

Malaysia. Japan's ODA disbursements to Malaysia, particularly the repayment and mutually agreeable settlement of loan aid, will continue to be one of the paramount issues in the economic relationship between Japan and Malaysia towards the twenty-first century.

Conclusion

Malaysia intends to become an Asian NIE by the end of the twentieth century. In so doing, she requires FDI, technology, managerial know-how, economic assistance/development aid as well as international markets. She has to expand her exposure to the world and attract foreign participation in her domestic economic activities not only from the industrialized countries but also from the NIEs. Being a developing country, she has managed to attract a substantial amount of FDI and development aid essentially from Japan. Japan will continue to be an important economic partner of Malaysia towards the twenty-first century.

Malaysia's economic development policy will continue to focus on resource-based industrialization, import-substitution industrialization,[10] and gradually shifting to export-orientation industrialization. By the twenty-first century, her economic structure is likely to be restructured and upgraded to reach a higher level of economic development. Malaysia is considering the NIEs as development models as they have succeeded in rapid economic development through export-oriented industrialization. Malaysia is now learning from the NIEs' development experience, and Japan's economic role (investment, foreign trade and development aid) is, therefore, indispensable.

A substantial amount of Japanese FDI and development aid has been poured into Malaysia's heavy industrial development projects, some of which have encountered serious problems in recent years. A lesson should be learnt from this failure. It is argued that nurturing a wide range of supporting industries, together with some promising local small-and medium-sized industries, will, in the long run, set up a healthy economy in Malaysia.

Malaysia should also change her vertical trade relationship with the outside world. Of course, resource-based industrialization and import-substitution policies will ultimately contribute to this move. Malaysia should increase exports of manufactured products to her major trading partners such as Japan, the US and the EU. On the Japanese side, the rising yen, increased domestic consumption of foreign goods and the additional Japanese FDI have all contributed towards imports of foreign manufactured products. The Japanese market is expected to import more Malaysian manufactured products in the years ahead.

Japanese development aid is commonly criticized as a tied-aid or a *yobimizu* (priming water) of Japanese economic expansion. This criticism of course can be heard everywhere in Malaysia. It is unrealistic to expect Japan to behave like Father Christmas. However, Japan should make a positive contribution toward Malaysia's economic development not merely toward her own economic expansion. *Sarakin* (consumer credit business) is not appreciated by the recipients. A mutually agreeable solution towards repaying Japanese development loan aid should be reached the sooner the better. Japan should keep in mind that a debtor is always less flexible than a creditor.

Notes

1 See Chapter 5 *Japan in ASEAN: Potential Trade Frictions*, for more information.
2 There are discrepancies between statistics published by the Japanese Ministry of International Trade and Industry and the International Monetary Fund. Here, the former is used.
3 For instance, the Perwaja Trengganu Sdn. Bhd. (M$0.25 billion) was jointly set up by the Nippon Steel Corporation and the Heavy Industries Corporation (HICOM) in Trengganu; Honda, Yamaha and Suzuki had set up joint ventures with HICOM and produced autobike engines in Malaysia separately.
4 The relaxation policies suggest that any new FDI or business expansion carried out during the period October 1966 to December 1990 is entitled to the following advantages. Firstly, FDI will be allowed to have up to 100 per cent equity shares provided that 50 per cent of its products are for export or are sold in the export processing zone, or has employed more than 350 employees. Secondly, a foreign company is allowed to reserve five posts (including one person in a key position) for foreigners for the first ten years if its paid-up capital exceeds US$2 million. Nihon Boeki Shinko-kai (JETRO), *1988 JETRO Hakusho Toshi-hen* [1988 JETRO White Paper on Investment] (Tokyo, 1988), p. 142.
   In July 1988, these relaxation policies had been further modified. JETRO, op. cit. (1989), pp. 140–141.
5 For a clearer picture about the extent of loans received by Malaysia from Japan one may find the following calculation useful. During the period 1966–1992, the per capita loan aid from Japan stood at ¥25,183 = M$633.6 (¥100 = M$2.516, as on 22 June 1994). (Total loan aid received ¥473,190 million divided by Malaysia's total population of 18.79 million [1992].)
6 In 1987, Malaysia received Japan's ODA which amounted to US$276.5 million (5.27 per cent of Japan's total ODA) which was only next to Indonesia (US$707.3 million: 13.48 per cent), China (US$553.1 million: 10.54 per cent), the Philippines (US$379.4 million: 7.23 per cent) and Thailand (US$302.6 million: 5.77 per cent). Gaimu-sho [Ministry of Foreign Affairs], op. cit., vol. 1 (1988), p. 138.
7 Total ODA volume of the US and Japan was US$8,776 million (21.3 per cent of total OECD share) and US$7,454 million (18.1 per cent) respectively. Japan has just become the largest donor country in the world.
8 *Japan Times*, 29 May 1993.
9 The Japanese currency has increased its value from US$1 = ¥242 just before September 1985 to the present US$1 = ¥100 (22 June 1994).
10 Malaysia implemented import-substitution policy in the 1960s. However, the second import-substitution policy, which is now being implemented, is essentially aimed at producing capital and intermediate products domestically to meet her rapid economic development and economic take-off.

CHAPTER 3

Japan–Singapore Trade Frictions: A Study of Japanese Non-Tariff Barriers

Introduction

Japan has been accused of imposing non-tariff barriers (NTBs) on imports of foreign products. NTBs form an important part in defining the closed and protectionist market in Japan. This chapter identifies — through a comprehensive survey of Singapore exporters and manufacturers and, to a lesser extent, Japanese importers and distributors — several suspected NTBs and examines them in detail. Singapore's lopsided trade relationship with Japan can be rectified if Japan is willing to look into measures to eliminate NTBs. On the other hand, it is an undeniable fact that Singapore's exporters and manufacturers have also created their own NTBs by ineffectively and less aggressively exploring the Japanese market.

It is widely known that the Singapore economy is very much outward-looking and trade-oriented due to its lack of natural resources and small domestic market. These two basic factors have made it necessary for Singapore to develop human resources aimed at promoting capital-intensive, high value-added, and high-technology industries. As a result of this industrial policy, Singapore-made manufactured products will be looking increasingly for potential foreign markets. It is anticipated that developed countries, such as the US, Japan, and the EC will gradually become important markets for Singapore's manufactured products. Obviously, Singapore has to explore wider markets among developed countries in order to maintain a balanced trade relationship with them, as rapid industrial development in Singapore requires substantial imports of machinery and equipment, and other high-technology supplies from technologically advanced countries. On the other hand, because of the world-wide economic recession which has led to an economic slowdown among developed countries, protectionist policies have been implemented to restrain import trade. Thus, manufactured products from developing countries find formidable constraints in penetrating the markets of developed countries.

In this context, Singapore has faced similar difficulties in exploring the Japanese market. The Japan–Singapore trade relationship is getting more and more serious in terms of the trade deficit suffered by Singapore in recent years. Singapore, as the only newly-industrializing country among the ASEAN member states, will suffer a further set-back in its industrial developmental process if appropriate quantities of manufactured products, such as petroleum products, electronic and electrical products, and pharmaceutical products, do not find outlets in the Japanese market.

This chapter analyses the trade relationship between Singapore and Japan. Emphasis is given to Japanese NTBs affecting Singapore's manufactured exports to the Japanese market. It is not designed to examine the features and substance of NTBs practised in Japan in general, but is basically an effort to provide a data-base on identified NTBs encountered by Singapore's exporters and manufacturers in their export trade with Japan.[1]

Trade between Japan and Singapore

Before examining Japanese NTBs encountered by Singapore manufacturers and exporters, it is perhaps essential to discuss the main features of the Japan–Singapore trade relationship and problems. There are trade deficits and difficulties in Singapore's export trade with Japan which undermine Singapore's intention to penetrate the Japanese market.

Basic Facts

During the 1988–1993 period, Malaysia, the US, Japan, and the EC have been the most important trading partners of Singapore (see

Table 3.1). Trade with these countries constitutes 55 to 57 per cent of Singapore's total international trade throughout the period under consideration. The Singapore economy cannot but be influenced by the economic situation in these countries.

Singapore's rate of export and import dependence on these countries has ranged from 50 to 54 and 59 to 61 per cent, respectively, over the period 1988–1993 (see Tables 3.2 and 3.3). Singapore's import dependence on these countries has been higher than its export dependence, that is, in terms of total values, Singapore imports more from this group of countries than it exports.

The US and Japan have been important importers of Singapore's products. Singapore's exports to the US, in absolute terms, increased substantially from S$18,826 million in 1988 to S$24,291 million in 1993 (but stagnated in the years 1989–1991); while its imports from the US increased from S$13,718 million to S$22,360 million during the same period. Its exports to Japan increased from S$6,828 million in 1988 to S$8,921 million in 1993; while its imports from Japan increased consistently from S$19,364 million in 1988 to S$30,111 million in 1993. It should be pointed out that, during the period under consideration (except in 1993), Japan has taken over from Malaysia as Singapore's second largest trading partner, next only to the US.

Malaysia and the EC rank next to the US and Japan as Singapore's major trading partners. Singapore's exports to Malaysia rose from S$10,721 million in 1988 to S$16,942 million in 1993; while its imports from Malaysia also increased from S$12,929 million to S$22,669 million during the same period. Singapore's exports to the EC also increased substantially from S$6,362 million in 1988 to S$10,081 million in 1993, while its imports increased from S$7,413 million to S$10,926 million during the same period. The EC has proven to be a more and more important trading partner to Singapore in recent years.

In 1991–1992, Singapore's exports to industrialized countries (excluding Japan), particularly the US and the EC, increased significantly. However, during this period, Singapore's exports to Japan, due to the sudden collapse of the bubble economy in Japan, declined from S$8,836 million to S$7,857 million (see Table 3.2). On

Table 3.1
Singapore's Trade with Major Trading Partners, 1988–1993

(In S$ millions)

	1988 Value	(%)	1989 Value	(%)	1990 Value	(%)	1991 Value	(%)	1992 Value	(%)	1993 Value	(%)
Malaysia	23649.8	(14.1)	24698.8	(13.4)	27412.0	(13.4)	32618.6	(15.1)	30212.6	(13.7)	39611.7	(15.4)
United States	32544.4	(19.5)	36896.1	(20.1)	37826.0	(18.5)	38132.6	(17.6)	41119.4	(18.6)	46651.5	(18.1)
Japan	26192.3	(15.7)	28117.1	(15.3)	30447.7	(14.9)	33206.0	(15.4)	32609.8	(14.8)	39032.2	(15.2)
EC*	13774.7	(8.2)	15883.5	(8.6)	18331.7	(8.9)	18402.1	(8.5)	19021.3	(8.6)	21007.5	(8.2)
Sub-total	96161.2	(57.5)	105595.5	(57.4)	114017.4	(55.7)	122359.3	(56.6)	122963.1	(55.7)	146302.9	(56.9)
All other countries	71116.8	(42.5)	78384.7	(42.6)	90994.6	(44.3)	93715.1	(43.4)	97917.6	(44.3)	110773.3	(43.1)
All countries	167278.0	(100.0)	183980.2	(100.0)	205012.0	(100.0)	216074.4	(100.0)	220880.7	(100.0)	257076.2	(100.0)

Source: *Computed from Ministry of Trade and Industry, Economic Survey of Singapore, various years.*
* EC includes United Kingdom, Federal Republic of Germany (figures from October 1990 include the former German Democratic Republic) and France.

Table 3.2

Singapore's Exports to its Major Trading Partners (1988–1993)

(In S$ millions)

	1988 Value	(%)	1989 Value	(%)	1990 Value	(%)	1991 Value	(%)	1992 Value	(%)	1993 Value	(%)
Malaysia	10721.1	(13.6)	11914.8	(13.7)	12448.5	(13.1)	15236.1	(15.0)	12925.4	(12.5)	16942.2	(14.2)
United States	18826.0	(23.8)	20290.8	(23.3)	20245.5	(21.3)	20103.0	(19.7)	21778.9	(21.1)	24291.8	(20.3)
Japan	6827.8	(8.6)	7447.7	(8.5)	8301.5	(8.7)	8836.4	(8.7)	7856.7	(7.6)	8921.3	(7.5)
EC*	6361.7	(8.0)	7495.4	(8.6)	8411.9	(8.8)	8534.6	(8.4)	8974.7	(8.7)	10080.8	(8.4)
Sub-total	42736.6	(54.1)	47148.7	(54.1)	49407.4	(51.9)	52710.1	(51.8)	515235.7	(49.9)	60236.1	(50.4)
All other countries	36314.7	(45.9)	39967.8	(45.9)	45798.6	(48.1)	49169.4	(48.2)	51815.3	(50.1)	59237.3	(49.6)
All countries	79051.3	(100.0)	87116.5	(100.0)	95206.0	(100.0)	101879.5	(100.0)	103351.0	(100.0)	119473.4	(100.0)

Source: Computed from Department of Statistics, Monthly Digest of Statistics, Singapore, various years.
* EC includes United Kingdom, Federal Republic of Germany (figures from October 1990 include the former German Democratic Republic) and France.

Table 3.3

Singapore's Imports from its Major Trading Partners (1988–1993)

(In S$ millions)

	1988		1989		1990		1991		1992		1993	
	Value	(%)	Value	(%)	Value	(%)	Value	(%)	Value	(%)	Value	(%)
Malaysia	12928.7	(14.7)	12784.0	(13.2)	14963.5	(13.6)	17382.5	(15.2)	17287.2	(14.7)	22669.6	(16.5)
United States	13718.4	(15.5)	16605.3	(17.1)	17580.5	(16.0)	18029.6	(15.8)	19340.5	(16.5)	22359.8	(16.2)
Japan	19364.5	(21.9)	20669.4	(21.3)	22146.2	(20.2)	24369.6	(21.3)	24753.1	(21.1)	30110.9	(21.9)
EC*	7413.0	(8.4)	8388.1	(8.7)	9919.8	(9.0)	9867.5	(8.7)	10046.6	(8.5)	10926.7	(7.9)
Sub-total	53424.6	(60.5)	58446.8	(60.3)	64610.0	(58.8)	69649.2	(61.0)	71427.4	(60.8)	86067.0	(62.5)
All other countries	34802.1	(39.5)	38416.9	(39.7)	45195.9	(41.2)	44545.7	(39.0)	46102.3	(39.2)	51535.8	(37.5)
All countries	88226.7	(100.0)	96863.7	(100.0)	109805.9	(100.0)	114194.9	(100.0)	117529.7	(100.0)	137602.8	(100.0)

Source: *Same as Table 3.2.*
* *EC includes United Kingdom, Federal Republic of Germany (figures from October 1990 include the former German Democratic Republic) and France.*

the other hand, Singapore's imports from Japan increased from S$24,370 million in 1991 to S$24,753 million in 1992, so that its trade deficit with Japan increased, exacerbating Singapore's overall trade balance in 1992 (see Table 3.4).

Between 1988–1993, Singapore's export trade has been encouraging. Increased exports to developed countries of chemicals and chemical products, machinery and transport equipment, and miscellaneous manufactured articles contributed to this sound export performance.

Lopsided Trade Relation

Singapore is heavily reliant on international trade. In 1985, her import/GDP and export/GDP ratios were 150 per cent and 131 per cent respectively. Traditionally, Singapore showed a deficit in its balance of merchandise trade, financed by surpluses in both the invisible trade (tourism, transportation and services, etc.) and capital inflow.[2]

Despite the fact that Singapore's foreign trade issues should not be restricted to her bilateral trade with Japan, Singapore's trade deficit with Japan is becoming more and more of a concern among the Singapore government officials and in business circles. Singapore's total trade deficit has been accounted for largely by the trade deficit with Japan which constituted 67.4 per cent of Singapore's total trade deficit with all foreign countries in 1985. Over the 1985–1993 period, Singapore's trade deficit with Japan exceeded Singapore's total trade deficit with all foreign countries between 1986–1989 and 1991–1993. Over the period under consideration, Singapore accumulated a trade deficit of S$113,798 million with Japan. This amount exceeded Singapore's total trade deficit of S$100,584 million with all foreign countries (see Table 3.4).

Singapore's exports to Japan increased steadily from S$6,828 million in 1988 to S$8,836 million in 1991 but dropped to S$7,857 million in 1992, due to Japan's sluggish economic situation as pointed out earlier. Exports of manufactured goods from Singapore to Japan increased substantially and have undoubtedly contributed to Singapore's export drive to Japan (see Table 3.5). However, as a result

Table 3.4

Singapore Trade with Japan (1985–1993)

(In S$ million)

	Exports	Imports	Bilateral Trade Balance	Total Trade Balance
1985	4722.2	9869.7	–5147.5	–7638.7
1986	4204.4	11052.2	–6847.8	–6649.9
1987	5449.3	14029.3	–8580.0	–8149.5
1988	6827.8	19364.5	–12536.7	–9175.4
1989	7447.7	20669.4	–13221.7	–9747.2
1990	8301.5	22146.2	–13844.7	–14599.9
1991	8836.4	24369.6	–15533.2	–12315.4
1992	7856.7	24753.1	–16896.4	–14178.7
1993	8921.3	30110.9	–21189.6	–18129.4
Total (1985–1993)			–113,797.6	–100,584.1

Source: *Department of Statistics, Yearbook of Statistics, Singapore, various issues.*

Table 3.5

Imports of Manufactured Products from Singapore, 1988–1993

(In US$ millions)

	(A) Japan's total imports of manufactured goods	(B) Imports of manufactured goods from Singapore	$\frac{(B)}{(A)}$ (%)
1988	91838.4	1187.4	1.3
1989	106110.5	1648.5	1.6
1990	118027.7	1816.1	1.5
1991	120340.8	1980.0	1.6
1992	116999.1	1983.2	1.7
1993	125203.9	2589.2	2.1

Source: *Computed from MITI, Tsusho Haku-sho [White Paper on International Trade], Japan, various issues.*

of Singapore's rapid industrial development, imports from Japan increased significantly despite the appreciation of the Japanese yen. Over the 1988–1993 period, imports of heavy industrial and chemical products have remained consistently at 86 per cent (compared to 79–83 per cent over the 1975–1984 period) of Singapore's total imports from Japan, and in absolute terms, have increased approximately 2.0 times from US$7,200 million in 1988 to US$14,326 million in 1993 (see Table 3.6). Some of these imports (for example, iron pipes and fittings) have been re-exported to neighbouring countries, such as Malaysia and Indonesia, for oil and gas exploration activities. Imports of machinery and equipment have increased significantly and have remained at 71 to 74 per cent of Singapore's total imports from Japan in 1988–1993.

Imports of machinery and equipment, especially electrical machinery, have constituted approximately 40 per cent of Singapore's total imports from Japan throughout the 1988–1993 period, and have undoubtedly become Singapore's largest import item. Singapore's industrial policy which focuses on high value added, high capital, and high technology industries especially after 1979, will continue to stimulate imports of intermediate and capital goods from Japan. Furthermore, rapid industrial development in ASEAN also stimulated Singapore's imports of intermediate and capital goods from Japan. As an intermediary country, Singapore has re-exported intermediate and capital goods to her neighbouring countries. Singapore's exports of machinery and transport equipment increased remarkably from S$18.9 billion (38.6 per cent of Singapore's total exports) in 1986 to S$37.9 billion (48.0 per cent) in 1988 and then to S$47.7 billion (50.1 per cent) in 1990.[3]

Mineral fuels have been the most important Singapore exports to Japan, comprising 70 to 80 per cent of total exports to Japan in 1975–1984. Exports of mineral fuel increased fourfold from US$295 million in 1975 to US$1,241 million in 1984. In 1982, these exports to Japan dropped owing to the fall in oil prices and reduced oil trade. Also, exports of petroleum products to Japan fell by 20 per cent in 1983 — the first such decline since 1976 — because of the depressed state of the petrochemical industry in Japan.[4] This, however, has not affected Singapore's position as the largest supplier of petroleum products to Japan. Since 1984, following a restructuring of Japan's petroleum industry which resulted in reduced refining capacity, Singapore's exports

Table 3.6

Composition of Singapore's Trade with Japan, 1988–1993

(US$ million)

	1991 Value	1991 %	1992 Value	1992 %	1993 Value	1993 %
Exports						
Foodstuffs	109	4.7	144	4.9	146	4.1
Raw materials	117	5.0	129	4.4	121	3.4
Mineral fuels	925	39.5	1031	34.9	1488	41.7
Manufactured goods	1015	43.4	1476	50.0	1606	45.0
Others	172	7.4	173	5.9	211	5.9
Total	2168.2	100.0	4124.0	100.0	5511.4	100.0
Imports						
Foodstuffs	57	0.7	66	0.7	68	0.6
Raw materials & fuels	51	0.6	94	1.0	71	0.8
Light industrial products	770	9.3	790	8.5	935	8.7
Heavy industrial &						
chemical products	7200	86.6	8032	86.9	9312	87.0
chemical products	454	5.5	479	5.2	557	5.2
metals	863	10.4	988	10.7	1022	9.5
machinery & equipment	5883	70.8	6565	71.1	7733	72.2
Others	233	2.8	257	2.8	321	3.0
Total	4330.1	100.0	5106.9	100.0	5401.6	100.0

	1991 Value	1991 %	1992 Value	1992 %	1993 Value	1993 %
Exports						
Foodstuffs	168	4.9	180	5.8	205	5.1
Raw materials	130	3.8	116	3.7	108	3.0
Mineral fuels	1137	33.3	818	26.4	700	19.4
Manufactured goods	1791	52.5	1820	58.8	2406	66.8
Others	189	5.5	164	5.3	183	5.1
Total	3415	100.0	3097	100.0	3602	100.0
Imports						
Foodstuffs	71	0.6	97	0.7	125	0.8
Raw materials & fuels	94	0.8	122	0.9	223	1.3
Light industrial products	1088	8.9	1183	9.1	1343	8.1
Heavy industrial &						
chemical products	10588	86.7	11143	85.9	14326	86.3
chemical products	639	5.2	666	5.1	816	4.9
metals	1131	9.3	1119	8.6	1202	7.2
machinery & equipment	8819	72.2	9357	72.1	12308	74.1
Others	372	3.0	430	3.3	584	3.5
Total	12213	100.0	12974	100.0	16601	100.0

Source: *Compiled and computed from Tsusan-sho [MITI], Tsusho Hakusho [White Paper on International Trade], various years.*

of mineral fuels/petroleum products, although substantial, have been affected by price fluctuations and are sensitive to developments in Japan's petroleum industry.

Apart from petroleum products, Singapore's other major exports to Japan are crude rubber,[5] machinery parts, and medicinal products (mainly penicillin, the export of which fell by 29 per cent due to increased use of other antibiotics).[6] Singapore's trade deficit with Japan, which has created economic and trade frictions between the two countries, can be improved by expanding the exports of these items (especially manufactured goods) or by diversifying exports.

In recent years, Singapore's exports of petroleum products to Japan diminished abruptly (in relative terms) compared to that in the 1970s and early 1980s. Over the 1988–1993 period, as shown in Table 3.6, Singapore's exports of mineral fuels to Japan have dropped drastically since 1991. Instead, exports of manufactured goods increased substantially. Exports of manufactured goods have maintained at 43 to 67 per cent throughout the 1988–1993 period. In other words, Singapore's exports of manufactured goods have surpassed exports of mineral fuels in Singapore's trade history. Among manufactured goods, exports of machinery and equipment (particularly electrical machinery), and chemical products have been particularly important. Over the 1988–1991 period, these items constituted 37 to 44 per cent of Singapore's total export trade to Japan. They further increased to 51 and 60 per cent respectively in 1992 and 1993.

It can be argued that for the following two basic reasons, exports of manufactured goods from Singapore to Japan increased substantially. First, Singapore's rapid industrial development. In recent years, Singapore has been in a better position to export better quality industrial products to suit Japan's domestic needs. Second, higher yen and foreign investment drive have prompted Japan to practise "reverse import" and to increase imports of Singapore's manufactured goods. Both heavy industrial and chemical products have constituted a substantial proportion of Singapore's export and import trade with Japan. The implication is that the complementary industrial relationship between the two countries has become closer and closer. However, as mentioned earlier, the increased exports of manufactured goods from Singapore to Japan have not been able to rectify the lopsided trade relationship between the two countries. To be more precise, Singapore's trade deficit with Japan has increased significantly year by year. Singapore has to explore the Japanese market more aggressively and persistently in order to reduce its trade deficit with Japan.

Singapore's manufactured products are, nevertheless, less competitive (in terms of quality, design and packaging etc.) compared to Japanese products. Besides, Singapore's manufacturers and exporters have not made the necessary effort to explore the Japanese market. On top of these, one of the accusations is that Japan's closed-market (commonly known as non-tariff barriers) has particularly restricted imports of manufactured products from Singapore. Exports from Singapore to Japan are therefore far from satisfactory. Singapore is getting more and more concerned about its increasing trade deficit with Japan. Trade frictions and economic conflict between Singapore and Japan may become more and more serious should Singapore's huge trade deficit with Japan not be rectified over time.

Singapore's Views and Perceptions of Japanese Non-Tariff Barriers

Looking exclusively from the exporter's perspective, Singapore's tremendous trade deficit with Japan can only be rectified by promoting exports of mineral fuels and manufactured products (in addition to machinery and equipment, and chemical products) to Japan. However, Singapore exporters and manufacturers have found difficulty penetrating the Japanese market. A questionnaire survey has indicated that local exporters and manufacturers are generally overawed by the Japanese "closed-market" image. Some have suggested with confidence that Japan has long been restricting foreign imports by implementing NTBs to protect its domestic industries. They have argued that Japanese NTBs restrict the inflow of petroleum products, electrical and electronic products, and pharmaceutical products, etc. from Singapore into the Japanese market.

Scope of Survey and Definition of NTBs

A questionnaire survey was conducted in October–November 1982 (there is, of course, an urgent need to conduct a questionnaire survey again in order to update all the relevant data) to collect data on Singapore exporters and manufacturers' views and perceptions of Japanese NTBs. A total of 1004 companies belonging to the following industrial groupings: (a) food, drugs, drinks and tobacco; (b) textile, jewellery, hair and feathers; (c) wood, paper and printing; (d) petroleum, chemicals and oils; (e) building materials, glass and ceramics; (f) metal, mechanical and engineering; (g) rubber, plastics, leather and footwear; (h) electronics, electrical, toys and musical instruments have been selected (based on the *SMA Directory 1981*) as targets of the survey.

The definition of NTBs the study employs does not conform to that used by the International Chamber of Commerce or the General Agreement on Tariffs and Trade. The definition follows that of Arthur D. Little, Inc., which categorizes NTBs as follows:

Category	Description
1.	Government regulation and control (e.g. quotas, import surcharges, customs problems)
2.	Government participation in trade (e.g. government procurement, administrative guidance, state trading practices, government subsidies)
3.	Product quality and testing requirements (e.g. product testing and certification procedures, labelling requirements, health and safety standards)
4.	Structural NTBs (e.g. cultural and business practices; domestic supplier preferences; distribution systems problems in Japan.[7]

Results of Survey and Analysis

Of the 1,004 questionnaires sent to members of the Singapore Manufacturers' Association (SMA), 136 responses were received. These respondents can be divided into the following four groups:

Group One consists of 62 companies whose questionnaires were returned undelivered due to change of address or closure. These companies were subsequently dropped from the survey.

Group Two is made up of 48 companies that indicated having no trading transactions with Japan because of the following reasons: (a) they have never attempted to explore the Japanese market as their manufactured products are subject to heavy import duties in Japan; (b) they are service industries and are not involved in exports; (c) they supply their products only to local end-users in Singapore; (d) their manufactured products are subject to expensive freight charges which make them uncompetitive in the Japanese market.

In the interviews, some of the companies raised grievances and complaints such as: the Japanese are interested only in importing raw materials from developing countries; the Japanese ask for good quality but cheap products; the Japanese are good at imitating and copying your sample products before you even export. Many manufacturers have expressed difficulties in overcoming Japanese cultural and linguistic barriers even after Japanese buyers or importers have been secured. Some suspect that Japanese NTBs such as quotas, import duty, and customs problems are preventing manufacturers of this group from exporting to Japan, although they have not in reality encountered such instances. Some manufacturers have been pre-occupied with the perception that Japan is a closed market and is implementing protectionist policies. Most cottage manufacturers have been unable to participate in product fairs in Japan to promote Singapore exports or engage in marketing research before sending products over to Japan.

Group Three consists of 13 companies that indicated having trading transactions with Japan but not having encountered any Japanese NTBs; some have, however, occasionally encountered certification procedures and customs clearance problems, none of which have been serious enough to affect their exports to Japan. This group of companies can be characterized as follows (see also Table 3.7).

First, seven of the 13 companies are Japanese subsidiaries. Of these seven, one belongs to Group A (food, drugs, drinks and

Table 3.7

Exports to Japan without Encountering NTBs,
by Industry Group

	Industry Group	Number of Respondents	Exports to Japan (% of Total Trade)		Ownership of Company
			1–10	41–70	
A.	Food, drugs, drinks & tobacco	1		1	Japanese
B.	Textile, jewellery, hair & feathers	1	1		Indian
C.	Wood, paper, & printing	2	1	1	Taiwanese; Singaporean
D.	Petroleum, chemicals & oils	0	–	–	–
E.	Building materials, glass & ceramics	0	–	–	–
F.	Metal, mechanical & engineering	2	1	1	Japanese; Taiwanese
G.	Rubber, plastics, leather & footwear	0	–	–	–
H.	Electrical, electronic, toys & musical instruments	7	6	1	5 Japanese; 2 American
	Total	13	9	4	7 Japanese; 1 Indian; 1 Singaporean; 2 Taiwanese; 3 American

Source: *Questionnaire Survey Data.*

tobacco) and exports 47 per cent of its fruit drinks and beverages to Japan. Another belongs to Group F (metal, mechanical, and engineering) and exports 50 per cent of its manufactured products — miniature ball bearings, industrial fasteners, mechanical components, stepper and synchronous motors, etc. — to Japan. The remaining five belong to Group H and export 1 to 60 per cent of their total exports of electrical and electronic goods, and musical instruments to Japan. Japanese subsidiaries tend to belong to Group H (electrical, electronic, toys and musical instruments) and have their own marketing network and distribution routes in Japan. They export up to 60 per cent of their manufactured products to Japan, or else regard Singapore as a production base from which to export to Europe and America.

Second, two are American subsidiaries and belong to Group H. Both export 10 per cent of their electronic, electrical, and mechanical products to Japan and have American subsidiaries in Japan.

Third, one is a Singapore company belonging to Group C (wood, paper and printing) and exports raw materials such as cane and rattan to Japan. It has a Japanese importer and distributor and has increased its exports to Japan from 65 per cent in 1982 to 80 per cent in 1984.

Fourth, one is an Indian subsidiary belonging to Group B (textile, jewellery, hair and feathers) and two are Taiwanese subsidiaries belonging to Groups C and F. These companies have reduced their exports to Japan; demand has dropped because their products and quality do not meet Japanese tastes. Moreover, they do not seem to have reliable Japanese importers and distributors.

In summary, Japanese subsidiaries in Singapore, mostly in Group H, do not have problems exporting their products to their motherland. Other companies, whether local or American subsidiaries, have potential markets in Japan provided they have subsidiaries or reliable distributors and importers in Japan. Taiwanese and Indian subsidiaries have experienced decreased exports to Japan due to less competitiveness in pricing and quality, but they do not regard NTBs as obstacles preventing them from penetrating the Japanese market.

Group Four consists of 13 companies that indicated having encountered Japanese NTBs in exporting to Japan. These companies are summarized in Table 3.8. A thorough survey of these companies was conducted through interviews with their chairmen, managing directors, finance directors, sales managers, etc. Some of the companies

Table 3.8

Exports to Japan Encountering NTBs, by Industry Group

Industry Group	Number Respondents	% of Total	Exports to Japan (% of total trade)						Ownership of Company
			1–10	11–20	21–30	31–40	41–50	51–60	
A	3	23.1	1		1			3	2 British; 1 Singaporean
B	1	7.7		1					Singaporean
C	2	15.4	1	1					Singaporean; Malaysian
D	3	23.1	3						2 American; 1 British
E	–	–	–	–	–	–	–	–	
F	2	15.4	1			1			American; Japanese
G	1	7.7		1					Singaporean & Japanese
H	1	7.7					1		Japanese
Total	13	100.0	6	3	1	1	1	1	3 British; 3 American; 3 Singaporean; 2 Japanese; 1 Singaporean and Japanese, and 1 Malaysian.

Source: Questionnaire Survey Data.

Table 3.9

Incidence of NTBs Encountered by Industry Group

Industry Group	Government regulation and control	Government participating in trade	NTB Product quality & testing requirements	Structural NTBs
A	1		1	1
B				1
C	1		1	
D	2	1		
E				
F	2			
G	1			1
H				1
Total	7	1	2	4

Source: *Questionnaire Survey Data.*

were unable to classify specific NTBs they encountered because of the complicated nature of these NTBs, for example, both import surcharges and customs clearance problems; product testing and certification procedures, etc.

Some have encountered NTBs only occasionally in their long period of trading transactions with Japan, as summarized in Table 3.9.

Seven companies of mixed origin and classification have encountered NTBs arising from government regulation and control — quotas, import surcharges, and customs clearance problems (see Table 3.9 for breakdown). Three have encountered NTBs related to domestic supplier preferences and distribution systems; in the case of two, the NTBs were related to product quality and testing requirements; the third one experienced administrative "interference" (or guidance).

Two Japanese subsidiaries in the metal and electronics industries indicated having occasionally encountered domestic supplier preference and minor customs clearance problems. They have reported that they compete, though favourably, with similar products produced in Japan including those manufactured by their subsidiaries in Japan. They have complained of Japanese customers' preconceptions, for example, that goods in Japan are superior to those produced overseas even though Japanese subsidiaries in Singapore have produced satisfactory or even better quality products.

Generally, Japanese subsidiaries do not encounter serious NTBs since they not only have marketing network and distribution routes in Japan, but are also familiar with Japanese commercial and business practices. However, one Singaporean and Japanese joint venture has indicated having encountered two serious customs clearance problems in their eight years of trading with Japan.

Japanese electronics subsidiaries do not encounter problems related to Japanese procurement practices that American electronics firms exporting to Japan see as severely penalizing telecoms equipment and semi-conductor manufacturers in Singapore. American manufacturers are being out-competed by Japanese firms in terms of product quality and service, partly as a result of government subsidies to Japanese firms for research and development activities. American manufacturers also face unfavourable customs clearance problems and domestic supplier preferences when exporting electronic and related products to Japan.

It has been argued that Japan has sufficient refinery capacity to produce petroleum products, and therefore, exports of petroleum products to Japan by American subsidiaries in Singapore have been kept at very low levels. Exports of petroleum products by American subsidiaries are restricted by Japanese government regulation and control (such as quotas) and government participation in trade (such as administrative guidance). These subsidiaries regard the administrative guidance, which through verbal and informal suggestions to domestic industry participants can restrain imports, as a typical NTB.[8] They insist that governments in Europe and the US do not usually practise administrative guidance to protect domestic petroleum industries and therefore find the Japanese market difficult to penetrate. Mobil Oil Singapore Pte. Ltd. has had to set up a Mobil subsidiary in Japan with 50 per cent Japanese equity. The timing and volume of exports of petroleum products from Singapore have been left totally to this Mobil subsidiary. It has been said that, because of many constraints and restrictions, the Japanese market for Mobil petroleum products has been smaller than that of Singapore.

The Japanese market has been very profitable and expansionary for certain British pharmaceutical subsidiaries from Singapore. These subsidiaries generally feel that NTBs are not a problem, this, despite the delay (about 18 months) experienced in having drugs registered in Japan where registration is quite meticulous and subject to the most demanding standards. They have had consignments rejected not because of NTBs but because of the product itself being defective or not meeting Japanese health standards which emphasize above-average quality. The rejection rate though has been at acceptable levels.

The high quality requirement demanded by the Japanese has made it necessary for a certain British pharmaceutical subsidiary in Singapore to set up a Tokyo office to monitor quality control and distribution in the Japanese market. The office does effective market research so that Japanese consumer preferences, such as presentation and packaging, are satisfactorily met. The British pharmaceutical subsidiary has established good trading relations and a marketing network in Japan and has direct links with Japanese distributors. About 65 per cent of its total sales in Japan are channelled through Japanese manufacturers and distributors (Fujisawa, Meiji, Taitoo, Takeda, Kyowahakko, and Taisho, etc.) who merely attach their own labels to British antibiotics produced in Singapore. This may probably be the best way to promote acceptability as Japanese consumers have more faith and trust in their own drugs.

Local firms, as a whole, do not make aggressive promotion efforts to penetrate the Japanese market. They are unable to set up subsidiaries, a marketing network, or distribution routes in Japan. Their products are either below the quality standards expected by Japanese consumers or do not suit Japanese tastes. These constraints result from their relatively small capital investment, less keenness towards technological improvement and, more importantly, their attitude towards penetrating the Japanese market.

Four local suppliers/manufacturers, primarily raw material suppliers and light industry manufacturers, were interviewed. Two exported substantially to Japan in 1982 with exports amounting to 12.8 and 20 per cent of their respective total exports. Exports of the first firm dropped drastically because of the gloomy market situation in Japan. Exports of the second firm were almost suspended because Mitsukoshi, a prestigious Japanese department store, terminated its sole agent distribution due to unsuccessful efforts to promote the firm's product. The two remaining firms had negligible exports to Japan — 1.5 and 2 per cent respectively.

The interviews revealed that these firms have encountered NTBs such as quotas, import surcharges, customs clearance, problems related to product testing, certification procedures, and Japan's distribution system. Some have had difficulty pinpointing the NTBs they encountered and have simply named those they are likely to encounter or which other firms in the same line have encountered. These firms are put off by the prospect of the "Japanese closed market" and "Japanese NTBs". Without making any aggressive effort to do market research and product development in Japan, certain local firms, after some preliminary frustrations, are quick to conclude that Japan is a "closed market".

Examples of Perceived Non-Tariff Barriers

This section presents cases of export items to Japan that have encountered suspected Japanese NTBs of one kind or another. A small number of the NTB cases are taken from newspaper reports and local publications. Most of the cases are from interviews with members of the SMA and the Singapore Chinese Chamber of Commerce and Industry (SCCCI) primarily, but some are from information provided by Japanese importers and distribution.

Example I: Frozen Beef
The export of frozen beef to Japan was initially proposed by Singapore's then Minister for Trade and Industry, Dr Tony Tan, to the Japanese government's special economic mission led by the former Minister of

International Trade and Industry, Mr Esaki Masumi, when he visited Singapore in August 1982. Later, the Japanese Minister of Foreign Affairs, Mr Abe Shintaro, promised his Singapore counterpart, Mr S Dhanabalan, that Japan would consider the proposal when Abe visited Singapore together with Prime Minister Nakasone Yasuhiro in May 1983. The Japanese government was initially very reluctant to allow Japanese tourists (approximately 350,000 who come to Singapore annually) to buy Australian frozen beef at Singapore's Changi Airport on their way home to Japan on the grounds that under a classification drawn up in 1983, Singapore was considered a Category Two country in terms of cleanliness for its meat exports. After sending experts to investigate Singapore's sanitary situation and after numerous talks with the Singapore authorities, the Japanese government eventually allowed frozen beef to be brought in from Changi Airport.[9] However, a year later the Japanese government banned the entry of frozen beef from Changi Airport.[10] This move seemed to be a shock to both the Singapore government officials and the owner of the frozen meat store at Changi Airport, but no reasons were given for the ban. After checking with the Japan Trade Centre and the Japan Embassy in Singapore on 28 June 1984, it was understood that the reason for the ban was the discovery by the Ministry of Agriculture, Forestry and Fisheries in Japan that although frozen beef sold at Changi Airport was imported from Australia which was regarded as a country free from foot-and-mouth disease, some beef consumed in Singapore was imported from South America, in particular Argentina which is among those countries with incidences of the disease. It was said that Argentinian beef might have been mixed with or affected Australian beef sold at Changi Airport. Some local sources claimed this to be a Japanese NTB.

Example 2: Quick-Frozen Pork

Owing to land constraints, the Singapore government is phasing out the pig-rearing industry in Singapore. However, in the early 1970s, the government was keen to explore its quick-frozen pork market in Japan following the success of the pig-rearing industry in Singapore.

The Japanese consume a large quantity of pork in addition to chicken and beef, and Japan was therefore considered a desirable market for Singapore pork. The Japanese Ministry of Agriculture and Forestry was concerned about potential foot-and-mouth disease and inquired about Singapore's quarantine facilities. After inspections, reports showed that facilities in Singapore had met their requirements. Yet even after three years of waiting, no quick-frozen pork had been allowed to be exported from Singapore to Japan.[11]

Example 3: Refined Petroleum

Japan has no significant reserves of oil and has to depend totally on imports. In 1983 it imported 4.1 million barrels of oil a day and refined 3.2 million barrels daily. Imported crude oil has been refined in Japan by 12 large refining and distribution companies licensed by the Japanese government to produce petrol and kerosene, etc. In Japan, there is a long-standing government policy of refining crude oil into petrol instead of importing petrol from abroad.

The owner of the Lions Petroleum in Japan, Mr Sato Taiji, planned to import petrol from the Singapore Petroleum Company (SPC) in January 1985. He hoped to further secure a contract estimated at S$1.32 million to import another 3,000 kilolitres of cheap petrol from Singapore. His plan was suspended by the Japanese Ministry of International Trade and Industry (MITI). Mr Matsumura Hiroshi, a spokesman for MITI's Petroleum Planning Division, reasoned that "a fierce price war would probably ensue, hurting small, financially-weak petrol stations" if petrol were indiscriminately imported into Japan. It was suspected that "administrative guidance" was given to the Jonan Credit Association, the major financial banker of Lions Petroleum. Subsequently, the Jonan Credit Association suspended credit and loans to Lions Petroleum. This left Lions Petroleum with no alternative but to drop the project. It was reported that Mr Sato Taiji "was forced to sell his first shipment of oil to the Nippon Petroleum Company . . . when the Japanese banks financing him backed out on the advice of MITI". Mr Matsumura later stressed that "if such imports are allowed, it would set a precedent which would have undermined Japan's policy of refining crude oil at home and disrupted the supply and price structure of other petroleum products here [in Japan]".[12]

Example 4: Pharmaceutical Products

Japan produces almost all kinds of both Western and Eastern (so-called Chinese medicine or *kanpoyaku*) pharmaceutical products. Japanese pharmaceutical products have not only saturated the Japanese domestic market but are also widely used abroad. Big pharmaceutical manufacturers such as Meiji, Fujisawa, Takeda, and Taisho have long been controlling the domestic pharmaceutical market in Japan. Japan has sufficiently produced, and to some extent has over-produced, pharmaceutical products. Therefore, foreign products have difficulty penetrating the Japanese market, unless they have particular functions or usages.

Singapore pharmaceutical products, apart from penicillin and penicillin drugs, can hardly be exported to the Japanese market. However, "Tiger" balm has been popular among the Japanese. It is common for Japanese tourists to buy a dozen or so jars of Tiger balm which they consider a valuable souvenir from Singapore, particularly for the elderly. In view of this, some Japanese pharmaceutical importers and trading companies have long planned to import Tiger balm. Companies in Osaka that were interviewed complained that their plan to import Tiger balm and other *kanpoyaku* from Singapore has been rejected by their Ministry of Public Welfare. Some of these companies have been instructed to set up laboratories and to employ pharmacists to examine the product's contents before applying for a licence to import the Tiger balm. Yet several of these companies cannot afford to carry out such experiments. It is still unknown whether today Singapore Tiger balm has been successfully imported by Japanese companies.

Example 5: Hoses

Tigers Polymer Singapore Pte. Ltd. is a Singaporean-Japanese joint venture based in Singapore. It produces PVC suction hoses, PVC delivery hoses, PVC vacuum cleaner hoses, and PVC washing-machine hoses. Products of this company can be regarded either as "semi-manufactured products" or "finished manufactured products" depending on their usage. It is said that the code numbers of semi- and finished manufactured products in Japan are inconstant. This restricts exports of Tigers Polymer's products to Japan.

Around 1980, a 20-foot containerload of Tigers Polymer's products exported to Kobe, Japan, was denied customs clearance on the ground that the Singapore exporter failed to specify the product's origin. The Japanese authorities had to send letters to Tigers Polymer Singapore Pte. Ltd. in Singapore for clarification, unnecessarily delaying the clearance of the products. Tigers Polymer felt that the Japanese customs should not have detailed the products nor insisted on asking the company to specify their place of origin since they already knew that the products were from Singapore. This has been interpreted by the company as a form of "obstruction" or "invisible tariff" on foreign products.[13]

Example 6: Canned Pineapple

Some time ago, a local trading company (which prefers to remain anonymous), exported a hundred cases of canned pineapple from Singapore to Japan. The Japanese customs refused the goods clearance and requested the Singapore trading company to specify the location of these products in the warehouse/cargo. The Japanese customs insisted that it would be easier for them to inspect the products before they were unloaded. The company considers this deliberate delay during customs clearance of foreign products a "suspected NTB".

Example 7: Beer

Heineken Oceania Pte. Ltd. in Singapore has experienced documentation problems when exporting beer to Japan under the GSP. For example, the Japanese customs would query them if the date on the GSP Certificate was later than the sailing date or if the crest stamp and the endorsement seal were not clear. The company has had to prepare a special type of packaging for products intended for the Japanese market. And as an added difficulty, Japan has plans to introduce a new labelling regulation for food and drink items requiring more details of the product to be shown on the label.[14]

Example 8: Black Tea

The Japanese customs refused to grant the Lipton Far East Pte. Ltd. company in Singapore the preferential duty of 2.5 per cent even though a GSP Form A was forwarded to the customs. Instead, the normal 5 per cent duty was imposed. In 1979, the Certificate of Origin Unit helped the company and issued five GSP certificates for their trial shipments. Unfortunately, the Japanese customs refused to accept the certificates. The reason given was that the tea from Singapore did not qualify for the Cumulative Working/Processing certificates as this only applied to goods originating in the ASEAN countries. The company's blends were made of tea originating in countries both in and outside ASEAN such as Indonesia, India, Sri Lanka, and Kenya. In view of the fact that Japan is liberalizing its imports, it has been suggested that perhaps the company could request the Japanese to ease the "Cumulative Working/Processing" rule of origin so that Singapore may enjoy the preferential duty. This will not only encourage exports, but will also save on costs for the company which exported about S$2–3 million worth to Japan in 1981.[15]

There are other exports items from Singapore that have encountered suspected NTBs in Japan. For instance, Japan has on occasion confiscated or destroyed considerable consignments of orchids from Singapore because insects have been found in one of the orchids;[16] shipments have been delayed by Japanese customs because labels on manufactures are not written in Japanese,[17] and so forth.

It can be argued that if the above-mentioned obstructive measures and practices had not been applied by Japanese authorities, Singapore products would have found easier access to the Japanese market.

Efforts and Constraints in Promoting Exports to Japan

Efforts to Promote Exports

On many occasions, the SMA, the SCCCI, and the Singapore Federation of Chambers of Commerce and Industry (SFCCI) have expressed dissatisfaction with the Japanese government and the Japanese private sector with regard to the importation of manufactured products from Singapore.[18] Rightly or wrongly, Singapore exporters and manufacturers consider Japan a closed market in spite of the fact that the Japanese government, through its trade promotion organizations such as the Manufacturers Import Promotion Organization (MIPRO) and the Japan External Trade Organization (JETRO), has helped exhibitions of Singapore's products in various cities in Japan; sent government missions to Singapore; and invited Singapore exporters and manufacturers to Japan to promote Singapore manufactured products. Unfortunately, Singapore manufactured exports to Japan have not increased satisfactorily to the level where it could remedy, in some way, Singapore's trade deficit with Japan.

The Japanese government — both the former Suzuki administration and the present one under Nakasone — has frequently promised to open the Japanese market to foreign manufactured products.[19] Numerous official missions and civilian delegations have been sent to ASEAN to promote export trade to Japan: the Ezaki Economic Mission in August 1983; two high-powered Japanese delegations, one led by Mr Murata Keijiro, the Minister of MITI and the other by Mr Inayama Yoshihiro, Chairman of the Federation of Economic Organizations (Keidanren) in January 1984; and the Fujio Trade Mission in May 1985. Meetings and negotiations have been held but the ASEAN countries seem to question any fruitful results or realistic policies to be implemented immediately by the Japanese government. For example, in the period December 1981–January 1983, the Japanese government adopted measures to open up the Japanese market by reducing or abolishing customs tariffs; easing import restrictions; and reforming distribution structures and business practices. But these do not seem to have had a great impact on promoting Singapore manufactured exports in the Japanese market — Singapore's exports of manufactures decreased from US$257 million in 1982 to US$254 million in 1983.

To help members of the SMA, the SCCCI, and other business associations in Singapore to explore foreign markets, the government created the Trade Development Board (TDB) in January 1983. Apart from exploring markets in the US and the EC, the TDB has made enormous efforts to explore the Japanese market. It has taken steps to encourage Singapore clothing manufacturers to penetrate Japan's fashion market and has encouraged Japanese manufacturers in Singapore to export their products (for example, electric motors and peripheral parts for computers) to Japan.[20]

The National Productivity Board (NPB) and the Singapore Institute of Standards and Industrial Research (SISIR) have been upgrading the productivity of various manufacturing industries and controlling the quality of Singapore's manufactured products. SISIR has been appointed by MITI as the first foreign institution to inspect goods for export to Japan bearing the Japan Industrial Standard (JIS) mark, thereby overcoming certain Japanese trade barriers. However, Singapore manufacturers have expressed pessimism, citing Japan's complex distribution system and government red tape as NTBs which hamper the growth of their exports to Japan.[21]

Constraints in Promoting Exports

Exports from Singapore to Japan cannot be expected to increase substantially because of the following factors: 1. Most Japanese affiliated companies have not been particularly interested in exporting their products to the Japanese market. However, after the yen appreciation in September 1985, more and more Japanese enterprises are shifting their production operations overseas. Japanese investments in Singapore have also increased substantially. It is therefore anticipated that exports of Singapore semi-finished and finished manufactured goods into the Japanese market will increase due to the "buy-back arrangements" between Singapore and Japan. 2. Most American-affiliated companies export to the US but little to Japan, except the oil refineries. 3. Domestic companies have not been successful in penetrating the Japanese market because of the relatively higher tariff imposed by Japan; the undervaluation of the Japanese yen before February 1973; the absence of firm trade routes in Japan and high-pricing of Singapore products compared with those produced in Korea and Taiwan.[22]

Our preliminary survey presented earlier indicates that: 1. most Japanese-affiliated companies in Singapore do not have difficulty penetrating the Japanese market because they have marketing networks and distribution routes in Japan, although the majority of them may not regard Japan as their main export market. 2. American-affiliated companies in Singapore have encountered various Japanese NTBs in their export trade with Japan. However, American-affiliated companies have invested heavily in the oil refineries in Singapore and their exports of petroleum products to Japan constituted 70 to 80 per cent of Singapore's total exports to Japan during the period 1975–1985. Therefore, should constraints on exports of petroleum products from Singapore be eliminated, it would definitely contribute to the rectification of Singapore's trade deficit with Japan. 3. As mentioned earlier, domestic companies have encountered various NTBs such as distribution systems problems, quotas, import surcharges, customs clearance, product testing and certification procedure problems. Most domestic companies do not have marketing networks and distribution routes in Japan. Furthermore, certain Singapore products are more costly than those produced in Hong Kong, Taiwan, and Korea. Therefore, unless productivity and quality-control are promoted to the level that will counterbalance the rapid increase of overhead charges derived basically from wages, Singapore products will lose their competitiveness in the Japanese market. Besides, less effort on the part of domestic companies has also contributed adversely to the penetration of the Japanese market.

It is widely known that the Japanese government has been actively involved in implementing policies to stimulate exports. To sustain Japan's export drive, the Japanese yen was maintained at a comparatively low level despite a strengthening as a result of the sizeable trade surplus that Japan has accumulated over the years. Statistics show that in 1982 and 1983, the exchange rates of the Japanese yen per US dollar were 249 and 238 respectively, compared with 240 in 1977.[23] Some prominent Japanese economists have suggested that owing to the persistent undervaluation of the Japanese yen,[24] exports of foreign products into the Japanese market have been restricted.

However, under the pressure of the Western industrialized nations (the US, West Germany, Great Britain, and France), the Japanese yen appreciated substantially from ¥230/US$ in September 1985 to ¥160/US$ in April 1986. The Japanese yen has since remained fairly strong, prompting imports of manufactured goods from overseas. Domestic consumption in Japan of imported goods from the US, the EC, and the NIEs increased year by year but has not reached the level to rectify Japan's favourable trade relationship with these countries. Among the NIEs, imports from Singapore have not increased much compared with those from Korea, Taiwan, and Hong Kong. This might be due to Singapore's heavy reliance on mineral fuels and petroleum exports to Japan as the petrochemical industries in Singapore and Japan still remained in a depressed state.

Conclusion

Japan is perceived by foreign exporters and manufacturers, both in developed or developing countries, as a closed market, although this perception is widely denied by Japanese government officials, businessmen, and academics. Foreign exporters and manufacturers regard it as extremely difficult, not to say impossible, to penetrate the Japanese market due to NTBs. The NTBs as perceived by Singapore exporters and manufacturers may be biased or may need further clarification, but from our survey, they unarguably have restricted exports of manufactured products, such as petroleum products, electrical and electronic and pharmaceutical products from Singapore to Japan. Singapore's increasing trade deficit with Japan can only be rectified by promoting exports to and restricting imports from Japan.

Singapore's imports from Japan are unlikely to be reduced but will possibly increase significantly as Singapore is still in the process of industrial development. Capital goods, such as machinery and equipment, base metals and products of chemical and allied industries, etc., will be needed by Singapore's various industrial projects and business activities. Japanese consumption goods and light manufactured products have flooded the Southeast Asian markets in general, and the Singapore market in particular. This tendency seems to have been strengthened by heavy Japanese investment and economic participation in the ASEAN region. Imports from Japan, both capital and consumption goods, are unlikely to decline in the foreseeable future. Accordingly, the only solution to rectify Singapore's sizeable trade deficit with Japan is for Singapore to explore the Japanese market for its manufactured products. In doing this, high quality and competitive pricing of products are required; and marketing networks and distribution routes have to be set up in Japan. If anticipated trade frictions between Singapore and Japan are to be minimized or avoided, much will depend on Japan's sincerity in opening up its markets by eliminating NTBs.

Notes

1   There are some comprehensive studies on Japanese NTB practices in Japan. For example, Kojima Kiyoshi and Komiya Ryutaro, *Nihon No Hi-Kanzei-Syoheki* [Japanese NTBs], (Tokyo: Nihon Keizai Shimbun-sha, 1972); Wee Mon-Cheng, *Economic Diplomacy in the Land of the Cherry Blossom* (Singapore: MPH Distributors, 1977), pp. 43–45. Arthur D. Little Inc., *The Japanese Non-Tariff Barrier Issue: American View and the Implications for Japan-US Trade Relations* (Tokyo: National Institute for Research Advancement, 1979); Kojima Kiyoshi, "Non-Tariff Barriers to Japan's Trade", in *Hitotsubashi Journal of Economics* (Tokyo, June 1980); Cai Can Wen, ed., *Ru He Da Kai Riben Shichang* [How to Penetrate the Japanese Market] (Taiwan: Jing Ji Ri Bao She, 1984).

2   Lim Chong Yah and Associates, *Policy Options for the Singapore Economy*, (Singapore, 1988), pp. 275–76. Singapore's international trade can not properly be judged owing to the following two reasons: Firstly, importation of goods for sale to tourists (4.2 million in 1988: 1.6 times Singapore's total population) do

not appear as merchandise exports. Secondly, figures on Singapore's trade with Indonesia (which is commonly believed to be quite substantial) were neither published nor included in Singapore's international trade statistics since 1964.

3   Department of Statistics, *Monthly Digest of Statistics*, (Singapore, February 1991), pp. 36 and 39.

4   Perhaps it is interesting to look into how much of Japan's decrease in imports of petroleum products from Singapore has been due to Indonesia's policy of refining Indonesian crude in its own refineries.

5   In 1983, the sales of rubber from Singapore to Japan, in response to large orders for tyres from Iran and the US, enjoyed the largest growth of 200 per cent (Ministry of Trade and Industry, Economic Survey of Singapore 1983 [Singapore], p. 39).

6   Ibid.

7   Arthur D. Little Inc., op. cit.

8   Manufacturers claimed that apart from MITI, the Ministry of Health and Welfare and the Ministry of Agriculture, Forestry, and Fisheries in Japan have also exercised administrative guidance.

9   *Straits Times*, 8 November 1982; interview with representatives of Japan External Trade Organization in Singapore on 10 May 1983; and *Lianhe Zaobao*, 26 May 1983.

10 *Straits Times*, 14 June 1984.

11 Wee Mon-Cheng, op. cit., p. 49, and Lim Hua Sing & Lee Chin Choo, "Japan–Singapore Relations: Trade and Development", in *ASEAN–Japan Relations: Trade and Development*, Narongchai Akrasanee, ed. (Singapore: Institute of Southeast Asian Studies, 1983), p. 135.

12 This is a summary derived from articles that appeared in the *Straits Times* on 22 January 1985, p. 40, entitled "Japan May Pressure Singapore to Stop Future Sales: Sato" and "Import Ban Won't be Lifted". The Lions Petroleum Company subsequently went to the Philippines and signed another contract with the Philippine National Oil Company (PNOC), which agreed to ship 4,500 kilolitres of oil to Japan. However, it was again obstructed by MITI, although it was denied that the Japanese government pressured the authorities in Manila to persuade PNOC to withdraw from the contract. It is said that "the Japanese government had threatened to freeze aid amounting to US$600 million to the Philippines if the contract of US$12 million was honoured to the Lions Petroleum Company". See *Straits Times*, "MITI Used Pressure to Stop Oil Deal", 27 April 1985.

13 Information gathered in an interview with Tigers Polymer Singapore Pte. Ltd. on 3 March 1983.

14 Based on information kindly provided by the SMA on 2 August 1982. It would be interesting to know whether such labelling requirements discriminate against imported products or apply to domestic products also.

15 Same as note 14.

16 Lim, op. cit., p. 135.

17 Information gathered in an interview of a Singapore manufacturer who insists on anonymity.

18 For example, the SMA and the SFCCI held a meeting at the World Trade Centre on 2 August 1982. The purpose of this meeting was to review the trade relations between Singapore and Japan and to sum up Singapore's view on trade with Japan in order to have fruitful discussions the following day with the

Ezaki Economic Mission, which was sent by the then Suzuki Cabinet. This meeting was overwhelmed by complaints and criticisms against the "Japanese closed market". Another meeting was organized by the SCCCI with the Nagoya Furniture Wholesalers Co-operative Association at the SCCCI conference room on 15 June 1983. In the meeting, frustrations and grievances against the Japanese closed market were also heard.

19 It is interesting to note that while the Japanese government is moving to open up the Japanese market, Mr Inayama Toshihiro, Chairman of Japan's powerful Federation of Economic Organizations (Keidanren) insists on stopping Japan's import drive because he thinks that Japan has nothing to buy from abroad since Japan can manufacture better products and at cheaper prices. See *Straits Times*, 28 May 1985.

20 *Straits Times*, "Assault on Japan. Singapore Will Go All-Out to Penetrate its Markets", 25 January 1984.

21 *Straits Times*, "Traders Expect No Jump in Japan Sales Though SISIR Does First Checks", 13 June 1984. Only one Japanese-affiliated company, Yokogawa Electric, has been successful in getting the JIS mark.

22 Kunio Yoshihara, *Foreign Investment and Domestic Response* (Singapore: Institute of Southeast Asian Studies, 1976).

23 Keizai Kikaku-cho Chosakyoku, *Keizai Yoran*, 1984, p. 25. According to Professor Nakamura, the yen-dollar rate was 243 in 1975, 236 in 1976, 219 in 1977, and 205 in 1978. He argues that the yen was undervalued in 1976, overvalued in early 1977, and undervalued once again in 1979. See Takafusa Nakamura, *The Postwar Japanese Economy* (Tokyo: University of Tokyo Press, 1981), pp. 242–43.

24 See also Okita Saburo, *Seikai Keizai Sindan* [To Diagnose the World Economy] (Tokyo: TBS Baritanika 1983), pp. 49–50.

CHAPTER 4

Japanese Foreign Direct Investment and Japanese-Style Management in Singapore

Introduction

Foreign direct investment has contributed greatly towards Singapore's rapid economic development.[1] Foreign investment commitments have dominated (in value) investment commitments to Singapore's manufacturing sector with the lowest of 65.6 per cent and the highest of 86.1 per cent in the 1980s. During the period 1975–1984, foreign-owned establishments (with more than 50 per cent of foreign capital investment) comprised 23 per cent of establishments, but generated 55 per cent employment, 73 per cent of gross output, and 65 per cent of capital expenditure.[2] The US, Japan, and Europe have been the predominant investors in Singapore. These three were responsible for 90 per cent in 1988 and 97 per cent in the first quarter of 1989 of total FDI in Singapore's manufacturing sector. The US had been the largest investor during the period 1980–1985 but was overwhelmed by Japan during the period 1986–1988. In 1980, Japan's investment commitments to Singapore's manufacturing sector were just 27 per cent of that of the US. The drastic yen appreciation in 1985 prompted Japan's investment in Singapore and in 1986 Japan exceeded the US with a new record of 42 per cent, leaving the US behind with 37 per cent and Europe with merely 18 per cent.

The Japanese presence in Singapore has accordingly attracted much attention. The adaptation to Singapore of Japanese-style management in Japanese companies in Singapore has become a great concern of not only the Singapore government but also the Japanese investors.

The aim of this chapter is, therefore, twofold: first, to examine the characteristics and recent development of Japanese FDI in Singapore, and second, to analyse the possibility of adapting the Japanese-style managerial system in Japanese enterprises to the heterogenous society of Singapore.

Investment Motivators for Japanese Foreign Direct Investment

Two comprehensive surveys have been conducted by Japanese organizations concerning the investment motivation of the Japanese in Singapore.

Survey I

This survey[3] was conducted just before the drastic yen appreciation began in September 1985. Issues such as "political stability" and favourable "economic infrastructure" are somehow excluded in this survey. Japanese firms regard Singapore as an important base of entrepôt trade, especially for exporting their manufactures to third countries, and as an important production base for supplying industrial parts and components (the combined affirmative responses to these two questions amounted to 33 per cent of the total number of responses received). Singapore is also regarded by the Japanese firms, as expected, as an important information centre, due to its strategic location and well-established transport and telecommunications system. Affirmative responses to these questions comprised 31 per cent (282 cases) and indicated the most important motivation for Japanese investment in Singapore. This is straightforwardly reflected in the rapid increase of Japanese liaison offices and branch offices in Singapore during the period 1979–1984. Besides, it is interesting to note that out of 282 cases, 196 cases (70 per cent) were non-manufacturers (Table 4.1). It is believed that, because a large proportion of Japanese liaison offices and branch offices is set up by non-manufacturers, one of their main activities must be related to information gathering and data analysis aiming for regional and global business expansion. Industrial restructuring and drastic economic changes in Singapore and in the region have prompted Japanese firms to treat the region more seriously. From time to time, Japanese firms are keen to make timely decisions conducive to business expansion. With this in mind, Japanese firms perceive Singapore as the most reputable information centre, despite the fact that operation costs in the country are the highest among Southeast Asian countries.

The survey also indicates that Japanese firms are rationally concerned about the supply of industrial parts and components in Singapore (92 cases, 10 per cent). Obviously, Japanese manufacturers in Singapore realize that a sufficient supply of high-quality and sophisticated industrial parts and components for its high-technology

Table 4.1

Japanese Investment Motivations in Singapore, 1985

Investment Motivation	Manufacturer	Non-Manufacturer	Total
Low labour cost	14	6	20
As a consumption market	43	59	102
Supply of industrial parts & components	62	30	92
As a base of entrepot trade	54	154	208
Preferential tariffs	52	22	74
Information centre	86	196	282
Financial centre	–	11	11
Hardly any merit	21	13	34
Others	25	55	80
Total	357	546	903

Note: *This survey was conducted in August-October 1985. It was based on multiple responses. The category "Financial Centre" was initially not included in the questionnaire survey; the 11 cases recorded here were responses given by the non-manufacturers that are included in "Others."*

Source: *Nihon Shingaporu Kyokai [Japan Singapore Association], Shingaporu no Nikei Kigyo (Japanese Business Activities in Singapore) (Tokyo 1986), p. 13.*

and knowledge-intensive industries is one of the important factors in doing business in Singapore. Had this survey been conducted after the drastic yen appreciation in 1985, when the Japanese economy had started to feel the impact, the additionally stimulated eagerness in looking for a supply of industrial parts and components, especially for the Japanese electrical and electronics industries, would have been reflected. This may be due to two reasons: first, Japanese firms in Singapore will reduce imports of industrial parts and components from Japan because of the high yen; second, procurement of industrial parts and components in Singapore's local markets will increase to coincide with Japanese firms shifting their production operations in Singapore.

Survey II

This survey has been conducted annually by the Toyo Keizai Shimposha. The survey reveals that over the period 1983–1989, Japanese motivation to invest in Singapore has been centred around: (a) increasing sales in Singapore and third countries; (b) utilization of the local labour force and reduction in operation costs; (c) collecting information; and (d) benefiting from the protective policies adopted by the Singapore government (Table 4.2). Singapore has also been regarded by Japanese firms as an important production base and centre for exploring international markets, as indicated in the previous survey.

Japanese manufacturing industries in Singapore benefited not only from the procurement of industrial parts and components from Japanese supporting industries in Singapore, but also from non-Japanese supporting industries, of Singaporean or other nationalities, though to a much lesser extent. Singapore's small and medium-sized businesses (SMBs) (mostly Chinese) are perceived as the least developed among the Asian newly industrializing economies (NIEs), due mainly to Singapore's heavy reliance since the separation from Malaysia in 1965 on multinational corporations (MNCs) and on developing public enterprises. Singapore's SMBs have consequently played a limited supplementary or supporting role to Japanese firms. Singapore's highly trained workforce and well-developed economic infrastructure, however, have ensured that the country develops high-tech, high-value-added, and knowledge-intensive industries. Labour-intensive industries are being phased out from Singapore. Some Japanese firms are therefore forced to relocate their production to neighbouring countries in Asia.[4] A Singapore objective has been to attract Japanese firms with advanced technology, especially after 1979 when it started restructuring toward export-oriented, high-value-added, high-tech, knowledge-intensive activities. Similar firms with advanced technology of other nationalities have also been attracted to Singapore. It is likely that the supply of industrial parts and components to Japanese manufacturing industries in Singapore will be partly substituted for by newly established Japanese and non-Japanese supporting industries in Singapore. Table 4.2 reveals that Japanese firms are optimistic (37 per cent in 1989) about securing or acquiring the necessary supply of industrial raw materials (that is, industrial parts and components) in Singapore. It is surprising, however, that despite drastic yen appreciation, imports of industrial raw materials from Japan have remained at fairly high levels during 1986–1989 (Table 4.2).

Protective policies, preferential tariffs, and the utilization of the labour force are considered important motivators for investment by Japanese firms. The concept of protective policies is rather vague from the macroeconomic viewpoint — it seems to refer to overall efforts made by the government to create a favourable environment in order to attract FDI; from the microeconomic viewpoint it seems to refer to various incentives and benefits given by the government, including incentives to pioneer industries and to expand established enterprises, investment allowances, warehousing and servicing incentives, international consultancy services, foreign loans for productive equipment, incentives for research and development, venture capital incentives, and royalties, fees, and development contributions.[5] The package of protective policies has undoubtedly facilitated Japanese FDI in Singapore.

Table 4.2
Japanese Investment Motivations in Singapore, 1983–1989

Investment Motivation	1983 Cases	1983 %	1984 Cases	1984 %	1985 Cases	1985 %	1986 Cases	1986 %	1987 Cases	1987 %	1988 Cases	1988 %	1989 Cases	1989 %
To ensure raw material supply	13	2.7	11	2.1	10	1.8	9	1.5	9	1.5	9	1.5	12	1.9
Easier to produce here due to the availability of abundant resources	8	1.7	8	1.6	8	1.5	9	1.50	10	1.7	12	2.0	12	1.9
Utilization of labour force; reduction of operation cost	86	18.0	81	15.8	88	16.0	93	15.4	91	15.4	95	15.6	103	16.0
Can benefit from the protective policies adopted by the Singapore government	64	13.4	68	13.2	70	12.7	73	12.1	69	11.7	69	11.3	73	11.4
To expand sales to markets in Singapore and to third countries	234	49.1	266	51.8	289	52.5	310	51.4	301	51.0	310	51.0	317	49.3
To collect information	71	14.9	79	15.4	85	15.4	96	15.9	95	16.1	92	15.1	95	14.7
To solve the export difficulties due to trade frictions	1	0.2	1	0.2	1	0.2	4	0.7	6	1.0	8	1.3	11	1.7
Royalty	N.A.	–	N.A.	–	N.A.	–	9	1.5	9	1.5	13	2.1	20	3.1
Total	477	100.0	514	100.0	551	100.0	603	100.0	590	100.0	608	100.0	643	100.0
Major Export Destinations for Manufacturers														
Total	240	100.0	261	100.0	281	100.0	313	100.0	318	100.0	340	100.0	351	100.0
Japan	30	12.5	31	11.9	35	12.5	38	12.2	43	13.5	47	13.8	52	14.8
Local markets	123	51.3	141	54.0	150	53.4	171	54.6	173	54.4	185	54.4	188	53.6
Third countries other than Japan	87	36.2	89	34.1	96	34.1	104	33.2	102	32.1	108	31.8	111	31.6
Major Sources of Industrial Raw Materials Import														
Japan	71	52.2	83	50.9	89	51.5	96	49.2	100	46.7	120	46.7	127	45.5
Local markets	47	34.6	59	36.2	63	36.4	74	38.0	83	38.8	95	37.0	104	37.3
Third countries other than Japan	18	13.2	21	12.9	21	12.1	25	12.8	31	14.5	42	16.3	48	17.2
Total	136	100.0	163	100.0	173	100.0	195	100.0	214	100.0	257	100.0	279	100.0

Source: *Compiled and computed from* Toyo Keizai Shimposha, Kaigai Shinshutsu Kigyo Soran *[Japanese Overseas Companies, Facts and Figures]* (Tokyo, *various years*).

Taking advantage of preferential tariffs in Singapore was also considered by Japanese firms as an important motivator for investment. As early as 1971, Japan had its first yen revaluation and the application of the GSP, which seriously affected Japanese labour-intensive industries (such as textile, lumber, and sundry processing industries) in their export drive.[6] Furthermore, prompted by increasing wage rates, higher energy prices, and higher prices for some natural resources, Japanese firms were forced to pursue radical industrial restructuring and overseas investment. By January 1989, Japanese firms were to a large extent entitled to the GSP, despite the fact that over the past few years protectionist tendencies have escalated due to the continuation of the worldwide economic recession. Some manufactures produced in Singapore, however, have been excluded from the GSP. The US graduated Singapore from the GSP in January 1989, and such other countries as Canada, European countries, Australia, and New Zealand are restricting imports of Singapore's manufactures by reducing Singapore's benefits from the GSP. American MNCs in Singapore suffered seriously from the protectionist measure, and Japanese firms were also affected. It is expected that manufactures produced in Singapore will be increasingly excluded from the GSP. Consequently, it is believed that Japanese firms have excluded the GSP as a motivator for investment in Singapore since January 1989. Japanese firms can, however, make themselves entitled to various preferential tariffs extended by the Singapore government when they shift their production operations to Singapore.

The quality of the labour force in Singapore has also been an important attraction for Japanese FDI. Singapore's educational level is comparatively higher among the ASEAN countries despite the fact that its labour quality in the manufacturing industries is the lowest among the NIEs. Singapore is said to have lacked middle-level managerial staff. Upgrading the quality of unskilled labour and creating a stratum of middle management are therefore crucial to Singapore's economic development. Singapore is, however, suitable for developing high value-added, high-tech, and knowledge-intensive industries because it has sufficient engineers, professionals, and high-level managerial staff. Singapore could recruit, as it has done before, professional personnel from all over the world whenever needed. By and large, high value-added, high-tech, and knowledge-intensive industries in Singapore have not, compared to other Southeast Asian countries, encountered any difficulty in recruiting professional personnel.

It should be pointed out that high labour cost in Singapore is one of the obstacles to attracting FDI. By 1985, Singapore's labour cost was the highest not only among the ASEAN countries but also among the NIEs.[7] Compared to Japan's labour cost,[8] however, Singapore appears to be attractive to Japanese firms. Besides, after the Economic Committee's recommendation on wage restraint and reform in February 1986, wages in Singapore were effectively restrained.[9] Singapore regained its international competitiveness thereafter. The National Wages Council (NWC) had further recommended that wage restraint continue to be exercised in 1987. In the end, Singapore succeeded in rapid recovery in 1987, and the economic growth from 1988 appeared promising.[10]

By 1986, the average wage of Singapore workers in manufacturing industries was the highest among the ASEAN countries and China. Among the NIEs, however, Singapore was lower than Korea and Hong Kong. Singapore was about one-seventh that of Japan. Therefore, from the viewpoint of Japanese firms, operation costs in Singapore are still manageable.[11] Japanese firms are usually good at technical innovation, improvement of manufacturers, and the collection of business knowhow. Within the investment environment in Singapore, Japanese firms are seen to be able to achieve these goals comfortably. Labour cost, which is estimated to comprise 10 to 15 per cent of the production costs of machinery industries, is therefore not a decisive factor in determining the competitiveness of manufactured goods produced.[12] Moreover, since Japanese FDI in Singapore is becoming increasingly capital and knowledge intensive, less and less manpower (especially unskilled workers) will be required. As long as Singapore can provide sufficient engineers, managerial staff, and other professional personnel, Japanese firms are likely to increase their business activities in the country.

Industrial Distribution and Type of Ownership

The precise number of Japanese-affiliated firms by sector in Singapore is difficult to ascertain for the reason that, in recent years, the Singapore government (Economic Development Board) has ceased to disclose detailed breakdowns, which is said to be because of industrial secrecy and sensitivity. A list of Japanese-affiliated firms by sector in Singapore can instead be gathered from the Registrar of Companies (ROC). Such a list lacks accuracy, however, for two reasons. First, some firms have not actually started their businesses although they have registered with the ROC. Second, some firms evacuate or cease activity without informing either the ROC or the local Japanese official representatives (for example, the Japanese Embassy in Singapore). In addition, paid-up capital of Japanese firms has always been smaller than authorized capital. Comprehensive statistics pertaining to the Japanese FDI in Singapore therefore cannot be acquired from the ROC.

Industrial Distribution

Statistics available here are from two sources. One is the regular surveys conducted by Japanese institutions in Singapore.[13] The second is the Ministry of Finance in Japan. There are discrepancies between the two. The figures from the Japanese institutions are said to include approximately 90 per cent of Japanese firms that responded to the surveys. Firms that have evacuated or ceased activities have been excluded from the surveys. The Ministry of Finance figures include cases of investment that have registered with the Ministry. It is believed that a single firm may have more than one case of investment due to business expansion. Furthermore, the dates and capital investment registered with the Ministry of Finance sometimes may not correspond to the actual Japanese FDI in Singapore.

These two sources are nevertheless thus far considered the most reliable and provide us with a pretty clear picture of industrial distribution of Japanese firms in Singapore.

Source One

Table 4.3 reveals Japanese investment by industry in Singapore in 1970, 1980, 1982, and 1985.[14] The following features can be identified. First, in the manufacturing sector, Japanese firms have a very high concentration in electronics and electrical fields.[15] In 1970, the textile industry together with the ferrous and non-ferrous industry, and the petroleum and chemical industry attracted substantial Japanese FDI.[16] However, the importance of Japanese FDI in the textile industry has diminished drastically — from five in 1982 to two in 1985. Japan has shifted her investment in Singapore from the relatively low-tech and labour intensive industries to capital and skill-intensive industries. Second, Japanese investment in Singapore's non-manufacturing sector has been gaining momentum. The ratios of manufacturing to non-manufacturing sectors during the years 1970, 1980, 1982, and 1985 were 1:1.7, 1:3.0, 1:3.1, and 1:3.2 respectively. The number of manufacturing industries has been overwhelmed by that of non-manufacturing industries. In addition, among the non-manufacturing industries, foreign trade and commerce have attracted substantial Japanese FDI. This is a reflection of Singapore's position as a trade and commercial centre in the Asia-Pacific region.

Between 1970 and 1985, the number of Japanese firms increased sixfold in foreign trade and commerce, sevenfold in construction and engineering, and ninefold in both finance and insurance and transportation and warehousing. If other "non-manufacturing" is included, the number of non-manufacturing firms had increased 7.4 times, from 63 firms in 1970 to 464 firms in 1985. If however we confine Japanese business activities to the years 1982 and 1985, data provided in Table 4.3 reveal a different picture. First, overall, the number of non-manufacturing firms decreased except for those belonging to "other non-manufacturing". The number of construction and engineering firms decreased from 77 in 1982 to 64 in 1985; foreign trade and commerce from 223 to 138; finance and insurance from 50 to 46; and transportation and warehousing from 61 to 55. On the other hand, during the same period, the number of Japanese firms in

Table 4.3

Development of Japanese Investment by Industry, 1970, 1980, 1982 and 1985

Industry	1970		1980		1982		1985	
	No. of Enterprises	%	No. of Enterprises	%	No. of Enterprises	%	No. of Enterprises	%
Manufacturer								
Food & Beverage	3	3.0	9	1.3	10	1.3	11	1.6
Textile & Textile Products	5	5.0	8	1.1	5	0.6	2	0.3
Ferrous & Non-ferrous Products	6	6.0	37	5.2	36	4.6	25	3.7
Electronics & Electrical Products	9	9.0	35	4.9	36	4.6	25	3.7
Petroleum & Chemical Products	1	1.0	14	1.9	13	1.6	23	3.4
Machinery	3	3.0	85	11.8	87	11.1	77	11.4
Transportation Machinery	2	2.0	9	1.3	17	2.2	5	0.7
Other Manufacturing	8	8.0	45	6.3	50	6.4	44	6.5
Subtotal	37	37.0	242	33.7	254	32.3	212	31.4
Non-Manufacturer								
Construction & Engineering	9	9.0	78	10.9	77	9.8	64	9.6
Foreign Trade & Commerce	23	23.0	198	27.6	223	28.4	138	20.4
Transportation & Warehousing	6	6.0	48	6.7	61	7.8	55	8.1
Other Non-manufacturing	20[a]	20.0	111[a]	15.5	121[b]	15.4	161[c]	23.8
Subtotal	63	63.0	476	66.4	532	67.7	464	68.6
	100	100.0	718	100.0	786	100.0	676	100.0

Notes: a. Indicates services firms, etc.

b. Indicates services firms comprising 34 wholly owned subsidiaries, 37 joint ventures, 8 branch offices, 25 representative offices, and 17 others.

c. Includes 44 liaison offices of manufacturers, 3 fishery and marine products firms, 1 mining firm, 61 services firms, 5 real estate firms, and 47 non-manufacturing firms (instead of 44 as stated in the reference source).

Source: Figures for the years 1970 and 1980 from Nihon Shingaporu Kyokai [Japan Singapore Association], Shingaporu no Nikkei Kigyo [Japanese Business Activities in Singapore] (Tokyo, 1986), p. 13.
Figures for 1982 from Japan Trade Centre (Singapore), Japanese Affiliated Firms in Singapore (March 1983), p. 164.
Figures for 1985 from Japan Trade Centre (Singapore), Japanese Affiliated Firms in Singapore (March 1986), p. 166.

Singapore's manufacturing sector also dropped from 254 to 212. In relative terms, Japanese FDI in Singapore's manufacturing and non-manufacturing sectors combined decreased from 786 in 1982 to 676 in 1985. In absolute terms, Japanese investment commitments in Singapore increased 3.3 times from US$73.7 million in 1982 to US$244.1 million in 1985.[17] Japanese FDI in Singapore is becoming more and more capital and technology intensive. Labour-intensive industries that are unable to automate or mechanize in time are forced to liquidate or to shift to neighbouring ASEAN countries. The persistent worldwide economic recession and particularly the sluggish economic situation in Singapore from 1985–1986 had threatened the survival of Japanese-affiliated firms with lower productivity, efficiency, and competitiveness. This group of Japanese firms appeared to be composed of textiles, ferrous and non-ferrous metals, transportation machinery, and electronics and electrical industries in the manufacturing sector; and construction and engineering, foreign trade and commerce, and transportation and warehousing firms in the non-manufacturing sector. During the period of Singapore's economic downturn in 1985–1986, Japanese firms in such areas as ferrous and non-ferrous, petroleum and chemicals, electronics and electrical, construction and engineering, and transportation and warehousing appeared to be badly affected.

Source Two

The Japanese Ministry of Finance has provided the breakdown of Japanese FDI in Singapore for alternate years during the period 1981–1987. Despite the possible shortcomings mentioned earlier, this source provides us with up-to-date Japanese cumulative investment, in both manufacturing and non-manufacturing, in Singapore in 1981, 1983, 1985, and 1987.

The following features can be observed in Table 4.4.1. First, both in relative and absolute terms, Japanese FDI in Singapore increased substantially during the period 1981–1987. Second, Japanese FDI in Singapore's manufacturing sector has been predominant but has shown a decline proportionately to non-Japanese FDI. Third, both in relative and absolute terms, Japanese FDI in Singapore's non-manufacturing sector has shown a substantial increase. Fourth, more and more Japanese firms are setting up branch offices in Singapore; their numbers increased from 77 at the end of 1981 to 106 at the end of 1987.

The latest breakdown of Japanese FDI in Singapore's manufacturing sector is shown in Table 4.4.2. The following features can be observed. First, Japanese FDI in Singapore's manufacturing sector increased substantially since 1985 but dropped in 1990. In relative terms, the cases of Japanese FDI increased 2.0 times, from 34 in 1985 to 69 in 1989. In absolute terms, Japanese FDI increased 6.8 times, from US$100 million to US$681 million during the same period. Second, Japanese FDI has been concentrating in electrical and electronics, petroleum and chemicals, and machinery. The greatest amount of Japanese FDI in 1985 was in machinery and constituted nearly 60 per cent of Japan's total manufacturing investment in Singapore, but food and beverage had become the recipient of the most Japanese FDI in 1989. Japan's investment in food and beverage constituted approximately two-thirds of Japan's total FDI in Singapore in 1989.

The breakdown of Japanese FDI in Singapore's non-manufacturing sector is also shown in Table 4.4.2. First, it is clear that Japanese FDI in Singapore's non-manufacturing sector increased substantially during the period 1986–1989 but dropped in 1990. In relative terms, the cases of Japanese FDI increased 2.4 times, from 46 in 1986 to 112 in 1989. In absolute terms, FDI increased 6.3 times, from US$194 million to US$1,222 million during the same period. Second, Japanese FDI has been concentrating on finance and insurance, transportation and warehousing, services, trade and commerce, and real estate. Japanese FDI in real estate increased 84 times, from US$4 million in 1985 to US$345 million in 1989, and constituted 28 per cent of Japanese FDI in Singapore's non-manufacturing sector in 1989. In recent years, real estate investment in Singapore has been proven to be particularly beneficial and can yield quick returns by Japanese investors.

Type of Ownership

Do Japanese investors prefer joint ventures or subsidiaries when they

Table 4.4.1

Japanese Cumulative Investment in Singapore, 1981–1987

Sectors	By End of March 1981			By End of March 1983			By End of March 1985			By End of March 1987		
	Cases	Amount (US$ million)	%	Cases	Amount (US$ million)	%	Cases	Amount (US$ million)	%	Cases	Amount (US$ million)	%
Manufacturing	527	686	73.5	706	1,006	73.0	826	1,352	70.1	894	1,550	60.3
Non-manufacturing	424	211	22.6	554	327	23.7	711	520	27.0	833	951	37.0
Branch Office	77	32	3.4	86	41	3.0	101	52	2.7	106	64	2.5
Real Estate	27	5	0.5	27	5	0.3	27	5	0.2	27	5	0.2
Total	1,055	934	100.0	1,373	1,382	100.0	1,665	1,929	100.0	1,860	2,570	100.0

Source: *Compiled and computed from Okura-sho [Ministry of Finance], Zaisei Kinyu Tokei Geppo [Statistics on Finance, Monthly Bulletin] (Tokyo, various issues).*

Table 4.4.2

Development of Japanese Investment in Singapore by Industry, 1985–1990

(Unit: No. of enterprises, US$ million)

Type of Industry	1985		1986		1987		1988		1989		1990	
	No. of Enterprises	Amount	No. of Enterprises	Amount	No. of Enterprises	Amount	No. of Enterprises	Amount	No. of Enterprises	Amount	No. of Enterprises	Amount
Manufacturer												
1. Food and Beverage	–	–	2	2.2	8	6.5	3	1.0	5	437.9	1	2.7
2. Textile and Textile Products	3	0.4	–	0.4	–	–	–	–	–	1.7	–	101.3
3. Wood and Plup	1	0.7	2	1.6	3	0.7	2	1.8	6	3.6	6	23.6
4. Petroleum and Chemical Products	5	5.9	7	10.9	19	145.9	30	41.8	19	41.6	13	52.5
5. Steel and Non-steel Products	2	6.2	5	6.2	15	13.7	8	16.1	6	13.6	3	9.9
6. Machinery	5	59.1	4	18.8	7	14.3	9	4.6	19	29.8	2	10.6
7. Electronics and Electrical Products	9	12.4	9	37.1	33	75.4	15	70.1	9	91.1	4	54.4
8. Transportation Machinery	–	4.1	1	8.3	3	0.7	–	–	–	–	–	–
9. Other Manufacturing	7	3.5	6	19.1	18	11.0	1	37.6	3	58.3	6	14.6
10. Liaison Office of Manufacturers	2	7.8	3	4.0	4	1.5	3	3.5	2	3.4	3	25.3
Sub-Total	34	100.3	39	108.6	110	269.7	83	176.5	69	681.0	38	294.9

Continued on next page

Table 4.4.2 (continued)

(Unit: No. of enterprises, US$ million)

Type of Industry	1985 No. of Enterprises	1985 Amount	1986 No. of Enterprises	1986 Amount	1987 No. of Enterprises	1987 Amount	1988 No. of Enterprises	1988 Amount	1989 No. of Enterprises	1989 Amount	1990 No. of Enterprises	1990 Amount
Non-Manufacturer												
1. Agriculture and Forestry	–	0.4	–	–	–	–	1	0.5	–	–	–	0.8
2. Fishery and Marine Products	–	–	–	–	–	–	–	–	2	1.3	–	–
3. Mining	–	–	–	–	–	–	–	–	1	–	3	4.3
4. Construction and Energy	2	0.6	–	0.1	4	1.2	2	45.5	1	91.1	2	2.1
5. Trade and Commerce	32	38.0	25	34.0	37	19.1	49	42.3	34	69.9	40	265.8
6. Finance and Insurance	23	119.9	10	84.9	4	39.0	17	225.2	12	338.5	10	86.6
7. Services	5	5.3	6	48.4	2	4.7	7	12.7	13	147.7	11	85.8
8. Transportation and Warehousing	12	69.2	2	0.7	15	101.4	18	136.1	23	228.2	14	46.1
9. Real Estate	–	4.1	3	25.6	10	59.2	20	108.1	27	344.9	20	52.3
10. Other Non-Manufacturing	2	1.3	–	–	–	0.1	–	–	–	–	–	1.0
Sub-Total	76	238.8	46	193.7	72	224.7	114	570.4	112	1221.6	101	544.8
Grand Total	110	339.1	85	302.3	182	494.4	197	746.9	181	1902.6	139	839.7

Source: *Compiled and computed from Okura-sho [Ministry of Finance], Zaisei Kinyu Tokei Geppo [Statistics on Finance, Monthly Bulletin] [Tokyo, various issues].*

invest in Singapore or elsewhere? The answer to this question is contentious for many reasons.

It depends, first, very much on investors' overall competence and efficiency, which include capital availability, management knowhow, technology, and familiarity with the host country (in terms of such factors as culture, commercial practices, market network, and so on). In the 1960s and 1970s, a large proportion of Japanese FDI in Asia was believed to be confined to labour-intensive industries and small and medium-sized industries. In terms of capital availability, management knowhow, and technology, such industries are unavoidably in a weaker position compared to big businesses or MNCs of other nationalities. Under such circumstances it is quite rational for Japanese investors to search for business partners mainly from the host country.[18]

Second, the preference of Japanese investors is related to the nature of Japanese FDI. It is argued that an export-oriented type of investment has a better chance of obtaining approval for 100 per cent ownership than an import-substitution type of investment.[19] By 1965, the strategy for industrial development in Singapore was based primarily on policies advocating import substitution. Therefore, an import-substitution type of investment, as long as it could make an impressive contribution to the creation of job opportunities and technological advance, was generally entitled to 100 per cent ownership. The import-substitution type of investment, however, appeared to have difficulty in getting 100 per cent ownership approved after 1965 (the year when Singapore was separated from Malaysia), as Singapore then shifted to promotion of export-oriented industries. Singapore switched its industrialization strategy from import substitution to export orientation in 1967. Import substitution industries became unattractive as they were restricted to products involving merely assembly.[20] Import substitution industries were discouraged as Singapore lost its domestic markets in Malaysia after 1965. Japanese firms, which considered Singapore as a production base in aiming for regional and international markets, were then entitled to 100 per cent ownership without much difficulty.

And last, Japanese investment preference is related to the Singapore government's involvement and participation. It is a well-known fact that the Singapore government has been actively involved in domestic economic activities.[21] A thorough study of government co-operation with Japanese firms and the development of such kinds of joint ventures is still not available. It is however clear that the Singapore government has a wide range of equity shares in Japanese firms, in both the manufacturing and service sectors.[22] There are several reasons for government participation in foreign firms: strategic importance, prospects of development, and technology transfer are the main considerations in the government's decision to set up joint ventures with foreign firms. The government obviously has the final say despite the fact that a substantial proportion of foreign firms is keen to have 100 per cent equity shares.

A survey conducted in Singapore in April 1974 revealed that 39.4 per cent of Japanese firms preferred joint ventures; 48.5 per cent declined to set up joint ventures (including those who wanted to set up subsidiaries but were rejected by Singapore); 6 per cent had no specific preferences; and the remaining 6 per cent belonged to the "others" category.[23] It is interesting that among the ASEAN countries, Singapore was the only country where Japanese firms chose subsidiaries over joint ventures.[24] Singapore's economic development has been heavily reliant on foreign investments and, compared to other ASEAN countries, it has less rigid rules and regulations that restrict equity shares of foreign firms, Japanese firms gave up their intention to set up subsidiaries in Indonesia, Malaysia, Thailand, and the Philippines as they knew that 100 per cent ownership applications would not be accepted in most of those cases.[25]

The number of Japanese industries by sector and type of possession in 1982 is shown in Table 4.5. The following features may be derived. First, the number of 100 per cent Japanese-owned companies is significant. The number of Japanese wholly-owned subsidiaries (271 firms), branch offices (101 firms), and liaison offices (127 firms) combined constituted 63.5 per cent of the total number of Japanese firms in Singapore in 1982. In the manufacturing sector, we find a high concentration of these three types of companies in trade and commerce.

In the non-manufacturing sector, the wholly-owned subsidiaries have concentrated particularly on the electronics and electrical industries. Second, next to the wholly-owned subsidiaries, joint ventures have still remained an important feature of Japanese FDI in Singapore. Aside from the comparatively high concentration in transportation, warehousing, and the chemical industries, joint ventures have particularly been significant in trade and commerce (65 firms) and to a lesser extent, in electronics and electrical sectors (19 firms). Third, as a result, Japanese firms in Singapore have concentrated on trade and commerce (233 firms; 28 per cent of Japan's total companies in Singapore in 1982), and to a lesser extent, on electronics and electrical sectors (87 firms; 11 per cent). Compared to the information gathered in Table 4.5 survey (which was conducted in May–September 1982), data shown in Table 4.6 indicate that Japanese-affiliated firms in Singapore decreased by 110 firms (14 per cent) in August–October 1985. This was a reflection of the worldwide economic recession and in particular the sluggish economic situation in Singapore. Singapore suffered a decline of 1.8 per cent in real GDP in 1985 after experiencing consistently high economic growth for the two decades following 1965. Japanese-affiliated firms in Singapore suffered at different levels. From 1982 to 1985 the number of Japanese firms engaged in trade and commerce decreased from 223 to 138; in construction and engineering from 77 to 64; in transportation machinery from 17 to 5; and in electronics and electrical products from 87 to 77. These are some notable casualties that have arisen in key industrial sectors where Japanese firms have a high concentration. Singapore's economic climate can thus partly be judged from the performance and vicissitudes of Japanese-affiliated firms in these industrial sectors.

If we compare the two surveys of Tables 4.5 and 4.6 closely, the following features can be identified. First, the number of joint ventures decreased by 33 per cent (82 firms), from 250 to 168, whereas the number of wholly-owned subsidiaries decreased by only 11 per cent (31 firms), from 271 to 240. Judging by the casualty rates, joint ventures seemed to be more vulnerable or inflexible than the wholly-owned subsidiaries during times of economic downturn in Singapore. Especially

Table 4.5

Number of Companies, by Industry and Type of Possession, May–September 1982

Industry	Wholly Owned Subsidiary	Joint Venture	Branch Office	Liaison Office	Others	Total
Total	271	250	101	127	37	786
(%)	(34.5%)	(31.8%)	(12.8%)	(16.2%)	(4.7%)	(100%)
Finance	5	9	15	9	–	38
Insurance	–	3	3	6	–	12
Transportation & Warehousing	10	32	2	16	1	61
Construction & Engineering	11	21	36	7	2	77
Other Services	34	37	8	25	17	121
Manufacturing						
Food & Beverage	3	6	–	1	10	
Textile & Textile Products	2	2	–	1	5	
Ferrous & Non-ferrous Metals	13	13	8	2	36	
Chemical Products	10	17	–	9	36	
Transportation Machinery	5	5	2	5	17	
Electronic & Electrical Products	57	19	2	8	1	87
Industrial Machinery	8	5	–	–	13	
Other Manufacturing	27	16	2	2	3	50

Source: *Japan Trade Centre (Singapore), Japanese Affiliated Firms in Singapore (March 1983), p. 164.*

Table 4.6

Number of Companies, by Industry, August–October 1985

Industry	N.A.	Joint Venture	Wholly Subsidiary	Branch Office	Liaison Office	Others	Total
Manufacturer							
Food and Beverage	0	4	5	0	1	1	11
Textile and Textile Products	0	1	0	0	1	0	2
Wood and Pulp	0	2	2	0	0	0	4
Petroleum and Chemical Products	0	14	9	1	1	0	25
Steel and Non-steel Products	0	11	5	3	6	0	25
Machinery	0	5	12	1	3	2	23
Electronic and Electrical Products	1	14	52	5	2	3	77
Transportation Machinery	0	2	2	0	1	0	5
Other Manufacturing	0	2	2	0	1	0	5
Liaison Office of Manufacturers	0	0	0	0	44	0	44
Sub-Total	1	63	109	15	59	9	256

Continued on next page

99

Table 4.6 (*continued*)

Industry	N.A.	Joint Venture	Wholly Subsidiary	Branch Office	Liaison Office	Others	Total
Non-Manufacturer							
Agriculture and Forestry	0	0	0	0	0	0	0
Fishery and Marine Products	0	0	1	0	2	0	3
Mining	0	1	0	0	0	0	1
Construction & Energy	0	16	8	36	2	2	64
Trade and Commerce	1	26	76	17	6	12	138
Finance and Insurance	0	7	10	23	6	0	46
Services	0	21	18	5	4	13	61
Transportation and Warehousing	2	25	6	2	18	2	55
Real Estate	0	1	0	1	1	5	
Other Non-Manufacturing	0	7	11	7	12	10	47
Sub-Total	3	105	131	90	51	40	420
Grand Total	4	168	240	105	110	49	676

Source: *Japan Trade Centre (Singapore), Japanese Affiliated Firms in Singapore (March 1983), p. 183.*

in the trade and commerce sectors, the number of Japanese joint ventures decreased by as much as 60 per cent (39 firms), from 65 in 1982 to merely 26 in 1985, whereas the number of wholly-owned subsidiaries decreased by merely 12 per cent (10 firms), from 86 to 76, during the same period. It is believed that if no restrictions are imposed by Singapore, which has been that country's consistent policy, an increasing number of Japanese investors will prefer 100 per cent shares in their future investments in Singapore. Second, the overall number of branch offices increased marginally from 101 to 105 whereas the number of liaison offices decreased slightly from 127 to 110. It is not easy to explain the change, as all of these offices are in Japanese-owned firms that exclude a third party's capital involvement. If we limit our observation to the trade and commerce sectors, it is not surprising to notice that the number of branch and liaison offices both decreased quite abruptly from 31 to 17 and from 30 to only 6 respectively due to the sluggish economy of Singapore. Perhaps one contributing factor to the overall decline was the setting up of a large number of branch offices and the closing down of liaison offices in the finance and insurance sectors. This is reflected in the fact that the number of liaison offices decreased abruptly from 15 to 6 and the number of branch offices in the finance and insurance sectors increased from 18 to 23. It remains unknown, however, to what extent liaison offices in the finance and insurance sectors have been upgraded to branch offices in Singapore. Nevertheless, the upgrading exercise should have taken place due to the important role played by Singapore as a financial centre in the Asia-Pacific region. Japanese investors have undoubtedly expanded their activities in the finance and insurance sectors. Third, as expected, Japanese-affiliated firms suffered a serious setback[26] during the period 1982–1985. Japanese firms decreased by 14 per cent from 786 in 1982 to 676 in 1985. The industries most affected during this period appear to be ferrous and non-ferrous (from 36 to 25), petroleum and chemical (from 36 to 25), transportation machinery (from 17 to 5), electronics and electrical (from 87 to 77), trade and commerce (from 223 to 138), and construction and engineering (from 77 to 64). Obviously,

Japanese-affiliated firms in trade and commerce suffered the most serious setback during this period. The overall decline in manufacturing industries has naturally adversely affected the performance of those firms dealing with trade and commerce.

Employment in Japanese Enterprises

One of the most important contributions of Japanese FDI in Singapore pertains to employment opportunities generated by Japanese firms. In 1980, 718 Japanese-affiliated firms in Singapore provided 70,323 employment opportunities for Singaporeans and guest employees mainly from Malaysia, together with 2,909 Japanese and 171 other expatriates. Employees working for Japanese firms formed 6.7 per cent of Singapore's total workforce.[27] In 1982, 786 Japanese firms provided 70,870 employment opportunities for Singaporeans and guest employees from Malaysia. In addition, 3,250 Japanese and 69 expatriates were also employed in these firms. They formed 6.2 per cent of Singapore's total workforce.[28]

The number of employees by type of ownership in 1980 is shown in Table 4.7. Japanese joint ventures employed 38,764 workers (52.8 per cent of the total workforce in Japanese firms), whereas wholly-owned subsidiaries employed 29,397 workers (40.1 per cent). Table 4.8 further reveals that 54,692 persons (74.5 per cent) were employed in the manufacturing sector, which comprised 16.9 per cent of Singapore's total manufacturing workforce.[29] Viewed from this aspect, it can be argued that some electronics and electrical industries were highly labour intensive. In 1982 the labour situation in Japanese manufacturing industries had remained almost unchanged. It is shown in Table 4.9 that 48,546 workers (68.5 per cent) were employed in the manufacturing sector, which comprised 14.4 per cent of Singapore's total manufacturing workforce. Again, the bulk of the manufacturing employees was engaged in the electronics and electrical sectors, which comprised 48.8 per cent of the total workforce in the manufacturing sector.

In 1988 Japanese firms in Singapore employed 69,179 persons (5.4 per cent of Singapore's total workforce), of which 67,441 persons

Table 4.7

Number of Employees, by Type of Ownership, 1981

	Local	Japanese	Other Expatriate	Total
Wholly Owned Subsidiary	28,377	969	51	29,401
Joint Venture	37,824	868	72	38,764
Branch Office	3,088	760	9	3,857
Representative Office	231	206	–	437
Others	803	106	35	944
Total	70,323	2,909	171	73,403

Source: *Nihon Boeki Shinko-Kai [Japan External Trade Organization] and Kaigai Keizai Joho Senta [Overseas Economic Information Centre],* Shingaporu ni Okeru Nikkei Shinshutsu Kigyo no Gensei *[The Present Situation of Japanese Affiliated Firms in Singapore] (publisher unknown, July 1981).*

(97.5 per cent of the total workforce in Japanese firms) were Singaporeans and guest workers other than Japanese, and 1,738 persons (2.5 per cent) were of Japanese origin (Table 4.10). The following additional features can also be identified. First, in contrast to the incremental growth in Japanese FDI in Singapore, the total workforce employed by Japanese firms is diminishing. Second, the manufacturing sector comprised 79.6 per cent of the total workforce employed in Japanese firms. Third, electronics and electrical industries (including general electricity) had 36,324 employees (66.0 per cent and 52.5 per cent of the total Japanese manufacturing industries and the total Japanese industries, respectively, in Singapore). Fourth, in the non-manufacturing sector, commerce industries constituted the largest share, with a total number of 8,288 employees (12.0 per cent of the total workforce in Japanese firms in Singapore).

Japanese manufacturing industries, especially electronics and electrical, require a large number of guest workers mainly from the Malay Peninsula. As early as 1968 the Singapore government relaxed its immigration policy in order to attract foreign workers. The number of foreign workers in 1973 constituted one-eighth of Singapore's total workforce. The number of foreign workers has since fluctuated

Table 4.8

Number of Employees, by Industry, 1981

	Local	Japanese	Other Expatriate	Total
Finance	734	109	1	844
Insurance	212	14	3	229
Transportation & Warehousing	739	98	8	845
Foreign Trade & Commerce	3,827	474	11	4,312
Construction & Engineering	8,391	693	22	9,106
Other Services	2,990	335	50	3,375
Manufacturing (total)	53,430	1,186	76	54,692
Food & Beverage	671	22	10	703
Textile	1,697	18	3	1,718
Ferrous & Non-ferrous	4,526	105	12	4,643
Chemical	1,769	103	13	1,885
Transportation Machinery	4,087	102	–	4,189
Electronic & Electrical	27,728	527	22	28,277
Industrial Machinery	6,236	161	–	6,397
Other Manufacturing	6,716	148	16	6,880
Total	70,323	2,909	171	73,403

Source: *Same as Table 4.7.*

but foreign workers have not disappeared from Singapore's labour market scene. Despite the fact that the Singapore government has discouraged the influx of foreign unskilled workers due to industrial restructuring particularly after 1979, the number of foreign workers still comprised 7 per cent of Singapore's total workforce in 1980.[30] In the manufacturing sector, the corresponding figure was as high as 46 per cent. It is clear that securing a sufficient supply of foreign workers is crucial to the development of Singapore's manufacturing industries, but the compulsory employers' Central Provident Fund (CPF) contributions and the heavy levy imposed by the government on employers of foreign workers have greatly perturbed investors and

Table 4.9

Number of Employees, by Industry, May–September 1982

Industry	No. of Companies	Total No. of Employees	Local	Guest Employees				
				Total	From Malaysia	Countries other than Malaysia	Japanese	Other Expatriate
Total	786	70,870	56,709	10,842	7,411	3,411	3,250	69
(%)		(100.0%)	(80.0%)	(15.3%)	(10.5%)	(4.8%)	(4.6%)	(0.1%)
Finance	38	1,036	874	156	1	155	3	3
Insurance	12	204	187	2	1	1	15	–
Transportation & Warehousing	61	1,348	1,087	130	8	122	4	12
Trade & Commerce	233	6,158	5,369	101	83	18	676	6
Construction & Engineering	77	10,524	6,688	3,132	1,885	1,247	698	6
Other Services	121	3,054	2,548	162	144	18	323	21
Manufacturing (total)	254	48,546	39,954	7,313	5,288	2,025	1,256	23
Food & Beverage	10	649	535	90	52	38	24	–
Textile & Textile Products	5	188	154	26	17	9	8	–
Ferrous & Non-ferrous	36	4,591	3,203	1,205	969	236	174	9
Chemical Products	36	1,888	1,408	289	242	47	185	6
Transportation Machinery	17	5,578	4,355	1,100	459	641	122	1
Electronic & Electrical Products	87	23,466	20,131	2,840	2,223	617	489	6
Industrial Machinery	13	5,080	4,433	582	394	188	65	–
Other Manufacturing	50	7,106	5,735	1,181	932	349	189	1

Source: *Japan Trade Centre (Singapore)*, Japanese Affiliated Firms in Singapore (*March 1983*), p. 166.

Table 4.10

Number of Employees in Japanese Industries in Singapore, 1988

	Local	Japanese	No. of Executives and Directors
Manufacturing (total)	54,087	982	218
Food & Beverages	651	45	11
Textile	841	5	3
Wood Products	832	14	1
Pulp & Paper Products	128	2	1
Publishing & Printing	1,603	13	6
Chemical	2,732	141	42
Rubber & Leather	786	21	5
Ceramics & Quarrying	691	15	7
Iron & Steel	407	11	4
Non-ferrous metal	1,635	39	11
Metal Products	2,198	36	11
General Electricity	5,887	115	15
Electronic & Electrical Products	29,887	435	81
Transportation Equipment	2,443	34	8
Precision Equipment	1,531	22	6
Others	1,835	34	8
Commerce	7,899	389	137
Finance & Insurance	572	152	60
Real Estate	29	4	3
Transport	1,235	78	29
Service	2,349	48	20
Construction	1,126	72	35
Others	93	10	2
Unknown	51	3	–
All Industries	67,441	1,738	504

Source: Toyo Keizai Shimposha, Kaigai Shinshutsu Kigyo Soran *[Japanese Companies, Facts and Figures]* *(Tokyo, 1989), p. 150.*

stimulated their protest.[31] The ultimate aim of readjusting CPF[32] and imposing a heavy levy is said to be to encourage investors to mechanize and automate their facilities. If, however, the labour-intensive nature and low productivity of the Singapore facilities are maintained, investors will be forced to liquidate or shift to neighbouring countries, where cheaper labour is available.

Japanese-Style Management in Singapore

A Move to Introduce Japanese-style Management
In the early 1980s the Singapore government started to look into the possibility of introducing the Japanese-style managerial system (which refers to a combination of a lifetime employment system, a seniority wage system, and an in-house union) into big enterprises, especially Japanese enterprises in Singapore. The government's rationale rested on three basic reasons. First, Japan's rapid economic development was perceived by the Singapore government as a developmental model. Second, Japanese FDI in Singapore was perceived as crucial to Singapore's industrial restructuring toward high-tech, high value-added, and knowledge intensive activities. Third, the number of Japanese affiliated enterprises in Singapore has remained at a high level among foreign enterprises.

Under the Singapore government's initiative, a comprehensive feasibility study was carried out through the following three measures. Japanese experts on management or productivity were invited to serve as advisers or consultants to the NPB; with the assistance of the NPB research staff, a number of books on Japanese management were published by these experts under NPB sponsorship. Japanese experts and academicians were invited to give lectures on Japanese managerial systems; such lectures were initiated mainly by the Economic Development Board (EDB) and the TDB together with the NPB. Government officials were sent to Japan to study Japanese management; they gathered first-hand information from companies, factories, and government organizations in Japan.

Through such thorough and comprehensive studies, the Singapore government was quick to realize that Japanese managerial systems were not applicable to enterprises in Singapore, even to Japanese-affiliated enterprises. No official reasons were given for this conclusion, as discussed in the following section.

The Impracticability of Adapting Japanese Managerial Practices to Singapore

The Singapore government had neither publicly nor officially announced that it was looking into the possibility of introducing Japanese management systems into enterprises in Singapore. Any subsequent official announcement pertaining to such a scheme's impracticability was thus unnecessary. Through bits and pieces of views and opinions as expressed by government officials in Singapore's local newspapers, however, it was revealed that the Singapore government had at one time seriously studied Japanese management. Although debate regarding the issue disappeared from the local mass media soon after, later arguments suggested that Japanese managerial practices without modification and rectification would not be applicable in Singapore.

The reasons for the impracticability of applying Japanese management systems — without modification and rectification — in Singapore can perhaps be derived from the following aspects of Singaporean culture.

First, Singapore is a society strongly influenced by Western culture. Singaporeans are said to be individualistic and economically pragmatic as are people in the Western countries. Job-hopping for better remuneration and career advancement is particularly common in Singapore. Remaining in the same job for a long period may be perceived as the result of an employee's inefficiency or incapability. In addition, the pledging of one's loyalty to a single company for life is totally unimaginable for most Singaporeans. A lifetime employment system is therefore impracticable and inapplicable in Singapore.

Second, Singapore is a heterogeneous society, with a population comprised of 77.6 per cent Chinese, 14.2 per cent Malays, 7.1 per cent Indians, and 1.1 per cent Eurasians and others (June 1992 census). (Although they are much influenced by Confucianism and qualify as part of the "chopsticks culture", Singaporean Chinese are also very much influenced by the West.) The nature of Singaporean society —

with its diverse races, religions, and cultures — makes the implantation of the lifetime employment system and the seniority wage system impossible. In addition, as mentioned earlier, Singaporean enterprises, particularly manufacturing industries, employ substantial numbers of foreign workers (mainly from Malaysia) on a contract basis and expect such employees to commute every day or to leave Singapore when the contracts expire. This farther adds to the impracticability of the lifetime employment and seniority wage systems in Singapore. Japan, on the other hand, is basically a homogeneous society, a nation of one people and one culture, despite the existence of approximately 0.7 million Koreans and 60,000–70,000 Chinese. Members of the "chopsticks culture" and very much influenced by Confucianism, the Japanese are loyal to their companies, and so the lifetime employment system and the seniority wage system are practicable in Japan.

Third, Singapore has a very large number of multinational enterprises of different nationalities. As mentioned earlier, Singapore has attracted multinational enterprises not only from Japan but also from the US and the EC. In recent years the NIEs (Korea, Taiwan, and Hong Kong) also increased their investments in Singapore. Even if Japanese managerial systems could be implanted in Japanese enterprises in Singapore, multinational enterprises of other nationalities might not follow suit. Mid-career employment, for example, discouraged in Japanese enterprises, is acceptable, not to say encouraged, in Western enterprises. Furthermore, Japanese enterprises may provide on-the-job training for their employees, but the trained employees may well be absorbed by Western enterprises at a later stage. Employees sent by Japanese companies to Japan for training may job-hop after returning to Singapore. Local employees are of course bonded, but Japanese employers always find it too troublesome to take the oath breakers to court. It can be seen, then, that Japanese managerial systems can never be practised solely by one enterprise of a particular nationality without the group consent of all the enterprises of other nationalities in Singapore.

What modifications and rectifications would make the practice of Japanese managerial systems in Singapore possible to some degree?

Japanese enterprises using modified Japanese-style managerial systems in Singapore have constituted a substantial amount of FDI in that country. The extent to which the Japanese-style management has been practised in Singapore will now be discussed in more detail.

Characteristics of Japanese-style Managerial Systems

Japanese-affiliated enterprises have applied a rather loose form of Japanese-style management system, in general observing the following practices.

(1) Japanese employers usually do not sign contracts with their employees, in contrast to the practice of local private, public, and Western enterprises, which often sign contracts for, say, one to three years with their employees. Successful local staff of Japanese enterprises become full-time employees after a three to six-month probation period. Such employees are allowed to work until the retirement age of 55 (it has recently been proposed to extend it to 60) if they do not commit any serious mistakes or offences.

(2) Midcareer employees are generally not recruited. Managerial staff are promoted from the rank and file.

(3) Wages are basically figured by seniority. The longer the period an employee has worked, the higher his or her wages. Wage increments or incentives are given once a year according to the employees' performance and the company's profits. The NWC provides guidelines to the public and private sectors every year. Wage increments, incentives, and bonuses are adjusted and determined accordingly although these guidelines are said to be noncompulsory.

(4) In practice, managerial staff are not allowed to join unions. Singapore's largest trade union, the National Trades Union Congress (NTUC), has a central committee that is staffed by high-ranking ministers and government officials. NTUC member unions are determined not by the profession of individuals but by enterprise (for example, Singapore Bank Union). The relationship between trade unions and enterprises has been harmonious. Labour disputes have been settled and wage adjustments made through collective bargaining. Inhouse unions are not implanted

in Japanese enterprises, despite the eagerness shown by the government to do so, because the relationship between employees and employers is harmonious.

(5) To a certain extent, on-the-job training and job rotation is applied. Employees, especially on the managerial staff, do not usually stay in one department or section for a long time. Employees are trained by working in different departments or sections, which differs distinctly from non-Japanese enterprises. Japanese enterprises prefer their employees to have comprehensive experience while non-Japanese enterprises demand specialization.

(6) Japanese enterprises demand overtime. Rank-and-file employees are entitled to an overtime allowance (OT allowance). Managerial staff (officers and above) are not entitled to OT allowance, but a "meal allowance" (usually S$10) is given if they work until 8:00 p.m.

Several reports (some prepared by JETRO in Singapore) and some public opinion hold that, in terms of the working environment, remuneration, and career advancement, Japanese enterprises are less attractive as compared to their Western counterparts. Furthermore, public enterprises in Singapore appear to be very attractive to university graduates. Among Japanese university graduates in Singapore, 28 per cent are working for the Singapore government and in the public sector, and 25 per cent for Japanese enterprises (including joint ventures). Entrepreneurial activities and non-Japanese enterprises have absorbed 20 per cent and 17 per cent respectively (Table 4.11).

After the phenomenal yen appreciation in 1985, Japanese FDI in Singapore increased remarkably. Japanese enterprises in Singapore are looking for increasing numbers of Japanese university graduates as well as for graduates of the National University of Singapore and the Nanyang Technological University. Japanese enterprises nevertheless appear to be less appealing than Western multinational corporations and public enterprises. Numerous posts in the Japanese enterprises remain unfilled, and job-hopping continues to be a common phenomenon. An additionally modified and rectified Japanese-style management is needed in order to adapt to the diverse races, religions, and cultures of Singaporean society.

Table 4.11

**Occupational Distribution of Japanese University Graduates
in Singapore, 1989**

	(%)
Government and Public Sector	27.97
Japanese Enterprises (including joint ventures)	24.90
Entrepreneurial Activities	19.92
Non-Japanese Enterprises	16.86
Others	10.34

Source: *Wong Len Poh, "The Roles of Japan Alumni in Singapore", paper presented at the Eighth ASCOJA Conference in Thailand, 30 September–3 October 1989 (September 1989).*

Conclusion

The twin engines of Singapore's rapid economic development, particularly after 1965, have been FDI and the Singapore government's active involvement in economic activities. Among direct foreign investors, the Japanese are becoming more and more important. The US used to be the single largest investor in Singapore but since 1986 it has been surpassed by Japan. Japanese FDI, together with American and European FDI, is indispensable to Singapore's objective of restructuring its economy into a high-tech, high value-added, and knowledge-intensive one. There are indications that some Japanese electronics and electrical industries, prompted by the 1985 yen appreciation, have expanded their activities in Singapore.[33] Singapore has become an important production base for Japanese manufacturing industries, especially for high-tech and high value-added industries.

Japanese non-manufacturing industries have also increased investments in Singapore. Japanese FDI since 1985 in Singapore's finance and insurance, commerce, service, and transportation sectors has particularly attracted attention. This trend seems to be further strengthened as Singapore's financial and commercial roles in the Asia–Pacific region gain momentum. The Singapore stated role in economic activities continues to remain paramount despite the fact that the government has hastened the implementation of its policies regarding the privatization and promotion of local enterprises. Singapore's local enterprises, mostly Chinese, have performed soundly in banking, finance, and other service sectors, but have been least effective in the manufacturing sector. The predominant proportion of Chinese enterprises in Singapore are SMBs and are highly labour-intensive. Together with some Japanese labour-intensive industries, they are faced with increasing operation costs (additional employers' CPF contributions and foreign workers' levy), and they will be forced to liquidate or shift to neighbouring countries if they are unable to upgrade or automate their facilities in a timely fashion.

Some Japanese manufacturing industries (even some electronics and electrical industries) in Singapore are still quite labour-intensive and require substantial numbers of non-Singaporean workers, mainly from the Malay Peninsula. Such industries are increasingly shifting these high-labour intensive operations to other ASEAN countries or to China, where cheap labour is readily available — and the trend will probably continue, as the Singapore government is unlikely to stop imposing higher employers' CPF contributions and heavy foreign worker levies while it aims at expanding high-tech, high value-added, and knowledge-intensive activities.

Singaporeans have shown more eagerness to work in Japanese enterprises due to the remarkable influx of Japanese FDI in Singapore in recent years. In terms of remuneration and career advancement opportunities, however, the Japanese enterprises still appear to be less attractive compared to Singapore government institutions, public enterprises, and Western multinational corporations. The Japanese-style managerial system without modifications and rectifications is not suitable for such heterogeneous societies strongly influenced by Western cultures such as Singapore. Owing to the growth of Japanese FDI in Singapore, a substantial number of employees, both managerial and rank and file, is severely needed by Japanese enterprises. Japanese investors should therefore modify and rectify their managerial systems in a more positive way in order to meet the requirements of Singapore's labour market. Japanese-style management must be internationalized and localized (so-called "internationalocalization") if it is to make greater positive contributions toward Singapore's rapid economic development.

Notes

1 There are quite a number of works dealing with this topic. For example: You Poh Seng and Lim Chong Yah, eds., *Singapore: Twenty-five Years of Development* (Singapore: Nan Yang Xing Zhou Lianhe Zaoboa, 1984); Walter Galenson, ed., *Foreign Trade and Investment: Economic Growth in the Newly Industrializing Asian Countries* (University of Wisconsin Press, 1985); Lawrence B. Krause et al., *The Singapore Economy Reconsidered* (Singapore: Institute of Southeast Asian Studies, 1987); Lim Chong Yah et al., *Policy Options for the Sikflapore Economy* (Singapore: McGraw-Hill Book Company, 1988); and Lim Hua Sing, *Singaporu no Taigai Keizai Kankei* [Singapore's Foreign Economic Relations], in Toshio Watanabe et al., eds., *Ajia NIEs Soran* [On the Asian NIEs] (Enterprise Press, 1989).

2 Krause et al., op. cit., pp. 24–25.

3 This survey was jointly conducted during August–October 1985 by the Japan Singapore Association (JSA), the Japan Trade Centre (JTC), the Japan Embassy (JE), and the Japanese Chamber of Commerce and Industry (JCCI). These four Japanese institutions are based in Singapore.

4 For instance, in 1987 Taiko Electronics, Sanyo Electronics Singapore, Singapore Kobe, Matsushita Electronics Pte., and Fujitsu Singapore shifted from Singapore to Malaysia. In 1988, Tanshin (Pekas Nanas) shifted from Singapore to Malacca.

5 For more information, see Peat Marwick, *Singapore Zeisei, Kaikei Seido, Kaisha-ho no Gaiyo* [Taxation, Accounting and Company Law in Singapore] (Singapore, July 1986), pp. 23–35.

6 Sekiguchi, S., ed., *ASEAN–Japan Relations: Investment* (Singapore: Institute of Southeast Asian Studies, 1983), pp. 246–48.

7 In 1984, the hourly wages of production workers of Asian NIEs were: Singapore US$2.37, Taiwan US$1.90, Hong Kong US$1.40, and South Korea US$1.32.

8 In 1984, the hourly wages in manufacturing industry in the selected countries were: US US$9.17, Canada US$8.18, Japan US$5.91, the Netherlands US$5.44, and the U.K. US$4.91.

9 Besides wage restraint, the following measures had also been taken. First, to reduce employers' CPF, contributions were decreased from 25 per cent to 10 per cent. Second, corporate taxes were reduced from 40 per cent to 30 per cent. Third, to introduce an across-the-board investment, allowance of 30 per cent on investments in machinery and equipment was made.

10 The Finance Minister of Singapore, Dr Richard Hu, predicted that the Singapore economy would chalk up 3 to 4 per cent growth for 1987 and 6 per cent from 1988 (*Straits Times*, May 25, 1987). As a matter of fact, Singapore succeeded in having an 8.8 per cent and 11.0 per cent economic growth in 1987 and 1988 respectively.

11 In October 1985, the JCCI in Singapore submitted a report based on a questionnaire survey of Japanese manufacturing industries in Singapore to the

Singapore government. The report urged the government to look into four areas of concern: high operation costs, inadequacy of the labour force and the working attitude of employees, support of industry, and economic policies (centred around high wage policy and restrictions on foreign workers) of the government. Since then, problems pertaining to high wage and operation costs in Singapore have been effectively remedied. Japanese firms in Singapore have now faced the problems of the working attitude of employees (that is, mainly job-hopping) and the inadequacy in nurturing supporting industries in Singapore.

12 Nomura Research Institute (NRI), *Nomura Ajia Joho* [Nomura's Information on Asia] (Tokyo, 1987), p. 7.

13 See note 3.

14 Japanese institutions (JSA, JTC, JE, and JCCI) in Singapore conducted questionnaire surveys on Japanese firms in these years.

15 In 1986, there were 166 foreign-affiliated firms invested in electronics and electrical products in Singapore. The breakdown includes the US 71, Europe 40, Japan 44, Australia and New Zealand 7, and others 4. Singapore deserves its status as an important production base for electronics and electrical industries for MNCs in Asia.

16 A study suggests that Japanese firms in Singapore were heavily concentrated in textiles and electronics in the early 1970s. Japanese firms were also heavily invested in textiles and electronics in Malaysia in 1978.

17 Economic Development Board, *Yearbook 1985/86* (Singapore), p. 18.

18 A questionnaire survey conducted in Singapore reveals that Japanese firms have acquired their business partners through the following routes: exporters or importers in Singapore (57 per cent); the Singapore government (11.4 per cent); Japanese trading companies or trading partners in Singapore (2.9 per cent); banks (5.7 per cent) and others (22.9 per cent). The date of this survey is not stated; however, it is likely that it was conducted in April 1974.

19 Kunio Yoshihara, *Foreign Investment and Domestic Response*, (Institute of Southeast Asian Studies, Singapore, 1976), p. 64.

20 Lim Hua Sing, "Singapore and Japan: Problems and Promises in Growing Trade", (*Marubeni Business Bulletin*, Tokyo, 1993, p. 7).

21 For a more detailed discussion, see Linda Low, "Public Enterprises in Singapore", in You Poh Seng and Lim Chong Yah, eds., op. cit., pp. 253–87.

22 To cite a few examples, the government has equity shares in Hitachi Electronic Devices (S) Pte. Ltd. (government equity holdings, 30 per cent), Jurong Shipyard Ltd. (79 per cent), Mitsubishi Singapore Heavy Industries Pte. Ltd. (49 per cent), Petrochemical Industry of Singapore (20 per cent), and Yaohan Singapore Pte. Ltd. (16.7 per cent).

23 Ichimura, Shinichi ed., *Nihon Kigyo in Ajia* [Japanese Enterprises in Asia], (Tokyo, 1980), pp. 12–13.

24 Ibid.

25 Among the ASEAN countries, both Indonesia and Malaysia have applied "Pribumi" and "Bumiputra" policies that limit foreign equity shares to 49 per cent. Thailand and the Philippines have practised rigid regulations, which were partly due to strong nationalism, that restrict foreign firms' ownership. However, in recent years, the ASEAN countries are allowing more and more foreign firms to have 100 per cent of the equity shares provided that they meet certain requirements and specifications (for example, capital requirement, export-oriented industry with a fixed number of employees, investment in certain type of industries, and so on) set by the respective countries.

26 There have always been casualties in Japan's FDIs, especially in Asia. The reasons for and significance of Japanese casualties in the 1970s have been examined by Ichimura Shinichi, ed., op. cit., pp. 183–201. The latest study further shows that during the period January 1985–December 1986, the number of withdrawals by Japanese-affiliated firms overseas amounted to 191 cases. The breakdown is as follows: Asia 65 cases (34 per cent); North America 41 cases (21.5 per cent); Latin America 26 cases (13.6 per cent); Africa 24 cases (12.6 per cent); Europe 20 cases (10.5 per cent); and others 15 cases (7.5 per cent). The industrial groups are as follows: commerce 36 cases; transportation 26 cases; textiles 18 cases; finance and insurance 17 cases; agriculture and fisheries 15 cases; and others. The highest casualties are seen in the manufacturing sector, which amounted to 67 cases (35.1 per cent of the total). See Toyo Keizai, op. cit., p. 7.

27 In 1980 the total workforce in Japanese firms was 73,403 persons (Nihon Boeki Shinko-kai, op. cit. [July 1981], p. 183) whereas Singapore's total workforce was 1,093,400 persons (Department of Statistics, *Economic and Social Statistics 1960–1982*, [Singapore, 1983], p. 32).

28 Nihon Boeki Shinko-kai, op. cit.; Department of Statistics, op. cit. At the end of 1984, 757 American firms in Singapore employed 71,130 workers, which formed 6.1 per cent of Singapore's total workforce, up from 5.5 per cent in 1982 ("American Investment: Singapore", Embassy of the US, unpublished paper [Singapore, June 1985], p. 8). 1000 Americans were employed in 757 American firms in 1984 compared to 2,909 Japanese who were employed in 718 Japanese firms in 1980 and 3,250 Japanese who were employed in 786 Japanese firms in 1982. Accordingly, it is clear that Japanese firms had a higher proportion of nationals compared to their American counterparts.

29 A similar feature can also be found in American firms in Singapore. At the end of 1984, slightly over two-thirds of the workforce were employed in the American manufacturing industries, which comprised 17 per cent of Singapore's total manufacturing workforce. In addition, the bulk of the manufacturing employees were engaged in the electronics industry (Embassy of the US, op. cit., p. 8).

30 The Singapore government declined to disclose the number of foreign workers from 1980 on.

31 Both employer and employee contribute to CPF. From the employees' viewpoint, the more CPF paid by their employers the better, as it ultimately belongs to the employees. CPF contributions have been adjusted again and again by the government. Employers' contributions were reduced from 25 to 10 per cent in 1986, after Singapore's economic downturn in 1985–1986. It was readjusted from July 1, 1989 to 15 per cent as Singapore experienced 8.8 per cent and 11.0 per cent GDP growth rates in 1987 and 1988 respectively. The levy, paid by employers to the government, brings no benefits to the employees. Since 1 July 1989 employers have been asked to pay S$240 to the government if they employed a foreign worker. In February 1993, the levy has been increased to S$300 for those manufacturing industries which have employed foreign workers below 35 per cent of the total workforce. However, if the proportion of foreign workers lies between 35 per cent and 45 per cent, the levy is set for S$450 per person. This is said to be aimed at restricting avoidable employment of foreign workers.

32 The Singapore government has also argued that as employers' CPF contributions were cut soon after the economic downturn in 1985–1986, and as Singapore has

continued to experience high GDP growth rates employers' contributions were raised again to 15 per cent from July 1, 1989. In July 1992, the employers' contributions rate was raised further to 18 per cent. The employees' rate was lowered to 22 per cent, giving a total CPF contribution rate of 40 per cent. This was in line with the move towards a long term contribution rate of 40 per cent, with equal contributions of 20 per cent each from both employer and employee (Ministry of Trade and Industry, *Economic Survey of Singapore 1992*, [Singapore], p. 47), which became effective in July 1994.

33 It is reported that AIWA and Kenwood, both audio product manufacturers, built additional plants to cope with rising demand. Matsushita also announced plans for a seventh factory, to build facsimile machines, first of its kind in the country. Yokogawa Electric Corporation extended its operation beyond software development for process computer systems to manufacturing as well. SMC established a world-scale pneumatic components plant, Teraoka Seiko invested in both the manufacture of electronic scales and software for system integration, and Hoxan transferred to Singapore its automated solar cell manufacturing facilities. Sony Corporation established a precision component production and engineering support facility, its only such facility outside of Japan. Sony also set up its operational headquarters the first Japanese operational headquarters in Singapore. (See Economic Development Board, *Yearbook 1987/88* [Singapore], pp. 27–28).

CHAPTER 5

Japan in ASEAN: Potential Trade Frictions

Introduction

After the second oil-shock in 1979–1981, trade frictions between Japan and the Western countries, that is the US and the EC, escalated. Relatively higher-quality and lower-priced Japanese manufactured goods have overwhelmed not only the markets in ASEAN but also those in Europe and North America. Japan's trade with the US and the EC has been in Japan's favour. In 1983, Japan's trade surpluses with the US and the EC reached US$21 billion and US$10.1 billion respectively.[1]

Both the US and the EC have been urging Japan to reduce its exports and increase imports from them in order to reduce Japan's trade surpluses. Despite numerous efforts by the parties concerned, trade relations between Japan and its foreign partners do not seem to have improved significantly. Thus, at a ministerial conference on 27 April 1984, the Japanese government adopted a six-point package of counter-measures in order to resolve contentious economic problems with the developed countries.[2] It is estimated, however, that these measures will reduce Japan's surpluses by only US$500–600 million at the most.[3] Trade frictions between Japan and the Western countries are unlikely to be resolved in the near future.

Trade frictions between Japan and Western countries have been sufficiently discussed and researched.[4] Much attention has been paid to efforts to rectify their distorted trade relationship, and this has been reported frequently in daily newspapers. The potential and/or actual trade frictions between Japan and ASEAN, on the other hand, have been overlooked, despite protestations made by governments and among business circles in this region against the closed nature of the Japanese market. For example, it was reported that Philippine President Ferdinand E. Marcos had asked the Japanese Prime Minister Suzuki Zenko to reduce tariffs on bananas when the latter visited the Philippines in January 1981.[5] Marcos in his keynote speech to the thirteenth meeting of ASEAN Economic Ministers in Manila in 1982 again voiced "the collective concern of the Philippines, Malaysia, Singapore, Thailand, and Indonesia over Japan's heavy tariff policies and non-tariff barriers against products from their region (ASEAN)".[6] The Malaysian Prime Minister Datuk Seri Dr Mahathir Mohamad, when he visited Japan in January 1983, also called on Japan "to open its markets wider to products from Malaysia and other developing nations".[7] He termed "the flow of primary commodities from ASEAN in return for finished and semifinished goods from Japan" anachronistic, and said that "this symbiotic relationship, which is based on the classical developed-developing economic dichotomy, is now very much obsolete".[8] In Singapore, Dr Tony Tan, formerly Minister of Trade and Industry (also Minister for Finance), in an interview with a Japanese fortnightly periodical, *Nikkei Shogyo*, criticized the closed nature of the Japanese market and cited examples of exports of meat and marine products which were required to meet Japan's sanitary standards, and exports of manufactured goods which must meet the Japanese Industry Standard (JIS), as typical non-tariff barriers imposed by Japan to restrict imports from the developing countries.[9] Mr Tan Keong Choon, President of the SCCCI, also urged Japan to look into its "trade barriers" and "obstacles imposed on imports" from Singapore.[10]

Governments and business circles in ASEAN feel frustrated in exploring the Japanese market. As a result of the rapid industrial development in this region and the close trade and economic relations between ASEAN and Japan, imports of industrial products from Japan are likely to increase substantially year by year. ASEAN will be in a difficult situation if the value of its exports to Japan do not match that of its imports from Japan. Statistics show that over the period 1979–1982, Japan's trade with ASEAN has been in ASEAN's favour because of its important supplies of industrial resources, such as crude oil, liquefied gas, timber, copper, and natural rubber to Japan. However, ASEAN's trade surplus with Japan diminished substantially from US$4,035 million in 1980 to merely US$841 million in 1982. Moreover, the trade surplus has been mainly due to Indonesia's exports to Japan. Taken individually, during the period 1981–1982, Malaysia, the Philippines, Singapore, and Thailand all experienced considerable trade deficits with Japan.

As a result of the world-wide decline in demand for crude oil, the export trade of Indonesia and Malaysia has been declining. Thailand and the Philippines have also been suffering from economic woes because of the decline in demand for their primary products, while Singapore does not seem to be much affected by the adverse international economic situation. ASEAN in general has been exploring the Japanese market for its finished and semi-finished products in order to rectify the grossly one-sided trade with Japan. These efforts have not been successful, implying the existence of various trade frictions between ASEAN and Japan.

This chapter examines the background of potential trade frictions between ASEAN and Japan through analysing their interdependent but asymmetrical trade relationships: ASEAN's unfavourable trade relationship with Japan and its stagnation of exports of manufactured goods (in relative terms) to Japan. More specifically, the significant features in ASEAN's trade relationship with Japan will be analysed in the context of trade relationships over the last decade or so, to provide a clearer picture of existing trade frictions between ASEAN and Japan.

Trade Relationship between ASEAN and Japan — Interdependence or Dependence?

Japan has been the most resource-poor country among the industrialized countries. Most of its industrial resources have had to be imported from abroad. Apart from crude oil, scrap and pig iron, iron ore and coal, Japan has had to import antimony, mercury, manganese, tin, tungsten, molybdenum, and chromium in large quantities. Furthermore, nickel, cobalt, and bauxite are not mined in Japan, and non-metallic minerals which have had to be imported in large quantities are borate, bromine, magnesite, phosphate rock, potash salt, and nitrates. Natural fibres, such as cotton, wool, flax, ramie, and jute, have also been supplied entirely from imports.[11]

The degree of Japan's dependence on imports of various key raw materials particularly attracts our attention. This dependence can be seen from Table 5.1. Japan's economic development has necessitated the supply of raw materials and industrial resources from abroad, mainly from Asia, for its export-oriented industries. The Japanese economy is primarily based on trade and the termination of the supply of certain industrial resources would certainly throw the industrial mechanism into confusion. Thus, the main theme of the Japanese policy-makers has been centred around the procurement of sufficient supplies of raw materials and promoting foreign trade. In the past, some extreme nationalists in Japan in several instances have tried to secure raw materials supply and foreign markets by military means. During World War II, the confessed purpose of the "Greater East Asia Co-prosperity Sphere" was to secure strategic industrial raw materials, particularly oil and iron ore supplies from China and the "South Seas" (Indonesia and Malaysia, in particular), and extensive markets in Asia.

In the early 1970s, influential figures in the Japanese parliament and business and academic circles proclaimed the Straits of Malacca as an "economic life-line" of Japan. Arguments for protecting the Straits of Malacca by some Japanese "nationalists" attracted serious attention, both domestically and internationally. Apart from military and political considerations, the Straits of Malacca were regarded by Japan as a vital trade route between Japan on the one hand and the Middle East, the EC, and Africa on the other. The EC, particularly, was regarded by Japan as an important market for its manufactured products such as metals, chemical products, and machinery and equipment, while the Middle East was important for the supply of petroleum to Japan. Petroleum, which has been vital to Japan's rapid

Table 5.1

**Japan's Degree of Dependence* on Imports of Selected Key Energy
and Mineral Resources, 1978, 1980, 1981**

(%)

Year	1978	1980	1981
Crude Oil & Petroleum Products	99.8	99.8	99.8
Natural Gas	89.0	90.5	90.5
Iron Ore	99.5	99.7	99.7
Coal	76.7	81.4	81.4
Copper	86.5	86.3	96.5
Lead	62.8	68.2	78.4
Zinc	57.8	54.5	61.0
Nickel	100.0	100.0	100.0
Tin	96.4	96.4	96.0
Bauxite	100.0	100.0	100.0
Manganese	91.2	95.9	94.9
Tungsten	68.5	74.1	63.3
Chrome	98.5	98.6	98.3
Phosphate	100.0	100.0	100.0

* *The degree of dependence is expressed here as:*

$$\frac{Imports}{Domestic\ production + imports}$$

Source: *Ministry of Foreign Affairs*, Waga Gaiko no Kinkyo *[The Recent State of our Foreign Policies] (Japan, 1980, 1982, and 1983).*

industrial development particularly after World War II, is imported mainly from the Middle East through the Straits of Malacca. In 1980, apart from other industrial resources Japan imported 221 million tons of petroleum (90 per cent of Japan's total petroleum imports) and 134 million tons of iron ore (89 per cent of Japan's total iron ore imports) through the Straits of Malacca and the Lombok Straits.[12] There has been a strong feeling among the Japanese, especially since the first "oil-shock" in 1973, that the stoppage of oil supply from the Middle East would be fatal to Japan's economy. This feeling strengthened after the second "oil-shock" in 1979–1981. Although

Japan was the largest beneficiary among the member countries of the OECD after the Organization of Petroleum Exporting Countries (OPEC) announced the price-cut on oil in 1983, wars in the Middle East, and particularly hostile relations between Iran (where the Mitsui Group has the largest petro-chemical industry in the world) and Iraq continued to pose a threat to a regular and sufficient oil supply from the Middle East to Japan.

It is therefore easy to understand why Japan has long been enthusiastic over China's "Four Modernization" plans and in expanding trade with the ASEAN countries. Oil and liquefied gas supplies from China and ASEAN[13] (mainly from Malaysia, Indonesia, and Singapore) have become increasingly important to Japan. In the years 1981, 1982, and 1983, exports of mineral fuel from Indonesia to Japan constituted 89, 89, and 87 per cent of Indonesia's total oil exports respectively. In the case of Malaysia, the proportions for those years were 38, 33, and 36 per cent; and in the case of Singapore (which does not produce oil but is an oil refinery centre for its neighbours and the Middle East countries), the figures were 77, 80, and 74 per cent, during the same period. Exports of mineral fuel from ASEAN to Japan amounted to US$14,472 million (69 per cent of ASEAN's total exports to Japan) in 1981, US$13,210 million (68 per cent) in 1982, and US$11,320 million (65 per cent) in 1983. In the case of liquefied gas from the ASEAN countries, Indonesia accounted for 31 per cent of Japan's total imports. Imports of this item from Malaysia are also increasing as new gas fields recently found in that country come on stream.

In 1981, Indonesian and Malaysian crude oil constituted 17 per cent of Japan's total imports. Japan was also highly dependent on certain natural and industrial resources of ASEAN, such as rubber (99.5 per cent), sugar (24.8 per cent), bauxite (30.2 per cent), copper (39.7 per cent), timber (42.2 per cent), vegetable oil (64.4 per cent), bananas (83.2 per cent), and nickel (51.0 per cent) (see Table 5.2).

On the ASEAN side, owing to its rapid economic and industrial development, imports of heavy industrial and chemical products from Japan increased remarkably. Imports of machinery and transport equipment from Japan increased from US$1,202 million in

Table 5.2

Japan's Imports of Primary Products from ASEAN, 1980

(US$ millions)

	World	ASEAN*	Indonesia	Malaysia	Philippines	Singapore	Thailand
Fish & Shellfish	3,026	429 (14.4)	228	40	33	–	128
Sugar	1,424	337 (24.8)	–	–	255	–	82
Bauxite	155	46 (30.2)	29	17	–	–	–
Copper	2,040	809 (39.7)	122	94	593	–	–
Natural Rubber	688	635 (99.5)	62	139	–	6	428
Timber	6,909	2,913 (42.2)	1,404	1,251	258	–	–
Vegetable Oil	186	114 (64.4)	–	90	24	–	–
Bananas	190	158 (83.2)	–	–	158	–	–
Crude Oil	52,763	8,882 (16.8)	7,567	1,315	–	–	–
Nickel	499	229 (51.0)	202	–	27	–	–
Liquefied Gas	7,671	2,399 (31.3)	2,399	–	–	–	–

Note: *Figures in brackets represent percentages. These percentages appear to be slightly larger as certain exports from individual ASEAN countries have not been included.*

Source: *Compiled from Ministry of Foreign Affairs, Japan, ASEAN (Tokyo, March 1982).*

1972–1973 to US$5,918 million in 1979–1980; while imports of chemicals increased from US$335 million to US$1,093 million during the same period.[14] ASEAN's total imports from Japan showed a substantial increase over the period 1974–1982. It seems likely that this trend will be sustained at least for some years, as long as ASEAN continues its ambitious industrialization and modernization programmes.

It is clear from the above analysis that Japan's industrial development depends heavily on ASEAN's supply of certain industrial and natural resources. In this sense, ASEAN is vital to Japan. However, ASEAN's share in Japan's import trade remained between 11 and 15 per cent over the period 1973–1983. In other words, in terms of value, imports from ASEAN have not constituted an important weight in Japan's total import trade. Similarly, Japan's exports to ASEAN have not constituted an important weight in Japan's total export trade; they have been between 9 and 11 per cent during the period 1973–1983. In short, from Japan's viewpoint and in terms of total value, Japan's trade with the ASEAN countries is not as important as it might appear at first sight.

From ASEAN's viewpoint, however, trade with Japan is particularly important. During the period 1973–1982, ASEAN's exports to Japan have been between 23 and 30 per cent of its total exports while its imports from Japan have been between 23 and 27 per cent. This is most significant in the case of Indonesia, followed by Thailand, the Philippines, and Malaysia. In some years during the period 1973–1982, about 50 per cent of Indonesia's exports went to Japan. As for ASEAN's import trade, about one quarter of the imports of Thailand, the Philippines, Malaysia, and Indonesia are from Japan. Among the ASEAN countries, Singapore's trade has been the most diversified. During the period 1973–1982, Singapore's exports to Japan have amounted to about 10 per cent while its imports from Japan have averaged around 18 per cent (see Table 5.3).

From the statistical evidence we can conclude that, firstly, Japan is a relatively important market for ASEAN but not vice versa; and secondly, Japan is a comparatively important supplier to ASEAN but not vice versa. Changes in Japan's import and export trade with ASEAN

Table 5.3

The Asymmetry in Japan-ASEAN Trade Relations, 1973–1983

(%)

	Exports											Imports										
	1973	1974	1975	1976	1977	1978	1979	1980	1981	1982	1983	1973	1974	1975	1976	1977	1978	1979	1980	1981	1982	1983
1. ASEAN's share in Japan's trade*	9.8	9.7	10.5	9.0	8.5	8.9	9.5	10.1	10.0	10.7	10.2	11.5	12.9	11.0	11.3	12.5	12.5	14.8	15.2	14.6	14.8	13.7
Japan's share in ASEAN's trade**	28.2	28.5	26.5	24.6	22.6	23.0	25.3	24.4	23.1	24.0	n.a.	27.3	25.5	25.5	24.6	25.1	25.9	23.7	22.6	23.3	22.8	n.a.
2. Indonesia's share in Japan's trade	2.4	2.6	3.3	2.4	2.2	2.1	2.1	2.7	2.7	3.1	2.4	5.8	7.4	5.9	6.0	7.0	6.6	8.0	9.4	9.3	9.1	8.2
Japan's share in Indonesia's trade	53.2	53.5	44.1	41.7	40.2	39.2	46.1	49.3	47.3	51.5	n.a.	29.3	29.4	31.0	26.2	27.1	30.1	29.1	31.5	30.1	28.3	n.a.
3. Malaysia's share in Japan's trade	P	13	10	10	11	1?	15	16	16	18	1Q	?0	1.6	1.2	2.0	2.2	2.4	3.0	2.5	2.0	2.3	2.5
Japan's share in Malaysia's trade	17.7	16.9	14.3	21.1	20.5	21.7	23.9	22.8	22.1	20.9	n.a.	21.6	22.0	20.1	21.2	23.4	23.1	23.5	22.8	24.4	24.2	n.a.
4. The Philippines' share in Japan's trade	1.7	1.6	1.8	1.7	1.4	1.6	1.6	1.3	1.3	1.3	1.2	2.1	1.8	1.9	1.2	1.3	1.3	1.4	1.4	1.2	1.2	1.0
Japan's share in Philippines' trade	36.0	34.9	37.8	24.3	23.2	24.0	26.4	26.6	21.8	22.9	n.a.	31.3	26.8	27.2	27.1	25.1	26.7	22.6	19.9	18.8	20.0	n.a.

Continued on next page

Table 5.3 (*continued*)

(%)

	Exports											Imports										
	1973	1974	1975	1976	1977	1978	1979	1980	1981	1982	1983	1973	1974	1975	1976	1977	1978	1979	1980	1981	1982	1983
5. Singapore's share in Japan's trade	2.5	2.5	2.7	2.3	2.1	2.4	2.6	3.0	2.9	3.9	3.0	0.6	1.0	0.7	0.9	1.1	1.3	1.1	1.4	1.4	1.2	
Japan's share in Singapore's trade	8.0	11.4	8.7	10.3	9.5	9.7	9.6	8.1	10.1	10.9	n.a.	18.3	17.9	16.9	16.0	17.5	19.1	17.0	17.8	18.8	17.9	n.a.
6. Thailand's share in Japan's trade	1.9	1.7	1.7	1.6	1.7	1.6	1.7	1.5	1.5	1.4	1.7	1.0	1.1	1.3	1.2	1.0	1.1	1.1	0.8	0.7	0.8	0.8
Japan's share in Thailand's trade	26.1	25.8	27.6	19.7	20.5	20.7	15.1	14.2	13.6	n.a.		36.0	31.4	32.4	32.5	32.4	30.7	26.3	21.2	24.3	23.8	n.a.

Note: n.a. = not available

   * Exports: $\dfrac{\text{Japan's exports to ASEAN}}{\text{Japan's total exports}} \times 100$ Imports: $\dfrac{\text{Japan's imports from ASEAN}}{\text{Japan's total imports}} \times 100$

   ** Exports: $\dfrac{\text{ASEAN's exports to Japan}}{\text{ASEAN's total exports}} \times 100$ Imports: $\dfrac{\text{ASEAN's imports from Japan}}{\text{ASEAN's total imports}} \times 100$

Source: JETRO, *White Paper on International Trade*, various issues.
Ministry of Foreign Affairs, *Statistical Survey of Japan's Economy*, (Japan, 1981).
Department of Statistics, *Economic and Social Statistics, Singapore 1960–1982*, (Singapore, 1983)
IMF, *Direction of Trade Statistics*, various issues.

can significantly affect the trade balances of the member countries. On the other hand, changes in ASEAN's import and export trade with Japan would hardly affect (in relative terms) Japan's trade balance. In this sense ASEAN is more dependent upon Japan than Japan on ASEAN.

Japan–ASEAN Trade, 1973–1983

During the period 1973–1983 (Tables 5.4, 5.5 and 5.6) ASEAN's trade with Japan was in favour of the former except in 1978 when ASEAN as a whole suffered a trade deficit of US$81 million.[15] This was primarily due to Singapore's substantial imports of heavy industrial and chemical products (which increased from US$1,405 million in 1977 to US$1,919 million in 1978) from Japan that year, particularly machinery and equipment which increased remarkably from US$974 million in 1977 to US$1,403 million in 1878. This reflected the need for Japanese supplies in Singapore's industrialization in 1978. To a lesser extent, this trade deficit was also due to the general increase in Japan's exports to the ASEAN countries that year, compared to the previous years.

Exports of mineral fuels and lubricants from Indonesia, and to a lesser extent from Malaysia, to Japan contributed tremendously to ASEAN's trade surplus with Japan.[16] Singapore, unlike its resource-rich neighbours, produces no crude oil itself but as an important refinery centre exported substantial amounts of mineral fuels to Japan throughout the period under consideration. (Exports of mineral fuels from Singapore into Japan increased substantially from US$148 million in 1973 to US$1,501 million in 1981.)[17] Therefore, it can be argued that ASEAN's export trade with Japan is primarily dependent on the quantity and more importantly on the prices of mineral fuels exported from Indonesia, Malaysia, and Singapore into Japan. In the 1970s, the oil-producing countries benefited greatly from the rising prices of mineral fuels. However, world crude oil prices dropped from US$35.49 per barrel in January 1981 to US$28.61 per barrel in January 1984,[18] and thus affected the oil-producing countries seriously. The export trade of Indonesia, Malaysia, and Singapore with Japan has been particularly affected by this adverse situation.

Crude oil prices in Indonesia have also experienced drastic changes over the last decade. They increased substantially from US$10.80 per barrel in January 1974 to US$27.50 per barrel in January 1980. This trend persisted until 1981 when it reached its peak at US$35 per barrel. However, the price dropped drastically thereafter and in February 1983 it was US$29.53. This persisted until June 1984 (see

Table 5.4
Japan–ASEAN Trade, 1973–1982
(In US$ Millions)

Year	ASEAN			Indonesia			Malaysia		
	Exports	Imports	Trade Balance	Exports	Imports	Trade Balance	Exports	Imports	Trade Balance
1973	3628	3575	53	1707	800	907	540	541	–1
1974	6906	5460	1446	3969	1131	2838	714	915	–201
1975	5611	5600	11	3132	1477	1655	546	707	616
1976	6754	5982	772	3565	1485	2080	1119	813	306
1977	7813	7157	656	4361	1689	2672	1245	1065	180
1978	8810	8891	–81	4566	2016	2550	1605	1372	233
1979	13484	10185	3299	7189	2101	5088	2595	1757	838
1980	17833	13798	4035	10793	3413	7380	2958	2471	487
1981	17377	16014	1363	10546	3989	6557	2470	2829	–359
1982	17123	16282	841	10298	4428	5870	2463	3039	–576

Year	Philippines			Singapore			Thailand		
	Exports	Imports	Trade Balance	Exports	Imports	Trade Balance	Exports	Imports	Trade Balance
1973	680	561	119	293	941	–646	408	732	–324
1974	932	924	8	660	1503	–843	631	987	–356
1975	858	1007	–149	466	1374	–908	609	1035	–426
1976	625	1072	–447	676	1453	–777	769	1159	–390
1977	732	1073	–341	767	1836	–1049	688	1494	–806
1978	828	1349	–521	981	2509	–1526	830	1645	–815
1979	1208	1480	–272	1366	3004	–1638	1126	1843	–717
1980	1540	1651	–111	1560	4311	–2751	982	1952	–970
1981	1241	1594	–353	2124	5188	–3064	996	2414	–1418
1982	1145	1645	–500	2262	5044	–2782	955	2126	–1171

Source: *International Monetary Fund (IMF)*, Directory of Trade Statistics, *various issues.*

Table 5.5

Commodity Composition of Japan's Exports to ASEAN, 1981–1983

	ASEAN			
	1981	1982	1983	Changing Rate (1982–1983) %
Foodstuffs	178,878	148,842	154,920	4.1
Raw Material & Fuel	150,857	120,279	114,603	-4.7
Articles of Light Industry	1,585,997	1,641,158	1,620,883	-1.2
Articles of Heavy Industry	13,121,348	12,747,696	12,854,747	0.8
Re-Export & Special Commodities	156,921	187,878	276,005	46.9
Total	15,194,002	14,845,853	15,021,158	1.2

	Indonesia			
	1981	1982	1983	Changing Rate (1982–1983) %
Foodstuffs	46,204	12,082	33,621	178.3
Raw Material & Fuel	42,974	43,974	36,654	-16.6
Articles of Light Industry	373,614	361,256	257,765	-28.6
Articles of Heavy Industry	3,637,879	3,793,546	3,143,102	-17.1
Re-Export & Special Commodities	22,152	49,696	80,943	62.9
Total	4,122,823	4,260,554	3,552,087	-16.6

	Malaysia			
	1981	1982	1983	Changing Rate (1982–1983) %
Foodstuffs	23,898	24,668	24,020	-2.6
Raw Material & Fuel	10,858	9,254	9,224	-0.3
Articles of Light Industry	193,066	204,506	217,161	6.2
Articles of Heavy Industry	2,173,997	2,238,095	2,487,206	11.1
Re-Export & Special Commodities	22,555	25,494	33,207	30.3
Total	2,424,374	2,502,017	2,770,818	10.7

	Philippines			
	1981	1982	1983	Changing Rate (1982–1983) %
Foodstuffs	33,696	35,631	8,491	-76.2
Raw Material & Fuel	36,215	33,173	27,822	-16.1
Articles of Light Industry	251,511	249,425	216,389	-13.2
Articles of Heavy Industry	1,587,776	1,469,970	1,474,633	0.3
Re-Export & Special Commodities	19,134	14,4770	16,222	9.8
Total	1,928,332	1,802,969	1,743,556	-3.3

Continued on next page

Table 5.5 *(continued)*

| | Singapore | | | | Thailand | | | |
	1981	1982	1983	Changing Rate (1982–1983) %	1981	1982	1983	Changing Rate (1982–1983) %
Foodstuffs	57,522	58,461	64,010	5.5	17,558	18,000	24,779	37.7
Raw Material & Fuel	11,522	12,940	16,370	26.5	49,287	20,937	24,533	17.2
Articles of Light Industry	590,622	658,427	727,773	10.5	177,184	167,545	201,795	20.4
Articles of Heavy Industry	3,734,999	3,568,508	3,521,185	–1.3	1,986,698	1,677,577	2,228,620	32.8
Re-Export & Special Commodities	37,728	45,956	78,115	58.8	19,766	22,274	24,775	16.1
Total	4,467,920	4,373,218	4,448,224	1.7	2,250,553	1,907,094	2,506,473	31.4

Notes:

Exports

Foodstuffs: fish, shellfish, and dried shitake.

Light Industrial Products: cotton fabrics, synthetic fibre fabrics, and secondary textile products (excluding clothing).

Heavy Industrial and Chemical Products: chemicals (organic compounds, plastic materials & artificial resins), metals (iron and steel) bars & shapes, wire rods, heavy plates & sheets, plates & sheets, tinned plates & sheets, galvanized plates & sheets, hoops & strips, tubes & pipes and tube and pipe joints). Non-ferrous metals, copper & copper alloys and metal products (construction & their building materials of iron). Machinery & equipment (boiler & boiler equipment, internal combustion engines, office machines, metalworking machinery, constructing & mining machinery, cargo handling machinery bearings, heavy electrical machinery, electrical circuit articles, telecommunication equipments, other electrical machinery, transportation and precision instruments).

Table 5.6
Commodity Composition of Japan's Imports from ASEAN, 1981–1983

(US$ '000s)

	ASEAN				Indonesia			
	1981	1982	1983	Changing Rate (1982–1983) %	1981	1982	1983	Changing Rate (1982–1983) %
Foodstuffs	1,226,232	1,325,859	1,288,344	-2.8	302,414	326,936	346,234	5.9
Raw Material	3,788,139	3,575,631	3,275,337	-8.4	984,863	769,092	711,314	-7.5
Mineral Fuel	14,471,749	13,210,199	11,320,048	-14.3	11,847,007	10,728,364	9,061,413	-15.5
Manufactured Products	1,311,750	1,190,754	1,361,910	14.4	163,590	168,853	298,563	76.8
Machinery & Equipment	350,368	252,517	261,100	3.4	1,911	943	433	-54.1
Chemicals	184,469	213,764	212,275	-0.7	10,097	9,411	7,854	-16.5
Other Articles	776,915	724,472	888,535	22.6	151,581	158,450	290,277	83.1
Re-Export & Special Commodities	170,555	155,141	110,044	-29.1	7,423	11,739	14,798	26.1
Total	20,968,426	19,457,583	17,355,684	-10.8	13,305,297	12,004,985	10,432,322	-13.1

	Malaysia				Philippines			
	1981	1982	1983	Changing Rate (1982–1983) %	1981	1982	1983	Changing Rate (1982–1983) %
Foodstuffs	69,229	64,612	81,536	26.2	448,247	430,442	398,125	-7.5
Raw Material	1,302,606	1,575,943	1,483,200	-5.9	1,018,865	879,437	675,997	-23.1
Mineral Fuel	1,114,940	995,169	1,114,889	12.0	8,958	22,537	50,625	124.6
Manufactured Products	421,733	353,304	427,145	20.9	178,638	183,034	168,344	-8.0
Machinery & Equipment	79,143	76,270	100,147	31.3	62,532	39,855	26,332	-33.9
Chemical	24,304	27,776	36,410	31.1	36,334	52,336	46,988	-10.2
Other Articles	318,286	249,257	290,587	16.6	79,771	90,844	95,024	4.6
Re-Export & Special Commodities	18,526	20,545	23,933	16.5	76,515	60,760	13,406	-77.9
Total	2,927,034	3,009,574	3,130,703	4.0	1,731,222	1,576,210	1,306,497	-17.1

Table 5.6 (continued)

(US$ '000)

	Singapore				Thailand			
	1981	1982	1983	Changing Rate (1982–1983) %	1981	1982	1983	Changing Rate (1982–1983) %
Foodstuffs	29,838	37,190	30,220	-18.7	376,504	466,678	432,229	-7.4
Raw Material	31,659	28,658	38,736	35.2	450,146	322,501	366,090	13.5
Mineral Fuel	1,500,844	1,464,123	1,093,112	-25.3	0	6	9	69.3
Manufactured Products	318,460	256,930	254,444	-1.0	229,329	228,631	213,413	-6.7
Machinery & Equipment	202,299	129,640	119,661	-7.7	4,482	5,809	14,527	150.1
Chemical	76,888	86,567	98,766	14.1	36,842	37,673	22,257	-40.9
Other Articles	39,273	40,723	36,018	-11.6	188,005	185,149	176,629	^.6
Re-Export & Special Commodities	62,978	39,218	50,992	30.0	5,114	22,879	6,915	-69.8
Total	1,943,780	1,826,119	1,467,504	-19.6	1,061,093	1,040,695	1,018,657	-2.1

Notes:

Imports

Foodstuffs: fish & shellfish, shrimps, prawns & lobster (crustacea & molluscs), cuttlefish & squid (crustacea & molluscs), cocoa containing food.

Raw Materials: metal materials and other raw materials (raw rubber, natural rubber [raw], and wood).

Mineral Fuels: petroleum products (petroleum spirits, kerosenes, and heavy fuel oils).

Manufactured Products: chemicals (medicinal & pharmaceutical products), machinery & equipment (office machines, pumps & centrifuges, heavy electrical machinery), transportation equipment, precision instruments, and watches & clocks.

Other Products: textile products and furniture.

Source: *Japan Trade Centre, Singapore, Bulletin 11, no. 131 (February–March 1984), Tables 1–12.*

Table 5.7

Crude Oil Prices in Indonesia

(US$ per barrel. Official selling prices)

Date effective		Minas (34 API)
1974	January 1	10.80
	April 1	11.70
	July 1	12.60
1972	October 1	12.80
1977	January 1	13.55
1979	January 1	13.90
	April 1	15.65
	May 1	16.15
	June 15	18.25
	July 15	21.12
	November 17	23.50
	December 1	25.50
1980	January 1	27.50
	February 4	29.50
	May 20	31.50
1981	January 1	35.00
	September 10	35.00
1982	November 11	34.53
1983	February 23	29.53
1984	June	29.53

Source: *OPEC*, Annual Statistical Bulletin of OPEC, 1983, *(Vienna, Austria: 1983), p. 158, and others.*

Table 5.7). It is clear that the change in Indonesia's export of crude oil has affected its export trade seriously since 1981.

Individual Country Review and External Debts

Among the ASEAN countries, Indonesia has been the main beneficiary of trade with Japan through its abundant exports of mineral fuels and, to a lesser extent, its raw materials (inedible) to Japan, resulting in a significant trade surplus with Japan throughout the period 1973–1983. ASEAN's trade surplus with Japan would turn into a severe deficit if exports of mineral fuels from Indonesia into Japan were excluded from Indonesian's export trade during the period under consideration. This simply implies that among the ASEAN countries, Indonesia has been the most important trading partner of Japan. Furthermore, exports of mineral fuels from Indonesia to Japan play a decisive role in Indonesian's balance of payments. Needless to say, as an economic bloc, ASEAN's trade surplus with Japan is due basically to Indonesian's export trade to that country. However, trade frictions between Japan and individual ASEAN countries do exist even though ASEAN as a whole has a favourable trade relationship with Japan. Statistics show that after the second oil-shock in 1979–1981, ASEAN's trade surplus with Japan decreased substantially from US$4,035 million in 1980 to US$1,363 million in 1981 and fell to US$841 million in 1982 (see Table 5.4). It was not difficult to anticipate ASEAN's trade situation with Japan in the years 1983 and 1984 as crude oil prices dropped drastically after 1982. The oil-producing countries in ASEAN, Indonesia and Malaysia, will be very much embarrassed by the decreased revenue from oil exports. In view of these facts, trade frictions between ASEAN and Japan will come to the surface once ASEAN suffers a trade deficit with Japan.

After Indonesia comes Malaysia, which had a trade surplus with Japan in 1976–1980. Malaysia is a resource-rich country and its exports of tin, petroleum (crude and partly refined), fixed vegetable oils (crude, refined, and purified), and natural rubber and latex to Japan have been promising. In 1981, however, Malaysia experienced a trade deficit with Japan because of the large increase in imports and the drastic drop in export trade with Japan. This situation worsened in the following year as a result of the stagnation in export trade and increased demand for Japanese light industrial products and heavy industrial and chemical products. The "Look East" policy publicly announced in December 1981 and the ambitious industrial projects carried out by the Malaysian government had undoubtedly stimulated imports from Japan.[19] This tendency seems to have escalated particularly in 1983, as far as statistical evidence shows.

The Philippines, compared to Singapore and Thailand, has had a moderate but persistent trade deficit with Japan during the period 1975–1983. Philippine exports to Japan decreased substantially from US$1,540 million in 1980 to US$1,145 million in 1982. On the import side, Philippine imports of light and heavy industrial products from Japan appeared to have stagnated as a result of the Philippines' lack of international reserves and sluggish economic development. The Philippine trade deficit with Japan increased substantially from US$111 million in 1980 to US$500 million in 1982. So far, there has been no indication that peso devaluations in June and October 1983 would stimulate Philippine exports to Japan greatly.

More notably, Singapore and Thailand suffered continuing and serious trade deficits with Japan throughout the period 1973–1983. In terms of total value, Singapore's trade deficits with Japan were greater than those of Thailand. However, it is understandable that Thailand's trade deficits with Japan have had more impact on Thai society than has been the case in Singapore. The reason is that Singapore is an entrepôt economy and its imports from Japan are not necessarily for domestic consumption.[20] Singapore's substantial imports of industrial products from Japan have also kept pace with its rapid economic development. Furthermore, Singapore's exports to Japan have been expanding since the mid-1970s while those of Thailand have been stagnating. Relatively poor economic performance in Thailand and protectionist measures against Thai products have restricted Thailand from expanding its export trade with Japan.

Certainly, foreign trade is not merely a bilateral issue but has to be considered from a broader perspective. Trade deficit with a certain country might be offset by gains from another country. However, ASEAN constitutes a resource-rich region which has a favourable trade balance with Japan. ASEAN's trade surplus with Japan reached its peak in 1980. It declined abruptly thereafter from US$4,035 million in 1980 to only US$841 million in 1982. ASEAN's favourable trade balance with Japan may soon be reversed if ASEAN's commodity prices continue to drop further (particularly for some crucial resources, such as petroleum, rubber, and tin), if ASEAN'S manufactured products cannot find a larger market in Japan, and if imports of Japanese industrial products continue to increase substantially as a result of ASEAN's modernization programmes. Imports of Japanese industrial products seem to have increased partly because of their quality and competitive prices, and partly because of the numerous industrial projects which have been carried out or planned by ASEAN. As a result of the world-wide economic recession, most of the ASEAN countries have been forced to adjust or to rephase some of their industrial projects. This will moderate their imports of industrial products from industrialized countries, particularly Japan. Should ASEAN wish to maintain its healthy economic growth, it has to explore foreign markets for its manufactured products so as to obtain foreign currency in order to strengthen its consuming power. ASEAN cannot develop further once its foreign currency reserves are drained; its consuming power will then be extremely weakened. This might pose potential trade friction between ASEAN and Japan.

It is unwise to strengthen consuming power through the use of external loans. ASEAN's external debt (including short-term debt) is not serious compared to that of some Latin American countries (such as Brazil, Mexico, Argentina, and Venezuela). However, the external debt of Indonesia, the Philippines, Thailand, and Malaysia in recent years has been serious enough to attract attention. In 1982, the external debt of these four ASEAN countries amounted to US$25.4 billion, US$16.6 billion, US$11.0 billion, and US$10.4 billion respectively.[21] It is predicted that these countries will borrow more than the International Monetary Fund (IMF) and other international commercial banks in future as a result of the world-wide economic recession which has adversely affected exports from ASEAN, and the ambitious industrial projects planned earlier which require substantial financial assistance.[22] On the other hand, statistics also show that financial assistance received by ASEAN from Japan has increased substantially in recent years. In 1970–1979, the aggregate amount of governmental development assistance extended by the OECD countries (through its Development Assistance Committee) to ASEAN amounted to US$8.22 billion, of which Japan contributed US$3.3 billion (40.1 per cent). In terms of bilateral ODA, Japan's lending to ASEAN increased substantially from US$450 million (29.4 per cent of Japan's total ODA) in 1978 to US$573 million (29.7 per cent) in 1979, and jumped to US$704 million (35.7 per cent) in 1980.[23] In November 1982, Japan's external credits to the Philippines amounted to US$2,357 million, symbolizing an unstable economic situation in the country.

ASEAN in general is thus facing a dilemma in its industrialization process and in maintaining its high economic growth rate. Sufficient funding must be secured through expanding the export of both traditional and non-traditional products, that is, industrial raw materials and manufactured goods, to Japan, and ASEAN has been putting emphasis on exploring the Japanese market for its manufactured goods.

ASEAN Exports of Manufactured Goods

Let us now examine further the performance of ASEAN manufactured goods[24] in the Japanese market. During the period 1970–1982 (see Table 5.8), ASEAN's exports of manufactured goods into Japan were between 2 and 5 per cent of Japan's total imports of manufactured goods. In absolute terms, ASEAN's exports of manufactured goods to Japan increased from US$725 million in 1977 to US$1,494 million in 1981 but dropped to US$1,356 million in 1982.

In relative terms, these exports to Japan have been stagnating during the period 1976–1982. The US and the EC have long been the most important suppliers of manufactured goods to Japan (see Table 5.9). In 1982, the shares of the US and the EC accounted for 55 per cent of Japan's total imports of manufactured goods. Despite Japan's healthy economic growth — at least in comparison to the OECD countries and in terms of economic growth rate and unemployment rate — the ASEAN countries have not benefited from their export trade with Japan, particularly in 1980–1982 when it dropped from US$17,833 million to US$17,123 million. ASEAN's share of exports of manufactured goods to Japan declined from 4.6 to 4.1 per cent during

Table 5.8
Japan's Imports of Manufactured Goods from ASEAN, 1977–1982

(US$ millions)

	(A) Japan's total imports of manufactured goods	(B) Manufactured goods from ASEAN	$\frac{(B)}{(A)}$ %	Compared with previous year (%)
1977	15213	725	4.8	110.8
1978	21224	928	4.4	128.0
1979	28775	1267	4.4	136.5
1980	32110	1485	4.6	117.2
1981	34778	1494	4.3	100.6
1982	32827	1356	4.1	90.8

Note: *ASEAN's share in Japan's total imports of manufactured goods in the early 1970s were: 1970–23%, 1971–2.7%, 1972–2.8%, 1973–3.1%, 1974–3.5%, 1975–3.5% and 1976–4.5%.*
Source: *JETRO, White Paper on International Trade, various issues.*

Table 5.9
Japan's Imports of Manufactured Goods, by Region and Country, 1978–1982

(%)

Country \ Year	1978	1979	1980	1981	1982
Communist Bloc	5.1	5.6	5.7	6.9	6.5
Oceania	3.2	2.7	2.8	2.9	2.7
Africa	3.8	4.8	4.7	3.9	3.2
Central and South America	3.0	4.4	4.6	4.1	4.4
North America	30.8	31.7	35.9	34.9	37.2
US	(28.9)	(30.0)	(33.5)	(33.0)	(34.9)
Western Europe	32.1	28.7	27.5	28.1	26.1
EC	(24.7)	(22.0)	(22.1)	(21.1)	(19.8)
Western Asia	1.7	1.1	0.9	1.0	1.3
Southeast Asia	20.3	21.0	17.8	18.1	18.5
ASEAN	(4.4)	(4.4)	(4.6)	(4.3)	(4.1)
Total	100.0	100.0	100.0	100.0	100.0

Source: *Tsusho Sangyo-sho [Ministry of International Trade and Industry], Tsusho Hakusho [White Paper on International Trade] (Tokyo, July 1983).*

the same period (see Table 5.8). In recent years, Japan has been accused, both at the governmental and non-governmental levels, of not promoting imports of ASEAN's manufactured goods.[25] It is argued that Japan's efforts in importing more foreign products, in modifying and abolishing both tariff and non-tariff barriers[26] are aimed merely at improving its trade relationships with the industrialized countries, namely the US and the EC. ASEAN has hardly benefited from these efforts. To some extent it can also be argued from this analysis that ASEAN's exports to Japan have decreased during the period 1980–1982, especially in manufactured goods.

Uncertain Response and Commitment from Japan

In the last decade, the Japanese economy has been performing relatively well among the OECD countries. The value of the Japanese yen has also strengthened substantially against the US dollar. In 1974, the exchange rate between the two currencies was ¥292: US$1. In 1982, this ratio changed to ¥249: US$1.[27] At the end of 1983 the Japanese yen remained fairly strong at the rate of US$1 = ¥232.[28] Under these circumstances, Japanese products would have faced fierce competition in the international market. Surprisingly, however, Japan's export trade has been growing steadily. Despite numerous efforts by the Japanese government to import more manufactured goods to reduce its lopsided trade surplus with developed and developing countries, Japan's trade surplus increased drastically from US$2.1 billion in 1980 to US$18 billion in 1982 and then to a staggering US$31.4 billion in 1983.[29] This large trade surplus in 1983 resulted from a combination of robust exports (mainly automobiles and electronics) and torpid imports (which fell by 4.1 per cent mostly in response to a 13.4 per cent dive in crude oil imports).[30]

Japan has been asked, particularly during this world-wide economic recession period, to reduce its trade surplus with the US and the EC. Japan has so far not paid much attention to a similar request by ASEAN, mainly because of the asymmetry in ASEAN–Japan trade relations. In terms of total value, ASEAN as a whole is not as important as the US or the EC to Japan. However, Japan should heed ASEAN's request, as 40 per cent of its total world imports pass through the Straits of Malacca and the ASEAN countries are important suppliers of certain industrial and strategic resources and important buyers of Japanese industrial products.

From ASEAN's viewpoint, its export and import trade with Japan is crucial. ASEAN depends on both the Japanese market and supplies from Japan. Japan does not find much difficulty in exporting to this region because of the better quality and competitiveness of Japanese products. However, ASEAN regards the Japanese market as typically closed with limited space for ASEAN's manufactured goods, as well as agricultural and marine products. Japan should therefore look into its commercial practices and tariff and non-tariff barriers in order to improve its trade relationship with ASEAN. ASEAN has also to consistently improve quality and make more efforts in exploring the Japanese market. It is indisputable that the Japanese market is very competitive. Almost all kinds of manufactured goods can be produced in Japan with competitive quality and prices. The Japanese government tends to protect its domestic industries by excluding foreign products which are seen as having inferior quality and unreasonable prices. However, some products with better quality and competitiveness have also been blocked from entering the Japanese market, owing to Japan's tariff and non-tariff barriers. Nowadays, non-tariff barriers are as effective in implementing a protectionist policy as tariff barriers. The only difference is that tariff barriers are "visible" while non-tariff barriers are frequently "invisible". Japan's non-tariff barriers have been attacked widely, although not systematically or persuasively, by both the developed and the developing countries. Japan insists that it maintains free trade and opposes a protectionist policy, and has promised to look into the 99 cases of non-tariff barriers in 1982.[31] Despite these efforts, Japan's trade relationship with the developed and developing countries has not improved significantly. More importantly Japan's trade surplus has increased year by year. This has led the Japanese government to seriously consider ways of expanding its imports of manufactured goods. The Japanese government decided either to eliminate or reduce import tariffs on 67 items (36 agricultural products and 31 industrial goods), starting from fiscal year 1985.[32] It is still too early to judge the impact of these measures on foreign manufactured goods. However, as has been pointed out by ASEAN, Japan has been trying to resolve contentious economic issues with the developed countries but has not seriously considered promoting imports of manufactured goods from ASEAN. It is thus hardly likely that there will be any significant improvement in ASEAN–Japan trade relationship in the near future.

Conclusion

Trade frictions between ASEAN and Japan are imminent but not conspicuous in the international trade arena. ASEAN's persistent trade surplus with the US and the EC might be an important contributing factor alleviating tensions between ASEAN and Japan.[33] If ASEAN had a trade deficit with the US and the EC, foreign currency would not have been utilized for purchasing manufactured goods from Japan. Tensions and frictions between ASEAN and Japan would then be expected to escalate. Nowadays, owing to world-wide economic recession, protectionist policies have been implemented particularly among industrialized countries. Exports from developing countries to developed countries have also been affected. The General Agreement on Tariffs and Trade (GATT) has lost its capability to maintain more equitable international trade relations. From the viewpoint of North–South relations, Japan's trade frictions with Korea and Taiwan, in terms of trade deficits suffered by Korea and Taiwan, and in terms of competitive relations such as in the shipbuilding, textile, construction, and electronics sectors, are more obvious than those with ASEAN. This indicates that once ASEAN's industrial development reaches the present stage of Korea and Taiwan, its frictions with Japan will increase accordingly. In other words, industrialization in ASEAN will farther stimulate imports of manufactured goods, both capital and intermediate, from Japan on the one hand, and change ASEAN from playing a supplementary role to a competitive one *vis-à-vis* Japan on the other hand. ASEAN can hardly compete with Japan in the international market. Trade deficits with Japan in most of the ASEAN countries seem to be indicated year by year. In view of these facts, trade and economic frictions between ASEAN and Japan are likely to gain momentum in the not too distant future.

There are already ominous signs of increasing criticism to "Japanese protectionist policy" against manufactured goods imported from ASEAN. For instance, the Thai Prime Minister, Prem Tinsulanond, urged Japan to lessen Thailand's trade deficit when the Japanese Foreign Minister Shantaro Abe visited Thailand on 16 July 1984.[34] It was also reported that Thai economic planners had decided to launch a "trade war" against Japan in retaliation for alleged unfair trading practices. Thai Industry Minister, Ob Vasuratna, had complained that "Japan has always been able to export anything to Thailand while it discriminated against Thai exports". He further claimed that it was time for Thailand to "retaliate".[35] Furthermore, at the First Malaysia–Japan Colloquium held in Petaling Jaya, Malaysia, on 27–28 August 1984, the Malaysian Prime Minister, Datuk Seri Dr Mahathir Mohamad, in a speech delivered on his behalf by the Minister of Trade and Industry, Tengku Razaleigh Hamzah, strongly condemned Japan for not buying Malaysian manufactured goods. He criticized the closed nature of the Japanese market, and stressed that "Japan bought practically nothing of our manufactured goods. The biggest single category — thermionic and cathode valves, tubes, photocells and diodes — amounted to only $170 million. ... We in fact bought more of those things from Japan than we sold to Japan". Japan was forcefully asked to rectify its unequal trade relationship with Malaysia so as to avoid the "tension" and, possibly, "turmoil" that might occur. Mahathir's accusation of Japan created tremendous repercussions both in Malaysia and Japan. It particularly gained, as anticipated, support and appraisal from academicians and the business community in Malaysia.[36]

Trade and economic frictions between ASEAN and Japan can develop into serious political and diplomatic issues if timely countermeasures are not taken. Rapid economic development requires ASEAN to export its manufactured goods to wider foreign markets. Exports of primary industrial resources, which are exposed to international fluctuations, are no longer a stable way of acquiring foreign exchange. Furthermore, foreign loans and debts can hardly provide ASEAN with healthy economic growth and rapid industrialization. Although exports of manufactured goods do not at present constitute a significant weight in ASEAN's export trade, this is in fact an important field for ASEAN to develop. As the Japanese have certain historical and cultural biases against buying manufactured goods from this region, ASEAN has to manufacture more well-designed, competitive, and better quality products through technical innovation and improvement, in order to compete in the Japanese market. It is unrealistic to claim that all products are prevented from entering the Japanese market because of its closed nature and more specifically, because of its non-tariff barriers. We have to bear in mind that the Japanese are becoming more and more, if not the most, quality conscious and design conscious community in the world. Its US$31.4 billion trade surplus in fiscal 1983 enabled the Japanese to be selective and to demand excellent products even at higher prices.

Notes

1 *Look Japan*, no. 339, June 1984.
2 These measures include: (1) market-opening and import promotion; (2) market-opening for high-technology products; (3) promotion of the liberalization of the domestic financial and capital markets and the internationalization of the yen; and (4) promotion of foreign direct investment in Japan (*Look Japan*, no. 339, June 1984).
3 Ibid.
4 Some of the latest publications are: (1) Arthur D. Little Inc. (1979); (2) Nihon Kanzei Kyokai [Japan Customs Association] (1982); (3) Kawata Tadashi (1982); (4) Okita Saburo and Sato Ryuzo, eds. (1983); and (5) Okita Saburo (1983).
5 It was reported that "Japan met this request by only decreasing the tariff on bananas cropped in October to March, from 45 per cent to 40 per cent, and that on crops in the April to September period from 30 to 25 per cent, effective from 1 April 1981" (*Daily Yomiuri*, 17 May 1982).
6 *Japan Times*, 21 May 1982.
7 *Straits Times*, 26 January 1983.
8 Ibid.

9   *Lianhe Zaobao*, 21 May 1983.

10 *Lianhe Zaobao*, 14 October 1983; *Straits Times*, 14 October 1983.

11 Hugh Kyung-Mo, *Japan's Trade in Asia* (New York, 1966), p. 8.

12 Ministry of Foreign Affairs *ASEAN* (Tokyo, March 1982).

13 Brunei is also an important petroleum supplier to Japan but it is excluded in this study as it joined ASEAN only in January 1984.

14 N. Akrasanee, ed., *ASEAN–Japan Relations: Trade and Development* (Singapore: Institute of Southeast Asian Studies, 1983), pp. 11–12.

15 There are some discrepancies between statistics published by the IMF and JETRO. (These might partly arise from whether the customs clearance is based on f.o.b. or c.i.f. values). Data used in this section are quoted from the IMF. However, for convenience, data provided in Tables 5.5 and 6.6 have been utilized to analyse the commodity composition of Japan's trade with ASEAN.

16 The Japanese government is planning to obtain more crude oil from non-Gulf states in future because of its precarious position in the face of the conflict in the Gulf. The advisory board of Japan's Petroleum Council has urged the government to amend existing regulations that restrict in principle the imports of oil products other than crude. The importation of most types of refined oil products has been banned or limited to strict quotas to protect Japan from price fluctuations on the international markets. The advisory board has now asked the government to expand its quotas on the imports of C-type heavy oil by 500,000 kilolitres per annum from 1985. The Japan National Oil Corporation, a government organization, is also expected to extend more subsidies for oil exploration work in Indonesia (*Straits Times*, 6 June 1984). Therefore, in time to come, Indonesia's exports of oil to Japan are likely to be promoted substantially.

17 However, due to the depressed state of the petrochemical industry in Japan and lower prices of oil, shipments of petroleum products from Singapore to Japan dropped by 20 per cent to S$3 billion in 1983. This was the first such decline since 1976 (Ministry of Trade and Industry, 1984).

18 The international energy journal, *Petroleum Economist*, LI, no. 2 (London: Feb. 1984). Prices represent weighted averages of internationally traded crude oil based on official sales prices or estimated term contract prices; spot transactions are not included. The averages are based on 27 grades of crude oil.

19 For a detailed discussion on Malaysia's "Look East" policy, which strengthened economic co-operation (through trade, investment, and aid) between Malaysia and Japan, see Chapter 1.

20 For a more detailed study on Singapore–Japan trade, see Lim Hua Sing and Lee Chin Choo, eds. in Akrasanee, op. cit. (1983).

21 Ichimura, op. cit.

22 Owing to the fact that Indonesia has been badly affected by the world economic recession and low oil prices, the World Bank and 12 nations (including the US and the Netherlands) have decided to grant Indonesia US$2.46 billion in financial aid (*Straits Times*, 7 June 1984). On the other hand, the Japanese government also granted a US$302 million loan to Thailand on 16 July 1984 carrying an interest rate of 3.5 per cent, to be repaid within 30 years (*Straits Times*, 17 and 18 July 1984).

23 Ministry of Foreign Affairs, March 1982, pp. 36–39.

24 Japan's imports of ASEAN's manufactured products are as follows:
    (i)   Indonesia: Chemical goods, machinery and other manufactured goods (such as unwrought tin).

(ii)   Malaysia: Chemical goods, machinery (electrical machinery: thermionic, etc., valves, tubes, photocells, transistors, etc) and other manufactured goods (wood chips, textile products, and unwrought tin).

(iii) Philippines: Chemical goods, machinery (electrical machinery: thermionic, etc., valves, tubes, photocells, transistors, etc), transportation equipment, precision instruments (watches and clocks) and other manufactured goods.

(iv)   Singapore: Chemical goods (medical and pharmaceutical products), machinery (general machinery: office machines, and pumps and centrifuges; electrical machinery; transportation equipment and precision instruments: watches and clocks) and other manufactured goods (textile products and miscellaneous goods: furniture, etc.)

(v)   Thailand: Chemical goods (medical and pharmaceutical products and other chemical products), machinery and other manufactured goods (textile products, precious and semi-precious stones, unwrought tin, etc.)

25   Apart from manufactured goods, governments and exporters in ASEAN expect Japan to import more agricultural and marine products from this region.

26   For detailed discussion on Japanese NTBs, please refer to Chapter 3.

27   Keizai Koho Centre [Japan Institute for Social and Economic Affairs], *Japan 1983, An International Comparison* (Tokyo, 1983), p. 43.

28   *Look Japan* 29, no. 336, March 1984.

29   The OECD further predicted that Japan's trade surplus would rise by more than 8 per cent to US$41 billion in 1984 and then to US$45 billion in 1985 (*Straits Times*, 30 June 1984). However, some Japanese voices point out that the Japanese current account balance showed a deficit of US$20.8 billion in 1983 although it was only US$6.9 billion in the previous year. Japan has had persistent huge deficits in its invisible trade. In 1983, Japanese deficits in technology (as measured by patent royalties), transportation and travel amounted to US$1.3 billion, US$3.6 billion, and US$3.3 billion respectively (*Look Japan* 30, no. 340, July 1984).

30   *Look Japan* 30, no. 340, July 1984.

31   These 99 cases of "non-tariff trade barriers" were released by the Special Committee for International Economic Measures of the Liberal-Democratic Party in Japan in January 1982. The details of these "non-tariff trade barriers" may be found in *Mainichi Daily News*, 31 January 1982.

32   The full text and discussion on these 67 items receiving elimination or reduction of import tariffs may be found in *Look Japan* 30, no. 339, June 1984.

33   In 1979, ASEAN's trade surpluses with the US and the EC were US$1,370 million and US$690 million respectively (Akrasanee and Rieger [1982], pp. 25–26). In 1980, these figures changed to US$1,595 million and US$366 million respectively (Akrasanee [1983], pp. 6–7).

34   *Straits Times*, 17 July 1984.

35   *Straits Times*, 18 July 1984; *Lianhe Zaobao*, 19 July 1984.

36   *New Straits Times* (Malaysia), 28–29 August 1984.

CHAPTER 6

Japan's Role in ASEAN's Economic Development — Trade and Investment

Introduction

ASEAN has been Japan's important supplier of raw materials, production base for manufacturing industries and market for manufactures. ASEAN supplies both industrial and agricultural raw materials, at reasonable prices, which have been instrumental in Japan's rapid economic development since the 1960s. Japan also uses ASEAN as an important production base for her manufacturing industries which have succeeded in penetrating international markets. ASEAN has been Japan's important market for light industrial products and now, as a result of ASEAN's rapid industrialization process, Japan's production of intermediate and capital goods is being increasingly consumed by the ASEAN countries.

From ASEAN's viewpoint, Japan has been ASEAN's important supplier of capital technology, managerial know-how and development aid. Japan has invested quite substantially in the manufacturing and service sectors in ASEAN. Particularly after the phenomenal yen appreciation in autumn 1985, Japan's FDI in ASEAN has gained in momentum and has exceeded the US in some ASEAN countries such as Singapore, Malaysia and Thailand. Technology transfer from Japan to ASEAN has been a great concern of the latter and, owing to rapid industrial restructuring in Japan, a comparatively lower standard of technology has been transferred to the recipient countries in parallel with the increase in Japanese FDI in ASEAN. Similarly, Japanese managerial know-how has also been introduced into the recipient countries due to Japanese active involvement in commercial and manufacturing activities in ASEAN. Besides, Japanese ODA has essentially been extended to ASEAN for setting up heavy industries and improving the infrastructure. As a result, Japanese ODA has further stimulated Japanese FDI in ASEAN.

The above-mentioned aspects portray a rather harmonious and complementary economic relationship between Japan and ASEAN. However, the Japan–ASEAN economic relationship has also hidden some serious problems, such as the vertical and asymmetrical trade relationship between Japan and ASEAN; the underdevelopment of peripheral or supporting industries in ASEAN due partly to Japan's propensity to rely on Japanese subcontractors; Japan has increasingly faced keen competition from the NIEs in its investment in ASEAN, etc.

This chapter is aimed at analysing the recent Japan–ASEAN economic relationship with special reference to trade and investment, taking the aforementioned serious problems into consideration.

Japan–ASEAN Economic Relations: Trade

An Overview of Japan–ASEAN Trade Relations

Japan has been ASEAN's most important trading partner. Among the ASEAN countries, the export trade of Indonesia and Brunei has been heavily reliant on Japanese markets. This is basically because of their rich natural resources, particularly petroleum. Table 6.1 reveals that in 1987, 43.8 per cent and 60.4 per cent of exports from Indonesia and Brunei respectively were directed to Japan. Japan imported less from Malaysia and the Philippines. However, in 1987, exports from these two countries to Japan amounted to 19.5 per cent and 17.2 per cent respectively. The US, ASEAN and the EC were Malaysia's and Indonesian's important export trading partners as well. As far as the Philippines is concerned, America has been the largest market. In 1987, 36.2 per cent of the Philippines' products were directed to the US.

Compared to the aforementioned ASEAN countries, Thailand and Singapore export much less to Japan. In 1987, exports from Thailand and Singapore to Japan constituted merely 14.7 per cent and 9.1 per cent respectively. Markets in the US and the intra-ASEAN region appeared to be particularly important to Singapore. Thailand's export trade is rather diversified, similar to Malaysia's.

Table 6.1

ASEAN's Major Trading Countries and Region (1987)

(Unit: US$100 million, %)

		Japan	Share	America	Share	ASEAN	Share	E.C.	Share	Others	Share	Total	Share
Indonesia	Total Trade	107	39.8	43	16.1	20	7.5	38	14.2	60	22.5	268	100.0
	Exports	72	43.8	33	20.2	13	7.8	16	9.4	31	18.8	165	100.0
	Imports	34	33.4	10	9.4	7	6.9	22	21.8	29	28.4	102	100.0
Malaysia	Total Trade	63	20.4	53	17.5	70	22.8	43	13.9	78	25.4	306	100.0
	Exports	35	19.5	30	16.6	43	24.2	26	14.3	46	25.4	179	100.0
	Imports	28	21.7	24	18.7	26	20.8	17	13.4	32	25.5	127	100.0
Philippines	Total Trade	21	16.9	36	28.5	12	9.2	19	15.2	38	30.2	126	100.0
	Exports	10	17.2	21	36.2	5	8.9	11	19.1	11	18.7	57	100.0
	Imports	11	16.6	15	22.2	7	9.5	8	12.0	28	39.7	69	100.0
Singapore	Total Trade	93	15.2	118	19.3	129	21.1	74	12.1	198	32.4	611	100.0
	Exports	26	9.1	70	24.5	71	24.7	35	12.2	84	29.5	286	100.0
	Imports	67	20.5	48	14.7	58	17.9	39	12.0	113	34.8	325	100.0
Thailand	Total Trade	50	20.7	37	15.4	36	14.7	45	18.5	74	30.6	243	100.0
	Exports	17	14.7	21	18.8	15	13.6	25	22.0	35	30.9	113	100.0
	Imports	34	26.0	16	12.5	20	15.6	20	15.5	40	30.5	130	100.0
Brunei	Total Trade	11	36.5	1	3.8	9	28.6	6	19.4	4	11.7	31	100.0
	Exports	11	60.4	0.2	0.8	4	21.7	0.5	3.0	3	14.1	18	100.0
	Imports	0.4	3.5	1	7.9	5	38.2	5	42.3	1	8.2	13	100.0
ASEAN	Total Trade	345	21.7	289	18.2	275	17.3	225	14.2	452	28.5	1,585	100.0
	Exports	171	20.9	175	21.4	151	18.5	112	13.4	209	25.6	819	100.0
	Imports	174	22.7	114	14.8	124	16.1	112	14.7	143	31.7	767	100.0

Source: *Ajia Shakai Mondai Kenkyu-sho [Institute of Asian Social Issues], Ajia to Nihon [Asia and Japan], no. 185 (1 June 1989), p. 44.*

With the exception of Brunei, a substantial proportion of ASEAN's imports comes from Japan. In 1987, Brunei had the lowest percentage of imports from Japan with only 3.5 per cent. At the other extreme, 33.4 per cent of Indonesia's imports came from Japan. The EC and ASEAN constituted 42.3 per cent and 38.2 per cent of Brunei's import trade respectively. As a whole, Japan constituted just more than one-fifth of ASEAN's export and import trade in 1987.

In 1987, ASEAN had a US$0.3 billion trade deficit with Japan, the Philippines, Singapore and Thailand had trade deficits, whereas Malaysia, Indonesia and Brunei had trade surpluses with Japan. Obviously, ASEAN's trade balance with Japan was in favour of resource rich countries.

The Philippines and Thailand cannot be considered as resource poor countries. However, the rather stagnant economic situation/ poor economic performance in the Philippines has restricted her export drive. Thailand's trade deficit with Japan was due to her recent rapid economic development which has stimulated the increase in imports of intermediate and capital goods from Japan.

Singapore's case is an exception as being an entrepôt or intermediary country, she re-exports a substantial quantity of intermediate and capital goods from Japan to neighbouring countries. Undoubtedly, in recent years, Singapore is also increasingly importing intermediate and capital goods from Japan for her own domestic consumption as a result of her active involvement in high-tech, value-added and knowledge-intensive activities.

Problems Hindering Trade between Japan and ASEAN
Presently, the following problems are seen to have hindered trade between Japan and ASEAN.

Vertical Trade Relationship
The vertical trade relationship between Japan and ASEAN has not been satisfactorily rectified. The exception is Singapore, the only Asian NIE among the ASEAN countries, whose exports of manufacturing products, such as electronic and electrical products

and machinery, have shown steady increases. However, the rest of the ASEAN countries have shown slower improvement in penetrating the Japanese market with their manufactured products.

As a matter of fact, ASEAN started implementing import-substitution policies in the latter half of the 1960s and, in the 1970s, export-orientation activities were heavily promoted. In the 1980s, export-orientated promotion had further gained in momentum among the ASEAN countries. This was basically due to two reasons:

(i) Industrial development in ASEAN had reached a higher stage, i.e. gradually moving towards capital-intensive from labour-intensive industrial activities; and

(ii) The success of the NIEs is perceived by ASEAN as a model based on the implementation of export-orientation policies.

Likewise, the ASEAN countries, especially Malaysia and Thailand, are considered to be able to become members of the NIEs by the end of the twentieth century. If this is the case, it will imply that ASEAN's exports of manufactured products, especially chemicals and chemical products, and machinery and transport equipment (office machinery, industrial and non-electrical machinery, telecommunication apparatus, electrical machinery and generators, and ships and other transport equipment), will increase proportionally year by year.

Is Japan going to increase imports of industrial products from ASEAN? Can ASEAN penetrate Japanese markets successfully? These are some important issues the ASEAN countries have to face and to tackle with tremendous efforts. Table 6.2 shows exports of ASEAN's manufactured products during the period 1965–1983. The following features can be identified:

(i) Exports of ASEAN's manufactured products to the world have increased steadily year by year.

(ii) Japan has imported far less manufactured products from the ASEAN member countries, throughout the years, compared to the US, the EC and the world as a whole.

Table 6.3 further reveals exports of ASEAN's total products, manufactured goods, textiles (as a symbol of light manufacturing

Table 6.2

Rate of Growth of Manufactured Products as a Percentage of ASEAN's Export Trade

(%)

		1965	1970	1975	1980	1983
Singapore	Japan	1.1	3.5	20.4	46.6	21:8
	US	19.7	35.3	56.1	80.7	84.8
	EC	5.2	14.2	51.3	55.6	66.0
	World	31.1	27.8	41.8	48.3	50.8
Malaysia	Japan	26.1	30.7	21.4	15.0	15.7
	US	68.4	61.4	52.2	44.4	76.6
	EC	18.8	25.1	34.9	43.5	48.3
	World	28.1	26.1	30.4	27.8	30.2
Thailand	Japan	0.9	3.9	14.3	21.8	21.9
	US	36.9	59.8	47.2	59.2	61.7
	EC	2.2	1.9	19.8	37.9	34.7
	World	5.8	16.4	20.3	35.3	35.0
Philippines	Japan	0.7	1.3	6.9	9.2	15.6
	US	10.5	11.4	20.1	28.9	32.4
	EC	0.8	3.5	15.9	32.1	27.2
	World	5.6	7.6	16.3	23.6	26.7
Indonesia	Japan	–	0.6	1.1	1.1	2.4
	US	–	0.6	1.5	0.8	6.6
	EC	–	6.6	14.2	19.4	33.9
	World	–	1.9	2.4	4.2	8.6

Source: Ajia no Kogyoka. Kodoka e no Tenbo *[Asia's Industrialization Aiming for Higher Development]*, Ajia Keizai Kenkyu-sho *[Institute of Developing Economies]*, *(Tokyo, 1988), p. 34.*

industries), and iron and steel (as a symbol of heavy manufacturing industries) to Japan and other countries and regions during the period 1970–1983. The following features can be identified:

(i)   Japan has been an important importer of ASEAN's products in general. Japan's share has exceeded that of the US, the EC, the NIEs and the intra-ASEAN region;

Table 6.3

ASEAN's Exports by Commodity and by Country of Origin

Country of Export	Total Products			Manufactured Products			Textiles			Iron & Steel		
	1970	1980	1983	1970	1980	1983	1970	1980	1983	1970	1980	1983
Japan	22.7	26.8	24.0	10.4	9.4	7.1	2.5	3.8	3.8	0.6	6.4	9.3
NIEs	4.8	7.2	7.5	3.9	6.9	6.7	4.5	6.4	5.1	1.3	22.1	11.4
ASEAN	12.3	15.7	20.5	8.2	20.0	21.8	9.4	10.9	10.7	15.3	47.3	44.6
Australia & New Zealand	2.5	3.0	2.4	1.6	2.9	2.1	2.1	3.7	2.8	1.1	3.8	4.3
US & Canada	18.7	17.5	19.4	29.4	23.0	31.2	22.0	18.7	33.1	15.2	1.0	2.9
Asia Pacific	60.9	71.1	73.8	53.6	62.2	68.9	40.7	43.5	55.5	33.5	80.6	72.6

Source: *Same as Table 6.2*

(ii) However, as far as ASEAN's manufactured products are concerned, Japan's share was smaller than the US, the EC and the intra-ASEAN region. Exports of ASEAN's manufactured products to Japan have even decreased from 10.4 per cent in 1970 to 9.4 per cent in 1980 and to 7.1 per cent in 1983. Likewise, we reached a conclusion that Japanese markets have been highly restrictive towards ASEAN's manufactured products. ASEAN's exports of manufactured products had been heavily reliant on the Western markets, in particular the US;

(iii) Both ASEAN's textiles, and iron and steel did not find Japan as an important outlet. Japanese markets absorbed the former at only 3.8 per cent, and the latter at only 9.3 per cent in 1983. Exports of ASEAN's textiles to the US, Canada, and the EC combined increased from 30.5 per cent in 1970 to 54.7 per cent in 1983. As far as iron and steel is concerned, the intra-ASEAN region and the NIEs constituted 44.6 per cent and 11.4 per cent respectively in 1983. The Asia–Pacific region's share amounted to 80.6 per cent in 1980 and

72.6 per cent in 1983. A distinct feature is that a very negligible share of ASEAN's iron and steel was consumed by the industrialized countries.

Asymmetrical Trade Relationship

The trade relationship between Japan and ASEAN is asymmetrical. ASEAN's export/GDP ratios have been higher than Japan. Table 6.4 shows that in 1970, Japan's export/GDP ratio was 9.5 per cent. The ratios for Singapore, Malaysia, the Philippines, Thailand and Indonesia were 81.9 per cent, 42.5 per cent, 14.5 per cent, 10.9 per cent and 12.0 per cent respectively. In 1986, Japan's export/GDP ratio increased to 10.8 per cent. The above-mentioned ASEAN countries increased their ratios yet further to 128.4 per cent, 49.9 per cent, 15.4 per cent, 21.1 per cent and 19.7 per cent. From these figures, it is clear that ASEAN's economic performance has been more reliant on its export drive than Japan.

Table 6.5 reveals that the US markets were particularly important to Japan, the NIEs and ASEAN. ASEAN's share in Japan's total trade was lower than that of the NIEs. If we look at it closely, we notice that ASEAN's share in Japan's total trade decreased from 7.0 per cent in 1980 to 4.9 per cent in 1988. However, from ASEAN's viewpoint, Japan's share of ASEAN's total trade was more significant than the US and the NIEs. In 1988, Japan's share in ASEAN's total trade amounted to 23.6 per cent. It is, therefore, clear that ASEAN's trade has depended on Japan rather than vice versa. In general, the asymmetrical trade relationship between Japan and ASEAN affects ASEAN more than Japan should economic downturn arise. Japan's economic performance has always had a direct impact on ASEAN. The recent drastic yen appreciation, for example, prompted Japan's FDI and Japan's "out-sourcing" activities. Japan's export trade was restricted due to the high yen. Subsequently, Japan's share in ASEAN's total trade decreased from 28.4 per cent in 1980 to 23.6 per cent in 1988. Japan has, however, managed to maintain a high percentage of ASEAN's total trade. This was due to ASEAN's increasing utilization

Table 6.4
Export/GDP Ratios of ASEAN and Japan

(%)

	1970	1975	1980	1985	1986	1987
Indonesia	12.0	23.3	30.2	21.8	19.7	–
Malaysia	42.5	41.2	52.9	49.4	49.9	–
Philippines	14.5	14.5	16.3	14.0	15.4	16.3
Singapore	81.9	95.3	165.3	128.9	128.4	144.2
Thailand	10.9	15.1	19.4	18.6	21.1	24.9
Japan	9.5	11.2	12.3	13.4	10.8	–

Source: *IMF, International Financial Statistics (1988), pp. 50–53.*

Table 6.5
Trade Interdependence among Countries in the Asia–Pacific Region

(Share of Total Trade of the Individual Countries, %)

		Japan	United States	NIEs	ASEAN 4
Japan	1980		24.2	14.8	7.0
	1987		36.5	17.2	4.1
	1988		33.8	18.8	4.9
US	1980	9.4		6.7	2.8
	1987	11.2		9.3	2.3
	1988	11.8		10.9	2.2
NIEs	1980	10.3	24.6	9.7	10.6
	1987	11.2	29.8	10.0	8.0
	1988	12.2	27.8	10.8	8.2
ASEAN 4*	1980	28.4	19.0	16.3	4.4
	1987	23.7	22.3	18.9	4.2
	1988	23.6	22.2	19.6	3.6

Notes: Excluding Singapore and Brunei.
Source: *Computed from JETRO, JETRO White Paper on Trade (1989), p. 31.*

of Japanese intermediate and capital goods caused by ASEAN's steady industrial development.

Japan–ASEAN Economic Relations: Investment

Features and Recent Development of Japanese Direct Foreign Investment

Features

Japan lost all of her FDI by the end of 1945 (i.e. World War II). Japan reopened her FDI in 1951 but, until the early 1960s, her FDI continued to be negligible. It was not until 1968 that Japan started to enjoy a positive trade surplus[1] every year (except 1973 and 1975) and consequently her FDI also increased significantly. The expansion of FDI was largely accelerated after the first liberalization step taken by the Japanese government in 1969. Subsequent liberalization measures taken in 1970, 1971, 1972, and also in the year 1978 have further accelerated the expansion of the FDI. In order to facilitate the process, Japan's Exchange Law was also amended twice in the years 1980 and 1984. Japan's FDI was seen to have been stimulated by these legislative measures.

The above-mentioned legislative measures were the contributory factors to Japan's expanding FDI and, in general, Japanese FDI has been prompted by the following objectives: (1) to obtain better access to natural resources, especially in the developing countries; (2) to protect the markets for the Japanese products; (3) to utilize low cost labour and overseas human resources; (4) to increase further exports to the host and third countries; (5) to avoid unfavourable conditions for expansion and obtain various institutional incentives provided by the host countries. More recently Japanese FDI was particularly stimulated by the phenomenal yen appreciations since Autumn 1985. (This will be discussed in more detail in the following sections.)

Japanese FDI has some peculiar features which can be summarized as follows:

Firstly, the crucial role played by the general trading companies (*sogoshoshas*). In Japan, there are some 6,000 "trading firms" (defined as wholesalers and retailers engaging in international trade), but only the largest of them, usually the top ten,[2] are called *sogoshoshas*. *Sogoshoshas* involve themselves in commercial and industrial activities. This is reflected in the *sogoshoshas'* numerous industrial investments, both domestic and overseas. *Sogoshoshas* possess numerous manufacturing subsidiaries or affiliated companies. They also set up joint ventures in the manufacturing sector all over the world. They are in an advantageous position, due to their international network, to handle almost anything under the sun — "from instant snack noodles to missiles". In 1986, nine sogoshoshas handled 45.8 per cent (16,163 billion yen) of Japan's total exports and 68.3 per cent (14,697 billion yen) of imports respectively.[3]

Secondly, the important role played by the SMBs. Japanese SMBs have also been actively involved in FDI. Particularly after 1985, the drastic yen appreciation, however, resulted in keen competition for trade with the NIEs. Besides, trade frictions between Japan and the West have also prompted the Japanese big companies to increase FDI abroad. As a result, many Japanese SMBs have to follow their parent companies in shifting their operations abroad. In 1987, FDI undertaken by Japanese SMBs amounted to 1,063 cases, of which 44.6 per cent were in Asia. Furthermore, as far as manufacturing industries are concerned, Japanese SMBs' FDI in Asia increased substantially from 57.9 per cent (of their total FDI) in 1978–1984 to 64.4 per cent in 1985–1986, and to 72.7 per cent in 1987.[4] Asia has therefore, been Japanese SMBs' largest overseas outlet.

Thirdly, imports increased in accordance with the immense increase in Japanese FDI. Most of the American overseas ventures have been undertaken by large oligopolists in high-technology industries which have been keen to re-export manufactured goods to American markets. However, Japanese-affiliated companies abroad have been keen to explore markets in third countries. This is basically due to two reasons:

One, it is argued that Japanese tariff and non-tariff barriers have been too restrictive against foreign manufactured goods, including those produced by Japanese-affiliated companies abroad[5] (except for the oil refineries).

Two, Japanese-affiliated companies abroad used to import parts and components from Japan and assemble for exports to third countries other than Japan. This has been considered as part of Japan's international industrial strategy to reduce trade surplus with the West. However, after 1985, the stronger yen has strengthened Japan's purchasing powers, especially for import-oriented industries, such as petroleum products, electric power, gas and foodstuffs. Besides, more and more Japanese companies are operating overseas, producing parts and components, together with a large quantity of manufactured products, all designed for re-export to Japan. Imports from the US and the EC increased from US$25.79 billion and US$9.3 billion in 1985 to US$31.49 billion and US$17.67 billion in 1987 respectively. Imports from the NIEs also increased substantially from US$9.84 billion in 1985 to US$18.82 billion in 1987.[6] This trend is likely to be sustained as long as Japan maintains her high level of FDI.

Recent Development

In the 1980s, Japanese FDI increased substantially, particularly since 1982 without interruption. Table 6.6 shows that Japanese FDI increased substantially from 2,613 cases (US$12,217 million) in 1985 to 6,589 cases (US$67,540 million) in 1989. Japan's cumulative FDI (1951–1992) amounted to 71,541 cases (US$386,530 million) by the end of 1992. However, it must also be pointed out that Japanese FDI started declining in 1990 due largely to the sluggish domestic economic performance (the collapse of the so-called "bubble economy").

Real estate acquisitions and the establishment of branch offices have constituted a negligible proportion of Japanese FDI. Japanese FDI has been predominantly concentrated in securities acquisition and bond acquisition. These two areas of acquisition contributed 98.8 per cent (US$8821 million) of Japan's total FDI in 1981. They even climbed to 99 per cent (US$33,777 million) in 1992, constituting 59.9 per cent (US$230,167 million) and 38.7 per cent (US$149,480 million) of Japan's total cumulative investment by the end of 1992. However, it is worth noticing that Japanese FDI has been moving toward securities acquisition rather than bond acquisition. Securities acquisition increased from 36.4 per cent (US$3,247 million) in 1981 to 63.5 per cent (US$21,667 million) in 1992 whereas bond acquisition dropped from 62.4 per cent (US$5,574 million) to 35.5 per cent (US$12,110 million) during the same period (see Table 6.7).

Some peculiar trends can be examined in Japanese FDI particularly after 1985. The following three points are particularly worth noticing.

Firstly, Japanese FDI has been concentrated in the industrialized countries especially in the US. In absolute terms, Japanese FDI in the US increased markedly from US$5,495 million (45 per cent of Japan's total FDI) in 1985 to US$33,902 million (50.2 per cent) in 1989. Japanese FDI in Europe increased even faster from US$1,930 million (15.8 per cent) to US$14,808 million (21.9 per cent) during the same period. Japanese FDI in the US and Europe declined sharply during the years 1990–1992. However, the US and Europe combined constituted 63.4 per cent of Japan's total FDI in 1992 (see Table 6.8).

Table 6.6

Evolution of Japanese Foreign Direct Investment

Year	Cases	Rate of increase or decrease ([]) over the previous year	Amount (US$ million)	Rate of increase or decrease ([]) over the previous year
1985	2,613	4.6	12,217	20.3
1986	3,196	22.3	22,320	82.7
1987	4,584	43.4	33,364	49.5
1988	6,076	32.5	47,022	40.9
1989	6,589	8.4	67,540	43.6
1990	5,863	[] 11.0	56,911	[] 15.7
1991	4,564	[] 22.2	41,584	[] 26.9
1992	3,741	[] 18.0	34,138	[] 17.9
Total (cumulative investment) (1951–1992)	71,541		386,530	

Source: *Okura-sho [Ministry of Finance], Okura-sho Kokusai Kinyu-Kyoku Nenpo [International Finance Bureau of the Ministry of Finance — Annual Report] (Tokyo, 1993), p. 161.*

Table 6.7

Types of Japanese Foreign Direct Investment

Year	Securities Acquisition		Bond Acquisition		Real estate Acquisition		Establishment of Branch Office		Total	
	Cases	Amount (US$ million)	Cases	Amount (US$ million)	Cases	Amount (US$ million)	Cases	Amount (US$ million)	Cases	Amount (US$ million)
1985	1,023	5,963 (48.8)	1,552	5,924 (48.5)	–	–	38	329 (2.7)	2,613	12,217 (100)
1986	1,419	12,546 (56.2)	1,728	9,208 (41.3)	–	–	49	566 (2.5)	3,196	22,320 (100)
1987	2,126	19,941 (39.8)	2,387	12,971 (38.9)	–	–	71	452 (1.4)	4,585	33,364 (100)
1988	2,724	28,638 (60.9)	3,263	17,801 (37.9)	–	–	89	584 (1.2)	6,076	47,022 (100)
1989	2,602	43,169 (63.9)	3,910	23,632 (35.0)	–	–	77	739 (1.1)	6,589	67,540 (100)
1990	2,249	38,507 (67.7)	3,565	17,598 (30.9)	–	–	49	806 (1.4)	5,863	56,911 (100)
1991	1,556	27,129 (65.2)	2,983	13,991 (33.7)	–	–	25	464 (1.1)	4,564	41,584 (100)
1992	1,397	21,667 (63.5)	2,318	12,110 (35.5)	–	–	26	360 (1.1)	3,741	34,138 (100)
Total (cumulative investment)	31,105	230,167 (59.5)	36,403	149,480 (38.7)	–	–	1,495	6,289 (1.6)	71,541	386,530 (100)

Notes: *Figures in parentheses represent percentages*

Source: *Okura-sho [Ministry of Finance], op. cit., p. 162*

Table 6.8

Evolution of Japanese Foreign Direct Investment, by Region

(Unit: US$ million, %)

Year	USA	Latin America	Asia	Middle East	Europe	Africa	Oceania	Total
1985	5,495	2,616	1,435	45	1,930	172	525	12,217
	(45.0)	(21.4)	(11.7)	(0.4)	(15.8)	(1.4)	(4.3)	(100)
1986	10,441	4,737	2,327	44	3,469	309	992	22,320
	(46.8)	(21.2)	(10.4)	(0.2)	(15.5)	(1.4)	(4.4)	(100)
1987	15,357	4,816	4,868	62	6,576	272	1,413	33,364
	(46.0)	(14.4)	(14.6)	(0.2)	(19.7)	(0.8)	(4.2)	(100)
1988	22,328	6,428	5,569	259	9,116	653	2,669	47,022
	(47.5)	(13.7)	(11.8)	(0.6)	(19.4)	(1.4)	(5.7)	(100)
1989	33,902	5,238	8,238	66	14,808	671	4,618	67,540
	(50.2)	(7.8)	(12.2)	(0.1)	(21.9)	(1.0)	(6.8)	(100)
1990	27,192	3,628	7,054	27	14,294	551	4,166	56,911
	(47.8)	(6.4)	(12.4)	(0.0)	(25.1)	2.0)	(7.3)	(100)
1991	18,823	3,327	5,936	90	9,371	748	3,278	41,584
	(45.3)	(8.0)	(14.3)	(0.2)	(22.5)	(1.8)	(7.9)	(100)
1992	14,572	2,726	6,425	709	7,061	238	2,406	34,138
	(42.7)	(8.0)	(18.8)	(2.1)	(20.7)	(0.7)	(7.0)	(100)
Total (cumulative investment)	169,580	46,547	59,880	4231	75,697	6,813	23,782	386,530
	(43.9)	(12.0)	(15.5)	(1.1)	(19.6)	(1.8)	(6.2)	(100)

Source: *Okura-sho [Ministry of Finance], op. cit., p. 163.*

As a countermeasure of the yen appreciation and trade friction, manufacturing industries such as electronics and electrical machinery, transport equipment and chemicals have rushed to the US and Europe together with finance and insurance, services and real estate industries in the non-manufacturing sector. Merger and acquisition (M&A) activities have also become more and more important in Japanese FDI in the West especially in the US. All in all, Japanese FDI in the non-manufacturing sector has by far surpassed that in the manufacturing sector in Europe and the US (see Table 6.9). In 1992, Japanese FDI in the non-manufacturing sector in Europe was 2.3 times that of the manufacturing sector and, in the US, it was 2.5 times (see Table 6.9).

Table 6.9

Evolution of Japanese Foreign Direct Investment (by sectors and regions), 1986–1992

(Unit: US$ million)

Sector	USA							Latin America						
	1986	1987	1988	1989	1990	1991	1992	1986	1987	1988	1989	1990	1991	1992
Manufacturing	2,199	4,848	9,191	9,586	6,793	5,868	4,177	273	161	442	196	649	364	267
Non-manufacturing	7,953	10,480	13,091	23,986	20,357	12,920	10,384	4,463	4,653	5,985	5,042	2,979	2,973	2451
Branch Office	289	30	46	331	42	35	11	1	2	0	0	1	–	8
Total	10,441	15,358	22,328	33,902	27,192	18,823	14,572	4,737	4,816	6,428	5,238	3,628	3,337	2,726

Sector	Asia							Europe						
	1986	1987	1988	1989	1990	1991	1992	1986	1987	1988	1989	1990	1991	1992
Manufacturing	804	1,679	2,370	3,220	3,068	2,928	3104	370	851	1,548	3,090	4,593	2,690	2,101
Non-manufacturing	1,457	3,141	2,983	4,915	3,891	2,891	3150	2,932	5,407	7,303	11,459	9,132	6,396	4,889
Branch Office	66	47	215	103	95	117	171	167	317	265	259	569	284	71
Total	2,327	4,867	5,569	8,238	7,054	5,936	6,425	3,469	6,575	9,116	14,808	14,294	9,371	7,061

continued on next page

Table 6.9 (*continued*)

(Unit: US$ million)

Sector	Oceania						
	1986	1987	1988	1989	1990	1991	1992
Manufacturing	151	291	239	184	383	405	247
Non-manufacturing	841	1,120	2,394	4,420	3,709	2,871	2,159
Branch Office	–	2	36	14	73	2	1
Total	992	1,413	2,669	4,618	4,166	3,278	2,406

Source: *Okura-sho [Ministry of Finance], op. cit., various issues.*

Secondly, both in relative and absolute terms, Japanese FDI in Asia is less significant than that in Europe, not to mention the US. However Japanese FDI in Asia has increased substantially since 1985 and its growth rate amounted to 254.0 per cent in 1989 compared to that in 1986. The US and Europe recorded 224.7 per cent and 326.9 per cent respectively during the same period. As mentioned before, the SMBs have constituted a substantial part in Japanese FDI in Asia. Besides, the drastic yen appreciation after 1985 has particularly prompted Japanese manufacturing industries, such as electronics and electrical machinery, ferrous and non-ferrous chemicals, together with non-manufacturing industries such as services, finance and insurance, and real estate, to rush to Asia. ASEAN is likely to attract more Japanese FDI than the NIEs as operation costs in the NIEs have been increasing quite rapidly in recent years. In addition, the US has disqualified the NIEs from GSP since January 1989. This has had a marked adverse effect on exports of manufactured goods to the US by Japanese manufacturing industries in the NIEs. Besides, one more new development indicates that, in recent years, the ASEAN countries are competing with each other fiercely in promulgating new rules and regulations in order to attract foreign investments, especially from Japan.

Thirdly, by international standards, the percentage of Japanese FDI in the manufacturing sector over Japan's total FDI is lower than other industrialized countries. Its percentage during the period 1951–1987 was 25.9 per cent, compared to 60.4 per cent of West Germany (based on cumulative investment by the end of 1986), 41 per cent of the US (based on the balance as at the end of 1987), and 28.5 per cent of Britain (based on cumulative investment by the end of 1984). However, Japanese FDI in the manufacturing sector is growing year by year, especially since 1985.

Japanese Foreign Direct Investment in ASEAN: Issues and Prospects

Japanese FDI in ASEAN increased substantially after 1985. Table 6.10 shows that ASEAN attracted substantial Japanese FDI during the period 1986–1992. In absolute terms, Japanese FDI in Indonesia increased 5.7 times from US$250 million in 1986 to US$1,676 million in 1992. In Malaysia, it increased 3.5 times from US$158 million to US$704 million; in the Philippines, it increased 6.6 times from US$21 million to US$160 million; in Singapore, it increased 1.2 times from US$302 million to US$670 million; and in Thailand, it increased 4.3 times from US$124 million to US$657 million, during the same period. Compared to 1985, Japanese FDI in Thailand and Malaysia experienced 1269 per cent and 791 per cent growth rates respectively in 1992. As a whole, Japanese FDI in ASEAN experienced 313 per cent growth rate during the same period. It is also important to point out that, during the period 1985–1992, Japanese FDI in Singapore (US$5,907 million) surpassed that of Thailand (US$5,175 million) and Malaysia (US$3,769 million), not to mention the Philippines (US$1,111 million) (see Table 6.10).

Viewed from the changes in the international economic environment, the following contributing push-factors (examined purely from the Japanese side) are seen to have prompted Japanese

Table 6.10

Japanese Investment in ASEAN, 1985–1992

(Unit: US$ million)

	1985		1986		1987	
	Cases	Amount	Cases	Amount	Cases	Amount
Brunei	–	1	1	1	1	0
Indonesia	62	408	46	250	67	545
Malaysia	60	79	70	158	64	163
Philippines	9	61	9	21	18	72
Singapore	110	339	85	302	182	484
Thailand	51	48	58	124	192	250
ASEAN	292	936	269	856	524	1,524

	1988		1989		1990	
	Cases	Amount	Cases	Amount	Cases	Amount
Brunei	–	0	–	0	–	–
Indonesia	84	586	140	631	155	1,105
Malaysia	108	387	159	673	169	725
Philippines	54	134	87	202	58	258
Singapore	197	7	81	1,902	139	840
Thailand	382	859	403	1,276	377	1,154
ASEAN	825	2,713	970	4,684	898	4,082

	1991		1992		1985–1992	
	Cases	Amount	Cases	Amount	Cases	Amount
Brunei	1	0	–	–	3	2
Indonesia	148	1,193	122	1,676	824	6,394
Malaysia	136	880	111	704	877	3,769
Philippines	42	203	45	160	322	1,111
Singapore	103	613	100	670	1,097	5,907
Thailand	258	807	130	657	1,851	5,175
ASEAN	688	3,696	508	3,867	4,974	22,358

Source: *Compiled from Okura-sho [Ministry of Finance]*, Zaisei Kinyu Tokei Geppo *[Statistics on Finance — Monthly Bulletin] (Tokyo), various issues.*

FDI in ASEAN after the phenomenal yen appreciation in Autumn 1985.

Firstly, Japanese firms can continue to benefit from the GSP if they invest in ASEAN (except Singapore) rather than in the NIEs. Japan has succeeded in making the NIEs her production base and penetrating the Western markets with her manufactured goods.

A considerable proportion of manufactured goods exported from the NIEs to the West is seen to have been produced by Japanese firms. The NIEs succeeded in penetrating the US's market, partly because of their privileges under the GSP. In 1985, the position of the NIEs in the US GSP were as follows: Taiwan (first, 24.2 per cent of the US's total GSP), Korea (second, 12.4 per cent), Hong Kong (fifth, 9.1 per cent) and Singapore (seventh, 5.1 per cent). Likewise, the NIEs were important beneficiaries of the US's GSP which had amounted to 50.8 per cent in 1985. The US's trade deficit with the NIEs increased year by year. In 1988 (January–August), the US's deficit with the NIEs was as follows: Taiwan US$8,820 million, Korea US$6,369 million, Hong Kong US$3,147 million and Singapore US$1,580 million.

The US came to review her double-deficit (fiscal and trade) situation and decided to reduce imports of manufactured goods by "graduating" the NIEs from the GSP. The US's new action came into force on 1 January 1989. Japanese affiliated firms in the NIEs were seriously affected. In order to continue to benefit from the GSP, some Japanese firms in the NIEs decided to shift to ASEAN. Furthermore, new Japanese investors prefer ASEAN to the NIEs if the GSP is an important consideration in their export drive. Likewise, Japanese FDI in ASEAN increased significantly in recent years.

Secondly, there is competition with the NIEs. It can be judged from two aspects:

One, Japan has to compete with the NIEs in Japanese domestic markets. The NIEs' manufactured goods, both light and heavy industrial products, are increasingly obtaining larger and larger shares of the Japanese markets.

Two, Japan is facing keen competition from the NIEs in international markets. In recent years, as a result of the currency appreciation and labour-management disputes in the NIEs, operation costs and wages have increased significantly. Firms in the NIEs are shifting to ASEAN. The influx of the NIEs' FDI in ASEAN increased substantially. In some ASEAN countries, the NIEs' investment has exceeded that of the Japanese. In 1988, for example, the NIEs' FDI in Malaysia (January–September) and the Philippines (January–November) have amounted to US$709.3 million and US$132.5 million respectively. Japanese FDI in these countries was US$561.1 million and US$105.9 million respectively. Accordingly, in order to be more competitive, Japanese firms have no choice but to increase their FDI in ASEAN.

Unlike Japan, both the NIEs and ASEAN do not have a fully developed industrial infrastructure. This is reflected in underdevelopment and an extreme lack of supporting industries. The influx of Japanese SMBs (i.e. supporting industries) into the NIEs and ASEAN, could be critically adjudged to have discouraged the development of local SMBs.

It is commonly argued that the FDI of the US and European MNCs in the developing countries do not usually accompany supporting industries of their own nationalists.[7] To a certain extent, Japanese firms, however, do either bring their supporting industries, or prefer Japanese subcontractors and subsidiaries which have already operated in a third country. It is said to be because of the reliability and competitiveness (quality, prices and delivery) provided by the Japanese subcontractors and subsidiaries.

A large proportion of Japanese subcontractors and subsidiaries comprises SMBs. The FDI of the Japanese SMBs is concentrated in Asia. It is true that supporting industries in Europe and the US are more developed than in Asia. Japanese SMBs seemed to have a smaller role to play in the West after the phenomenal yen appreciation in 1985. The FDI of the Japanese small and medium-sized manufacturing industries in the US and Europe dropped from 45.8 per cent in 1981–1984 to 34.1 per cent in 1985–1986.[8] Compared to the big firms, in terms of the availability of paid-up capital, technology and managerial know-how, Japanese SMBs are in a weaker position when they have to invest abroad. The following advantages and considerations, therefore, appeared to be more appealing and attractive to the SMBs if they invest in Asia: (a) religious and cultural similarity, (b) geographical proximity, (c) low operation costs, (d) cheap raw materials, (e) to make use of Chinese investors and distribution routes, (5) regional markets in Asia, (g) to benefit from GSP, and (h) to benefit from the pioneer status awarded by governments in Asia.

The FDI of Japanese SMBs in Asia increased from 30.1 per cent in 1980 to 45.6 per cent in 1985 and remained at the level of 44.6 per cent in 1987.[9] However, as far as Asia's manufacturing sector is concerned, the FDI of Japanese SMBs increased from 47.2 per cent in 1982–1983 to 59.8 per cent in 1984–1985. In the US and Europe, it dropped from 39.4 per cent to 30.9 per cent, and from 10.6 per cent to 6.9 per cent respectively during the same period. Among the Asian countries, Korea, Taiwan and Hong Kong have been the three major recipients of FDI from the Japanese SMBs. In 1987, these three countries combined constituted 28 per cent of the total FDI of the Japanese SMBs. Data on ASEAN's breakdown are not available. It is, however, believed that ASEAN has also attracted a substantial amount of Japanese SMBs' FDI. ASEAN's local manufacturers usually, we observe, complain about the Japanese firms' subcontracting only to the Japanese supporting industries, i.e. Japanese SMBs. It is important to find out whether parts and components provided by the Japanese supporting industries are distinctively competitive or simply that the Japanese firms in ASEAN have a bias in favour of the Japanese supporting industries.

Conclusion

The economic relationship between Japan and ASEAN will be strengthened further in the years ahead. This is basically for the following reasons:

(i) The high yen has come to stay and has prompted Japan to proceed rapidly with industrial restructuring. Japan will further increase her FDI in ASEAN in order to compete with the NIEs and to expand into international markets, and into the US in particular.

(ii) The establishment of economic blocs in the West, for example, European economic integration and the US–Canada Trade Agreement etc., will further stimulate Japan's economic involvement and expansion in the Asia-Pacific region. ASEAN, as an economic identity, has naturally attracted special attention from Japan.

(iii) Currency appreciation and labour-management disputes in Taiwan and Korea have raised operation costs and have weakened the NIEs' international competitiveness. Two phenomena can be observed. One, the NIEs increased their FDI in ASEAN. Two, Japan has turned to ASEAN for her future investment (the GSP issue is, of course, taken into consideration) and some Japanese affiliated firms in the NIEs have redirected FDI to ASEAN.

On the ASEAN side, the economic infrastructure has been improved and restrictions on foreign equity shares have been removed to attract FDI. Likewise, ASEAN will continue to proceed to steady economic growth in the years ahead. Learning from the NIEs, ASEAN will move forward to promote export-oriented industries. However, to what extent can the US import manufactured products from ASEAN? The US is keen to reduce her huge trade deficit with Japan and the NIEs. The US does not wish ASEAN to replace Japan and the NIEs. ASEAN economic development is, therefore, very much reliant on the trade expansion in China, intra-ASEAN region, the NIEs and Japan.

China's economic development is rather unpredictable, despite the fact that it has succeeded in rapid economic growth over the last decade. China's shares in ASEAN's total trade have remained at 1.5 per cent in 1981 and 1984, and 2.6 per cent in 1987. Intra-ASEAN trade was 3.8 per cent in 1981, 4.3 per cent in 1984 and 4.5 per cent in 1987. The ASEAN–NIEs' trade was 16.4 per cent, 18.6 per cent and 19.4 per cent during the same period. ASEAN–NIEs' trade had amounted to 29.5 per cent, 27.9 per cent and 25.5 per cent during the same years. It is, therefore, clear that ASEAN's future economic development is reliant heavily on its trade and economic co-operation relationship with the NIEs, and with Japan in particular.

Notes

1   In December 1967, Japan's reserves (gold and dollars) stood at just over US$2,000 million. They increased nine times by December 1972, but fell back after the oil shock in 1973. Japan soon overcame the effects of that crisis, and by December 1978 they amounted to over US$33,000 million. Japan's reserves decreased to US$25,000 million by December 1980 after experiencing the other oil shock in 1979.

2   These *sogoshoshas* include, among others, C. Itoh, Sumitomo, Marubeni, Mitsui, Mitsubishi, Nissho Iwai, Toyo Menka, Nichimen and Kanematsu-Gosho.

3   The *sogoshoshas* also handled offshore trade amounting to ¥14,876 billion in 1986. See Keizai Koho Centre [Japan Institute for Social and Economic Affairs], *Japan 1988, An International Comparison* (Tokyo, 1988), p. 46.

4   Nihon Boeki Shinko-kai (JETRO), 1989 *Jetro Hakusho Toshi-hen* [1989 JETRO White Paper on Investment], (Tokyo, 1989), pp. 32–34.

5   See Chapter 3 for detailed discussion.

6   Lim Hua Sing, "Azia Niizu no Oiage to Jiba Sangyo no Tai-o" [Competition and Complementarity between the SMBs in the NIEs and Japan], *Journal of Economics*, no. 46 (Niigata University [Japan], March 1989).

7   It is worthwhile to look into the co-operation and relations between the Western firms and their supporting industries of different nationalities in the NIEs and ASEAN.

8   By 1985, the FDI of the Japanese small and medium-sized manufacturing industries in the West increased from 28.1 per cent in 1977–1980 to 45.9 per cent in 1981–1984. It is believed to be for the following reasons: (a) to secure markets in the West, (b) to set up sales bases, (c) to alleviate trade friction between Japan and the West, and (d) to follow their parent companies.

9   Chusho Kigyo-cho [Board of Small and Medium-sized Businesses], *Chusho Kigyo Hakusho 1988* [White Paper on Small and Medium-sized Businesses 1988] (Tokyo), p. 49.

CHAPTER 7

Japanese Economic Involvement in Asia and Chinese Partnerships

Introduction

This chapter is divided into three parts. The first part analyses recent Japanese foreign direct investment (FDI), especially in Asia. It also highlights some characteristics of industrial co-operation between Japan and the Asian countries.

The second and third parts are analyses based on the results of a questionnaire survey, which was conducted in Japan in June 1992. It was carried out by the Japanese Enterprises Internationalization Study Group of Chukyo University. Questionnaires were sent out to 114 selected large enterprises throughout Japan. These enterprises are predominantly manufacturing industries and a few companies which belong to the service sector, such as prominent department stores. In any case, these enterprises are found to have overseas investments in one way or another.

Based on the questionnaire survey results, Part Two attempts to analyse the main reasons why Japanese enterprises invest in Asia. It also attempts to identify some major problems encountered by Japanese enterprises when they invest in Asia.

Part Three examines the reasons for either choosing or not choosing Chinese entrepreneurs as partners when Japanese enterprises invest in Asia.

Japanese Foreign Direct Investment and Industrial Co-operation

Japanese Foreign Direct Investment

Japanese foreign direct investment (FDI) increased by 4.6 times from US$49.220 billion between 1978–1984 to US$227.157 billion between 1986–1990. It was apparently stimulated by the drastic yen appreciation in September 1985. Japan experienced a "high yen economic boom" for four to five years during the 1986–1989 period, but the "bubble economy" collapsed by the end of 1989. The Japanese economy has not shown any sign of recovery since 1990 despite various economic and fiscal measures implemented by the government. Japanese FDI has decreased significantly since 1990 due to sluggish domestic economic performance. This has been caused largely by stagnant consumption and despite the strong yen which should have stimulated a Japanese overseas investment drive like that of the 1986–1989 period.

Japanese FDI increased by 5.5 times from US$12.217 billion in 1985 to US$67.540 billion in 1989. However, it dropped to US$56.911 billion in 1990 and to US$41.584 billion in 1991. The latest statistics show that in 1992, Japanese FDI decreased further to US$34.138 billion.

Japanese FDI in Asia decreased abruptly from US$8.238 billion in 1989 to US$5.936 billion in 1991. This was the period when Japan fell into a stagnant economic dead-end and increasingly felt the impact of sluggish domestic consumption. This means that despite the yen appreciation, Japanese enterprises have not increased overseas investment since 1990 mainly due to sluggish economic performance in the industrialized countries, and more importantly, to Japan's domestic economic stagnation. However, Japanese FDI in Asia increased slightly to US$6,425 million in 1992 as a result other abrupt investments in China and South Asia (India, Bangladesh and Sri Lanka).

As a "detour production base" of Japanese enterprises, Asians exports of machinery and equipment, and electronics and electrical products to American and European markets have also declined in recent years. Similarly, exports of manufactured products by Japanese manufacturing industries in Asia to Japan were also limited. However, Japanese enterprises in the Asia-Pacific region were able to operate without much interruption. This was mainly because of sound economic performance in Asia, particularly in the NIEs, ASEAN and China. In other words, it is believed that rapid economic development among the Asian countries has consumed a substantial quantity of manufactured products produced by Japanese enterprises in the region.

Industrial Co-operation between Japan and Asia

According to the "JETRO White Paper on Investment" (1993), during the 1991–June 1992 period, Japanese enterprises experienced 803 cases of industrial co-operation and collaboration with America (288 cases), the EC (237 cases), Asia (215 cases) and others (63 cases). These cases of industrial co-operation and collaboration are shown as follows:

(1) Technology transfer (308 cases)
(2) Joint R&D (152 cases)
(3) OEM (original equipment manufacturing) (85 cases)
(4) Sales co-operation (47 cases)
(5) Business co-operation (86 cases)
(6) Other types of co-operation (125 cases)

The above-mentioned cases consist of the following three categories: first, co-operation extended by foreign countries to Japan (188 cases); second, mutual co-operation between Japan and foreign countries (266 cases); third, co-operation extended by Japan to foreign countries (349 cases).

Two major phenomena can be further derived from the above information: one, technology transfer (the provision of technology, technology co-operation and the provision of licences) constitutes the highest proportion of industrial co-operation (38 per cent of the total);

two, industrial co-operation extended by Japan to foreign countries shows the largest percentage (43 per cent of the total). Owing to: (a) Japan's active involvement in overseas investments, (b) the eagerness to obtain Japanese technology in order to improve productivity and (c) the increased competitiveness of manufacturers, technology transfer from Japan to overseas countries will continue to be the main concern of both policymakers and investors, especially among Asian countries.

In recent years, industrial co-operation between Japan and Asia has gained momentum. Table 7.1 indicates industrial co-operation between Japan and Asia (NIEs, ASEAN, China and Vietnam) by sector during the July 1991–June 1992 period. Machinery (43 cases), automobiles (23 cases), electronics and electrical machinery (16 cases), and textiles (16 cases) appeared to be the most important sectors for industrial co-operation (provision of technology and licences, OEM, etc.) between Japan and Asian countries. The Asian countries, especially the NIEs and ASEAN, are increasingly placing emphasis on developing capital- and technology-intensive industries. Likewise, industrial co-operation between Japan and Asia appeared to have been concentrated in capital-and technology-intensive industries, such as machinery, automobiles, electronics and electrical machinery. These constituted 64 per cent (82 cases) of Japan's total industrial co-operation with Asia during the July 1991–June 1992 period.

During the same period, the provision of technology and licences by Japan to the Asian countries can be broken down as follows: the NIEs 45 cases, China 29 cases and ASEAN 15 cases. Furthermore, the OEM from Japan to the Asian countries can be broken down as follows: the NIEs 10 cases, China 10 cases, ASEAN 9 cases and Vietnam 5 cases. The provision of technology and licences by Japan to the NIEs played a larger role compared to the rest of Asian countries; whereas the OEM by Japan to the non-NIEs (ASEAN, China and Vietnam) is higher than the NIEs. In general, as can be expected, the OEM by Japanese labour-intensive industries normally goes to the less developed countries (for instance, textile OEM predominantly goes to Vietnam). Industrial cooperation (provision of technology and licences, OEM, etc.) provided by Japanese capital and technology-intensive industries is extended primarily to the NIEs and, to a lesser extent, to ASEAN and China.

Table 7.1

**Industrial Co-operation between Japan and Asia by Sectors
(July 1991–June 1992)**

	Asia		The World	
	Cases	%	Cases	%
Semiconductors	5	11.4	44	100.0
Computers	10	9.9	101	100.0
Automobiles	23	30.3	76	100.0
Electronics and Electrical Machinery	16	28.6	56	100.0
Precision Machines	6	26.1	23	100.0
Machinery	43	32.1	134	100.0
Chemistry	10	18.5	54	100.0
Textiles	16	45.7	35	100.0
Total	129	24.7	523	100.0

Source: *Compiled and computed from JETRO, op. cit., pp. 90–91.*

Japanese Investment in Asia: Reasons for and Constraints against

Why Should Japan Invest in Asia?

The main motivators for Japanese FDI in Asia can be analysed from the following two perspectives:

Firstly, Japan is looking to secure markets in the Asia-Pacific region. The NIEs, ASEAN and China are particularly important markets for Japanese manufacturing industries. Asia has experienced high economic growth over the last decade or so. Consequently, living standards in Asia have been upgraded significantly and domestic consumption power has also increased tremendously in recent years. Demand for complex manufactured products, such as automobiles, electronics and electrical products, has gained momentum, especially among urbanites. Year by year, the Asia-Pacific region has increasingly become an indispensable outlet for Japanese manufactured products.

Secondly, Asia is seen as a "detour production base" for Japanese enterprises in order to alleviate economic conflicts and trade friction between Japan and Western nations. In 1992, America and the EC suffered trade deficits with Japan of US$43.6 billion and US$31.2 billion respectively. These trade deficits are difficult to rectify largely for the following reasons: (a) domestic consumption in Japan has remained inactive due to the collapse of the "bubble economy". The sluggish economic situation has been further discouraged by a series of scandals and corruption by politicians and bureaucrats. In addition, disposable income and wages have not been adjusted to allow the Japanese to consume more freely in recent years; (b) American and European products have encountered problems, such as tariff and non-tariff barriers, in penetrating the Japanese market. The Western nations are inclined to believe that Japanese distribution systems are particularly complicated, and that Japanese business practices (for instance, bribes are given by big enterprises to bureaucrats in order to win bids) are unfair to non-Japanese investors. The strong perception of Japan as a "closed-market" has kept many Western enterprises from even considering exploring markets there; (c) Japan is basically a "production giant" and high quality manufactured products have overflowed the domestic market. Except for some brand manufactured products, Western products are perceived as being of mediocre quality which can hardly satisfy choosy Japanese consumers. Western nations have found only a limited outlet in Japan for their products.

Western nations, through diplomatic and political measures, have repeatedly urged Japan to open up her closed market. On the other hand, Japanese currency has been pressured to increase its value in order to restrict Japanese exports. Nevertheless, all these measures have only had limited impact, and Japanese trade surpluses with Western nations have still remained at high levels.

Japanese enterprises were quick to invest overseas in order to alleviate economic conflicts and trade friction with Western nations particularly during the 1986–1990 period. This move was obviously prompted by the development of the EC economic integration and economic co-operation amongst countries in North America. In addition, Japanese FDI in Asia, as mentioned earlier, has also aimed at exploring markets in the Asia-Pacific region, and at creating a "detour production base" in Asia for penetrating markets in the West.

Reasons for Japanese Enterprises to Invest in Asia

Table 7.2 reveals motivators of Japanese FDI in Asia. It clearly indicates the main motivators for Japanese enterprises to invest in Asia, namely sale expansion (27 per cent) and production base expansion (27 per cent). If the item "supply of manufactures/services" (13 per cent) is included, the three above-mentioned items constitute as much as 68 per cent of Japan's total motivators to select Asia for overseas investment. This is clearly related to our earlier hypothesis that Japanese FDI in Asia is aimed at exploring international markets (both the Asia-Pacific and the Western markets), and that Asia is considered an important "detour production base" for the Japanese enterprises.

Viewed from different angles, the questionnaires identify the main reasons for the selection of Asia for investment by Japanese enterprises, which is shown in Table 7.3. It is not surprising to notice that Japanese enterprises invest in Asia to "take advantage of geographical proximity" (31 per cent) and to "explore regional and international markets" (41 per cent). The results found in Table 7.3 support the findings in Table 7.2 that Japan considers Asia an indispensable production base from which Japan's manufactured products can be sold not only in regional, but also in international markets.

Table 7.2

Japanese Motivators to Invest in Asia*

Investment Motivators	Number of Enterprises (%)	
Supply of manufactures/services	8	(12.9)
Sale expansion	17	(27.4)
Production base expansion	17	(27.4)
To secure labour force	7	(11.3)
To secure entrepot base	3	(4.8)
Procurement of raw materials/parts	3	(4.8)
To avoid trade frictions	0	(0.0)
To avoid foreign exchange risks	0	(0.0)
By invitation from local government	6	(9.7)
Others (please specify): Technology supply	1	(1.6)
Total	62	(100.0)

Note: *Up to three reasons have been identified by each responding Japanese enterprise.*
Source: *Questionnaire Survey Data.*

Table 7.3

Main Reasons for Selection of Asia for Investment by Japanese Enterprises

Main Reasons for Selecting Asia to Invest	Number of Enterprises (%)	
To do business in an area with a similar religion/culture	2	(5.1)
To take advantage of geographical proximity	12	(30.8)
To explore regional/international markets	16	(41.0)
To benefit from the generalized system of preferences	1	(2.6)
To benefit from policies of foreign pioneer investments	5	(12.8)
To make use of Chinese investors and their distribution networks	2	(5.1)
Others (please specify): High economic growth rate	1	(2.6)
Total	39	(100.0)

Note: *Up to two reasons were chosen by each responding Japanese enterprise.*
Source: *Questionnaire Survey Data.*

Constraints against Japanese Enterprises Investing in Asia

Japanese enterprises have encountered some major problems when investing in Asia. These problems include a poor industrial infrastructure (22 per cent), a low quality labour force (15 per cent), wage increases (15 per cent) and, to a lesser extent, a small domestic market (9 per cent), country risk (9 per cent), insufficient intermediate managerial staff (7 per cent) and a high job-hopping rate (6 per cent) (see Table 7.4).

Table 7.4

Major Problems Encountered by Japanese Enterprises in Asia*

Major Problems	Number of Enterprises (%)	
High job-hopping rate	3	(5.5)
Lack of reliable local partnership	2	(3.6)
Low quality labour force	8	(14.5)
Rejection of sole capital investment	1	(1.8)
Poor industrial infrastructure	12	(21.8)
Wage increases	8	(14.5)
Obligations to export manufactured products	2	(3.6)
Country risk	5	(9.1)
Procurement of parts and components	4	(7.3)
Small domestic market	5	(9.1)
Insufficient intermediate managerial staff	4	(7.3)
Others (please specify): Small financial market	1	(1.8)
Total	55	(100.0)

Source: *Questionnaire Survey Data.*

* *The two major problems encountered by each Japanese enterprise have been chosen.*

These problems have been encountered elsewhere when Japan invests overseas. In Asia, "poor industrial infrastructure" has been quoted as the most significant problem for Japanese enterprises. Industrial infrastructure in the NIEs has basically met the needs of Japanese FDI. Among the ASEAN countries (excluding Singapore), industrial infrastructure in Malaysia and Thailand has been improved significantly in recent years, while that in Indonesia and the Philippines is still below expectations. In China and Vietnam, obviously the pace of industrial infrastructure development lags far behind the significant inflow of foreign investment. China started its open-door economic reform in 1979 and the development of industrial infrastructure has gained momentum particularly in big cities and in the coastal special economic zones. Insufficient electrical supply has, however, slowed down industrial production especially in the inland areas. Vietnam's economic reform and construction only started in recent years, but rapid development of its industrial infastructure has been thwarted by the war-torn economy, and is therefore far below the expectation of foreign investors.

With the exception of the NIEs, Asian countries are seen to have a "low quality labour force". Even in the NIEs, a sufficiently high quality labour force is required by Japanese enterprises to expand their R&D activities. In general, human resource development programmes have become more and more important in ASEAN, especially in Malaysia and Thailand. These countries are securing and upgrading the quality of the labour force, as they are shifting steadily from labour-intensive to capital-and technology-intensive industrial activities. The quality of the labour force in the rest of the ASEAN countries, China and Vietnam, requires constant upgrading to attract more and more capital- and technology-intensive industries from Japan.

Together with increases in the cost of land and property, wages also increased substantially in the NIEs. The NIEs have successfully shifted from labour-intensive to capital- and technology-intensive activities. Wages, therefore, have to be kept in accordance with the increase of productivity and industrial restructuring processes. More and more Japanese enterprises have, however, perceived rapid "wage increases" as the main constraints to investment and business expansion, and have started shifting to ASEAN, China and Vietnam. The constraints of "small domestic market", "high job-hopping rate" and "insufficient intermediate managerial staff", can be found in the rapid industrialized economies of urban states, such as Singapore and

Hong Kong. Singapore and Hong Kong have small populations of 2.9 million and 5.9 million respectively. Unless Japanese investment in these two regions is aiming for market expansion in ASEAN and mainland China, domestic markets in Singapore and Hong Kong are extremely limited, despite high per capita growth rates.

In Singapore in particular, the constraints of "high job-hopping rate" and "insufficient intermediate managerial staff" coincide with rapid economic development. These two issues have become serious impediments for business activities and expansion not only for foreign enterprises but also for local firms.

Japanese investors are concerned about "country risk" when they invest in Asia. Resistance against China's open-door economic reform by some Chinese conservative politicians; the 4th of June Tiananmen Incident in 1989 and the post Deng Xiao Ping issue, etc., are seen by Japanese investors as uncertainties which may create social or political instabilities in China. On the other hand, Japanese investors have taken a "wait and see" attitude towards exploring opportunities in Vietnam. They agree that Vietnam is a very attractive country to invest in, but so far their approach has still remained cautious.

Japanese Investment in Asia and Chinese Partnerships

Capital Composition and Investment Classification of Japanese Investment in Asia

Japan experienced high economic growth in the 1960s. Her FDI increased significantly after 1968 when she started to enjoy a positive trade surplus. Japan's FDI was farther stimulated by liberalization measures taken in the 1970s (four times in the years 1970, 1971, 1972 and 1978) and because the exchange law was amended in the 1980s (twice in the years 1980 and 1984). Japan's FDI was particularly significant after the yen appreciation in 1985 until the collapse of the "bubble economy" at the end of 1989.

Japan has investments all over the world and has become one of the largest investors among the industrialized nations. However, Japanese enterprises were seen to be rather conservative and defensive in terms of their attitude or eagerness to secure control over the management and equity in their overseas ventures.

Firstly, Japan was a latecomer in the world-wide investment arena compared to European countries and America. In the 1960s and 1970s, Japan gained her stronghold in overseas investments, but compared to her European and American counterparts, in general she lagged behind in terms of technology, capital and managerial know-how. Therefore, Japan preferred local partnerships or local investment participation rather than sole capital investment when making overseas investments.

Secondly, Japan tends to avoid "country risk" in her FDI. Japanese investors used to be more cautious compared to their European and American counterparts when they invested in China, Indo-China, Myanmar and some Islamic countries (such as Brunei, Indonesia and Malaysia) in Asia. They were concerned about social and political instability in the socialist countries and nationalistic sentiments in the Malay-predominant nations.

In recent years, both the socialist countries and the Malay-predominant nations have changed their policies quite significantly. The former have applied "open-door economic policies" and "socialist free-market economies"; while the latter have relaxed their "bumiputra" or "prebumi" policies to attract foreign investments. Fears about the nationalization of foreign assets in the socialist countries, or even in Indonesia under the Sukarno regime before 1965, diminished. The Asian countries are now keen to attract foreign investment in order to speed up industrialization and the modernization process.

Japan, has also gained confidence in her FDI especially over the last decade. Japan's accumulation of capital, technology and managerial know-how has increased significantly to enable her to be more aggressive and offensive in her FDI. Japanese investors are not only eager to take the initiative in their management of overseas ventures,

Table 7.5

Capital Composition of Japanese Investment in Asia

Capital Composition	Number of Enterprises (%)	
100% (Sole Capital Investment)	7	(31.8)
Between 50% and 99%	7	(31.8)
50% Each	0	(0.0)
Between 30% and 49%	6	(27.2)
Below 30%	2	(9.1)
Total	22	(100.0)

Source: *Questionnaire Survey Data.*

Table 7.6

Investment Classification of Japanese Enterprises in Asia

Investment Classification	Number of Responses (%)	
Setting up a new factory	15	(37.5)
Setting up sales dealerships	8	(20.0)
R&D	2	(5.0)
Setting up a branch	3	(7.5)
Setting up a business office	1	(2.5)
Technology co-operation	6	(15.0)
Others	5	(12.5)
Setting up a local corporation and sale centre		
Setting up a new company under a different name		
Involvement in Joint-ventures		
Total	40	(100.0)

Note: *Each company may have more than one response.*
Source: *Questionnaire Survey Data.*

but also keen to make sole capital investment in their overseas business activities. Japanese investors are inclined to make vast investments, to have a final say in management and quality control, and to make decisions about overall production. Likewise, as shown in Table 7.5, our survey suggests that 32 per cent of Japanese investors chose "sole capital investments" and the other 32 per cent of Japanese investors chose "between 50 per cent and 99 per cent" in their FDI in Asia. In other words, 64 per cent of the Japanese investors have above 50 per cent in capital composition in their FDI in Asia. Table 7.6 farther suggests that 38 per cent of Japanese investors have set up new factories, whereas 20 per cent of them have set up sales dealerships. It is therefore clear from Tables 7.5 and 7.6 that more and more Japanese investors are taking the initiative in the manufacturing sector in their FDI in Asia in order to explore markets in the Asia-Pacific region as well as in the rest of the world.

Japanese Foreign Direct Investment and the Selection of Chinese Partnerships in Asia

The Chinese population is concentrated in Asia. The distribution of the Chinese population in some major Asian countries is as follows: Peopled Republic of China 1.2 billion, Taiwan 20 million, Hong Kong 5.9 million, Macau 0.4 million, Indonesia 6.2 million, Malaysia 4.5 million, Thailand 4.5 million, Singapore 1.9 million, the Philippines 1 million, Vietnam 0.7 million and Myanmar 0.7 million, etc. The total Chinese population in China, Taiwan, Hong Kong and Macau amounts to 1.226 billion, whereas in the rest of the Asian countries, the number amounts to approximately 20 million.

Mainland China started its open-door economic policy in 1979 and 1.2 billion of the Chinese population have been actively involved in economic activities since then. In Taiwan, Hong Kong and Macau, of the Chinese population, 26.2 million have traditionally participated in economic activities. On the other hand, in the rest of the Asian countries, the proportion of Chinese people playing a more and more important role in the economic development of their respective countries is increasing.

Over a long period of involvement in economic activities, Chinese in Asia have accumulated capital, technology and managerial know-how in one way or another. Some Chinese have succeeded in setting up conglomerates or financial cliques. They have substantial investments all over the world, and in the Asia-Pacific region in particular. They have close industrial co-operative relationships with foreign countries and have set up joint ventures in many sectors (manufacturing, commerce, services and others) with foreign investors. Their manufactured products have been widely sold in domestic and international markets.

Our survey reveals that out of 24 Japanese enterprises responding, 17 (71 per cent) of them have business relationships with Chinese entrepreneurs in Asia. They are concentrated in transport equipment (21 per cent of the total), food and beverage (13 per cent), electronics and electrical products (13 per cent), chemical products (8 per cent), and iron and steel products (8 per cent) (see Table 7.7).

Table 7.7

Japanese Enterprises having Business Relationships with Chinese Entrepreneurs in Asia

Types of Industry	Total Number of Enterprises Responded	Have Business Relationship with Chinese Entrepreneurs in Asia
Food & Beverage	3	3
Textile & Textile Products	0	0
Pulp & Paper	0	0
Chemical Products	3	2
Petroleum Products	0	0
Quarrying & Ceramics	0	0
Iron & Steel Products	2	2
Non-ferrous Metals	0	0
Metal Products	1	0
Machinery	1	0
Electronics & Electrical Products	3	3
Transport Equipment	8	5
Precision Equipment	0	0
Other Manufacturers	1	0
Distribution Industries	2	2
Total	24 (100.0)	17 (70.8)

Source: Questionnaire Survey Data.

Japanese investors are keen to have Chinese partnerships in Asia.
The main reasons for co-operating with Chinese entrepreneurs to do
business in Asia are highlighted in Table 7.8. Japanese investors are
particularly keen to utilize Chinese managerial know-how (26 per
cent), capital (21 per cent), distribution network (21 per cent) and
network of contacts (21 per cent) in Asia. Technology (5 per cent)
accumulated by Chinese entrepreneurs in Asia is far less important
for Japanese investors.

Table 7.8

**Reasons for Co-operating with Chinese Entrepreneurs to Do
Business in Asia***

Reasons for Co-operating with Chinese Entrepreneurs	Number of Enterprises (%)	
Capital	8	(20.5)
Technology	2	(5.1)
Managerial know-how	10	(25.6)
Distribution network	8	(20.5)
Network of contacts	8	(20.5)
Political influence	2	(5.1)
Information	1	(2.6)
Others (please specify)	0	(0.0)
Total	39	(100.0)

Source: *Questionnaire Survey Data.*
* *Two main reasons were chosen by each Japanese enterprise.*

Table 7.9 provides a negative picture of Chinese entrepreneurs in
Asia. Japanese investors do not choose Chinese entrepreneurs as
business partners simply because of the Chinese "lack of long-term
vision on industrial development" (30 per cent) and because they are
"family-management oriented" (30 per cent). These two reasons
constitute as high as 60 per cent of the reasons for Japanese investors
not choosing to do business with Chinese entrepreneurs in Asia. In
general, compared to Western and Chinese entrepreneurs, Japanese
entrepreneurs are good at planning and have long-term vision for

industrial development. They prefer capital re-investment or production expansion to dividend distribution to shareholders when their companies make profits. Big Japanese enterprises are also not "family-management oriented", but of course there are numerous exceptions, especially for small and medium-sized businesses. Japanese enterprises used to be "family-management oriented" but nowadays Japanese enterprises recruit talented employees from outside the family. This is considered necessary to secure stable development and smooth transition of their enterprises.

Table 7.9

Reasons for Not Choosing Chinese Entrepreneurs to Do Business in Asia*

Reasons for Not Choosing Chinese Entrepreneurs	Number of Enterprises (%)	
Lack of long-term vision on industrial development	10	(30.3)
Prefer dividend to re-investment	3	(9.1)
Lack of capital, technology and managerial know-how	4	(12.1)
Rather speculative and risky	1	(3.0)
Being family-management oriented	10	(30.3)
Non-separation between ownership and management	3	(9.1)
Lack of interest in making an investment in the manufacturing sector	2	(6.1)
Others (please specify)	0	(0.0)
Total	33	(100.0)

Source: *Questionnaire Survey Data.*
* *Two main reasons were chosen by each Japanese enterprise.*

We pointed out earlier in Table 7.8 that Japanese investors prefer Chinese partnerships because they are keen to utilize Chinese managerial know-how and capital. To a certain extent, this perception is legitimate because compared to other Asian races, Chinese are in a better position in terms of managerial know-how and capital. However, in Table 7.9, Japanese investors also cited Chinese "lack of capital, technology and managerial know-how" (12 per cent), as a reason for not choosing Chinese entrepreneurs to do business with in Asia. Japanese investors may experience frustration if their expectations for these factors are too high.

In addition, Japanese investors have negative appraisals of Chinese entrepreneurs in Asia because they maintain that Chinese "prefer dividends rather than re-investment" (9 per cent), have "non-separation between ownership and management" (9 per cent) and a "lack of interest in making investment in the manufacturing sector" (6 per cent). These are some of the main reasons cited by Japanese enterprises for not choosing Chinese entrepreneurs as business partners in Asia.

Conclusion

Asia's economic development has been promising and Asia will continue to grow rapidly toward the twenty-first century. In Asia's economic development process, Japan plays an important role in terms of FDI, technology transfer and the introduction of managerial know-how, etc. Japan considers Asia as having important markets and a "detour production base". Economic and industrial co-operation between Japan and Asia are expected to be farther strengthened in time to come.

Chinese entrepreneurs have been playing an important role in the economic development of Asia. Chinese in Asia have long been involved in economic and commercial activities, and have accumulated a substantial quantity of capital, technology and managerial know-how. Despite some shortcomings of Chinese enterprises, Chinese entrepreneurs will continue to contribute toward modernization and industrialization in Asia.

Like American and European multinational corporations, Japanese enterprises regard the Chinese as important partners when they decide to invest in Asia. To what extent foreign enterprises can penetrate markets in Asia is very much dependent on their economic and industrial co-operation with the Chinese in this region.

CHAPTER 8

Economic Superpower and International Roles

Introduction

Japan is the only highly industrialized country in Asia. Japanese economic development has been promising, despite setbacks and stagnation. As an economic giant, Japan is expected to make contributions to peace and economic development in the world in general, and to the Asia–Pacific region in particular. Through making contributions to the world, Japan can benefit reciprocally from the world's economic development in order to make further progress and to improve the quality of life of the Japanese people.

This chapter is divided into two parts. The first part analyses Japan's real economic strength, as an economic superpower, by examining her per capita gross national product, international balance of payments, external balance of assets and liabilities, and disposable income and savings. Japan is obviously a rich country but the quality of life of the Japanese people could be much improved. For example, the high disposable wages of the Japanese are essentially offset by high commodity prices. The high savings of the Japanese are specifically reserved for the education of their children, medical expenses, wedding ceremonies and old age. The quality of life of Japanese people needs to be further improved to reach the standard of Western nations.

The second part examines Japan's international role as an economic superpower. Japan's economic, political, diplomatic and military roles are discussed at length. Japan should emphasize its economic and diplomatic roles (through trade, investment and official development assistance) but limit its political role in international affairs. In particular Japan's military role is not welcomed by Asian countries.

This chapter proposes that economic co-operation between Japan and especially the Asia–Pacific region should be further strengthened. Japan's economic advancement depends greatly on the prosperity of the Asia–Pacific region. Japan should open up her domestic markets and import manufactured goods at much more reasonable prices from the region. Likewise commodity prices in Japan can be stabilized further and the quality of life of the Japanese people significantly upgraded.

Has Japan Become an Economic Superpower?

An Economic Superpower

Has Japan become an economic superpower? Most would answer "Yes". However, it is not easy to define whether Japan can really be classified as an economic superpower. By what criteria or according to what definition can one judge whether a specific affluent country has reached the status of a so-called "economic superpower". By examining Japan's per capita gross national product (GNP), international balance of payments, external balance of assets and liabilities and disposable income and savings, we can obtain a clearer picture of the level of Japan's economic development. This will help to decide whether Japan qualifies as an "economic superpower".

Table 8.1 shows the per capita GNP of selected countries in 1992. Japan ranked third, below only Switzerland and Luxembourg. The US ranked eighth, with its per capita GNP US$5,100 lower than that of Japan.

Table 8.2 shows the Japanese international balance of payments during the 1991–1992 period. Japan's trade surplus with the US increased substantially from US$43.4 billion in 1991 to US$50.2 billion in 1992.

Table 8.1

**Per Capita Gross National Product of
Selected Countries (1992)**

	(Unit: US$)
Switzerland	36,230
Luxembourg	35,260
Japan	28,220
Sweden2	6,780
Denmark	25,930
Norway	25,800
Iceland	23,670
US	23,120
Germany	23,030
Finland	22,980

Source: *JETRO, (Japan, 1994), p. 17.*

Similarly, its trade surplus with the EC increased remarkably from US$33.4 billion to US$39.4 billion during the same period. Japan's trade balance with all countries increased substantially from US$103.0 billion in 1991 to US$132.3 billion in 1992. Despite the collapse of the "bubble economy" since 1991, and the persistence of a sluggish economy, Japan's enormous international trade surplus has enabled her to win the title of "economic superpower".

Table 8.2

Japan's International Balance of Payments (1991–1992)

	Balance with all countries		Balance with US		Balance with EC	
	1991	1992	1991	1992	1991	1992
Current balance	72.9	117.6	40.0	44.5	25.2	37.4
Balance of trade	103.0	132.3	43.4	50.2	33.4	39.4
Balance of trade in non-material goods and services	–17.7	–10.1	–2.7	–4.8	–8.0	–1.9

(Unit: US$ billion)

Source: *Same as Table 8.1.*

Table 8.3 compares the external assets and liabilities of Japan and the US. The total assets of Japan and the US do not differ much over the 1991–1992 period. However, the total liabilities of the two countries differ substantially.

Table 8.3

External Assets and Liabilities (Japan and the US)

(Unit: US$ billion)

	Japan		US	
	End of 1991	End 1992	End 1991	End 1992
Total Assets	2,006.5	2,035.2	1998.4	2,003.4
Direct investments	231.8	248.1	655.3	666.3
Securities	632.1	655.5	294.2	327.4
Total Liabilities	1,623.4	1521.6	2,363.2	2,524.7
Net Assets	383.1	513.6	–364.9	–521.3

Source: *Same as Table 8.1.*

As a result, by the end of 1992, Japan had net assets of US$513.6 billion while the US had net liabilities of US$521.3 billion. These figures indicate the strength of the Japanese economy and the weakness of the US economy. Internationally, Japan has become one of the largest creditor nations, while the US has become the largest debtor nation.

By looking at Japanese per capita GNP, its international trade surplus and net assets, it is clear that Japan is one of the most affluent nations in the world. Its affluence is also demonstrated by the level of disposable income and savings of the Japanese people. Table 8.4 shows that the disposable income of an individual Japanese was nearly 2.4 million yen in 1991. It was the highest among the industrialized countries, and probably the highest in the world. This is also reflected in its high savings rate.

Table 8.4

Disposable Income and Savings in Selected Countries (1991)

(Unit: ¥1000)

Country	Disposable Income	Savings	
Japan	2389	357	(15.0)
US	2159	105	(4.9)
Germany	2076	278	(13.4)
France	1942	250	(12.8)
UK	1611	92	(5.7)
Italy	1956	305	(15.6)
Canada	1998	213	(10.7)

Note: *Figures in parentheses indicate savings rates.*
Source: *Compiled from Nihon Ginko Kokusai-Kyoku [Bank of Japan, International Bureau]*
Gaikoku Keizai Tōkei Nenpo [Annual Report on Foreign Economic Statistics], (Japan, December 1993), p. 28.

Myth and Reality

Japan is no doubt a rich and industrially advanced country. However, the living standard of the Japanese people is not high in comparison with Western countries. As mentioned earlier, Japanese disposable income is the highest among the industrial countries. However, commodity prices are also high compared to those in the West. In 1990, the hourly wages of employees in Japan and the US were ¥2,164.7 and ¥1,452.2 respectively. The former was 1.5 times that of the latter. However, average wages in Japan in 1990 were ¥1563.8 an hour, or about equal to those in the US.[1] In fact, commodity prices in Japan are much higher than one would expect. If we look at Table 8.5, gasoline in Tokyo costs 3.2 times more. In the case of rice, the ratio is 3.8:1.

Most Japanese, after working all their lives, find it difficult to purchase a house in any of the big cities such as Tokyo, Osaka, Yokohama or Nagoya. Land and property prices in Japan are extremely high. The price of a new home in Japan costs 5.7 times the annual salary of an average company employee, compared to 3.5 times in the US. If Tokyo is compared with the most expensive northeastern part of the US, the ratio becomes 8.5:4.0.[2]

Table 8.5

A Comparison between Commodity Prices in Japan and the US

(Unit: US$)

Commodity	Tokyo	New York
10 kilograms rice	48.90	13.00
100 grams beef	4.50	1.75
1 litre milk	1.98	0.90
1 can Coca-Cola	1.05	0.75
1 can Budweiser	2.20	0.89
1 litre reg. gasoline	1.26	0.40
Taxi flagfall	6.00	1.50
1 Sony TR1 camcorder (with accessories)	1,450.00	1,030.00

Note: *As of 1 September 1993, when 100 yen = US$1*
Source: Far Eastern Economic Review, *5 May 1994.*

More and more Japanese company employees, especially the younger staff, feel frustrated by this and, as a result, are becoming less enthusiastic about their work. In general, they are less loyal and less hardworking than their seniors: they tend to job-hop and look for better career advancement. It is not surprising then that life-time employment and the seniority system in Japan are now rapidly losing popularity. The government and the business community are concerned about the work attitude of the younger generation. As a result, improving the quality of life in Japan (*seikatsu taikoku*) became an important policy of the previous Miyazawa Administration. The Japanese government disclosed the Five-Year Economic Plan in 1992 which aimed to reduce the price of a new home in the big cities in Japan to 5 times the annual salary of an average company employee. At about the same time, an increasing number of Japanese companies began to invest in building dormitories and residential housing for employees. Employees, who were loyal and committed themselves to the company, were entitled to free houses (or houses at reasonable prices) when they retired.

These efforts, however, were in vain. The intense power struggle and the split of the LDP forced Miyazawa to dissolve his Cabinet in

1993. The new coalition government under Hosokawa Morihiro was kept busy fulfilling the long-awaited political and tax reforms. Furthermore, he had to pay more attention to stimulating the domestic economy and to easing trade frictions, especially with the US. The Hosokawa Cabinet collapsed in April 1994 as a result of alleged scandals and the split among his coalition party members. The Hosokawa Administration was taken over by the minority government under Hata Tsutomu, without serious attention being given to solving the housing problems or to improving the living standard of the Japanese people.

Housing problems still remain unsolved. Japanese companies have seen hard times since the collapse of the "bubble economy" in 1989, and therefore are not in a position to improve the living conditions of their employees. Land and property prices have not dropped drastically despite the sustained sluggishness of the economy. Most Japanese in cities are still living in "rabbit hutches". They are unable to own homes despite having, by international standards, high disposable income and high savings.

As mentioned earlier, the high disposable income of the Japanese is essentially offset by high commodity prices. The phenomenal appreciation of the yen since September 1985 has benefited Japanese consumers. However, cheaper prices are restricted to certain commodities. Generally, commodity prices in Japan remain high, if not the highest, among the industrialized nations.

In Japan, high savings do not necessarily reflect real economic well-being for the Japanese people. One should note that the Japanese are generally very thrifty. They have to save but not because they can afford to keep some money in the banks. It is because they live in society with many uncertainties and therefore need to save for the education of their children, medical expenses, wedding ceremonies, old age, etc. Japan can be said to be the world's most expensive country in which to live.

Since everything is expensive in Japan, the Japanese have to work longer hours in order to increase their income. It is argued that the Japanese are inefficient compared with their Western counterparts and thus have to work longer hours, or, that they work longer hours and in the end become inefficient. However, the main concern here is to compare the working hours of the Japanese and the Americans.

The latest statistics show that in 1990, the working hours of the Japanese and the Americans were 2,052 per annum and 1,799 per annum respectively. Thus, the Japanese work 253 hours more than their American counterparts despite the fact that, over the last ten years, Japanese working hours have decreased by about 45 hours. A substantial part of salary is derived from overtime in Japan. Overtime has been cut because of the present economic stagnation. Consequently, Japanese workers have received less and less pay over the last few years.

As a result, the Japanese are becoming more cautious in spending their money. This explains why domestic consumption activities have slowed down, despite the strong yen and despite the consequent reduction in commodity prices in Japan.

Economic Superpower and International Roles

Although Japan is regarded as an economic superpower, the quality of life of the Japanese is unsatisfactory and living conditions are poor. Some people have been inclined to comment that "Japan is rich but the Japanese are poor". This argument is somewhat ambiguous as the Japanese government has been running fiscal deficits. However, if one identifies the Japanese government as synonymous with the big enterprises, one can be forgiven for saying that "Japan is a rich country" because the big enterprises are rich and strong.

Japan is seen to be rich because millions of Japanese are working day and night and have made tremendous contributions to the Japanese economy. The Japanese economy is strong because it has thousands of big enterprises supported by millions of small and medium-sized enterprises. The *Keiretsu* (the systemization of enterprises) has gained a good reputation for Japan as the only "economic superpower" in Asia.

What international roles can Japan play as an economic superpower? The following discussion will focus on Japan's economic, political, diplomatic and military roles.

Economic Role

Japan's economic role can be divided into three parts: international trade, foreign direct investment (FDI) and official development assistance (ODA). Technology transfer and transfer of managerial know-how can be included when we examine Japanese FDI and ODA.

Japan's international trade with the US, the EC and Asia has been in Japan's favour. Japan's trade surplus has been increasing. Her economic conflict and trade friction with the US have particularly attracted attention. The US, together with the EC, forced Japan to increase her currency value in September 1985. This was aimed at restricting Japan's exports to the Western nations. The Japanese currency has since then been maintained at a high level. Despite some fluctuations, the currency has grown stronger and stronger. The currency ratio was US$1: ¥240 just before the G5 meeting in September 1985. The ratio has increased to US$1: ¥99.9 (18 January 1995).

Export industries (especially automobiles, electronics and electrical products and machinery, etc.) have suffered from the strong yen. However, contrary to Western nations' expectations, the strong yen has had a limited impact on curtailing Japan's exports. Through industrial restructuring, mechanization and the rationalization of management, Japanese manufacturers have managed to maintain their international competitiveness. On the other hand, in order to benefit from the strong yen, Japanese manufacturers increased their foreign direct investment forcefully over the 1986–1990 period before the collapse of the "bubble economy" in 1991.

The US, the EC and Asia have large trade deficits with Japan. Japan needs to work on expanding her domestic consumption and stimulating imports from overseas. She is gradually opening up her market but still has a strong "closed-market" nature, as claimed by Asia and the Western nations. Non-tariff barriers and complex distribution systems have especially restricted imports from overseas. Making use of the strong yen to import manufacturing products from overseas would kill two birds with one stone: it would alleviate trade frictions with trading partners as well as increase the quality of life in Japan. These important tasks have been put forward to the policy-makers under the present Murayama Administration.

Japan's foreign direct investment has slowed down since 1991. Asia, as a "detour production base" for Japanese enterprises which sought to explore the international markets in order to alleviate economic conflicts between Japan and Western nations, absorbed substantial investments from Japan during the 1986–1990 period. The newly industrializing economies (NIEs) in particular have successfully transformed themselves from import-substitution activities to export-oriented activities. The member countries of ASEAN have become more outward-looking and have moved towards export-oriented activities. China and Vietnam are also carrying out economic reform policies to attract foreign investments so as to speed up the economic development process. Asian nations have also been seen by Japanese manufacturers as attractive investment locations.

Japan's FDI in the US and the EC has always played an important role in Japan's industrial internationalization process. The Western nations have big domestic markets. Besides the phenomenal appreciation of the yen, the protectionist tendency (EC economic integration and the setting up of the North American Free Trade Agreement) has also prompted Japan to invest in Western nations. This is, of course, also aimed at reducing Japan's economic trade surplus with the US and the EC.

The "reverse imports" (*gyaku yunyu*) phenomenon has also been stimulated by Japan's immense overseas investment. Despite moving to open up her markets and import more from overseas, Japan has not satisfactorily rectified her lop-sided trade relationship with the West. The Western nations have become impatient and have even threatened to break the GATT agreement in order to force Japan to import a fixed quantity of manufactured goods from the West in general, and the US in particular (the so-called numerical trade). The West has also found it difficult to invest in Japan. Commercial practices in Japan are complex, and tenders are made illegally through "*dango*" (arrangement through consultation) between big enterprises and government bureaucrats. These are some of the major issues the Japanese government has to examine in order to rectify the estranged economic relationship between Japan and the West.

The "reverse imports" from Asia into the Japanese market have also been increasing. Most Asian countries are, however, suffering from trade deficits with Japan. Moreover, trade relationships between Japan and Asia have remained "vertical", that is, the Japanese export manufactured products to Asia, and import industrial and agricultural raw materials from Asia. In recent years, exports of manufactured products from Asia to Japan have increased steadily, but the trade relationship will require some time to shift from "vertical" to "horizontal". In 1992, the ODA provided by Japan was US$11.15 billion (excluding that for Eastern European countries) exceeding that of the US (US$10.76 billion) and Germany (US$7.59 billion). Japanese ODA can be divided into two parts: bilateral assistance (74.9 per cent) (including uncompensated financial assistance) and those directed towards international organizations (25.1 per cent). In the same year, the breakdown of the distribution of Japan's bilateral ODA by field is as follows: (a) social infrastructure (17.5 per cent) (including education, health, water supply, sanitation, population, etc.), (b) economic infrastructure (27.3 per cent) (including transportation, communications, riparian development, energy, etc.), (c) production sector (27.0 per cent) (including agriculture, industry, construction, trade, etc.), (d) multisector (1.1 per cent) and (f) others (27.1 per cent) (including structural adjustments, commodity loans, debt relief, etc.).[3]

Asia has been Japan's largest ODA recipient. Japan's bilateral ODA to Asia increased by 2.6 times, from US$1.73 billion in 1985 to US$4.52 billion in 1991. Asia constituted 51 per cent of Japan's total bilateral ODA in 1991. Over the 1987–1991 period, the top six recipients of Japan's ODA were Indonesia (US$4.77 billion; representing 13.9 per cent of the total), China (US$3.37 billion or 9.8 per cent), the Philippines (US$2.42 billion or 7.1 per cent), Thailand

(US$1.98 billion or 5.8 per cent), India (US$1.72 billion or 5.0 per cent) and Bangladesh (US$1.54 billion or 4.5 per cent).[4] Undoubtedly, through Japanese ODA, Asia has managed to improve its social and economic infrastructure, and production sector greatly. Through utilizing Japanese ODA and DFI, Asia has benefited from the transfer of technology and managerial know-how from Japan.

Japan has undoubtedly contributed greatly to Asia's economic development. Without Japanese capital, technology and managerial know-how, the industrialization and modernization process in Asia would have been much slower. Japan's contribution will continue to be an important pull-factor, if not indispensable factor, in the rapid economic development of Asia and in the world.

Nevertheless, there are some shortcomings to Japan's economic contribution. Many people, including academics, entrepreneurs and government officials, argue that the Japanese are reluctant to transfer technology, that the Japanese are too calculating when they invest overseas, and that Japan's ODA is too Japan-centred and inflexible. Japan should pay serious attention to these grievances and criticisms and make continuous efforts to build up cordial economic relations with the rest of the world.

Political and Diplomatic Roles

It is said, with cynicism, that Japan is "an economic giant but a political dwarf". In general, in the international arena, a country which is strong economically also has strong political and diplomatic influence. In contrast, the US, which has changed from the largest creditor nation to the largest debtor nation, still maintains its superpower status. It is the only superpower which has influence in all areas — economic, political, diplomatic and military.

It is also interesting to note that China is just the opposite of Japan. In this sense, China is also a rare exception. It is the only developing country which does not have much economic power, but one cannot disregard its political, diplomatic and military influence.

China's economic development has been significant since the introduction of economic reform in 1979. After a decade or two, China is likely to become, at least, a medium-sized economic power equipped with political, diplomatic and military strengths.

The USSR has been torn apart. The CIS will never be able to restore it again. The former Soviet Union was a superpower with tremendous political, diplomatic and military influence, although her centrally-planned economy had been deteriorating for some time: She has now lost almost everything, and no one can predict her future development with confidence.

The main concern is thus Japan. The US, China and the former Soviet Union have been changing quite rapidly. Under these new circumstances, will Japan continue to be "an economic giant but a political dwarf"?

Japan is expected to have more say on international issues as a result other economic strength. In other words, it is quite natural for Japan to wield political and diplomatic influence commensurate with her economic strength. Presently, the cold war structure has collapsed. The influence of the former Soviet Union in the Asia–Pacific region has receded. No single nation is able to fill this vacuum nor would it be welcomed by the developing countries in Asia. The Asia–Pacific region has hopes that a balance can be maintained by powers such as the US, China, Japan and India. Japan is hoping to be elected as a permanent member of the Security Council of the United Nations. It will, therefore, have more say in international affairs in general, and in affairs in the Asia–Pacific region in particular. Presently, the outcome is unpredictable.

On the domestic scene, Japanese politics have long been contentious. Scandals, factional infighting and power struggles have consumed much of the politicians' energy. The political leadership and the premiership have seen constant changes. The government leadership is extremely vulnerable and inefficient. The country is thus left to the well-trained bureaucrats. The bureaucrats are good at administrative work but do not have political power. In the international arena, the Japanese stand on views expressed by the politicians are, in most cases, not taken seriously.

Japan's weak political and diplomatic position is not only due to weak leadership. It also been argued that Japan does not really have an independent political and diplomatic stand. Japan's policies toward international affairs have been very much influenced by the US. Of course, there are some spectacular exceptions. For example, the previous Tanaka Kakuei Administration established diplomatic relations with China in 1972, which surprised the American government; the former Prime Minister Hosokawa Morihiro also did not concede to the Clinton government when he visited the US in February 1994, when the latter urged Japan to open up her markets in order to effectively rectify trade imbalance.

Before Japan can gain an influential position in the international political arena, she needs drastic political reform in order to select a clean administration staffed with effective and powerful politicians. As an economic superpower and a highly industrialized nation, Japan cannot afford to have numerous small parties without a centripetal force. The everlasting factional infighting will further weaken the role of the government, as well as the political and diplomatic roles played by Japan in the international arena.

Military Role

The Minister of Justice, Nagano Shigeto, was forced to resign on 7 May 1994. The reason for the resignation was that he made a statement denying that the "Rape of Nanking" occurred in December 1937 in China. He said the "Rape of Nanking" was a "fabrication". In fact, before Nagano, two other Japanese Cabinet members were also forced to resign from their ministerial posts for making statements denying Japan's responsibilities during World War II. Other politicians, such as the influential figure of LDP, Ishihara Shintaro, had also described the "Rape of Nanking" as a "fabrication", just before Nagano made his statement. Ishihara's statement had, of course, gained some sympathy among the Japanese, but as can be expected, it had also received strong protests and criticism from Asia in general, and from

China and Korea in particular. Ishihara, however, was not a minister, and so he was not asked to resign from any post. Recently, Ishihara made a proposal to the previous Hata Administration, to form a joint investigation mission to look into the number of Chinese people killed by the Japanese soldiers during the Japanese military occupation in Nanking in 1937. The Chinese claimed that the number of the people killed by the Japanese soldiers amounted to 300,000–360,000, but some Japanese have said that it was only 5,000. The Hata government, as did the former Hosokawa government, apologized for the Japanese military incursion into China and rejected Ishihara's suggestion, since it would jeopardize Japan's relations with China.

Likewise, there are some perception gaps among the Japanese, and between Japan and Asia, pertaining to the Japanese military expansion in Asia in the 1930s and 1940s. The Asian countries are particularly cautious about Japanese political and military moves. This is basically due to two reasons: first, the Asian countries suffered tremendously from Japanese military expansion during World War II; second, Japan has been either reluctant or unwilling to admit to the damage caused to the Asian people by her military expansion during World War II.

During the war between Iraq and Kuwait, as a result of the US demand through the United Nations, Japan was asked to send troops, and make a US$15 billion contribution, to fight against Iraq. Japan was reluctant at first to send troops or to make a speedy contribution to assist the Allied Forces. The Japanese Constitution Bill No. 9 prohibits Japan from sending its self-defence forces overseas. Japan had to amend the Constitution or to approve the PKO (peace keeping operations) Bill in order to send troops to Kuwait. The Japanese government under Kaifu Toshiki at the time needed not only the understanding and support of the Japanese, but also of the Asian countries. After a long discussion, which did not reach any consensus, the Japanese government passed the PKO Bill by force. At the same time, the Japanese government sent delegates to the Asian countries to explain Japan's policy toward the Iraqi invasion of Kuwait. Governments in the ASEAN countries, with some reservations, supported Japan's stand. On this issue, there was a distinct perception gap between the Japanese and the Asian mass media. The Japanese mass media provided the Japanese readers with a strong impression that the Asian countries had fully supported Japan to send troops to Kuwait. However, a careful reading of the newspapers and magazines published in Asia at that time reveals that Asian countries expressed their understanding of Japan's stand, but had reservations about Japan sending troops to Kuwait. The Asian people in general had strong feelings against the despatch of Japan's self-defence forces to Kuwait.

There is a consensus amongst the Asian countries that Japan should play a more important international role but without sending troops overseas. Japan has already made some outstanding contributions to the world. Japanese non-military personnel, such as medical staff and overseas youth co-operation groups, have been sent to various countries. Japan's contribution to the peaceful solution in Kampuchea has earned her high praise and its economic sanctions against South Africa's apartheid policies were appreciated. Material assistance (foodstuffs, clothing and medical products, etc.) from Japan to thousands of refugees in the Middle Eastern countries has also been well-received. Thus Japan can play a more positive role towards world peace and development.

Conclusion

The quality of life of the Japanese does not compare well with Japan's economic strength. The strong Japanese currency can be used to stimulate Japan's domestic consumption and the importation of manufactured goods from overseas. The quality of life in Japan could be improved considerably if cheaper manufactured goods were available in the country. Japan should strengthen its economic relations through trade, investment and development aid, particularly with the Asia–Pacific region. Japanese capital, technology and managerial know-how are useful for the rapid economic development of the Asia–Pacific region. Japan can in return benefit from the economic advancement and prosperity of the region.

As an economic superpower, Japan is expected to make an important contribution to the world. However, Asian countries are particularly cautious of Japan's political and military ambitions essentially because of its past military expansion in the 1930s and 1940s, and its unwillingness to admit to the atrocities carried out during its military occupation in the region. Japan should, therefore, minimize its political and military roles but needs to increase its contribution in other areas. It is to Japan's benefit to maximize its economic and diplomatic roles in order to make distinct contributions to the world's economic development in general, and to the Asia–Pacific region in particular.

Notes

1 JETRO, US and Japan in Figures, (Japan, November 1992), p. 8.
2 Ibid, p. 31.
3 See JETRO, (Japan, 1994), pp. 82–83.
4 Kaigai Keizai Kyoryoku Kikin [The Foundation of Overseas Economic Co-operation], *Kaigai Keizai Kyoryoku Binran* [Annual Report on Overseas Economic Co-operation], (Japan, 1993), pp. 7 & 15.

CHAPTER 9

Japan's ODA and Economic Performance in Asia

Introduction

Japan experienced 0.7 per cent GDP growth rate in 1994 and 1.9 per cent in 1995. During the same period, GDP growth rates for China were 11.0 per cent and 8.5 per cent; for ASEAN (excluding Singapore) they were 7.1 per cent and 7.4 per cent (Indonesia's were 7.0 per cent and 7.2 per cent) and for the NIEs they were 7.4 per cent and 7.0 per cent (Singapore's were 10.0 per cent and 8.5 per cent). Obviously, Japan's GDP growth rates have been much lower than other countries in Asia. The Japanese economy has not shown strong recovery since the collapse of the "bubble economy" in 1991. Earlier this year, the Japanese economy was widely expected to recover with some sort of stamina, but statistics just released show that Japan suffered –2.9 per cent GDP growth in April–June 1996.[1] In the meantime, Japan watchers are unable to predict the Japanese economy with optimism and confidence. One of the detrimental reasons for Japan's sluggish economic performance was seen to be due to the drastic appreciation of the Japanese currency. The Japanese yen appreciated from 242 per US dollar in September 1985 (just before the G5 meeting) to 100 in June 1994, and later to 80 in May 1995. Japanese export industries (automobiles, electronics, electrical and machinery industries in particular) suffered seriously. Japanese industries were forced to invest overseas and to increase imports especially from Asia. In the meantime (12 September 1996), Japanese currency depreciated and reached the level of 110 per US dollar. The Japanese economy, especially Japanese export industries, should now benefit from the depreciation of the yen. Yet, it is hard to say that Japan will soon bring its sluggish economic deadlock to an end.

Nevertheless, despite all these negative images of Japan, Japan still qualifies as an economic giant. There are some indicators to show that Japan is still economically strong. For instance, Japan's trade surplus increased from US$69.86 billion in 1990 to US$144.37 billion in 1994. During the same period, Japan's current balance increased from US$33.72 billion to US$124.28 billion, foreign reserves from US$69.89 billion to US$141.2 billion, net assets abroad from US$328.06 billion to US$688.97 billion, GDP from US$2,957.9 billion to US$4,590.9 billion, and per capita national income from US$18,979.2 to US$29,165.4. Japan is therefore expected to make greater contribution through official development assistance (ODA), to the rest of the world.

Japan's ODA disbursement to developing countries and less developed countries has been a controversial issue.[2] Does Japan's ODA disbursement really contribute to social and economic development of the recipient countries? How can the abuses of Japan's ODA disbursement be avoided? Why should a Japanese contribute more than ¥10,000 (Japanese population was 125.5 million and Japan's ODA disbursement was ¥1.38 trillion in 1995) to help other countries when the quality of life (for instance, housing and welfare facilities) in Japan is still low compared to other industrialized countries? These are some questions commonly raised by the Japanese populace.

This chapter attempts to examine closely Japan's ODA disbursement to China, Indonesia and Singapore, China and Indonesia having been important recipient countries of Japan's ODA. China's introduction of a "socialist market economy" since 1979 required a substantial amount of foreign aid especially from Japan. On the other hand, among the ASEAN countries, Indonesia received the largest ODA disbursement from Japan due to its country's size, and partly to its keen desire to speed up the construction of its social and economic infrastructures. As for Singapore, since it has become an advanced developing country, Japan's ODA disbursement has become almost non-existent. Technical cooperation between Singapore and Japan, and the joint efforts of these two countries to assist other developing countries have instead increased dramatically.

This chapter also attempts to examine some important issues related to the ODA disbursement to these countries. These issues include China's nuclear test and Japan's reactions, both the positive and negative effects of Japan's ODA, and the immense debt accumulation due to the drastic appreciation of the yen. There are numerous obstacles laid between Japan and Japan's ODA recipient countries. These obstacles must be cleared in time in order to create a healthy and mutually beneficial relationship between the donor and the recipient countries.

Characteristics of Japan's ODA

Japan's ODA in the World

Japan's ODA is divided into bilateral aid and subscriptions and contributions to international organizations. Bilateral aid is further divided into grants (grant aid and technical cooperation) and ODA loans (project loans, non-project loans and debt rescheduling), which are shown in Figure 9.1.

In recent years, most of the industrialized countries have had difficulties in increasing their ODA budge due to sluggish economic performances and tight fiscal constraints Figure 9.2 shows the trends of major DAC (Development Assistance Committee of the OECD) countries' ODA over the period 1987–1996. The ODA budgets of the US and Italy declined during the period 1992–1995. Japan's ODA has shown steady improvement since 1989 but dropped in 1997. (Japan was the largest ODA disbursement country in the world during the period 1991–1997.) Despite the long-standing stagnation of the economy since March 1991 and the need to rehabilitate the areas struck by the great Hanshin–Awaji earthquake in January 1995, Japan's ODA budget increased from US$13.46 billion in 1994 to US$ 14.72 billion in 1995 but dropped to US$9.43 billion in 1997.

Figure 9.1
ODA Category

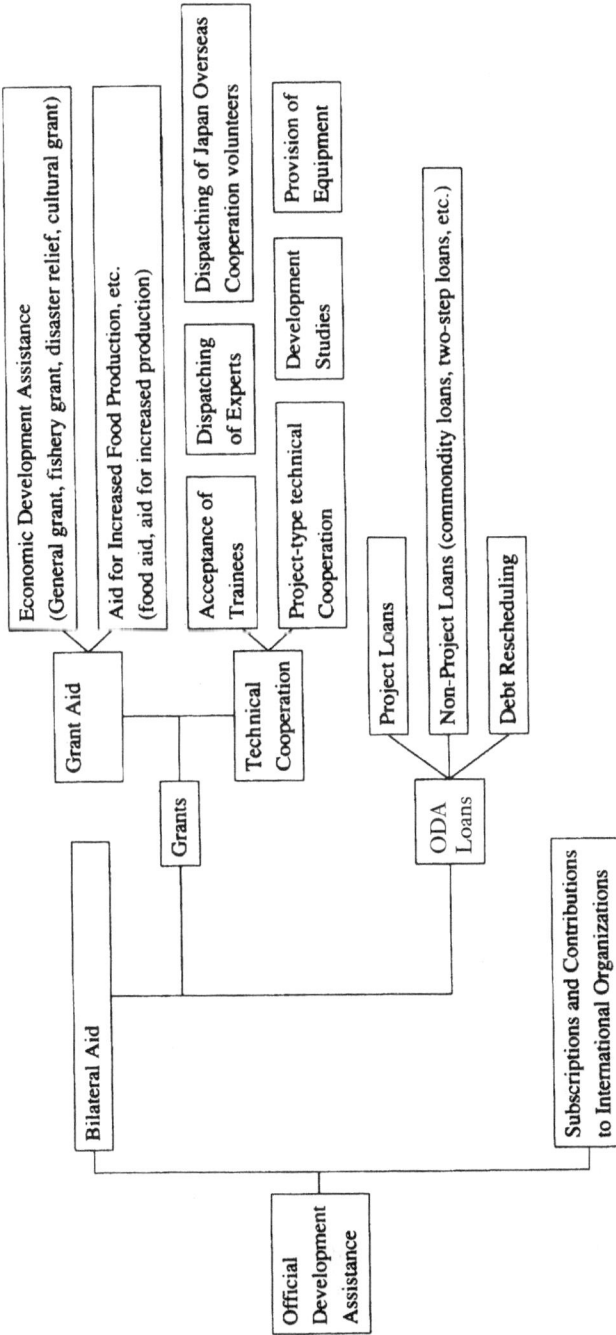

Source: *Ministry of Foreign Affairs, Japan's ODA Annual Report, Tokyo, various issues*

Figure 9.2

Trends in Major DAC Countries' ODA (Net Disbursement Basis)

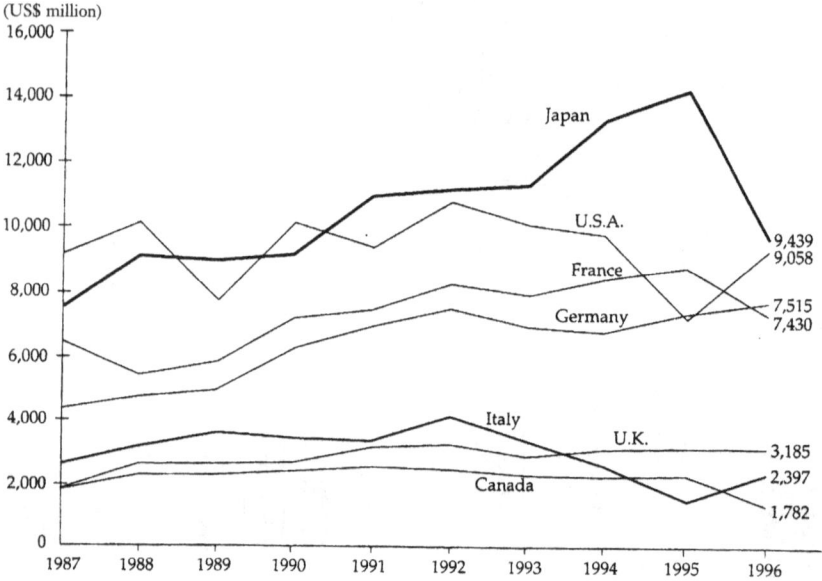

Note: *Excluding aid to Eastern Europe.*
Source: *Ministry of Foreign Affairs, op. cit.*

On 29 July 1996, the tripartite ruling alliance in Japan discussed a new budget for the ODA disbursement the following year. The Japanese government (The Liberal Democratic Party and the Ministry of Foreign Affairs) had taken the recent weakening yen into consideration, and demanded a 3.5 per cent ODA increase at the Japanese tripartite ruling coalition meeting in Tokyo. However, the Social Democratic Party (the second largest party in the coalition) opposed the 3.5 per cent increase and insisted on a 2.5 per cent increase instead. The party felt that Japan's ODA should shift from emphasizing "quantity" to "quality". (This is seen to be a reflection of the common sentiment of the Japanese people.) The ODA budget for the year 1997 was concluded at a 2.6 per cent increase (compared to the previous year) after lengthy discussions.[3]

Figure 9.3   **ODA of DAC Countries**

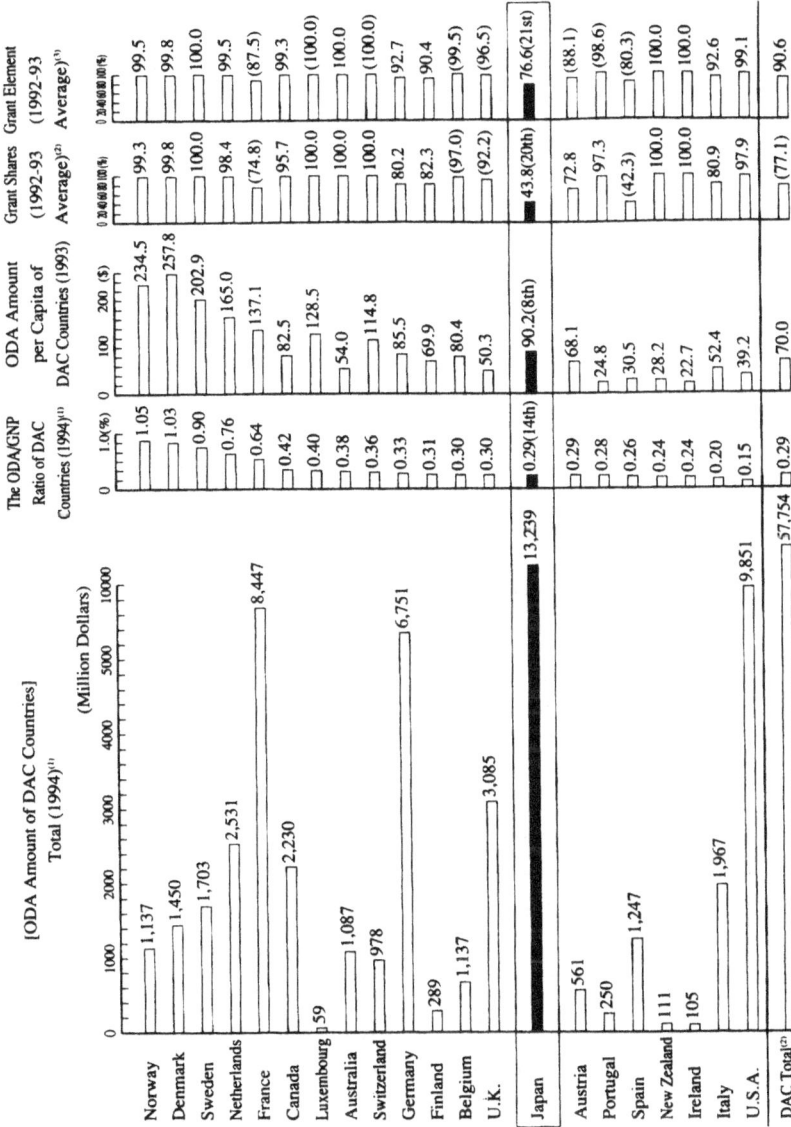

Country	ODA Amount of DAC Countries Total (1994)[1] (Million Dollars)	The ODA/GNP Ratio of DAC Countries (1994)[1] (%)	ODA Amount per Capita of DAC Countries (1993) ($)	Grant Shares (1992-93 Average)[2] (%)	Grant Element (1992-93 Average)[3] (%)
Norway	1,137	1.05	234.5	99.3	99.5
Denmark	1,450	1.03	257.8	99.8	99.8
Sweden	1,703	0.90	202.9	100.0	100.0
Netherlands	2,531	0.76	165.0	98.4	99.5
France	8,447	0.64	137.1	(74.8)	(87.5)
Canada	2,230	0.42	82.5	95.7	99.3
Luxembourg	59	0.40	128.5	100.0	(100.0)
Australia	1,087	0.38	54.0	100.0	100.0
Switzerland	978	0.36	114.8	100.0	(100.0)
Germany	6,751	0.33	85.5	80.2	92.7
Finland	289	0.31	69.9	82.3	90.4
Belgium	1,137	0.30	80.4	(97.0)	(99.5)
U.K.	3,085	0.30	50.3	(92.2)	(96.5)
Japan	13,239	0.29(14th)	90.2(8th)	43.8(20th)	76.6(21st)
Austria	561	0.29	68.1	72.8	(88.1)
Portugal	250	0.28	24.8	97.3	(98.6)
Spain	1,247	0.26	30.5	(42.3)	(80.3)
New Zealand	111	0.24	28.2	100.0	100.0
Ireland	105	0.24	22.7	100.0	100.0
Italy	1,967	0.20	52.4	80.9	92.6
U.S.A.	9,851	0.15	39.2	97.9	99.1
DAC Total[2]	57,754	0.29	70.0	(77.1)	90.6

(1) Except for Japan, ODA figures for 1993 are provisional (excluding aid for Eastern Europe). (2) DAC total excludes U.S. military debt forgiveness (3) Excluding debt relief ( ) Figures in parentheses are DAC secretarial estimates.

Sources: *Ministry of Foreign Affairs, op. cit.*

DAC's total aid increased by merely 0.1 per cent to US$59.2 billion in 1995 compared to the year 1994. The ODA extended by the US and Italy decreased by 26.4 per cent and 43.8 per cent respectively during the same period. Japan's ODA increased by 9.4 per cent in 1995 over the previous year. Japan's ODA disbursement accounted for 22.9 per cent in 1994 and 24.5 per cent in 1995 of the total amount of aid given by DAC countries. In 1995, Japan's ODA was 1.7 times that of France and approximately 2 times that of Germany and the US.[4]

However, Japan's ODA in 1995 accounted for 0.28 per cent of the gross national product, down from 0.29 per cent in 1994.[5] In 1994, the ODA/GNP ratio of Japan ranked 14th among the 21 DAC countries (see Fig. 9.3). Japan should contribute more towards its ODA in relation to the size of its gross national product. Figure 9.3 also shows that in 1993, the ODA amount per capita of Japan amounted to merely US$90.2 which ranked 8th among DAC countries.

The nature or the quality of Japan's ODA programmes has always been contentious. Japan's grant shares[6] and grant element[7] have long been below the DAC average. In 1994, Japan's grant share increased to 52.4 per cent, up from the 1992–1993 average of 43.8 per cent (the DAC average was 77.1 per cent during the same period. Japan ranked 20th among the DAC countries). Its grant element also rose to 80.6 per cent in 1994, up from the 1992–1993 average of 76.6 per cent (the DAC average was 90.6 per cent. Japan ranked 21st among the DAC countries)[8]. There is no doubt that Japan should improve the quality of its ODA in the future.

Regional Distribution of Japan's Bilateral ODA

Due to close cultural, historical, geographical, political and economic relationships, Japan's bilateral ODA has been concentrated in Asia. Asian countries, particularly the NIEs (newly industrializing economies) and ASEAN (Association of Southeast Asian Nations), have succeeded in rapid economic development until the so-called financial and economic crisis erupted in July 1997. However, Asian

Table 9.1

Ten Major Recipient Countries of Japan's Bilateral ODA

(Net disbursement basis; US$ million)

Rank	1994 Country	Amount	1995 Country	Amount	1996 Country	Amount
1	China	1,479.41	China	1,380.15	Indonesia	965.53
2	India	886.53	Indonesia	892.43	China	861.73
3	Indonesia	886.17	Thailand	667.37	Thailand	664.00
4	Philippines	591.60	India	506.42	India	579.26
5	Thailand	382.55	Philippines	416.13	Philippines	414.45
6	Syria	330.03	Mexico	288.29	Pakistan	282.20
7	Pakistan	271.04	Sri Lanka	263.70	Mexico	212.84
8	Bangladesh	227.60	Bangladesh	254.89	Egypt	201.32
9	Sri Lanka	213.75	Egypt	242.75	Bangladesh	174.03
10	Egypt	188.99	Pakistan	241.03	Sri Lanka	173.94
	Total above 10	5,457.68	Total above 10	5,153.15	Total above 10	4,529.30
	Bilateral Aid Total	9,680.48	Bilateral Aid Total	10,557.06	Bilateral Aid Total	8,356.26

Source: *Ministry of Foreign Affairs, op. cit.*

countries are expected to regain high economic growth rates from the beginning of the 21st century. Asia's social and economic developments will therefore require substantial amounts of ODA from Japan in the years to come.

Table 9.1 shows the geographical distribution of Japan's bilateral ODA over the 1980–1994 period. Asian countries have been the main recipients of Japan's bilateral ODA. As early as 1970, 98.2 per cent of Japan's bilateral ODA was directed to Asia. It dropped to 70.5 per cent a decade later in 1980. Japan's bilateral ODA has since been redirected to the Middle East, Africa, Central and South America. In 1996, 49.6 per cent (US$4.14 billion) of Japan's ODA was allocated to Asia.

Among Asian countries, ASEAN received 35.8 per cent of Japan's bilateral ODA in 1980. ASEAN's share dipped to 20.3 per cent (of which Indonesia accounted for 11.5 per cent) in 1996. In contrast, Northeast Asia's share increased remarkably from merely 4.2 per cent

Table 9.2

Distribution of Aid by Form to the Ten Largest Recipient Countries of Japan's Bilateral ODA

(On a net payment basis; US$ million, %)

		1994				
Rank	Country	Amount	%	Breakdown Grant Aid	Technical Cooperation	Loans
1	China	1,479.41	15.28	99.42	246.91	1,133.07
2	India	886.53	9.16	34.64	23.61	828.28
3	Indonesia	886.17	9.15	72.28	177.69	636.20
4	Philippines	591.60	6.11	138.41	110.41	342.78
5	Thailand	382.55	3.95	27.36	137.36	217.84
6	Syria	330.03	3.41	16.53	8.57	304.93
7	Pakistan	271.04	2.80	50.72	19.44	200.88
8	Bangladesh	227.60	2.35	204.71	35.93	−13.05
9	Sri Lanka	213.75	2.21	53.59	27.51	132.66
10	Egypt	188.99	1.95	129.51	20.85	38.63
	10 country total	5,457.67	56.37	827.17	808.28	3,822.22
	Worldwide Total	9,680.48	100.0	2,402.90	3,020.31	4,257.27

Source: *Ministry of Foreign Affairs, op. cit.*

to 10.4 per cent (of which China's share was 10.3 per cent) during the same period. China opened up her markets in 1990 and that required huge amounts of foreign direct investment as well as ODA from industrialized countries, especially from Japan. China alone absorbed almost 100 per cent of Japan's bilateral ODA extended to Northeast Asia in 1996.

As mentioned earlier, China and Indonesia were the largest recipients of Japan's bilateral ODA in Northeast Asia and Southeast Asia (ASEAN) respectively, in 1996. In recent years, China and Indonesia have been the leading countries in the top 10 recipients of Japan's bilateral ODA. In 1992, there were 9 Asian countries among the top 10 largest recipients of Japan's bilateral aid. The figure was 8 in 1994, 1995 and 1996 (see Table 9.1). China and Indonesia combined received US$2.41 billion (28.4 per cent) of Japan's bilateral ODA in 1992, US$2.36 billion (24.4 per cent) in 1994, US$2.27 billion (21.5 per cent) in 1995 and US$1.83 billion (21.9 per cent) in 1996. Japan has therefore played an important role in the social and economic developments of China and Indonesia.

As expected, in bilateral ODA, loans are always larger than technical cooperation and grant aid. In 1994, loans extended by Japan to China were 11.4 times as large as grant aid, and 4.6 times as large as technical cooperation. Furthermore, loans extended by Japan to Indonesia were 8.8 times as large as grant aid, and 3.6 times as large as technical cooperation (see Table 9.2).

Japan's ODA to China

Among the DAC countries, Japan was China's largest ODA donor over the 1991–1995 period. Japan's ODA disbursement to China overwhelmed all DAC countries such as France, Germany, Italy, Spain and Australia. Japan's ODA disbursement to China increased substantially from US$585 million (46.7 per cent of DAC countries) in 1991 to US$1.38 billion (54.5 per cent of DAC countries) in 1995 (see Table 9.3). Japan's ODA disbursement to China has even surpassed all international organizations[9] combined over the 1992–1995 period (see Table 9.3).

Over the 1992–1996 period, Japan's accumulative grants to China amounted to US$1.62 billion (grant aid US$334.0 million and technical cooperation US$1.28 billion) whereas its accumulative net loan aid to China amounted to US$4.50 billion. Loan aid was 2.8 times that of grants (see Table 9.4).

Over the 1990–1994 period, both Japan's grants and loan aid to China increased substantially except in 1991. Japan's grants to China dropped from $201.3 million in 1990 to US$194.1 million in 1991. Its loan aid to China dropped from US$521.7 million to US$391.2 million during the same period. The Tiananmen incident occurred on 4 June 1989 and Western countries led by the US were quick to

Table 9.3

DAC Countries and International Organizations' ODA Disbursements to China (US$ million)

DAC Countries, ODA Net

Year	1	2	3	4	5	Others	Total
1993	Japan 1,350.7	Germany 247.8	Spain 140.1	Italy 135.5	France 102.6		1,976.7
1994	Japan 1,479.4	Germany 300.0	Spain 153.1	France 97.7	Australia 75.6		2,105.8
1995	Japan 1,380.2	Germany 684.1	France 91.2	Austria 66.2	Spain 56.0		2,277.7
1993	IDA 865.1	UNDP 44.8	WFP 23.8	EDF 19.5	UNICEF 17.6	59.2	1,030.0
1994	IDA 671.0	UNDP 38.4	WFP 24.9	UNICEP 22.5	ADB 16.7	46.6	820.1
1995	IDA 798.2	UNDP 38.3	CEC 32.7	WFP 21.2	UNICEF 20.0	57.1	967.5

Table 9.4

Japan's ODA Disbursements to China

(US$ million)

Year	Grants			Loan Aid		Total
	Grant Aid	Technical Cooperation	Total	Gross	Net	
1992	72.05	187.48	259.53	871.27	791.23	1,050.76
1993	54.43	245.06	299.49	1,189.06	1,051.19	1,350.68
1994	99.42	246.91	346.33	1,298.46	1,133.08	1,479.41
1995	83.12	304.75	387.87	1,216.08	992.28	1,380.15
1996	24.99	303.73	328.72	774.08	533.01	861.73
Total (1992–96)	334.01	1,287.93	1,621.94	5,348.95	4,500.79	6,122.73

impose economic sanctions on China and suspended economic aid as well. Japan tried not to be influenced by the West but Japan's continuous ODA disbursement to China was severely criticised, both domestically and internationally. This is seen to have affected Japan's ODA disbursement to China in 1991. Japan's ODA disbursement to China also dropped from US$1.48 billion in 1994 to US$61.7 million in 1996. This was basically due to China's nuclear test in August 1995 and Japan's consequent freezing of its grant aid to China.

After the incident, together with the economic sanctions imposed by the Western countries, foreign direct investment in China dried up. China was forced to restructure its economy. China later experienced an economic slowdown in 1989–1990. It regained 8 per cent economic growth rate in 1991, and it was only from 1992 that China regained an ODA disbursement increment both from Japan and DAC countries.

Over the last few years, China's economic performance has been outstanding. China's real GDP annual growth rates were 12.6 per cent in 1994, 10.5 per cent in 1995, 9.6 per cent in 1996, and 8.8 per cent in 1997. China's rapid economic development has been centred around special economic zones such as Pudong, Hainan-dao, Xiamen, Zhuhai, Shantou and Shenzhen; and coastal economic free zones such as Changjiang Delta and Zhujiang Delta. Besides, economic and technological development areas, such as Shanghai, Dalian, Tianjin, Qingtao, Guangzhou and Fuzhou, new high-tech areas, such as Wuhan, Chongqing, Shenyang and Nanjing, have also gained economic development momentum.

China's rapid economic development, however, has caused some serious problems. The fast expansion of income disparity among the Chinese, and the fast development in the coastal areas at the expense of China's inland areas are some important issues which require special attention. The Chinese authorities were aware of the seriousness of this situation and had taken measures to cool down the "over-heating economy" over the years. At the same time, foreign aid and investments had been lured to develop China's inland provinces.

However, due to the underdevelopment of the social and economic infrastructures in the inland areas, foreign industries are reluctant to penetrate into China's rural areas.

Even in the coastal areas in China, the development of social and economic infrastructure has always been left behind in the rapid economic development process. Even for overseas Chinese investments in China from Asia, the emphasis has always been put on the development of housing, hotels, department stores, resorts and trade centres. Only in recent years, have overseas Chinese ventures from Asia begun investing in the social and economic infrastructures in China. Investments from Hong Kong, Malaysia, Singapore, Indonesia and Thailand have always been lured to construct highways, bridges, harbours, railways, telecommunications, power stations and hospitals in China. However, due to China's large size and its rapid industrial development, foreign aid and investments from the West and Japan, together with overseas Chinese investments are obviously much needed to develop social and economic infrastructures in China.

Some serious problems faced by China interruptions in manufacturing production due to the shortage of power supply; traffic congestion due to poor transport systems; air and sea pollution due to lack of purification systems in factories, and workers' welfare not taken care of due to the shortage of hospitals. Foreign investments and ODA loans (especially from Japan) have therefore had important roles to play in helping China overcome these shortcomings.

Some of Japan's ODA loans are used to overcome the above-mentioned problems faced by China. Some of the latest assistance include the following: 1) The comprehensive transportation development programme of Dalian City; and 2) Yen loans to China in FY 1991–1996 to finance the Second Phase of the Subway Construction Project of Beijing which was aimed at diffusing traffic congestion. (The subway systems of Beijing were all built or revamped with funds provided by Japan's ODA.) Over the 1990–1996 period, numerous projects were financed by Japan's ODA (both loan aid and grant aid). It is clear that Japan has played a crucial role in the development of China's social and economic infrastructure. Japan is expected to play an even more important role as China's "socialist market economy" gather momentum, after 17 years of economic reform and restructuring since 1979.

Japan's ODA and China's Nuclear Tests

China's continued nuclear tests caused some excitement in Japan and among members of the Japanese tripartite ruling coalition. On 8 June 1996, China conducted its 44th nuclear test since 1964 at its Lop Nor test site in the Western Xinjiang Uygur Autonomous Region.[10] China had insisted that it was entitled to carry out one more nuclear test in September 1996, and then join a test moratorium observed by the other declared nuclear powers — Britain, France, Russia and the United States — while signing the proposed comprehensive nuclear test ban treaty (CTBT).[11]

The House of Representatives in Japan expressed "regrets" and unanimously adopted a resolution on 14 June that condemned China's nuclear tests and demanded that China immediately cancel any plans for further tests.[12] The House of Councillors in Japan also adopted a similar resolution soon after.[13]

Takemura Masayoshi, former leader of the New Party Sakigake, the smallest component of the tripartite ruling alliance in Tokyo, urged Beijing not to conduct any more nuclear tests.[14] He further suggested the suspension of future talks for Japanese official yen loans and cautioned about extending economic aid to China.[15] The Japanese government was quick to express "strong protest" against China's nuclear tests to the Chinese envoy in Japan. However, the then Japanese Prime Minister Hashimoto Ryutaro, former president of the Liberal Democratic Party, the largest party in the tripartite ruling coalition, reiterated that he was only considering freezing the loans, saying that it would "leave scars" in bilateral relations if he did.[16]

Murayama Tomiichi, a former prime minister who headed the Social Democratic Party, concurred with Hashimoto, saying that it was "taken for granted" for Tokyo to continue suspension of grant aid to Beijing but that a freeze of yen loan aid would negatively influence China's efforts to push ahead with its policy towards an open economy.[17]

Grant-in-aid (with the exception of emergency relief and humanitarian assistance) to China was suspended again by Japan pending the termination of Chinese nuclear testing. This reflected the general sentiment in Japan against China's nuclear tests. Japan had pledged that it would extend ¥580 billion in soft loan assistance (as the fourth package of yen loans) to China for the first three years of the fiscal 1996–2000 aid package. For fiscal 1996, ¥200 million was planned to be disbursed.[18] In the meantime, however, it is likely that China's persistent nuclear tests will have a negative impact on Japan's yen loan assistance to China (in terms of the deduction or the postponement of Japan's ODA disbursement).

China's "socialist market economy" requires foreign aid especially from Japan. However, China will not abandon its nuclear test policy to obtain yen loan assistance from Japan. Chinese leader Jiang Zemin became impatient and criticized Japan at the meeting with Takemura Masayoshi saying that "people with full stomachs can never understand the feeling of the people with empty stomachs".[19] China's *People's Daily* further accused Japan of having "nuclear ambitions" and further questioned whether a country that enjoys US nuclear protection can really be considered a non-nuclear state.[20] The *Daily* commented that "with Japan's present technology, it can easily produce an intercontinental ballistic missile, while Japanese supercomputer technology can simulate nuclear explosions in three dimensional space, thus eliminating the need for underground nuclear tests".[21] The row over China's nuclear test has somehow developed from the arguments about the legitimacy of Japan's ODA disbursement, to national nuclear stance between China and Japan.

The General Assembly of the United Nations voted overwhelmingly on 10 September to endorse a treaty banning all nuclear test blasts. This action opened the door for the CTBT to be signed by UN member states, although it must overcome strong opposition from India if it is to become law.[22] Together with the other four major nuclear powers (the United States, Russia, France and Britain), China signed the CTBT on 24 September. Japan was one of the strong supporters of the treaty. It was therefore expected that Japan would favourably re-examine its ODA to China should China abandon nuclear tests after signing the CTBT.

Recent reports suggest that Japan is ready to "re-open" its ODA loans to China.[23] The postponed fourth yen loan (approximately ¥580 billion) and the grant aid which was frozen in summer 1995 were the two major ODA disbursements which required the prompt attention and fast settlement between Japan and China. The Japanese government (especially the Ministry of Foreign Affairs) was keen to improve its diplomatic relations with China after the Diaoyu-Tai incident, and before the 25th Anniversary of China–Japan diplomatic relations which fell in 1997. Japan was particularly keen to participate in the construction of the power station of the Sanxia Dam (Three Gorges) (dam construction work started in 1994) in China.[24]

Sanxia Dam will be the largest dam in the world when it is completed in the year 2009. The construction cost is about ¥2 trillion and the dam will have a 18.2 million kilowatt capacity. With a credit

Table 9.5

DAC Countries and International Organizations' ODA Disbursements to Indonesia (US$ million)

						DAC Countries, ODA Net
Year	1	2	3	4	5	Total
1991	Japan 1,065.5	Neth. 139.4	Germany 135.8	France 126.5	Australia 72.9	1,772.3
1992	Japan 1,356.7	France 168.8	Germany 116.4	Austria 104.8	Australia 77.0	1,971.4
1993	Japan 1,148.9	Germany 279.4	France 113.8	Austria 96.7	Australia 85.7	1,924.5
1994	Japan 886.2	Germany 265.8	France 107.7	Australia 93.1	Austria 90.8	1,557.0
1995	Japan 892.4	Australia 107.9	Austria 98.1	France 88.4	U.K. 56.2	1,303.3

Source: *Ministry of Foreign Affairs, op. cit.*

221

loan (same as ADA) from the Export and Import Bank of Japan and the application of trade insurance approved by the Ministry of International Trade and Industry in Japan, a Japanese industrial group[25] has decided to tender for the construction of the power station (approximately ¥60 billion) with much confidence. Despite some criticism (environmental destruction, destruction of historical ruins and the enforced removal of 1.5 million residents for the purposes of development) from various peace organizations, the Japanese government has given full support to the industries to go ahead.

Japan's ODA to Indonesia

Table 9.5 shows that among DAC countries, Japan was the largest donor country to Indonesia over the 1991–1994 period. Japan's ODA disbursement to Indonesia overwhelmed the Netherlands, France, Germany and Austria. In 1994, Japan's share amounted to US$886 million (56.9 per cent of all DAC countries).

Compared to China, Indonesia received much lesser ODA disbursement from international agencies. For example, in 1994 China

Table 9.6
Japan's ODA Disbursements to Indonesia

(US$ million)

| Year | Grants | | | Loan Aid | | |
	Grant Aid	Technical Cooperation	Total	Gross	Net	Total
1990	58.38	108.68	167.06	964.81	700.72	867.78
1991	79.73	133.07	212.80	1,169.73	852.71	1,065.51
1992	85.73	141.72	227.45	1,469.06	1,129.26	1,356.71
1993	67.61	157.93	225.54	1,303.45	923.35	1,148.89
1994	72.28	177.69	249.97	1,084.37	636.20	886.17
1995	66.46	203.67	270.13	1,155.14	622.28	892.41
1996	64.41	163.31	227.72	1,234.15	737.81	965.53
Total (1990–96)	494.60	1,086.07	1,580.67	8,380.71	5,602.33	7,183.00

and Indonesia received US$818 million and US$86 million respectively from international organizations. China received 9.5 times as much as Indonesia. The fact that China's "socialist market economy" attracted much more attention and economic assistance from international organizations is obvious.

In 1994, Japan's ODA disbursement to Indonesia was 10.3 times as much as all international organizations combined. Japan's ODA disbursement to Indonesia is particularly important to Indonesia's social and economic development. Japan's total grants (grant aid and technical cooperation) and loan aid to Indonesia amounted to US$1.58 billion and US$7.18 billion respectively over the 1990–1996 period. Grants were equal to 22.0 per cent of loan aid (see Table 9.6).

According to Japan's ODA Report (1995), Japan's yen loans to Indonesia financed the construction of waterworks, electric power, highway systems, railroads and telecommunications. The details are as follows: 1) Waterworks — 55 per cent (380,000 t/d) of the costs of construction of Jakarta's water purification facilities were financed by yen loans; 2) Electric power — 20 per cent (2,064 MW) of the costs of construction of Indonesia's power generation capacity were financed by yen loans; 3) Highway systems — 15 per cent (56 km) of the costs of construction of Indonesia's toll road systems were financed by yen loans; 4) Railroads — 12 per cent (779 km) of the costs of construction of Indonesia's railroad systems were financed by yen loans; 5) Telecommunications — 50 per cent (2,500 km) of the costs of construction of Indonesia's microwave cables across the country were financed by yen loans, and 60 per cent of the costs of laying transmission cables (connecting telephone offices in Jakarta) were financed by yen loans. Obviously, at least in recent years, compared to the Western countries, Japan's role in Indonesia's social and economic infrastructure development has been particularly significant.

In the agricultural sector, Japan's role in financing irrigation projects is also worth noticing. Figure 9.4 shows a steady increase in the area of irrigated farmland in Indonesia and facilities (irrigation projects) financed with Japan's ODA yen loans. Figure 9.5 shows that

Figure 9.4

**Japan's ODA Yen Loan Contributions and the Increase of
Irrigated Areas in Indonesia since 1981**

1,000MW

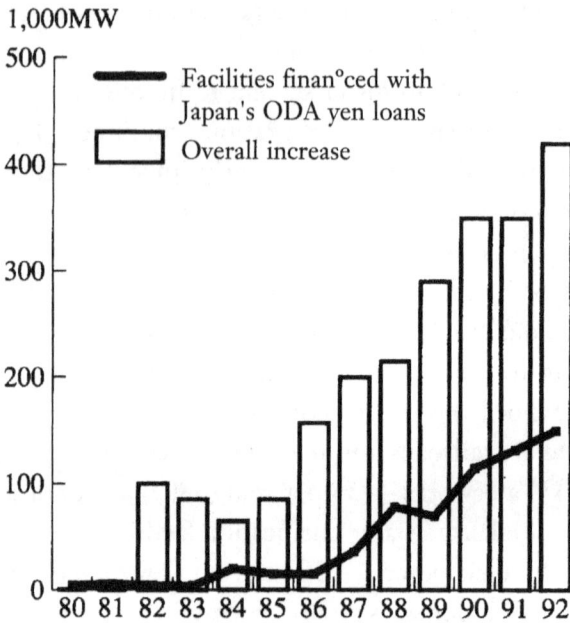

Source: *Ministry of Foreign Affairs, op. cit.*

Figure 9.5

**Japan's ODA Yen Loan Contributions in the Total Area of Irrigated
Land in Indonesia (as of 1992)**

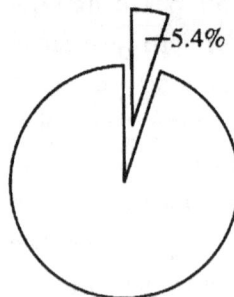

Of the total area of irrigated farmland of Indonesia, 5.4% was covered, by facilities built with
Japan's ODA yen loans.

Source: *Ministry of Foreign Affairs, op. cit.*

the cumulative total area of irrigated farmland covered by Japan's ODA by 1992 amounted to 5.4 per cent (150,000 hectares) of the total irrigated land of Indonesia.

It is clear that without Japan's ODA loans, the development of Indonesian's social and economic infrastructure would be very much delayed. To be more precise, without foreign ODA loans particularly from Japan, Indonesia would be unable to sustain rapid economic development. In recent years, Indonesia, together with China and Thailand, have been among the top three recipients of Japan's bilateral ODA. As has been seen in the case of China, where economic development has been centred around coastal areas and cities, income and development disparity in Indonesia appeared to be one of the major national issues. Judging from this aspect, the task of spreading Japan's ODA disbursement and technical cooperation to Indonesia's inland areas and less developed/underdeveloped islands has yet to be carried out.

Indonesia's economic development had been promising before Suharto resigned in May 1998. In the years 1995 and 1996, Indonesia's real annual growth rates were 8.2 per cent and 8.0 per cent respectively. As a big country with 13,500 islands has yet and a 192 million population (1994), Indonesia's economic success has naturally attracted much attention. Not only big ports and cities, such as Jakarta, Bandung, Surabaya, Medan, Semarang and Bogor, are well developed, but also the resort Mecca Bali has become a symbol of Indonesia's development. These places have received substantial amounts of Japan's ODA disbursement for social and economic infrastructure development. Again, it is clear that Japan's ODA has been particularly important for Indonesia's development.

Riau Islands, especially Batam and Bintan islands, have developed remarkably after forming the growth triangle together with Singapore and Johor in Malaysia since December 1989. Batam and Bintan received substantial amounts of foreign direct investments not only from the NIEs (Singapore in particular) but also from Japan, the US, England, the Netherlands and Sweden. Besides huge investments in

Table 9.7

Japan's ODA Disbursements to Singapore

(US$ million)

Year	Grant Aid	Technical Cooperation	Total	Gross	Net	Total
		Grants			Loan Aid	
1990	—	14.34	14.34	—	−24.78	−10.44
1991	—	18.43	18.43	—	−2.45	15.98
1992	—	16.43	16.43	—	−0.97	15.46
1993	—	18.40	18.40	—	−0.24	18.16
1994	—	13.56	13.56	—	—	13.56
1995	—	13.53	13.53	—	—	13.53
1996	—	8.54	8.54	—	—	8.54
*Total (Cumulative)	24.63	234.53	259.16	77.27	−10.76	248.40

Notes: *Includes data from preceding years.*
Source: *Ministry of Foreign Affairs, op. cit*

Table 9.8

DAC Countries and International Organizations' ODA Disbursements to Singapore (US$ million)

DAC Countries, ODA Net

Year	1	2	3	4	5
1991	Japan 16.0	USA 3.0	France 2.9	Australia 1.7	Finland 0.5
1992	Japan 15.5	USA 3.0	France 2.9	Australia 1.1	Canada 0.8
1993	Japan 18.2	USA 3.0	France 3.0	Australia 0.7	Canada 0.6
1994	Japan 13.6	France 3.6	Canada 0.8	Australia 0.5	Finland 0.0
1995	Japan 13.5	France 2.3	USA 1.0	Canada 0.6	Australia 0.1

Source: *Ministry of Foreign Affairs, op. cit.*

the manufacturing sector, the development in the resort and services sectors has also shown great momentum. The quick development on the Riau Islands will be contributing more and more to overall economic development in Indonesia. Judging from this aspect, there is an important role for Japan's ODA to play in developing social and economic infrastructures on the Riau Islands. In other words, the Riau Islands (especially Batam and Bintan) should become new main targets for Japan's future ODA disbursements.

Japan's ODA to Singapore

Singapore was ranked the world's 11th richest nation in 1995. Recently, according to a statement from Taiwan's Council for Economic Planning and Development, Singapore will become the world's wealthiest nation by the year 2020 with a per capita GNP of US$145,729.[26]

Likewise, as a newly industrializing country, Singapore is considered a fairly rich country. Singapore is basically no longer qualified to receive ODA (except technical cooperation but not grant aid or loan aid) from developed countries. Table 9.7 shows that Singapore did not receive either loan aid or grant aid from Japan over the 1990–1996 period.

Singapore did, however, receive technical cooperation consistently from Japan over the 1990–1996 period. Japan's cumulative grants on technical cooperation to Singapore had amounted to US$0.23 billion by 1996. Japan's loan aid to Singapore was negative over the 1990–1996 period. It is interesting to note that Japan's cumulative loan aid to Singapore had amounted to minus US$10.76 million by 1996 (see Table 9.7).

Table 9.8 shows that Japan (despite the negative loan aid) was the largest donor country to Singapore among the DAC countries. ODA disbursement from the US, France, Australia, Finland and Canada to Singapore was obviously negligible. Similarly, as shown in Table 9.8, ODA disbursement by international organizations to Singapore can also be ignored totally.

Singapore has, in fact, become an advanced developing country. Singapore has basically graduated from the status of developing country and has stepped up to be a donor country. "Singapore–Japan partnership programme" supports Singapore's effort. The programme is aimed at increasing the number of third-country training programmes which are implemented in the countries concerned with Japanese cooperation. The programme also includes the idea of technical cooperation through jointly dispatching experts to other developing countries.[27] Recently, it is reported that the foreign ministries of Singapore and Japan have agreed to set up a high-level working group to boost technical assistance to developing countries.[28] Singapore–Japan joint efforts in assisting developing countries are likely to be strengthened.[29]

The Singapore–Japan partnership programme requires further technical assistance from Japan and a closer technical cooperative relationship to be set up between the two countries. As a city-state without natural resources, Singapore has been systematically developing human resources particularly through tertiary education. Besides, together with its well-developed social and economic infrastructure, Singapore has been in an excellent position to transfer technology from the industrialized countries. As early as 1979, the Singapore government had already urged Japan to transfer high technology in the fields of machinery tools, automobile parts, camera and electronic products to Singapore. Since then the Singapore government has lured the supporting industries of Japanese high technology (for instance, the development of computer software and IC expansion technology) industries to invest in Singapore. Furthermore, in recent years, Japanese enterprises had set up operational headquarters (OHQ) inclusive of research and development (R&D) departments in Singapore in order to benefit from human resources and tax privileges in the country. These enterprises include Sony, Toshiba, Fujikura, Omron, Matsushita, NEC and Hitachi. Some years ago, Singapore's manufacturing sector had already been ranked second in the world (next only to Japan) where robot machinery was being utilized. Singapore is well qualified to be a "technology entreport country" to transfer technology to other Asian countries. In view of this, through Japan's ODA disbursement, technical cooperation between the two countries should be encouraged and strengthened.

In the meantime, one of the main problems which has thwarted the transfer of Japanese technology and technical cooperation is the lack of Japan experts in Singapore. Very few Singaporeans understand Japan or Japanese technology compared to those in the western countries. There are some technological institutions funded and set up by Japan in Singapore to promote technical cooperation between the two countries. Singaporean technicians find it hard to understand Japan or Japanese technology mainly due to a language handicap. The Department of Japanese Studies of the National University of Singapore was funded and set up by Japan which enrols a few hundred students every year. It remains unknown how many students have been trained to become Japan experts by now. Grants or scholarships provided by Japan, although extremely limited in number, sometimes do not attract sufficient promising candidates. There is a tendency for Singapore's top students to go to either England or the US. In the end, the Singapore–England and Singapore–US relationship have deepened, whereas the Singapore–Japan relationship has continue to dwindle. These are some issues which need to be looked into and rectified.

Conclusion

In Japan's bilateral ODA to China and Indonesia, loans have been larger than grant aid and technical cooperation. Due to the drastic yen appreciation after 1985, loans from Japan have become serious debt problems for recipient countries in Asia, particularly China and Indonesia. With China signing the CTBT and pledging to terminate nuclear test blasts, Japan is likely to increase its ODA loans to China, as China is seen by Japan as a gigantic market for Japanese manufactured products and investment. At the same time, Indonesia's ambitious economic development programmes and the rapid development in the Riau Islands, in particular, are likely to acquire substantial ODA especially from Japan. In the long run, therefore,

China and Indonesia are likely to become highly indebted countries to Japan.

China and Indonesia have been negotiating with Japan for help in alleviating their ballooning repayment burden. The Japanese government is, however, not willing to respond to growing calls from China and Indonesia for debt relief.[30] In fact, the Japanese government's stance has been clearly expressed in the Ministry of Foreign Affairs, Japan's ODA Annual Report 1995, "Exchange risks are, however, concomitant with international financial transactions under the floating exchange rate system, and basically it is the responsibility of the borrowers to manage such risks. In addition, it should not be overlooked that the yen appreciation has a positive side. . . Therefore, arguments which stress only the increased debt service do not necessarily grasp the whole picture in the proper perspective."[31]

Instead, the Japanese government is considering reductions in interest rates on fresh yen loans to China and Indonesia.[32] The government reaffirmed that "even if the interest rates are slashed again in 1996, the new rates will not be applied to yen loans that Japan has already disbursed or pledged to extend."[33]

The Japanese government's fiscal budget is now one of the worst among the major industrialized countries because of revenue shortfalls caused by the prolonged economic stagnation. The situation will not change much although the consumption tax is to rise from 3 to 5 per cent soon. Under these circumstances, the Japanese government has said that it will not be in the position to respond positively to China and Indonesia. Undoubtedly, Japan's intention to reduce interest rates on fresh yen loans to China and Indonesia will be highly regarded, but the status of "highly indebted countries" will certainly remain unchanged. The Japanese government is therefore urged to look into these problems more seriously.

Next to the issue related to the seriousness of debt burdens suffered by China and Indonesia, is the effectiveness of Japan's ODA disbursement to the recipient countries. Japan's ODA has long been a contentious issue, both domestically and internationally. The Ministry of Foreign Affairs in Japan has just conducted a survey on the effectiveness of Japan's ODA to the developing countries. The results were released on 5 July 1996 in "Kyuzyu-roku-nen-ban Keizai Kyoryoku hyoka hokoku-sho" (A Report on the Appraisal of Economic Cooperation in 1996). Among 110 projects examined, 67 projects (60.9 per cent) are considered as "successful", 41 projects (37.3 per cent) "requiring improvements", and 2 projects (1.8 per cent) "failed".[34]

This is an astonishing report. Only 60 per cent of projects financed by Japan's ODA (loan aid, grant aid and technical cooperation) are considered as successful and 40 per cent required improvements inclusive of 2 unsuccessful projects, even based on reports provided by the Japanese authorities. Both Japan and the recipient countries should study these 43 projects carefully in order to improve future ODA loans extended by Japan.

There are some contentious projects widely argued in China and Indonesia. For instance in China, the Beijing–Qinhuangdao Project is particularly controversial due to cost-overruns, mismanagement (on purchase of materials) and the delay of project completion.[35] In Indonesia, the Wonogiri Dam Project in Surakarta and the Borobudur–Prambanan Historical Park Project in Yogyakarta are particularly controversial due to environmental destruction and enforced resident removal with minimal compensation (suppressed human rights).[36] These are some important cases which require further investigation and examination.

Notes

1 *Nihon Keizai Shimbun*, 14 September 1996.
2 In Japan, there are numerous publications dealing with Japan's ODA. Some are critical and some are supportive. The typical works for the former include:
1) Sumi Kazuo, *ODA enjo no genjitsu* (The Reality of ODA), Tokyo, 1993. 2) Murai Yoshinori (ed.), *Kensyo Nippon no ODA* (Japan's ODA — An Inspection), Tokyo, 1994; *Dare no Tame no enjo* (Assistance For Who), Tokyo, 1990. 3) Nishikawa Jun, *Seikai Kenzai nyumon* (An Introduction to World Economy), Tokyo, 1991. 4) Dot Takako et al., *ODA Kaikaku* (The ODA Reform), Tokyo, 1990.
The typical works for the latter include: 1) Iida Tsuneo, *Enjo suru kuni sareru kuni* (The Donor Country and the Recipient Country), Tokyo, 1974. 2) Kusano Atsushi, *ODA iccho ni-sen-oku en no yukue* (The Future of ODA), Tokyo, 1994. 3) Nishigaki Akira & Shimomura Yasutami, *Kaihatsu enjo no keizaigaku* (The

Economics of Development Assistance), Tokyo, 1995. 4) Kohama Hirohisa, *ODA no keizaigaku* (The Econmics of Development Cooperation), Tokyo, 1993.

3   *Nihon Keizai Shimbun*, 10, 11 and 30 July 1996.

4   *Nihon Keizai Shimbun*, 18 June 1996.

5   The ratio of Japan's ODA to its GNP in 1994 had just reached the DAC average. As early as in 1970, the General Assembly of the United Nations adopted a resolution, the 'International Development Strategy for the Second UN International Decade for Development', urging donor countries to raise their ODA/GNP ratio to 0.7 per cent (Japan's official Development Assistance Annual Report 1995, Ministry of Foreign Affairs, September 1995, Tokyo).

6   The share of grants, i.e. grant aid, technical cooperation and contribution of funds to international institutions, out of the total amount of aid provided by a country (Japan's Official Development Assistance Annual Report 1995, p. 8).

7   Grant element is an index of financial terms of assistance, which measures the concessionary nature of aid, taking into account interest rate, grace period and maturity. The grant element of a loan on a commercial basis (10 per cent interest rate) is 0 per cent, and as the terms and conditions are alleviated, the figure of the grant element becomes higher, reaching 100 per cent in the case of a grant (op. cit., see Explanatory Notes and p. 8).

8   Ibid, p. 8.

9   These international organizations include the International Development Association (IDA), UN Development Program (UNDP), World Food Program (WFP) and UN Children's Fund (UNICEF) etc.

10 Paul Krugman and Kent Calder are particularly pessimistic about China's economic performance while Ezra Vogel has even suggested that China would achieve an annual GDP growth rate of 10 per cent in 20 to 30 years.

11 *Nihon Keizai Shimbun*, 9 June 1996.

12 *Nihon Keizai Shimbun*, 9 June 1996; *Japan Times*, 11 July 1996.

13 *Japan Times*, 15 June 1996.

14 *Japan Times*, 22 June 1996.

15 *Japan Times*, 11 June 1996; *Nihon Keizai Shimbun*, 11 June 1996.

16 Ibid.

17 Ibid.

18 Ibid.

19 Ibid.

20 *Nihon Keizai Shimbun*, 14 July 1996.

21 *Japan Times*, 22 June 1996.

22 Ibid.

23 *Japan Times*, 12 September 1996. The vote was 158 for the pact. India, Bhutan and Libya voted against it, and Cuba, Lebanon, Syria, Tanzania and Mauritius abstained.

24 *Nihon Keizai Shimbun*, 3, 14 and 15 November 1996.

25 *Nihon Keizai Shimbun*, 4, 17, 18 and 19 December 1996.

26 Led by the Hitachi Manufacturing Industry; Toshiba, Mitsubishi, Itochu, Mitsui and Sumitomo, etc. are participating.

27 *Straits Times*, 28 August 1996.

28 Japan's ODA Annual Report 1995, op. cit., p. 216.

29 *Straits Times*, 3 September 1996.
    Singapore and Japan also agreed to cooperate closely at the upcoming Asia–Pacific Economic Cooperation (APEC), World Trade Organization (WTO) and Asia–Europe meetings. Ibid.

30 *Japan Times*, 4 July 1996.

31 Ministry of Foreign Affairs, Japan's ODA Annual Report 1995, op. cit., pp. 143–44.

32 Japan now charges four different interest rates on yen loans — 1 per cent, 2.3 per cent, 2.7 per cent and 4 per cent — according to the per capita income level of borrowing countries. The interest rates on fresh yen loans were last slashed in June 1995, by an average of 0.4 percentage points (*Japan Times*, 4 July 1996).

33 *Japan Times*, 4 July 1996.

34 For detailed discussion, see *Gaimo-sho Keizai Kyoryoku-Kyoku* (The Cooperation Bureau of the Ministry of Foreign Affairs), Keizai Kyoryoku Hyoka Hokoku-sho (A Report on the Appraisal of Economic Cooperation), Tokyo, July 1996.

35 Watanabe Toshio & Kusano Atsushi, *Nihon no ODA wo do suru ka* (How To Do About Japan's ODA), Tokyo, 1991. pp. 87–99.

36 Op. cit., pp. 112–21 and pp. 132–39.

CHAPTER 10

Japan and the Asian Economic Crisis

Introduction

Some years ago, people started talking about the slowdown of the economic development among the Asian countries and ASEAN in particular. However, it was not only until the summer of 1997, that the Asian economic crisis erupted with the collapse of currencies and stock markets in Southeast Asia. On 2 July, a drastic drop in the Thai currency and stock market indicated the beginning of the Asian economic crisis. Nowadays, most of the Asian countries (Indonesia, Korea, Thailand and Malaysia in particular) are in one way or the other, suffering from economic depression, political chaos and social instability. Indonesian President Suharto was forced to resign on 21 May 1998, indicating that the chaotic situation in Southeast Asia had reached its most serious level.

In Japan, Hashimoto Ryutaro resigned after a crushing defeat in Upper House elections in July 1998. Hashimoto was the fourth leader (following General Chavalit Yongchaiyudh in Thailand, Kim Young Sam in Korea and Suharto in Indonesia) to resign in Asia within a year after the eruption of the Asian economic crisis. On 24 July 1998, Obuchi Keizo was elected as president of the Liberal Democratic Party and subsequently became the Prime Minister of Japan. Very few observers within and outside Japan expected him to efficiently rectify the Japanese economy and put it on the right track within a year. If the sluggish economic situation in Japan were to drag on for another year and the Japanese currency were to depreciate further, it would definitely delay the recovery of the Asian economies much beyond our expectations.

In the meantime, China's economic development is the main concern, particularly within the Asia-Pacific region. Can China successfully restructure its state-owned enterprises within three years, as promised by the Chinese Premier Zhu Rong Ji? Can China succeed in attaining 8 per cent GDP growth without depreciating the Renminbi? (China has maintained approximately 8.3 Renminbi to the dollar over the period 1994–1997). Chinese leaders have on many occasions, particularly during the period March–July 1998, announced that China will not depreciate its currency so as to avoid further jeopardizing the economic crisis in Asia. However, if the Japanese Yen drops further (say around 150 to the US dollar) or if the Southeast Asian economies, like Indonesia, Korea and Thailand are further jeopardized, China will depreciate her currency (as she did in 1994 by depreciating the Renminbi by more than 33 per cent). This is simply because China has already felt the impact since January 1998 and cannot afford to substantially reduce her exports or direct foreign investments, if she intends to gain 7-8 per cent GDP growth in 1998.

All in all, Asian countries are suffering from serious economic difficulties. At this moment, do we perceive the Asian currency crisis and a slump in stocks in Asia as an economic crisis, or simply due to Southeast Asian economies having just entered into a transitional period of economic restructuring? In other words, do we perceive the currency crisis and a slump in stocks in Asia as a common syndrome and a defect in the economic structure among the Asian countries, or simply a temporary economic confusion due to the mismanagement of macroeconomic (both monetary and fiscal) policies?

This chapter is aimed at analysing the substance of the Asian currency crisis and to predict the recovery prospects of the Asian economies. The Asian currency crisis is perceived here as an economic crisis accompanied by a serious economic downturn and is basically due to the failure of macroeconomic policies implemented by the Asian countries. However, it is believed that this economic crisis can be overcome and the Asian economic recovery can be put back on the right track (say within 2 years), should resolute and timely rectification macroeconomic policies be implemented.

The Asian currency crisis erupted in Thailand and spread to the ASEAN countries and then to the NIEs (newly industrializing economies). The so-called Blue Monday occurred on 27 October 1997. It was caused by the drastic drop in currency and stocks in Hong Kong, which in turn forced stocks in the USA and Japan to drop almost simultaneously. The Blue Monday was just 10 years after the Black Monday that occurred on 19 October 1987. Stocks in the USA dropped by 554.26 points on Blue Monday compared to 508.00 points on Black Monday. A slump in stocks in the USA caused chaos in stock markets in Europe, South America, Mexico and then throughout the World.

Fortunately, between the 29–31 October, stocks in the USA and Japan rebounded, and the Blue Monday crisis was resolved, at least temporarily. Likewise, the Asian currency and economic crisis can never be treated in isolation. Should the Japanese economy drag on with no sign of rapid recovery since the bubble economy collapsed in March 1991, the Asian economies in general and the Chinese economy in particular, will no doubt be adversely affected. The sluggish economies in Asia will further adversely affect the economies in Europe and the USA. The world economy is now facing its most difficult time since the 1930s.

Current Balance Deficit — A Failure of Monetary and Fiscal Policies

Current balance consists of the following items:[1]
- Trade balance (balance of export and import trade)
- Balance of invisible trade (transportation, insurance, travel, investment earnings etc.)
- Balance of transfer (services and the sum of cash transactions etc.)

Here we are only discussing the trade balance, as it is the most important part of the current balance.

As can be seen from Tables 10.1 and 10.2, the ASEAN countries have been suffering from current balance deficits seriously in recent years. In 1996, Thailand, Indonesia and Malaysia suffered from current balance deficits amounting to US$14.4 billion (8.1 per cent in terms of GDP), US$7.8 billion (3.4 per cent) and US$4.8 billion (4.9 per cent) respectively. It can therefore be suggested that one of the detrimental factors that contributed to the collapse of the currencies and stocks in ASEAN was the weak monetary and fiscal condition of these countries.

Table 10.1

Current Balance of the Asian Countries

(Unit: US$ million)

		1993	1994	1995	1996	1997	1998
ASEAN							
	Indonesia	–2,106	–2,792	–7,023	–7,801	–5,824	–
	Malaysia	–3,079	–5,628	–8,644	–4,840	–5,031	9,199
	Philippines	–3,016	–2,950	–1,893	–3,953	–4,351	1,294
	Thailand	–6,364	–8,085	–13,554	–14,691	–3,024	14,290
NIEs							
	Korea	890	–2,867	–8,508	–23,005	–8,167	40,039
	Taiwan	7,042	6,489	5,474	11,027	7,688	3,728
	Hong Kong SAR	9,872	3,135	–3,401	–2,133	–5,184	–
	Singapore	4,272	11,452	14,361	14,743	14,803	17,524
	USA	–90,771	–133,538	–129,095	–148,184	–166,446	–
	China	–11,902	7,657	1,620	7,242	29,717	–
	Japan	131,915	130,540	110,421	65,802	94,523	121,167

Source: *Compiled from* Keizai Kikaku-cho, Ajia Keizai *(Asian Economics), various issues.*

Among the NIEs, over the period 1993–1997, Singapore and Taiwan recorded a substantial amount of current balance surpluses. In 1997, Singapore and Taiwan benefited from US$14.8 billion (15.6 per cent in terms of GDP) and US$7.7 billion (2.7 per cent) current balance surpluses respectively. Hong Kong SAR's current balance surpluses decreased from US$9.9 billion in 1993 to merely US$3.1 billion in 1994. In 1995, Hong Kong SAR suffered a current balance deficit that amounted to US$3.4 billion. As for Korea, it suffered current balance deficits during the period 1994–1997. In 1996 in particular, Korea's current balance deficit amounted to US$23.0 billion (4.4 per cent in terms of GDP).

The figures mentioned earlier have somehow explained why the present Asian economic crisis has so far only marginally affected the economies in Singapore and Taiwan. However, with tremendous current balance deficits, Hong Kong SAR and Korea are suffering from continuous economic downturn, political instability and social chaos. In 1998, Hong Kong SAR and Korea suffered from –5.1 per cent and –5.8 per cent GDP growth.

Table 10.2

Current Balance of the Asian Countries in terms of GDP

(Unit: %)

	1993	1994	1995	1996	1997	1998
ASEAN						
Indonesia	–1.3	–1.6	–3.5	–3.4	–2.7	–
Malaysia	–4.8	–7.8	–10.0	–4.9	–5.1	13.0
Philippines	–5.5	–4.6	–2.7	–4.8	–5.3	2.0
Thailand	–5.1	–5.6	–8.1	–8.1	–2.0	12.3
NIEs						
Korea	0.3	–1.0	–1.7	–4.4	–1.7	12.5
Taiwan	3.2	2.7	2.1	4.0	2.7	1.4
Hong Kong SAR	8.5	2.4	–2.4	–1.4	–3.0	
Singapore	8.9	15.9	17.0	16.1	15.6	20.7
China	–2.0	1.4	0.2	0.9	3.3	–
Japan	3.1	2.8	2.1	1.4	2.3	3.2

Source: *Same as Table 10.1*

It is therefore clear that the recent currency crisis and stock market collapse struck first in those economies with tremendous current balance deficits. The tremendous current balance deficits have become a great pressure on the overvalued currencies in Asia and have functioned as a determining factor in the depreciation of currencies and the collapse of the stock markets in Asia.

International Trade Deficit — A Fatal Result of Rapid Industrialization

Particularly after the second half of the 1980s, Southeast Asian countries had enthusiastically been implementing industrialization policies in order to speed up the economic development process. The implementation of industrialization policies implied that Southeast Asian countries needed to import a substantial amount of capital goods, intermediate goods and durable consumption goods from the industrialized nations, especially from Japan, Europe and the USA. International trade relationships between Southeast Asian countries and the industrialized nations have been shifting from vertical to horizontal trade structure. However, apparently Southeast Asian countries require a long period of time to break away from the vertical trade structure.

It is particularly essential for Southeast Asian countries to promote horizontal trade relationships with the West in order to correct trade deficits. Especially for resource rich countries such as Indonesia and Malaysia, when prices of primary products are stable or increasing, it would definitely contribute favourably to the international trade of these countries. However, as in the first half of the 1980s, countries producing natural resources suffered a serious blow when prices of petroleum and natural gas dropped drastically. As a matter of fact, most of the Southeast Asian countries have been suffering from substantial trade deficits even when prices of primary products remained stable. Generally, ASEAN and the NIEs' trade deficits against Japan have been balanced by trade surpluses with the USA. However, as seen in Table 10.3, most of the Southeast Asian countries have been suffering from international trade deficits.

Over the period 1993–1997, resource rich Indonesia was the only country in ASEAN to benefit from a trade surplus. Malaysia, the Philippines and Thailand were trade deficit countries, with trade deficits in Thailand and the Philippines being particularly serious. In 1996, trade deficits in these two countries amounted to US$16.6 billion and US$11.8 billion respectively (see Table 10.3).

Among the NIEs, Taiwan was the only trade surplus country over the period 1993–1997. The re-export trade factor should be taken into consideration, as Hong Kong SAR and Singapore are entrepot economies. Besides, as mentioned earlier, Hong Kong SAR and Singapore had recorded current balance surpluses as they had healthy invisible trade balances. Korea's trade deficit increased substantially year by year over the period 1993–1997. In 1996, it amounted to US$20.6 billion.

Judging from the above-mentioned figures, it is not surprising to notice that the recent Asian currency crisis and the collapse of the stock markets occurred in countries with substantial trade deficits (weak financial base) (i.e. Thailand and Malaysia among the ASEAN countries and Korea among the NIEs).

Table 10.3

Trade Balance of the Asian Countries

(Unit: US$ million)

		1993	1994	1995	1996	1997	1998
ASEAN							
	Indonesia	8,495	8,069	4,789	6,886	11,763	21,745
	Malaysia	1,489	–762	–3,737	–101	–16	14,893
	Philippines	–6,268	–7,808	–9,168	–11,884	–10,706	–159
	Thailand	–9,147	–9,329	–14,317	–16,602	–3,749	11,446
NIEs							
	Korea	–1,564	–6,335	–10,062	–20,624	–8,452	39,031
	Taiwan	8,030	7,700	8,109	13,572	7,656	5,917
	Hong Kong SAR	–3,410	–10,437	–19,001	–17,800	–20,555	–10,583
	Singapore	–11,219	–5,938	–6,207	–6,320	–7,404	8,302
	China	–12,215	5,391	16,696	12,230	40,420	43,600
	Japan	120,241	120,858	106,843	61,941	82,501	106,886

Source: *Same as Table 10.1*

Accumulation of Foreign Debts — A Heavy Burden of Economic Development

It has been a common feature that the Asian countries financed their domestic industries, social and industrial infrastructure and big industrial projects by borrowing heavily from the highly industrialized countries and international financial institutions (for example the International Monetary Fund, the World Bank and the Asian Development Bank). Presently, there are many countries in Asia whose foreign debts have accumulated substantially in recent years so that they are unable to pay back the debts.

The Asian countries have been borrowing heavily from Japan. Since 1989, Japan has wrested from the West the title of the world's largest official development assistance (ODA) nation. Japan's ODA increased remarkably from US$8.9 billion in 1989 to US$14.7 billion in 1995. In 1970, 98.2 per cent of Japan's ODA was concentrated in Asia. However, in 1995 the degree of concentration dropped to 54.4 per cent. In recent years, China, Indonesia, India, the Philippines and Thailand have been Japan's largest recipient countries among the Asian countries.

Financial loans have been extensively utilized by the Asian countries to speed up development. However, financial loans from overseas have always been accompanied by foreign exchange risks. The strong and appreciated Japanese currency during the period 1985–1995 has forced the Asian countries to adopt a policy of postponing the repayment of loans or refinancing. In April 1995, the yen debtor countries in Asia fell into chaos, as the yen soared to 78 to the dollar. Loan repayment by Asia to Japan became impossible. Fortunately, the yen depreciated there after and now the weak yen has continued to deteriorate. It is now a great chance for the Asian countries to repay the loans to Japan. However, at this juncture, the Asian currencies have suffered an even greater drop than the Japanese yen.

The fall of the Asian currencies and the accumulation of foreign debts are somehow interrelated. Table 10.4 reveals that the Asian countries particularly Indonesia, China and Thailand, have suffered

Table 10.4

External Debt Balance of Asian Countries

(Gross, US$100 million)

	1992	(D/SR)*	1993	(D/SR)	1994	(D/SR)	1995	(D/SR)	1996	(D/SR)
Indonesia	880	32.6	891	33.6	1,078	30.7	1,244	30.9	1,290	36.8
Philippines	330	24.4	359	25.6	400	18.9	394	16.4	412	13.7
Malaysia	200	9.2	261	8.6	295	9.3	344	7.0	398	8.2
Thailand	418	13.8	427	13.7	481	13.5	832	11.6	908	11.5
Vietnam	239	12.7	249	13.2	256	7.3	258	5.0	268	3.5
China	724	10.2	859	11.1	1,005	8.9	1,181	9.9	1,288	8.7

Note: *D/SR means debit service ratio. D/SR indicated the degree of external debt owed by an individual country. It shows the ratio of external debt repayment compared to the total amount of exports of an individual country. The burden of external debt is high if the ratio is high.*

Source: *Same as Table 10.1*

from serious foreign debts. In 1996, the foreign debts of these three countries amounted to US$129.0 billion, US$128.8 billion and US$90.8 billion respectively. Even in 1995, according to a *Nihon Keizai Shimbun* editorial, Indonesia's foreign debt amounted to US$110.0 billion and was the highest among the Southeast Asian countries. It was reported that government loans and private loans amount to US$50.0 billion and US$60.0 billion respectively, and if the unreported portion were to be included, the latter should increase to US$80.0 billion.[2]

Among the NIEs' foreign debts, data on Taiwan, Hong Kong SAR and Singapore are not available. Probably the foreign debts of these countries are satisfactory. However, as far as Korea is concerned, its foreign debt had amounted to US$47.2 billion in 1993. As an OECD country next only to Japan in Asia, Korea's case is astonishing.

As for China, her foreign debts have particularly attracted much attention. China's foreign debts have been substantial and comparable to Indonesia over the 1992–1996 period. (See Table 10.4.) By June 1997, China's foreign debts had amounted to US$118.6 billion and had exceeded Indonesia's US$110 billion. China has become the largest debtor country in Asia. Undoubtedly, the substantial amount of foreign debt has become a detrimental factor in China's economic development.

In the meantime, fortunately, the foreign debts issue has not become a serious obstructive or destructive factor in China's economic development, as her other economic fundamentals (in terms of current balance surplus and foreign currency reserves) are in good order. China is now facing some other serious problems. The problems include a task to restructure state-owned enterprises, a drastic decrease in export trade (20 per cent decrease in the first half of 1998), an abrupt decrease in foreign direct investments in China (dropping from US$64 billion in 1997 to probably US$40 billion–US$50 billion in 1998) and an immense increase in unemployment. (The unemployed will most likely increase from 10 million in 1997 to 16 million in 1998 due to the mismanagement of the state-owned enterprises) The most serious problem faced by China at the moment is a drastic increase in bad loans. Presently, the total amount of China's domestic bad loans is as high as 37 per cent of the GDP, compared to 20 per cent of Thailand's.

The accumulation of foreign debts among the ASEAN countries, Korea and China implies the weaknesses of the economic institutions and economic fundamentals of these countries. Foreign investors may lose confidence and foreign direct investments could diminish abruptly in these countries. All these factors in one way or the other prompted the collapse of currencies and stock markets in Asia.

International Turbulence — Three Big Undercurrents of the Economic Crisis

The Asian economic crisis erupted initially from the collapse of currencies and stock markets in ASEAN and the NIEs. This economic confusion that occurred in countries in ASEAN and the NIEs was basically due to macro mismanagement — current balance deficit, international trade deficit and accumulation of foreign debts. However, it cannot be ignored that the following international turbulence also contributed adversely to the outbreak, expansion and intensity of the Asian economic crisis. For convenience, all this international turbulence can here be termed as Chinese turbulence, Japanese turbulence and American turbulence.

The Chinese Turbulence

Twenty-one years have passed since China implemented an open-door policy and reformed economic policies in 1978. The Chinese style socialist market economy has been carried out with unprecedented impetus. China's relationship with ASEAN and the NIEs has been complementary as well as competitive. China's relationship with ASEAN and the NIEs in the fields of international trade, foreign investment, technology transfer and economic cooperation have no doubt had many complementary aspects. However, the following competitive aspects cannot be ignored. First, the competitiveness of ASEAN and the NIEs in international markets has been lowered, as wages and raw materials in China are much cheaper than those in ASEAN and the NIEs. Especially in recent years, the Chinese government has depreciated the Renminbi by 33 per cent against the dollar.[3] Chinese industrial products (labour intensive light industrial products and consumer goods in particular) have therefore speedily overwhelmed international markets. Since 1993, China's trade surplus with the USA increased remarkably. In 1996, China's trade surplus (inclusive of Hong Kong's exports to the USA) with the USA amounted to US$40 billion. The abrupt increase in China's exports to the USA implied the sudden decrease of ASEAN and NIEs exports to the USA. In other words, exports of ASEAN and NIEs industrial products within the same category as China's have been restricted. Second, European, American and Japanese direct foreign investments in China increased substantially while those in ASEAN and the NIEs decreased abruptly. Foreign direct investments to be invested in ASEAN and the NIEs have been redirected to China. Ironically, investments from ASEAN and the NIEs have also been lured to China. A large proportion of labour-intensive industries, with less comparative advantages, are also shifting to China. China has not only become an important recipient country of the foreign direct investments of Europe, the USA and Japan, but has also become a large recipient country of ASEAN and NIEs' investments. Viewed from this perspective, China is apparently the opponent of ASEAN and the

NIEs. As a result of sufficient foreign capital in China, ASEAN and the NIEs suffer from lack of foreign capital in their domestic markets.

The Japanese Turbulence

In December 1971, Japan shifted from the peg system (US$1=¥360) to the floating rate system. Since then, the Japanese currency has fluctuated according to the realities of the Japanese economy. The Japanese currency reached a turning point when the G5 meeting was held in autumn 1985. Just before the G5 meeting, the yen was pegged at ¥242 to the dollar in the Japanese exchange market. The USA currency depreciated drastically and in June 1994, the yen was pegged at ¥100 to the dollar. The yen continued to appreciate and in April 1995, the Japanese yen reached its peak and US$1 was transacted to ¥78. After the second half of the 1980s, due to the strong yen, Japanese direct foreign investments in Asia increased remarkably. Until the collapse of the Japanese bubble economy in March 1991, Japan had, both from supply and demand sides, contributed tremendously to the economic development of the Asian countries.

From January 1991 to April 1995, the Japanese currency maintained its strength. Over the above-mentioned period, both Japanese direct investments in Asia and the reverse export from Asia to Japan should have been strengthened. However, Japanese domestic markets were extremely sluggish due to the collapse of the bubble economy. Exports from Asia to Japan had not been satisfactorily stimulated as deregulation and the opening up of Japanese domestic markets had not fruitfully materialized.

The Japanese currency started to depreciate soon after it reached its peak in April 1995. Over the period April 1995–October 1997, Japanese exports were largely stimulated due to the drastic depreciation of the yen. Japan's trade surplus, especially against the USA, increased abruptly. In parallel with the immense increase of Japan's international trade, Asian export trade stagnated.

Actually, in 1995, ASEAN's exports were promising. Exports of machinery from ASEAN (especially Malaysia and Thailand) to Japan increased substantially to such a high level that it constituted one-third of Japan's total machinery imports in the same year. Exports of machinery from ASEAN to the USA and the NIEs had also increased remarkably. However, in 1996, the growth rate of exports from Asia including ASEAN decreased abruptly. Total growth rate of exports from the NIEs dropped from 21.0 per cent in 1995 to merely 4.3 per cent in 1996. Both growth rates of exports from ASEAN (Indonesia, the Philippines, Malaysia and Thailand) and China dropped drastically from 22.7 per cent to 5.1 per cent, and from 22.9 per cent to 1.5 per cent, respectively.[4]

In 1996, the growth rates of exports from Asia to Japan had also shown a similar tendency. For Singapore, it decreased from plus 47.3 per cent to plus 5.7 per cent. For Thailand and Malaysia, it decreased from plus 23.8 per cent to plus 0.8 per cent, and from plus 28.2 per cent to plus 11.4 per cent respectively. Even for China, it also decreased from plus 30.3 per cent to plus 12.6 per cent. Furthermore, if we confine it to machinery exports from Asia to Japan, Korea's exports dropped from plus 57.8 per cent in 1995 to minus 13.2 per cent in 1996, Thailand's exports decreased from plus 51.5 per cent to plus 10.5 per cent and Malaysia's exports decreased from plus 53.1 per cent to plus 22.2 per cent.[5]

From the above analysis, it is clear that Japan's exports had been stimulated after the yen depreciation from 1995 onwards. However, due to the sluggish domestic markets in Japan, ASEAN and the NIEs' exports to Japan dropped substantially. Obviously, a drastic drop in the export trade of ASEAN and the NIEs to Japan had in general worsened further both the current balance and trade balance of the Asian countries. Japanese turbulence has, in this sense, no doubt contributed adversely to the present Asian economic crisis.

The American Turbulence

After the second half of the 1980s, ASEAN and the NIEs succeeded in rapid economic development. One of the most important contributing factors, as mentioned earlier, was Japan's heavy investment in Asia. The other essential factor for the Asian success was undoubtedly due, as an enormous absorber of Asian manufacturing products, to gigantic domestic markets provided by the USA.

Ronald Reagan started promoting domestic consumption as soon as the Reagan regime was formed in 1981. Reaganomics produced a substantial amount of "twin deficits" (fiscal and trade) on the one hand, and stimulated a great flow of manufacturing products from Asia and Japan in particular on the other hand. The USA eventually started "bashing Japan", starting from the G5 meeting in autumn 1985, when the USA was no longer able to bear the burden of the "twin deficits". Almost at the same time, the USA started "bashing the NIEs" by forcing the currencies of the NIEs (except Hong Kong SAR, as its currency has been pegged to the dollar) to appreciate. Exports from Japan and the NIEs to the USA were then efficiently restricted. The sustainable Asian economic development was then seriously affected.

In January 1988, the Reagan regime had further announced that the Generalized System of Preferences (GSP) practised by the NIEs should be removed from January 1989. This announcement shocked the NIEs.[6] Thus since the removal of the GSP in January 1989, exports from the NIEs to the USA have been seriously restricted. The international trade mechanism of the NIEs, trade deficits with Japan being financed by trade surpluses with the USA, was totally disrupted.

ASEAN's international trade mechanism has been similar to that of the NIEs. ASEAN's exports to the USA had been stagnating when it met with the Chinese and Japanese turbulence. ASEAN's trade deficits were jeopardized, as ASEAN's trade deficits with Japan were not covered by trade surpluses with the USA.

As mentioned earlier, stimulated by the yen depreciation, Japan's exports increased substantially after April 1995. In the same year, despite the fact that exports from ASEAN and the NIEs to Japan increased substantially, ASEAN and the NIEs suffered from serious trade deficits with Japan. Table 10.5 reveals that in 1995, both ASEAN (Indonesia, the Philippines, Malaysia and Thailand) and the NIEs recorded US$25.7 billion and US$67.0 billion of trade deficits with Japan, respectively. These trade deficits could hardly be counterbalanced by ASEAN and the NIEs' trade surpluses with the USA (US$7.6 billion and US$25.1 billion respectively). ASEAN and the NIEs' trade deficits amounted to US$60 billion. Thus their current balance and trade balance were reduced due to their diminishing exports to Japan and the USA.

Disturbing Factors of the International Speculators — Thirty Per cent Responsibility

It is not easy to prove that international speculators or investors have thrown currencies and stock markets in Asia into confusion. It is also unfair to suggest that international speculators were real criminals in the Asian economic crisis. However, it would be ignorant of Asia, if someone suggests that the present economic chaotic situation had nothing to do with international speculators.

It was Malaysian Prime Minister Mahathir Mohamad who, for the first time, criticized an international speculator by mentioning his name. Soon after the Thai currency depreciated on 2 July 1997, Mahathir repeatedly and angrily criticized George Soros for his immoral speculative activities. His fierce criticisms against international speculators have shocked the world.

Malaysian currency and stock markets dipped whenever Mahathir criticized Soros. The former Malaysian Deputy Prime Minister and Finance Minister, Anwar Ibrahim, had to make statements to clarify the situation. The Malaysian opposition party, the Democratic Action Party, had asked the Prime Minister to "make statements with caution". However, Mahathir did not stop and instead increased his criticism of international speculators.

The spokesman of the US Department of State, Barnes, has totally denied that international speculators had plotted the Asian currency crisis, as implied by Mahathir. He backed Soros by saying that, "Mr. Soros is a brave man." He further suggested that "I don't think that Mr. Soros' activities are conspiratorial. Only economic forces are at work. The market price can only be rectified by healthy economic policies."

Figure 10.1

Supplementary Relationship in the Asia-Pacific Region (1995)

Unit: US$ million

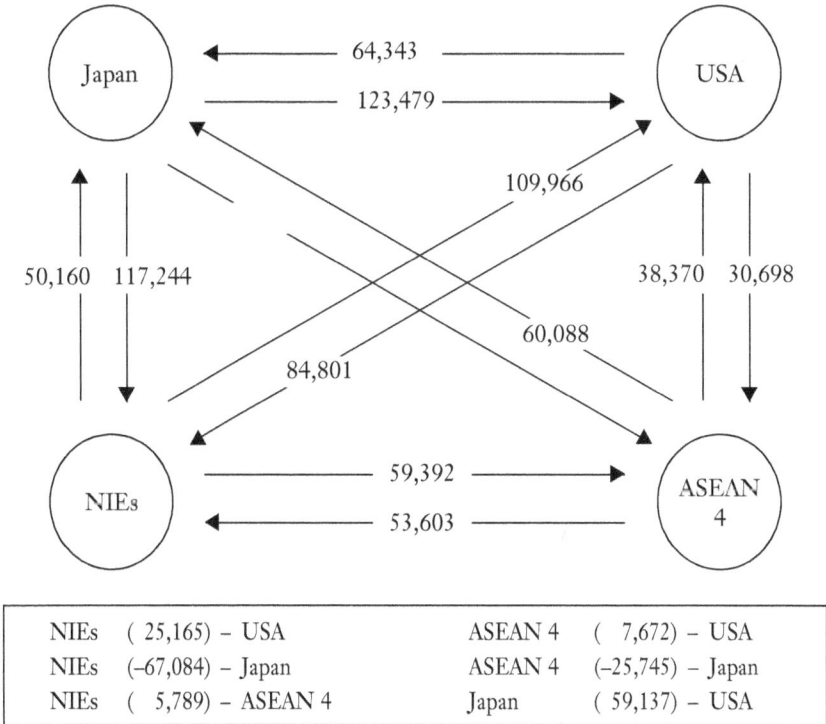

NIEs	(25,165) – USA	ASEAN 4	(7,672) – USA
NIEs	(–67,084) – Japan	ASEAN 4	(–25,745) – Japan
NIEs	(5,789) – ASEAN 4	Japan	(59,137) – USA

Source: *Same as Table 10.1*

He added, "we respect Mr. Soros. He has done a lot of good deeds all over the world."[7] It was significant that Barnes made such statements in Malaysia when he accompanied the US Secretary of State, Madeleine Albright, on a tour of the country on 26 July 1997.

It was reported that Soros (with estimated assets amounting to US$20 billion) speculated on British currency during the European currency crisis and had made a profit of US$1 billion in 1992. However, he made more than US$2 billion losses in currency speculation in the midst of the recent Asian economic crisis.[8]

Perhaps having this information in mind, the Emeritus Professor of Yale University, J. Tobin, replied impatiently, "the judgement of speculators cannot be always correct as they are also human beings," when questioned about Asian people criticizing international speculators. The international MIT economist, Professor Paul Krugman, added, "I am very surprised as to why the Premier should comment so much."[9] He further warned that, "it takes two to three years for investors to regain their confidence and succeed in smooth economic development, should policy makers of the Asian countries review the present currency crisis humbly and tackle the problems with pragmatism. However, a complete Asian economic recovery would take a much longer time, should they hysterically look for scapegoats such as Soros."[10]

The mass media in the West were overwhelmingly supportive of international speculators. In Asia, however, criticisms against speculative activities involving international speculators were conspicuous. The following comments were some examples:

- The Chinese former Premier Li Peng commented, "We should consider both the internal factors (the weaknesses of economic fundamentals) and external factors (disruptive activities carried out by international speculators) of Southeast Asian countries", when he was on a tour in Malaysia and Singapore and currency and stock markets collapsed in Thailand.

- The Bank of Thailand criticized Soros by name. The Bank commented that "Soros speculated US$2 billion in currency. He also intends to use US$6 billion to attack the Thai currency."[11]

- A Hong Kong finance source argued that "On 15 August 1997, Soros' hedge fund has plotted to sell Hong Kong dollars in the Hong Kong foreign exchange market. The Hong Kong dollar exchange dropped instantly, the Hong Kong central bank intervened and purchased a large quantity of Hong Kong dollars."[12]

In addition, Chinese bank representatives attributed Blue Monday (27 October) to the collapse of the Hong Kong currency and stock markets, and argued that "the hedge fund related to Soros had sold Chinese Hong Kong shares (red chips) in the Hong Kong market."[13]

- The former president of Indonesia, Suharto, argued in his annual parliamentary speech (16 August 1997) that speculative transactions by a specific speculator (referring to Soros implicitly) had "worsened the situation of the collapse of the recent Southeast Asian currency and stock markets."[14]

- Comments on international speculators in Singapore have been rather cautious. Singapore Prime Minister Goh Chok Tong avoided attributing the disruptive factors affecting the Southeast Asian currency crisis to international speculators. He emphasized the importance of economic fundamentals and the rational management of monetary and fiscal policies. However, Finance Minister Richard Hu affirmed that "Singapore will beat back the international speculators should they come to disrupt the exchange market in Singapore." Deputy Prime Minister Lee Hsien Loong observed that "international speculators do not attack Singapore currency as Singapore fundamentals are sound."[15] It is clear that the Singapore government is also taking the disruptive factors against the Asian currencies by international speculators into consideration.

International hedge funds have always speculated in countries with weak economic fundamentals (current balance deficits, trade deficits, accumulation of foreign debts and low foreign currency reserves). This explains why international hedge funds have so far not attacked Japan, China, Hong Kong SAR and Singapore on a large scale, as these countries have impressive records of current balance surpluses. Besides, as can be seen from Table 10.5, the above-mentioned countries have, at least, over the 1993–1997 period, accumulated a substantial amount of foreign currency reserves. These substantial reserves can be mobilized to protect and stabilize local currencies whenever there are ill manipulations of international speculators. International speculators have so far aimed at Thailand, Indonesia and Korea and have played a role in further disclosing countries with weak economic fundamentals. It is, therefore, clear that the present Asian economic crisis is not unrelated to speculative activities led by international speculators headed by Soros. It can be argued that the present Asian economic crisis is due 70 per cent to the weaknesses of economic fundamentals of specific countries, and the remaining 30 per cent due to disruptive activities in foreign exchange markets by international speculators.

Conclusion

Thai Tom Yam crisis (currency depreciation and stock market collapse) affects not only the ASEAN region but also Hong Kong SAR — a place displaying stability and prosperity. The Hong Kong SAR shock had then spread to Japan, Europe and the USA, and then to the whole world. It was termed the Blue Monday of 27 October 1997.

Asia used to have high economic development potential but has become the seismic centre of the worldwide economic crisis. It is hard to predict from which country the next Asian economic crisis will erupt in the Asia Pacific region. Recently, the drastic drop of currencies and stocks in the NIEs has also attracted much attention. Korea, as an OECD member next to Japan in Asia, has reached a level that without foreign assistance she is not in a position to rescue herself by being self-reliant. Korea is now receiving loans amounting to US$20 billion from the International Monetary Fund (IMF) and US$37 billion emergency loans from the world (essentially from Japan, Europe and the USA) to tackle her economic crisis.

The impact of the Asian economic crisis on Japan is potentially important. Currency and stocks in Japan dropped together with currencies and stocks in Asia. The weak Japanese economy has, in turn, affected the Asian economies quite seriously. Exports from Asia,

Table 10.5

Foreign Currency Reserves of the Asian Countries

(Unit: US$ million)

	1993	1994	1995	1996	1997
ASEAN					
Indonesia	10,988	11,820	13,306	17,820	16,088
Malaysia	27,249	25,423	23,774	27,009	26,100*
Philippines	4,546	5,866	6,235	9,902	7,147
Thailand	24,473	29,332	35,982	37,731	26,179
NIEs					
Korea	20,228	25,639	32,678	33,237	20,406
Taiwan	83,573	92,454	90,310	88,038	83,502
Hong Kong	42,990	49,250	55,400	63,810	75,320
Singapore	48,361	58,177	68,695	76,847	122,600*
USA	74,938	76,656	88,397	—	68,100**
China	22,387	52,914	75,377	105,000	139,900
Japan	98,524	125,860	183,250	216,648	219,648

* Indicates figures of September 1997
** Estimate

Source: *Same as Table 10.1*

however, have been stimulated due to weak currencies in the region while exports from Japan to the world have been restricted. Exporting industries in Japan are facing difficulties. However, the weak yen has spurred Japanese exports in recent years. The weak yen has not only intensified price competition among the Asian countries but has also had an adverse impact on the recovery of the Asian economies. If the Japanese economy worsens and the yen depreciates further, China might have to depreciate her Renminbi in order to stimulate export trade and to attract foreign direct investments. Price competition among the Asian countries is likely to intensify.

Japanese enterprises in Asia have also suffered quite seriously during the present economic crisis. It is estimated that more than

3,000 Japanese enterprises have invested in Thailand. The present Thai Tom Yam crisis has forced Japanese enterprises to reduce or stop production. Not only Japanese manufacturing industries but also Japanese banks and financial institutions in Asia, and in Thailand and Indonesia in particular, have suffered heavily from bad debts. It partly explains why financial reforms in Japan, since the collapse of the bubble economy in March 1991, have so far not been successful.

Due to the Asian currency crisis, a substantial amount of foreign exchange lost by the Japanese enterprises and financial institutions can not be ignored. Real assets held by Japan in Asia dropped drastically (for instance in Thailand, Japanese assets dropped by 30–40 per cent). The Asian economic crisis is not a fire on the opposite bank. Japan needs to implement economic reform policies forcefully and decisively under the new Obuchi administration, in order to get out from its blind alley as quickly as possible. The Asian economies will not recover easily without the recovery of the Japanese economy. A strong Japanese economy is essential for the recovery of the Asian countries.

Japan should initiate bilateral or multilateral supportive institutions (for instance through the Asian Development Bank, the World Bank, IMF or some sort of ASEAN Fund or Asian Fund) in order to strengthen cooperation with the Asian countries. Japan is expected to actively participate in mutual assistance, pertaining to Asian economic development, and to extend loans to solve the problems arising from the economic crisis in Asia. It is crucial for the Asian countries to get out of the economic crisis, as soon as possible, in order to allow the Asia Pacific region to proceed to rapid economic development in the 21st century.

Notes

1 *Nihon Keizai Shimbun-sha-hen*, Keizaishingo Jiten 92 Edition, p. 94.
2 *Nihon Keizai Shimbun Shasetsu*, "Indonesia Shien no Jyoken" (Conditions for assisting Indonesia), 22 October 1997.
3 Shogaku-kan, SAPIO, 22 October 1997, p. 23.
4 *Nihon Keizai Shimbun*, 23 June 1997.
5 Ibid.

6   The size of USA's GSP increased from US$3.2 billion in 1976 to US$10.8 billion in 1983. The NIEs constituted 50.8 per cent of the USA's GSP. The breakdown is Taiwan (1st, 24.2 per cent), Korea (2nd, 12.4 per cent), Hong Kong (5th, 9.1 per cent) and Singapore (7th, 5.1 per cent).

7   *Nihon Keizai Shimbun*, 27 July 1997.

8   *Nihon Keizai Shimbun*, 31 October 1997.

9   *Nihon Keizai Shimbun*, 20 October 1997.

10 Paul Krugman, "Wrong, It Never Existed", *Time*, 29 September 1997, p. 41.

11 *Straits Times*, 27 June 1997.

12 *Nihon Keizai Shimbun*, 16 August 1997.

13 *Nihon Keizai Shimbun*, 25 October 1997.

14 *Nihon Keizai Shimbun*, 1 August 1997.

15 *The Straits Times* (weekly edition), 11 October 1997.

CHAPTER 11

Japan's Bubble Economy and Asia's Economic Recovery

Introduction

The collapse of the so-called bubble economy in March 1991 in Japan and the long entrenchment of Japan's economy in the doldrums of recession and financial despair can be considered one of the important factors contributing to the Asian financial crisis that erupted in July 1997. Similarly, it is one of the main reasons why the recovery from the crisis is still on an uncertain footing.

This chapter examines the background and causes of the bubble economy, focusing on stock and real estate market issues. Next, it delves into the various government policies (such as monetary and fiscal policies, banking and foreign exchange rate systems and crisis management measures) implemented, their impact and limitations as to re-energizing the economy, discussing them in detail and putting forward criticisms and suggestions. Lastly, it considers the complementary relationship between Japan and Asia and analyzes in some detail Japan's role in the recent financial crisis. This chapter is particularly aimed at examining the potential effects of the so-called New Miyazawa Plan on the nascent economic recovery of Asia.

Despite their high degree of interdependence the Asian countries have few and weak formal organizations that can help them coordinate their economic policies. Setting up a new international organization or institution among the Asian countries to strengthen economic cooperation in the region is an important focal point in the future.

The Background and Causes of Japan's Bubble Economy

The Western nations, led by the USA, put pressure on Japan to let the yen appreciate in the mid 1980s. This happened at the G5 meeting held in September 1985 ("the Plaza Accord"). Since then the Japanese currency appreciated rapidly from 242 yen to the US dollar just before the G5 meeting, to 100 yen in June 1994, and later to 80 yen in May 1995. As a result, asset values in Japan, in dollar terms, tripled within a decade. The reason behind the move was that the USA suffered from serious "twin deficits" (fiscal and international trade), and wanted to restrict imports from Asia, Japan in particular.

Meanwhile in Japan, asset (stocks and land property) values increased substantially but abnormally from the second half of the 1980s to the end of 1990. It was even referred to as "asset price inflation" or "stock inflation". The situation was characterized by strong increases in asset prices, while prices of commodities and services in general remained stable. The Nikkei Index jumped threefold from approximately 13,000 in January 1986, to approximately 39,000 by the end of 1989. Land prices also tripled during the same period. *Table 11.1* indicates that total land prices in Tokyo alone increased from 176 trillion yen in 1985, to 517 trillion yen in 1990. Market capitalization (total equity of listed companies on the Tokyo Stock Exchange) increased from 160 trillion yen to 478 trillion.[1]

Obviously this did not reflect the economic reality in Japan. If we take a closer look at the GDP in Japan, it increased only from 324 trillion yen to 434 trillion yen during the same period. Table 11.1 further shows that both land prices (in Tokyo) and market capitalization (as described above) exceeded Japan's GDP during the 1987–1991 period and the 1988–1990 period respectively. Hence Japan created a "bubble economy" during the period between the second half of the 1980s and the end of the year 1990.

What made the bubble economy possible? The large scale financial deregulation policy implemented since the second half of the 1980s was a major reason. Following the drastic yen appreciation in September

Table 11.1
GDP, Stock and Real Estate Values

(Unit: Trillion yen)

Year	GDP	Stock	Real estate
1985	324	169	176
1986	338	230	280
1987	354	301	449
1988	377	394	529
1989	403	527	521
1990	434	478	517
1991	457	373	504
1992	484	297	428

Notes:
* Stock value represents the total value of partially listed companies by Tokyo Stock Exchange.
** Real estate value represents the total amount of residential assets in Tokyo yen during this period.
Source: Noguchi Yukio, Baburu No Keizaigaku (Bubble Economics), Nihon Keizai Shimbun-sha, 1993, p. 23.

1985, the tempo of the financial liberalization process in Japan escalated and current account surpluses fuelled the liquidity of the market. At the same time, the already huge demand for business offices in big cities in Japan, Tokyo in particular, increased significantly. The government could not play any active role as it had fiscal expenditure constraints and was in urgent need to cover deficits incurred by various governmental departments. Under these circumstances, measures pertaining to the privatization of city development projects and deregulation policies were introduced. Later in autumn 1987, the "Black Monday" incident occurred and this further prompted the deregulation process in Japan.[2]

In retrospect, the bubble economy in Japan was partly created by the government. After the second half of the 1980s, the deregulation policies prompted investors to concentrate on land speculation for capital gains, partly because there was no rational land property taxation system. Land prices were pushed further skywards by government sales of state land, in particular land owned by the Old

National Railways, at high prices. The Old National Railways (now called JR, for Japan Railways) suffered from serious deficits, before it was privatized. Land owned by the state was sold at high prices to cover part of the railway company's losses. Land prices were hiked up in this way by measures taken by the government.

The low interest rates policy had also power as long as the value of their stocks kept on increasing. Bank managers could not refrain from lending money to real estate speculators as they thought it was a profitable venture with little risk involved.

Because the financial liberalization (liberalization of the rate of interest in particular) process was underway, banks were able to accumulate substantial amounts of capital through "free interest rate deposits" (MMC and large fixed deposits), parked in banks by customers. The total amount of these "free interest rate deposits" accumulated by city banks skyrocketed. The proportion of this type of deposits in city banks' overall portfolio increased from 37.1 per cent in 1988 (by the end of March), to 47.2 per cent in 1989, to 61.1 per cent in 1990 and to 69.8 per cent in 1991. In the case of local banks, the figure for this proportion was 60 per cent in 1991, and for credit houses, 50 per cent in the same year.

Thus both city and local banks continued to extend loans to real estate investors and speculators directly or through finance houses. It was somehow restricted when the government enforced "controls over loans towards real estate businesses" in April 1990. However, the controls were abolished again in January 1992. There were signs of policy inconsistencies, which implied that the government was undecided as to how the problem of the bubble economy should be tackled, or even at the very least, how to solve the lingering real estate problem.

Fiscal Policy

Japan is a big trading country. The economic development of Japan relies very much on export trade. An export-led growth policy has been Japan's survival mantra, and export industries (particularly automobile, electrical and electronics industries) contributed to a stable currency. The other members of the G5 meeting in September

1985 pressured the Japanese government to appreciate its currency drastically and this had a tremendous impact on Japan's export trade. Japan's export trade was seriously restricted and this also created a high yen stagnant economy soon after.

Countermeasures to a high yen stagnant economy are a low interest rate climate and, in general, an economic stimulus policy. These had already been implemented for years. As pointed out earlier, low interest rates had prompted speculative activities in real estate. In May 1987, as an emergency economic measure, a supplementary budget amounting to 6 trillion yen (5 trillion yen for public infrastructure and 1 trillion for tax deductions) was introduced. This supplementary budget, together with the "Black Monday" incident happened in autumn 1987, prompting deregulation sentiment in Japan. All this worked as a catalyst for speculative activities in real estate, which fuelled the bubble economy in the country. In other words, the stimulation package, intended to make up for the decrease in economic activity caused by stagnant exports, backfired as the stimulation effect was channeled mainly into the asset markets.

Banking System

We mentioned earlier that the deregulation of the financial sector had enabled banks (city banks, local banks and credit houses) to accumulate substantial amounts of capital through utilizing the MMC and the "huge fixed deposits" facilities. One serious side effect of this maneuver was the inordinate increase in operational costs. At the same time, bank managers were more inclined to supply lending to speculative activities in real estates for quick returns and possibly better profits. Over the last few years, numerous scandals, relating to illegal loans extended by financial institutions to speculators, unlawful individuals or organizations, have been disclosed.

As described already, the stock market flourished from the middle of the 1980s till February 1990. Centred around big enterprises in Japan, the equity finance companies were in a better position to raise funds, compared to other banking institutions. Within 3 years, from 1987 to 1989, these equity finance companies managed to raise funds amounting to 56 trillion yen out of a total of 58 trillion yen raised. The equity finance companies were not interested in investing in equipment or production, but in the so-called "assets technology", such as the "huge fixed deposits", the "special monetary trust" and the "fund trust".

At the other end, banking institutions encountered difficulty mobilizing funding. They then took two approaches. First, they became more aggressive and looked for speculative investments such as in real estate. Secondly, they switched their loan facilities from big enterprises and manufacturing industries to small and medium-sized industries and, of course, to real estate concerns.[3]

Exchange Rate System

Drastic yen fluctuations have been typical for the Japanese economy since 1985. A strong yen has both beneficial and adverse effects on the economy. Yen appreciation contributes to import industries such as the foodstuff, petroleum and natural gas industries. It also contributes to Japan's purchasing power and hence has stabilizing effects on domestic markets. However, the strong yen limits exports of manufactured goods such as automobiles, electrical and electronic products to international markets and forces outsourcing of industrial activities. On the other hand, yen depreciation reduces Japan's purchasing power and has inflationary effects on the Japanese economy, although it stimulates Japan's export trade and contributes favourably to her international trade balance.

As mentioned earlier, since the G5 meeting in September 1985, the yen has been fluctuating drastically. The *yen-daka* (yen appreciation) and the *yen-yasu* (yen depreciation) have been major concerns of Japan as well as the world. Japan has been particularly annoyed by the drastic fluctuation of the yen. The Japanese economy has been disturbed by the abrupt changes of Japan-USA currency exchange rates, particularly over the last 15 years. In general, it has been quite flexible and has been quick to adjust to the international monetary environment. This is due to Japan's strong industrial infrastructure and the strengths of numerous manufacturing industries. When the yen started appreciating substantially from September 1985, the Japanese economy was thrown into a chaotic situation, however. Many Japanese believed that 100 yen to the US dollar was the lifeline of the Japanese economy. However, Japan managed to survive even when the yen reached its peak of 80 yen to the US dollar in April 1995.

Presently the exchange rate is 108 yen to the US dollar (5th August 2000), but the rate has been on a rising trend lately and this has not worked to the advantage of Japan, as the Japanese economy has just started to show signs of recovery. The Japanese authorities intervened many times by buying US dollars and selling the Japanese yen but all to no avail.

One serious problem is that Japan has lost control of the Japanese currency. Without the so-called Kyocho Kai'nyu (harmonious interference) with the USA, nothing much can be accomplished by Japan. Although Japan has managed to survive from the "yen shocks", the Japanese economy has remained in bad shape. Recently (24th December 1999), the Bank of Japan (BOJ) injected US$2.4 billion into the forex market in its yen-selling intervention but only managed to pull the yen from 101.57 to 103.1 to the dollar. The former vice-finance minister Mr. Sakakibara Eisuke suggested that the yen's current level of then 102 should be pulled to the 110 level. In doing so the BOJ should make its yen-selling intervention an "unsterilized intervention", meaning that any excess currency created through intervention by BOJ should be allowed to stay in the market rather than being absorbed via daily money market operations.[4]

Crisis Management

The Government of Japan has pumped in billions of dollars to rescue the country's economy. Public funds have been used to bail out banks and finance houses, to expand construction of social and industrial infrastructure, to reduce income taxes and corporate taxes and to give out promotion (free) tokens (Chi'iki Sinko-ken) to children and the elderly, etc. Initially, the Japanese in general had a very strong objection to using public funds for private purposes, especially for rescuing ailing corporations. After 9 years of recession, the Japanese have become indifferent to this government strategy and pay less attention to how public funds are being utilized.

Despite announcing numerous economic rescue packages and pumping billions of dollars into the Japanese economy, Japan Inc. has remained sluggish. Why? Does the Japanese economy have structural defects or cyclical problems?

If the collapse of the bubble economy in Japan were limited to merely cyclical problems, the macro-economic policies pursued (including expansionary demand policies such as tax reductions, public expenditure increases, financial deregulation, distribution of regional promotion tokens or free tokens to children and elderly) should have pulled Japan out from the economic doldrums over these 9 years.

After the sluggish economy has dragged on for nearly a decade, with no effective, efficient and consistent policy being implemented to put the economy back on track, it has begun to show signs of structural defects, with no easy cures in sight. One such defect is evident from the extremely low level of domestic consumption. This is due to the long-term uncertainty over unemployment opportunities (the unemployment rate has now reached 5 per cent and this is the highest rate since World War II) and uncertain pensions scheme (evidently the government will be unable to pay pensions to retirees due to huge fiscal deficits). Tax reductions only encourage the Japanese to save more for the uncertain future. They apparently do not work toward stimulating domestic consumption or to reenergize the domestic economy.

In fact, the Japanese government has come under heavy criticism for not being bold enough to embark on significant reforms of the economy. Instead it has resorted to old-fashioned Keynesian pump-priming in order to keep the economy going. Despite the fact that enormous amounts of money have been spent, the effect has been rather insignificant. The main outcome instead has been an enormous public debt now amounting to 1.3 times the value of the GDP.[5]

Various suggestions to break the deadlock have been put forth. Large-scale urban reconstruction projects have been suggested, rather than the general increase of public expenditures (construction of social and industrial infrastructure). By doing so, the declining real estate market could be revitalized and the urban living environment could be upgraded at the same time. In the end, the Japanese economy would be lifted once again from the depths of gloom.[6]

It is commonly argued that by taking advantage of a strong yen, through deregulation and opening up of the domestic market and totally amending housing and land systems in Japan, products from overseas could be cheaply imported. The Japanese domestic market could then be expanded and living standards in Japan could be improved.

On the other hand, one important aspect that must be taken into consideration here is that the collapse of the bubble economy was related to the restructuring of the financial sector. Solving the problems in that sector can be viewed either as a short-term crisis management problem or a long-run structural reform problem. The Japanese government has been racking its brains on how to settle the problem of bad debts incurred by banks and other financial institutions. The focus of its plan is protecting the depositors (up to a limit), improving the accounting system and making sure that loans are available for reliable borrowers.

However, prices of real estate and stock have continued to fall as the Japanese public in general does not have confidence in the country's economic prospects and have remained largely pessimistic about the direction of asset prices (i.e., real estate and stocks) in the future. (During the last year considerable improvements in the general trend of share prices have occurred but whether this trend is sustainable is still a moot point.) It is argued that in order to prevent future drops in asset prices, improving the outlook of the Japanese economy has become a matter of paramount importance. In the long run, the government undeniably has to create an environment conducive to development of leading industries. In order to do so, Japan has to create a new and healthy financial system, the sooner the better.[7]

The Japanese government has recently tried to revitalize the financial sector through carrying out a reform programme (the so-called Big Bang) since fiscal year 1997. The reform covers the financial sector as a whole, including banking, securities and insurance and removes restrictions on organizational structures and financial products and services. It also aims at improving the protective rules for customers and providing improved mechanisms for dealing with financial failures. Some institutions had to be closed down or taken over by the state (such as the Long-Term Credit Bank and the Nippon Credit Bank). While these measures are likely to make the financial system more efficient they may not, as such, help boosting the level of demand in the short term. The conventional way to do this is through low interest rates. For over three years now, the Bank of Japan has kept the interest rate very close to zero. This has not had much effect, however. The households are too pessimistic to take up new loans, while the excess capacity of many firms discourages new investment.

Japan is a highly industrialized country and has accumulated numerous advanced technologies. Using its strong technological bases to nurture some new industries should not be a big problem. In fact, new industries have been nurtured all the time. The problem is that under the present gloomy economic environment, growing leading industries in time to pull Japan out of the doldrums is obviously a difficult task. In any case it takes time to do so. To follow the example of the USA, using information technology to lead the Japanese industries to engineer a third industrial revolution is a task yet to be fulfilled.

Japan's Role in Asians Financial Crisis – Effects of the New Miyazawa Plan on the Economic Recovery

Over the last 9 years, to the surprise of most people, Japan's economy, as we have seen, has not shown any promising signs of recovery. Actually, the economy has already bottomed out several times, but has not recovered with consistency and dynamism. Nobody could have predicted that this situation would have dragged on for such a long period. Nor could anybody have anticipated precisely when the economy really would bottom out and then start to recover steadily. Japan's economy has lost its direction and is in a state of confusion.

The Japanese government has so far pumped in billions of dollars,[8] in the form of rescue packages, in order to put the Japanese economy back on the right track. Despite several attempts, the Japanese economy would at best succeed in achieving a 0.6 per cent growth rate for the fiscal year 1999 and perhaps 1.0 per cent in the year 2000.

In terms of GDP, Japan is the largest economy in Asia (it is about twice as large as that of the rest of East Asia taken together), and the second largest in the world, next only to the USA. Japan's poor economic performance has been detrimental to the economic development of the other Asian countries. Japan's decreasing investment in Asia, especially after 1995, and its diminishing import of manufactured products (machinery and equipment in particular) from Asia in the second half of the 1990s, have contributed adversely to Asia's economic performance. Japan's economic collapse and prolonged stagnation in the 1990s contributed largely to the contagious economic malaise that spread to the other Asian countries.

The present strong yen situation in Japan, after the drastic currency appreciation, stunts the country's recovery. Most of its export industries suffer from the strong yen. Japan has again been put in a difficult situation, as it has to adjust to the new international environment and has to restructure its weak economy. Many Japanese experts estimate that the US dollar should be kept at the 115–125 yen level, for the country to be able to proceed along the path of smooth economic recovery. Japan seems to be in for hard times. The USA believes a "weak" US currency (i.e., against the yen) will continue to benefit its economy, and has no intention of interfering with the currency market. The Japanese government and the Ministry of Finance in Japan have had limited success adjusting the yen level despite continuous interference. Without "harmonious interference" by the USA and Japan, the Japanese currency will not be weakened significantly in the foreseeable future.

The strong yen encourages exports from Asia to Japan. The Asian countries are thus in a great dilemma. They hope for the Japanese economy to recover quickly and for their exports to Japan to increase. However, it would be preferable that exports to Japan rise because of an economic recovery of Japan rather than because of a strong yen.

The Asian economies have shown some signs of recovery, after the devastating Asian financial crisis. Some critics still question whether the recovery is sustainable, however, since most of the affected countries in Asia have not gone through a thorough industrial and financial restructuring. Some Asian countries may not have learnt their lesson and might have become complacent or too confident. In a way the Asian economies are still vulnerable.

Japan, still in the midst of a possible recovery, is expected to make a contribution also to Asia's economic recovery. The so-called New Miyazawa Plan (Shin Miyazawa Koso) originally allocated US$30 billion to assist Asian countries recovering from the Asian financial crisis. This amount has so far been increased to US$80 billion.

It is clear that a quick recovery in Asia is also to Japan's benefit. Economic relations between Japan and Asia are complementary. Japan's economic recovery relies very much on the quick recovery of the Asian countries. Japan dispenses the largest amounts of Official Development Assistance (ODA) of all countries in Asia. Corporations in Asian countries have been suffering seriously from bad debts since the Asian financial crisis erupted and Japan is the most important country extending loans to the rest of Asia, especially to Thailand and Indonesia. Japan would suffer the worst consequences should the Asian countries not be able to solve their bad debt problem. In other words, only when the corporations and banks in Asia have solved this problem are they in the position to repay their loans to Japan (i.e., Japanese corporations, financial institutions and the government).

The New Miyazawa Plan is aimed at helping the Asian countries overcome the Asian financial crisis contagion. In doing so, corporations' bad debt issues must be solved and industrial restructuring must be carried out as smoothly as possible. Loans can be repaid to Japan only when Asia is economically sound. The New Miyazawa Plan is designed to help the Asian countries and Japan can also be benefit in return. Judging from this aspect, Japan's recovery greatly depends on Asia's overall recovery.

The crisis has prompted new efforts at strengthening formalized economic cooperation in Asia. The New Miyazawa Plan could contribute to the formation of an Asian Monetary Fund (AMF). Government officials among the Asian countries unofficially mooted the AMF idea soon after the Asian financial crisis. The USA was quick to respond and opposed the idea of forming the AMF, however. The USA insisted that the AMF should either act subordinately to, or as a supplement to the International Monetary Fund (IMF), should the plan materialize. However, the initiative for forming the AMF has gradually subsided for now without much fuss.

The USA was less involved in the Asian financial crisis as compared to the previous crises in the Latin American countries, in particular Mexico. From the USA's point of view, Latin America is in its backyard while Asia is rather far away. Under the initiative of the USA, the IMF extended loans to, and prescribed deflationary policies for the Asian countries, especially in the cases of Thailand and Indonesia. But unlike Japan, the USA provided limited amounts of loans to the Asian countries. Furthermore, the Asia-Pacific Economic Cooperation (APEC) has hardly played any active role to help tackle the financial crisis in Asia. As a consolidated entity in Asia, ASEAN has almost had no role to play in alleviating the Asian financial crisis. None of the existing organizations is really equipped with instruments to deal with a major economic crisis. Besides, they are consensus-based and thus slow-moving by nature.

If the AMF were to be established, it should play an important role as a separate "IMF" in Asia. In future, the AMF can monitor or supervise economic development of the Asian countries. Member countries of the AMF can mutually keep an eye on each other before a crisis erupts. If a new financial crisis erupts, they can also extend assistance, both financial assistance and remedy measures, promptly and efficiently with immediate results.

In general, Asia has to take more responsibility for Asian affairs. ASEAN, APEC or the IMF cannot take care of Asia alone. An international organization by the Asian countries, for the Asian countries, should be set up. Of late, the USA seems less inclined to object to an AMF and Japan has developed an intention to set up an AMF among the Asian countries through realizing the New Miyazawa Plan. Malaysia gained China's support to push for an East Asian Monetary Fund in Asia. The EMF is no different from the AMF, and the grouping is the same as the East Asian Economic Caucus (EAEC) which was proposed by the Malaysian Prime Minister, Dr. Mahathir Mohamad in December 1990 but which has been dormant, by and large, since.

It would be ideal for the Asian countries, in the time to come, to set up an international institution for strengthening economic cooperation among themselves, adding to the organizations already existing. It does not matter whether the name chosen is the AMF or the EMF, as long as it can prevent another financial crisis from erupting in a country in Asia, or to assist that country effectively before the crisis catches on in the Asia region. In general, Asia has an important role to play, through implementing the New Miyazawa Plan.

Conclusion

In May 2000, China, Japan and Korea, together with the ASEAN 10, have reached a mutual agreement in Chiangmai, Thailand. They agreed to sign the ASEAN Currency Swap Agreement. This was both a big development and a break-through. Based on this agreement, it is believed that economic harmony and cooperation among the Asian countries will be further strengthened and deepened. It is expected that in the foreseeable future, say in 1-2 years time, members of these thirteen countries in Asia will form an international and functional organization (whether it is called the AMF or EMF or some other name), aimed at maintaining political stability and promoting economic development in the Asia-Pacific region.

Notes

1   Noguchi Yukio, Baburu No Keizaigaku (bubble economics), Nihon Keizai
    Shimbun-sha, 1993, pp. 21–23.
2   Tanaka Naoki, Saigo NoJyunen, Nihon Keizai No Koso (Towards the Twenty-
    first Century - A Vision for the Japanese Economy), Nihon Keizai Shimbun-
    sha, 1992, pp. 62–64.
3   Noguchi Yukio, op. cit., pp 35–37.
4   *Straits Times*, 27th December 1999, p. 43; Lian He Zao Bao, 27th December
    1999, p. 23.
5   *Asiaweek*, February 21, 2000.
6   Noguchi Yukio, Nihon Keizai Saisei No Senryaku (Strategies for the Resuscitation
    of the Japanese Economy), Chukyo Shinsho, 1999, pp. 22–24.
7   Ibid., pp. 24–26.
8   The Japanese government approved another biggest-ever draft budget totaling
    84.98 trillion yen to stimulate the domestic economy on 20th December 1999.
    This brings Japan's National Debt to 364 trillion yen and if the debt of local
    governments is included, to a staggering 647 trillion yen – or roughly equivalent
    to 1.3 times Japan's GDP. (*Straits Times*, 21st December 1999, p. 57)

CHAPTER 12

Japan's Initiatives and Asia's Revitalization

Introduction

Nowadays, the economic development of Asia is both uncertain and unpredictable. The Asian countries (Japan, NIEs, ASEAN and China) have in recent years, displayed both economic might as well as economic slump. Three years have passed since the Asian financial crisis first erupted and some optimists have forecast Asia on the path to sustainable economic development. Pessimists, on the other hand, have highlighted the bleak picture of economic performance among some of the Asian countries, which might again lead to overall regional economic setback, given the intimate interwoven economic relationships among partners within the region.

Japan together with China and the USA, have important roles to play in the Asia-Pacific region, in terms of influencing the economic performance of the Asian countries. Japan's New Miyazawa Plan should be in the long run designed to make contributions toward Asia's economic revitalization and sustainable economic development. Japan is expected to take initiatives or explore ways and cooperate closely with China, Korea and the ASEAN 10, in order to contribute to Asia's economic recovery. And, as a result, they expect to succeed in reintroducing the rapid economic growth experienced by most of the Asian countries from the 1980s until the eruption of the Asian financial crisis in 1997.

Potential for Asia's Rapid Development After the Crisis

Western critics tend to relate the Asian financial crisis to the corruption, collusion and cronyism so prevalent among Asian countries. It is further said that economic development and prosperity in Asia has been lacking in technological innovations and a manufacturing base. The Asian economies are therefore weak and termed ersatz capitalism or simply crony capitalism.

To a certain extent, their criticisms are correct and justified. One cannot ignore that the above-mentioned syndromes are indeed the weaknesses of some Asian societies. Overcoming these weaknesses will be the key if the Asian countries intend to succeed in sustainable economic development.

However, the Asian countries deserve success in economic development due to the following strengths and advantages:

High Savings Rates

Over the 1966–94 period, the average savings rates of Japan and the NIEs were 33.7 per cent and 30.6 per cent respectively, compared to that of EU's (fifteen countries) 22.5 per cent and the USA's 18.4 per cent. In general, high savings rates contribute to domestic capital formation and investments in social and industrial infrastructure development. After the Asian financial crisis, the savings rates in Asia have remained at high levels. In 1998, savings rates among the Asian countries were: China 41.5 per cent, Korea 42.3 per cent, Taiwan 25.1 per cent, Hong Kong SAR 30.5 per cent, Singapore 52.2 per cent and Japan 29.9 per cent (1997).

Especially in Japan, high savings rates are due to children's high education fees, savings for an aging population, high medical expenses and an uncertain future in general. This is also a reflection of low quality welfarism.

On this note, one should not ignore the fact that high savings rates inactivate domestic economic activities. Presently, Japan and China have failed to revive domestic consumption due to high savings rates. The governments are trying to reduce savings rates and stimulate domestic consumption in order to emerge from the doldrums of economic recession.

However, with the exception of China and Japan, high savings rates tend to do more good than harm among developing countries in Asia.

High Investment Rates and Low Welfare Expenditure

Over the 1991–1993 period, the welfare expenditures of the NIEs (in terms of GDP) were: Taiwan 4.4 per cent, Korea 1.2 per cent, Hong Kong 0.5 per cent and Singapore 0.4 per cent. However, over the 1976–1993 period, the welfare expenditures of the Western countries (in terms of GDP) were: the USA 7.2 per cent, Germany 14.7 per cent, France 18.3 per cent and Italy 14.8 per cent, as compared to Japan's 8.4 per cent.

Japan's welfare expenditure is marginally higher than that of the USA. But on the whole, the welfare expenditures of the rest of the Asian countries are much lower than that of the Western nations. Low welfare expenditures imply high investment rates in Asia and high investment rates have no doubt contributed to economic development throughout Asia. Should the developing countries, such as some of the Asian countries, put more emphasis on developing welfare systems, or should they develop their national economies at the expense of welfarism. This is a contentious issue among policy makers. Richer nations tend to put more emphasis on welfarism, whereas poorer nations tend to prefer economic development to welfarism.

Efficient Technocrats and Policy Makers

The Asian nations, especially Japan and the NIEs, have put more emphasis on education compared to the Western nations. Some people even relate it to the influence of Confucianism. The Asian nations have come to realize that human resource is the main driving force behind economic development. Higher education, beyond the first basic degree, has particularly been promoted by the leaders in the Asian countries. Asia is increasingly being known as an education and research hub and also a production line for thinkers as well as researchers. Leaders in Asia are either graduates of prestigious universities at home or abroad. Waseda and Tokyo Universities in Japan, National Taiwan University in Taiwan, Seoul University in Korea and the National University of Singapore in Singapore etc. have produced numerous leaders and capable technocrats in Asia. Some of these leaders have, of course, furthered their studies in Western countries, the USA in particular. A large number of these scholars have proven to be efficient technocrats and have formulated both industrial and economic policies, which have led to rapid economic development in the Asian nations.

Technocrats and policy makers in Asia are all-rounded. They have knowledge ranging from industrial management to overall economic development policies. Some are particularly knowledgeable on and keen to develop leading industries of the future, such as telecommunications, information technology, and recently, biotechnology.

The world has become a borderless and a more competitive place since the rapid development of the telecommunication and information technology industries. A new product can be developed and marketed all around the world at great speed, and a substantial amount of transactional agreements can be signed within minutes through information technology. Efficient technocrats and policy makers also do well by equipping themselves with advanced managerial skills as well as multidisciplinary training. Asia has, to its benefit, over the last 2-3 decades, developed substantial numbers of energetic and knowledgeable professionals, who form a ready pool of potential technocrats and policy makers.

The above-mentioned points such as high savings rates, high investment rates and low welfare expenditure and efficient technocrats and policy makers, which characterize much of Asia, are some of the strong elements conducive to Asia's rapid economic development in Asia. However, a sustainable and rapid economic development in Asia (the NIEs and ASEAN) is also very much dependent on the following three factors: the China factor, the Japan factor and the America factor.

The China Factor

Over the last twenty-two years since China implemented economic reform and open-door policies, her economy has taken off and she is now a major player on the world economic stage. China has, on one hand, become a keen competitor of the Asian developing countries (in terms of attracting foreign direct investments and competing in international markets with their manufactured products), and on the other hand, provided opportunities to the Asian developing countries (in terms of providing markets for their products and attracting labour-intensive industries from the region). China has contributed to overall regional stability and economic development since 1994, as the Renminbi was kept at a stable level. Even after the Asian financial crisis in 1997 and despite severe domestic and international conditions, the Renminbi was maintained at a stable level. Should the Renminbi have been depreciated by 10-15 per cent (it depreciated by 33 per cent against the dollar in 1994) after the Asian crisis, as put forward by some prominent Chinese economists, the Asian economies would have been adversely affected and the Asian economic recovery would have been prolonged. China was thus a stabilizing force among regional economies.

The Chinese currency will remain stable if the currencies in Asia do not depreciate drastically. The Chinese economy is now generally in good shape (despite some setbacks such as increasing unemployment, environmental pollution, growing disparity between coastal and internal areas etc.) and is likely to develop steadily, for at least another 20-30 years. China will join the WTO very soon and the Chinese economy will be further opened up and geared to the world. The opening-up of the Chinese economy will definitely further enhance and strengthen economic cooperation between China and the rest of the Asian countries.

Recently, the Chinese government has announced the development of the western areas in China. This is a big and long-term development plan, which requires a substantial amount of capital, technology and managerial know-how, domestically and internationally. The central government in China has decided to allocate billions of dollars to develop the western areas and at the same time, investments from industrialized nations are also expected. The ethnic Chinese in Asia have also shown great interest in joining the queue to explore opportunities in the western areas, although concrete plans have yet to be worked out.

A sustainable economic development in China is an important factor for Asia's continued political stability and economic development.

The Japan Factor

From September 1985 to March 1991 (during which the Japanese currency appreciated abruptly after the G5 meeting until the collapse of the bubble economy in Japan), Japan's foreign direct investment in Asia contributed greatly to the region's economic development. Japan not only provided capital but also technological and managerial expertise to the Asian countries. The industrial sector in Asia expanded and manufactured products were consumed in the region as well as exported to international markets. Japan also imported substantially from Asia, as she was then experiencing a booming economy.

However, from 1991 until now, the Japanese economy has stagnated. The punctured Japanese economy has had a detrimental effect on economic development in Asia. This was witnessed by the diminishing economic role played by Japan (such as reduced investment in Asia and decreasing imports from Asia). Especially from 1991 to the outbreak of the Asian financial crisis in 1997, the Asian economies were very much affected by the gloomy Japanese economy. The prolonged economic recession in Japan is beyond our expectation. The Japanese government has been running an unprecedented fiscal budget deficit amounting to 645 trillion yen. This fiscal budget deficit has so far not been able to put Japan back on the track of economic recovery and development.

Despite the gloomy economy, Japan's economic fundamentals have been encouraging. This is manifested by possessing the highest foreign currency reserves, the highest GDP per capita and the highest foreign assets in the world, huge international trade surpluses and a reasonable unemployment rate. This unemployment rate is presently about 5 per cent and is the highest since the Second World War. However, considering unemployment standards among the highly industrialized nations, it is relatively low. Although it can be said, that the way of calculating the employment rate does differ from country to country. Besides, Japan has been the largest ODA donor country (1 trillion 404.7 billion yen in 1998) in the world, and the Asian countries have been the biggest recipients among the developing countries. During the Asian financial crisis period, Japan was the country that extended the most financial assistance to various Asian countries.

Japan has been struggling over the last decade. Her economy has recently shown some signs of recovery and is expected to bottom out soon. The complementary economic relationship between Japan and Asia indicates that Japan's recovery will contribute to Asia's overall recovery and revitalization. Together with Japan's ODA, the New Miyazawa Plan, amounting to US$ 80 billion, can be utilized to assist economic development in Asia, through nurturing small and medium-sized industries, constructing social and industrial infrastructure, environmental improvement for better economic development, monetary assistance conducive to industrial and financial restructuring, etc. Japan is in the position, and is expected by Asia, to assist the Asian countries overcome the financial crisis and move forward to rapid economic development. In return, Japan's prolonged stagnated economy will also be reactivated by the Asian economies.

The America Factor

The USA is the largest economic power as well as the largest market in the world. The vicissitudes of the American economy have always had impacts on the world economy in general and the Asian economies in particular. The Reagan Administration started in 1981 and introduced Reaganomic policies soon after, which stimulated domestic consumption and international trade. In the end, the 'twin deficits' of fiscal and international trade were created. The 'Japan bashing' and the 'NIEs bashing' policies were then introduced after the second half of the 1980s. Exports from Asia to the USA were restricted but the 'twin deficits' were not effectively rectified even during the Bush

Administration, which followed. The USA economy was in bad shape during the Bush Administration but the democratic Clinton Administration has created a booming economy in the USA today. The fiscal deficit has been totally rectified while the international trade deficit has remained unsolved. The USA does not seem overly concerned about the trade deficit as long as the economy is well. Some people in the USA have even made a point that 'Japan has tremendous trade surpluses but her economy is in bad shape, so what is wrong if the USA has trade deficits while her economy is booming?'

The booming economy in the USA is now helping the Asian countries pull out of the financial crisis. Asia's recovery and revitalization are also very much dependent on the buoyant economy of the USA. However, the USA has been experiencing economic fertility for many years and her economy, or bubble economy, can collapse anytime. Once it collapses, the Asian economies will be the first to feel its effects. The foundation of the present USA economy is very much built on developing the information technology industries. This is a new trend of the worldwide economic development, and the USA is by far the leading trendsetter. The Asian countries are particularly keen to develop their information technology industries in order not to be left behind the western nations, and the USA in particular. Japan, the NIEs, ASEAN and China are pushing very hard, but some of the ASEAN countries will be gradually left behind. In the foreseeable future, the development standard of the Asian economies will be judged by the development and performance of these information technology industries.

The Tripolarization of the Asia Pacific

The economic development of Asia (the NIEs and ASEAN 10) is very much dependent on the above-mentioned three countries. The USA is setting standards for the rest of the world and is continuing to influence the world economy. When Japan established a double-income (shotoku-baizo) economy in the 1960s, and forged continuous industrial development from the 1970s till the time before the bubble economy collapsed in 1991, she was considered the USA's main economic rival. However, the USA is now industrially and economically much more superior than Japan. Japan has been in the doldrums of a stagnated economy over the last decade, and has now suddenly realized that she has lagged behind the USA in the sectors of finance, telecommunications and information technology. During the Okinawa Summit in July 2000, Japan showed great concern over its position in the New Economy and has decided to play catch up with renewed vigour.

The USA policy towards China has been seesawing between the 'containment' and 'engagement' approaches. The USA has only recently extended the Most Favourable Nation (MFN) status to China permanently. In the same vein, after years of negotiations, the USA has recently also agreed with China's participation in the World Trade Organization (WTO). After twenty-two years of reform and open-door policy, China has at last managed to become a member of the international economic world. It is clear that China's international trading status has been very much influenced by the Western nations in general and by the USA in particular.

China, Japan and the USA constitute the tripolarization of the Asia and Pacific region. The USA is a vital market for China's comparatively low value added manufactured products. On the other hand, China forms an important market for the USA and Japan's high value added manufactured products as well as direct foreign investments (especially automobile, electronics and electrical, telecommunications, banking and information technology). China's international competitiveness will be upgraded and China's economy will be prompted to restructure in response to this change, once China has officially joined the WTO. Evidently, due to the collapse of the bubble economy and the prolonged stagnated economy of Japan, Japan's DFI in China has been squeezed and Japan's domestic industrial development has lagged behind the USA. However, Japan has always had sound production base and technologies, so she can proceed with rebuilding her economy once the decline has bottomed out.

The USA is leading the race, but China and Japan have tremendous development potential. China has succeeded in rapid economic development over the last twenty-two years, and it is argued that by 2050 she could well be the second largest trading nation in the world. By 2040, China and Japan's combined GDP will exceed that of the USA. The USA, Japan and China are, and will increasingly be the most important economic powers not only in the Asia-Pacific region but also in the world. The rest of Asia's (the NIEs and ASEAN 10) economic development is therefore dependent on how well they gear towards and integrate with this tripolarization.

Recovery Without Thorough Restructuring and Reform

The Asian economic development depends very much on the China factor, the Japan factor and the America factor. These three factors will continue to affect Asia's recovery and revitalization, after the Asian financial crisis. The Asian countries expect these three nations to perform well and contribute positively to the development in the Asia-Pacific region.

Three years have passed since the Asian financial crisis. Judging from Asia's economic fundamentals (visible and invisible trade balances, foreign currency reserves, unemployment rates, currency depreciation rates, fluctuation of share prices, fluctuation of land and property prices, and the GDP growth rates, etc.), the Asian countries have overall recovered.

Is Asia's recovery sustainable? Is Asia's recovery on track? Will Asia develop rapidly without interruptions over the next five or eight years? Unfortunately, very few people will be able to answer these questions with confidence. Many people are sceptical as the Asian countries recovered without thorough industrial restructuring and reform. In general, among the Asian nations, the financial and banking reforms have not been fully implemented, and bad debt issues have not been resolved. Over the last decade, Japan has been trying to restructure her industrial and financial systems, but without much success. It was therefore unrealistic to expect the Asian countries to have their industrial and financial systems restructured over 2-3 years. On this note, most of the Asian countries have not conducted their industrial and financial reforms seriously. The Asian economies have somehow recovered, due partly to the expansion of the domestic consumption markets, and partly to the booming economy of the USA which has stimulated exports from Asia to America.

Some of the Asian countries have not learnt much from the Asian financial crisis. They have become too complacent and over confident. They have not reviewed their long-term industrial development strategies and macro-economic management policies. They have not worked out policies or measures against short-term speculative investments in currencies, stock and shares, or other portfolio investments, especially from overseas. The 3-C issues (corruption, collusion and cronyism) or the so-called crony capitalism in Asia have not been rectified. Thus the economies in Asia remain vulnerable.

Uncertainties in Asia

From the politico-economic viewpoints, the Asian economic development process has long been disrupted by the following factors. Firstly, prices of industrial materials have been dropping. Indonesia, Malaysia and Brunei are important producers of crude oil and natural gas. These countries will be affected economically should prices of these industrial products drop drastically. In the 1930s, Malaya (including Singapore), Thailand and Indonesia suffered seriously when the rubber prices dropped. In the middle of the 1980s, Indonesia, Malaysia and Brunei were set back when oil prices dropped abruptly. And as a crude oil refining centre in the Asia-Pacific region, Singapore also suffered a great deal.

Secondly, foreign debts have always been a burden to bear. China, Indonesia, Malaysia, Thailand and the Philippines, etc. have been borrowing substantially from the industrially developed countries (particularly Japan) and international financial organizations (such as the World Bank) for their economic development. This burden was especially painful during the 1985–1995 period, when the Japanese currency appreciated substantially (from 242 yen to 78 yen to the dollar). Meanwhile, the Chinese Reminbi depreciated by 33 per cent in 1994, and after the Asian financial crisis in 1997, the Asian currencies in general have also depreciated drastically. These currency shifts have forced some of the Asian countries to become highly indebted countries and have undoubtedly been detrimental to Asia's economic development.

Thirdly, the prolonged gloomy economic outlook of some major industrialized countries has dampened overall economic development in the region. As mentioned earlier, over the last decade, the collapse and then the prolonged bleak Japanese economic situation, has adversely affected the Asian economies. Before that, the weak USA economy from the early 1980s to the beginning of the 1990s also adversely affected the Asian economies. On top of that, poor economic performance in Europe over the last one or two decades has also had a negative effect on Asia's economic development. These are basically reflected by the diminishing capital investments in Asia and Asia's stuttering export trade. At the present, in order not to be left behind in the information age, the NIEs and other countries in the Asia-Pacific region require more and more high technology investment, especially information technology investment from Japan.

Fourthly, the disruptive regional disputes and conflicts are derailing economic development in the region. The Southern and Western Spratly islands' dispute, the Taiwan Cross Strait problems, the Northern Island's dispute between Japan and Russia, the North-South Korea's problem, the Takeshima Island dispute between Japan and Korea and the Diaoyu Island dispute between China and Japan, etc. may create instability and be detrimental to economic expansion in these countries and beyond. The North and South Koreas have moved to reconciliation while the Taiwan issue has become more complicated since Chen Shui Bian was elected as the new president of Taiwan. The cross-strait dispute has so far become the most dangerous dispute, which may seriously affect the stability and economic development in the region.

Fifthly, the political instability in Asia has also become a concern. Asia has witnessed several race riots in the past, such as the 30th September riot in 1965 in Indonesia and the 13th May incident in 1969 in Malaysia. Furthermore, the democracy movement's anti-military regime in Burma, the Western Irian dispute, the East Timor independence and the Aceh dispute have also attracted our attention. Furthermore, political instabilities due to the transfer of political power in Asia, such as from Marcos to Aquino, from Kim Young Sam to Kim Dae Jung, from Suharto to Wahid, etc. have also caused much political anxiety in Asia. With regard to the above-mentioned political instabilities and other power transfers, some are major shifts while others are small, some have limited influence but others have widespread impact on the region, especially on the countries involved.

Sixthly, the religious disputes in Asia are becoming a serious problem. These religious problems are very much related to racial problems in Asia. We have witnessed how religious problems have caused racial disputes in the multi-racial societies in Asia. The uprising of the Islamic movement in the Southern part of the Philippines and the East Timor independence movement's activities are in fact very much related to the difference in religious beliefs in Asia. All these disputes have no doubt affected economic development in Asia.

The above-mentioned uncertainties have in one way or the other, been detrimental to the economic development of the Asian countries. It remains an uphill task for these Asian countries to recover from the Asian financial crisis, revitalize themselves and resume rapid economic development.

Conclusion

What Roles should Japan Play in Asia?
Japan has to make every effort to recover from the collapse of the bubble economy, should she intend to play an active role in Asia's

economic development. Japan lacks forceful and consistent macro-economic policies as Japanese Prime Ministers change frequently, not to mention bureaucrats in various ministries. The policy makers are reluctant to assume responsibility and so they need to reach a consensus to formulate policies. In the Japanese society, it always takes a long time to reach a consensus. The economic reform policies based on consensus are quite often without immediate effect and hence become untimely. The policies implemented can hardly meet the rapidly changing environment of today. It is difficult to predict precisely when the Japanese economy will bottom out and then rebound to develop steadily. Japan is still expected to play an important role even if her economy has not fully recovered. This is because a substantial amount of bad debt suffered by enterprises in Asia is funded by Japan. Japan will suffer considerably if the bad debt issues in Asia are not solved in time. It is therefore to Japan's benefit, if she can resolve the bad debt issues in Asia quickly. Understandably, Japan is keen to help the Asian countries to restructure their industries and financial institutions. It is important for the Japanese government to pass this message to her people and gain strong support from them. Some of the Japanese taxpayers are puzzled with the Japanese governments assistance policies (together with the ODA) toward the Asian countries. The Japanese government requires their support and understanding should she want to proceed with forceful and consistent policies toward the Asian countries.

The New Miyazawa Plan is designed to help the Asian countries recover in a more forceful manner. This plan can be substantiated and developed to set up the AMF in the Asia-Pacific region. In the beginning, the USA had strong objections towards the setting up of the AMF soon after the Asian financial crisis. Obviously, the USA did not want to see strong Japanese initiatives or her dominance in the Asia-Pacific region. The USA insisted that should the AMF be set up, it should function in a supplementary or complementary role to the IMF. In other words, the AMF should in all aspects be subordinated to the IMF.

The USA did not extend financial assistance to Thailand when the Asian financial crisis erupted in 1997. She extended limited financial assistance, incommensurate to her economic status, directly to the other nations in Asia affected by the crisis, but only at a later stage. However, through the USA's initiatives, the IMF played a very active role in assisting the Asian countries. The IMF's rescue packages (deflationary policies and conditionalities) in Thailand, Korea and Indonesia have earned both praise and critique. The IMF's approach has its own merits and demerits, and thus has limitations in assisting the Asian countries to fully recover from the Asian financial crisis.

The USA has come to realize that Japan should play a more important role in Asia. The USA has toned down her objections on the establishment of the AMF, and has not displayed any strenuous objections to the New Miyazawa Plan. It seems that Japan intends to set up the AMF through realizing the New Miyazawa Plan. It has encountered less resistance pushing the New Miyazawa Plan compared to the AMF. Among the Asian nations, China and Korea, especially the former, are sceptical about and have reservations on the setting up of the AMF. They are concerned about Japan's intentions and initiatives in Asia. Implicitly and unofficially, China and Korea maintain that Japan's hegemony in the Asia Pacific region should be checked.

Except for Singapore, the ASEAN countries have either not expressed any opinion or have welcomed Japan's bigger role in Asia. Singapore has also had no objection to the setting up the AMF, but is rather pessimistic about the role the AMF can play. It is argued that Japan will be unable to play an important role in the AMF, the way the USA plays in the IMF.

A collective role should be played by Japan, China and Korea, together with the ASEAN 10. Presently, China and Korea are less sceptical about Japan's ambition, as they are invited to participate more actively in the Asia and Pacific region. They are invited by Japan to take initiatives in Asia, and cooperate closely with the ASEAN 10 to revitalize the Asian economies. They seem to have reached a consensus. This was reflected by the signing of the ASEAN Currency Swap Agreement in May 2000, in Chiangmai, Thailand. The Asian countries have agreed to organize themselves and to set up an international institution in order to monitor and assist each other to revitalize and develop their economies. This international institution, say, the AMF or the EMF, is likely to be formed in a year or two, with initiatives jointly taken by Japan, China and Korea, with close cooperation and strong support from the ASEAN 10. The details and functions of this international institution have yet to be worked out.

CHAPTER 13

Chinese Abroad: Problems and Adaptation

Chinese Living Abroad Face Multiple Problems[1]

Chinese Descent, Overseas Chinese and Ethnic Chinese

According to a 1998 estimate, about 27.19 million kaei Chinese descent (people of Chinese ancestry who live outside China) lived in Asia (not including those residing in continental China, Hong Kong, Macau and Taiwan), in particular in countries of the Association of Southeast Asian Nations (ASEAN).

Kaei are made up of kakyo overseas Chinese (those of Chinese ancestry who live in Asia but have not acquired the nationality of the countries in which they live) and kajin ethnic Chinese (those who have taken the nationality of the countries in which they live). There is currently an advancing shift from kakyo to kajin. Although it is difficult to establish the exact number of kakyo, there are estimated to be slightly more than 4 million. Although kajin have Chinese blood and are historically and culturally Chinese, legally, they are not. Chinese emigration dates back to the Tang Dynasty in the ninth century but did not start in earnest until the 19th century after the Qing Dynasty was forced to open itself to the outside world after having lost the Opium War (1840–1842). The development triggered the move for a large number of Chinese mainly from Fujian and Guangdong provinces to immigrate to the South Seas. Since then, kakyo, who made a fortune starting their business from scratch in the South Seas, returned to their native land in triumph. Others who stayed behind thought of China, hoping to eventually return there. With the passage of time, however, their awareness as Chinese began to fade. In particular, the inclination not to identify themselves as Chinese grew stronger among second-, third- and fourth-generation kakyo.

Southeast Asian kaei have inseparable ties with China. First, kaei drifted to the South Seas as "displaced" Chinese. Exposed to severe conditions that forced them to choose between life and death with no one to help them, they somehow survived. To overthrow the Qing Dynasty, Sun Yat Sen received powerful personnel, material and financial support from Southeast Asian kakyo and kajin. He left the words, "Kakyo are the mother of revolution." Mao Tse-tung also received the strong backing of kakyo and kajin when he liberated China from the aggression of major Western powers and Japan. However, during the 1966-1976 Cultural Revolution, kakyo and kajin were criticized and purged by the Gang of Four. After 1978, however, with Deng Xiaoping's policy of reform and openness and the development of a "socialist market economy," China made an about turn and encouraged the advancement of kakyo and kajin businesses to China. Consequently, Asian kajin business leaders may come to be dubbed "the leading players of China's economic development" in the future.

However, China may need to re-examine its policy toward and estimation of kakyo and kajin, both of which need to be consistent. The Chinese central government has "a committee of overseas Chinese affairs." Local governments across China, in particular in Fujian and Guangdong provinces, also have "kakyo committees." In other words, China still regards Asian kakyo and kajin as people of Chinese ancestry living outside China.

Consider another example. In 1998, a mob of Indonesian rioters attacked local kakyo and kajin. When countries around the globe criticized the atrocities of the Indonesian rioters, the Chinese government alone remained silent. Out of consideration to China-Indonesia relations, China positioned the attack on local Chinese residents as an internal problem of Indonesia. China was afraid that if it criticized the incident, it would cause misunderstanding that it was siding with overseas Chinese. It took quite a long time before China officially criticized the incident from "a humanitarian viewpoint." However, when humanitarian problems occur, China should immediately take measures to deal with them.

New Overseas Chinese

In recent years, the term "new kakyo" has emerged. After China began promoting its reform and open-door policy in 1978, the number of Chinese students going to the USA, Japan and other countries to study has steadily increased. After graduating from university, instead of returning to China, many of these students land jobs in their host countries. While many retain their Chinese nationality, China calls these people, some of whom acquire the citizenship and permanent residency status of their host countries, "new kakyo."

Under a broader interpretation, Southeast Asian kajin who are active in Western countries and Indochinese kajin refugees who emigrate to and work in Europe and the USA are also called new kakyo. The term is ambiguous and misleading. But people of Chinese ancestry who hold the nationality of the countries where they emigrate to and live are neither kakyo nor new kakyo. In other words, they are the people-the leading players-of those countries. While they still may feel nostalgia for China, they have an obligation to their countries of residence. They must blend with their host countries and contribute to their social, economic and cultural advancement. At the same time, China should not be bound by sentimentalism that they are of Chinese descent, but evaluate their ability from an objective viewpoint.

Chinese Adopt Patriotism of Their New Homes[2]

Chinese Heritage

Over a long period of time, Chinese people have assimilated themselves into the Asian countries they emigrated to. Former Thai Prime Minister Chatchai Choonhavan and former presidents of the Philippines Ferdinand Marcos and Corazon Aquino, for example, have Chinese heritage. The Thai royal family has Chinese blood.

President Aquino visited her family grave in Fujian province when she made an official visit to China. Indonesian President Abdurrahman Wahid also said his ancestors migrated to Indonesia from Fujian province about 500 years ago and openly acknowledges himself as half-Chinese. In short, many Asian leaders are related to China by their blood. But it is also true that antipathy against "kajin" (ethnic Chinese living overseas who have taken the nationality of their countries of residence) is still strong in Asia.

Do Asian kajin have a patriotic spirit? Kajin businesses are aggressively advancing into China, supported by China's strong desire to attract them. As a result, ethnic Chinese representing such businesses always are seen with a wary eye by the local communities where they live. Is their patriotism directed at China or their country of residence?

A Sensitive Issue

Asian kajin capital accounts for about 80 per cent of China's overall foreign capital. However, such concentrated advancement of kajin capital into the Chinese market is aimed solely at profit and not as an outflow of capital. Nevertheless, investment of kajin capital in China is always a sensitive issue in Asia, where it tends to develop into political, social and ethnic problems.

Is the homeland of kajin the countries of their residence or China? In the 1950s and 1960s, many kajin thought of China as their homeland. Back then, it was a well-known practice for kajin to send items to their relatives in China, such as clothing and large quantities of canned dried pork. Sending cash was also common. A Chinese proverb has it that no matter how tall a tree is, fallen leaves eventually return to its root. Such a sense of belonging and a desire to return to one's hometown in glory and boast of one's success were still predominant.

A Drastic Change

But in the last four decades, the awareness of overseas Chinese underwent a drastic change from that of "kakyo" (people of Chinese ancestry who live outside China but have not taken the nationality of the countries in which they live) to kajin. In other words, emigrants who kept their Chinese nationality hoping to eventually return have been replaced by permanent residents who acquire the nationality of their countries of residence. As a result, while kajin in Asian countries maintain close ties with China in terms of history, culture and language, they are no longer Chinese. They feel uncomfortable when others refer to them as Chinese or kakyo. Many Asian kajin still observe traditional Chinese culture at formal ceremonial occasions such as weddings and funerals. At the same time, they are becoming increasingly diversified and localized. It is easy to find a kajin who cannot speak Chinese and is neither a Buddhist nor a Taoist. In particular, many young ethnic Chinese do not know which part of China their ancestors came from, showing how they identify with their countries of their residence rather than China.

Patriotism of Ethnic Chinese

In fact, there is doubt about whether there is a single Asian kajin born after World War II who thinks of his homeland as China: The countries where they were born and live are indisputably their homelands. Many young kajin do not even know how to write their names in Chinese characters. Doubting the loyalty and patriotism of Asian kajin is nothing but an anachronism. Many Asian kajin businesses were hit hard by the Asian economic crisis in 1997. Still, as kajin businesses expand internationally, their advancement into China also is expected to intensify. I do not think the loyalty and patriotism of kajin to their countries of residence will be questioned again or made into political, social and ethnic issues anytime soon.

What Japan Should Do With Chinese Economies[3]

Awareness of Chinese Studies in Japan

In Japan, awareness of "Kakyo" and "Kajin," Chinese living overseas, has been important since before World War II.

Kakyo refers to people of Chinese ancestry who live outside China but have not acquired the nationality of the countries in which they live. Kajin are ethnic Chinese living overseas who have taken the nationality of their countries of residence. During the 1930s and 1940s, Kakyo studies that mainly focused on how to deal with and make use of these people became active with Japan's overseas expansion policy. Later, prompted by Japan's postwar economic recovery, in particular during the high economic growth period in the 1960s, research on development of cooperative relations with Kakyo and Kajin became active. After a temporary slump, with a sharp rise in the advancement of Japanese capitals triggered by the strong yen in the late 1980s, research on promoting cooperation with Kakyo and Kajin boomed. Although interest in the subject somewhat declined during "the lost decade" following the collapse of Japan's asset-inflated economy in 1991, it is still very much a matter of concern in Japan. Despite this fact, however, the Japanese media still confuse the concepts of Kakyo and Kajin.

Emergence of Chinese Economies

Kakyo-Kajin studies in academic circles also still tend to be centred on Kakyo studies. The Japanese public also mixes up Southeast Asian Kajin, calling them Chinese, people of Chinese ancestry, Kakyo or Kajin, and makes no clear distinction between them. Kakyo-Kajin studies are closely tied with China's reform and open-door policy and the advancement of socialist market economy. Research on Kakyo-Kajin economies also became active with the establishment of the concepts of the Kajin, or ethnic Chinese, economic community (ECEC) and the Chuka, or Chinese, economic community (CEC).

Of course, ECEC and CEC are not established organizations like the European Union, the North America Free Trade Agreement, the Association of Southeast Asian Nations or the Singapore-Johor-Indonesia Growth Triangle. They are not more than vague groupings of economies such as the newly industrialized economies and the Sea of Japan economic zone.

As it is well known, Kajin economies started showing signs of growth in the 1960s in Southeast Asian countries. From the late 1980s to 1997, when the region was hit by an economic crisis, they attained rapid growth and development. Transcending conventional trade associations as well as family and community ties, Kakyo and Kajin made themselves leading players on the world economic stage centring on the Asia-Pacific region. Sharing a common language (Chinese plus local dialects spoken in such provinces as Fujian, Guangdong, Hainan and elsewhere), culture (philosophies and ethics rooted in Sino-centrism and Confucianism) as well as human networks, overseas and ethnic Chinese have continued to advance, showing the strength of their economic power. Kajin business groups and financial combines are now more prosperous than ever. They are actively tying up with each other and advancing into regional and global markets. As a result, the concepts of ECEC and CEC have come to be proposed.

Four Chinese Areas

Strictly speaking, the 1.28 billion Chinese who live in the four Chinese areas – continental China, Hong Kong, Macau and Taiwan – are not called Kajin. Hence, these four areas do not form part of ECEC. Likewise, Southeast Asian Kakyo-Kajin societies comprised of 27.19 million Chinese living overseas are not called greater Chinese societies because they are of a different nature from the Chinese societies in the four Chinese areas. Since Southeast Asian nations are multi-ethnic, it is common sense to distinguish local ethnic Chinese societies from the Chinese societies and people in the four areas. Therefore, it is not right to include Southeast Asian Kajin economies in the greater Chinese economic community. The Chinese government is also intent on avoiding the advocacy of the concept of greater Chinese economies and the Chinese economic community.

Actually, however, the terms Kajin and Chinese economic communities as they are conventionally used include the economies of the four Chinese areas as well as those of Southeast Asia. The English translation of Kajin economies would be "ethnic Chinese economies" but the term "Chinese economies" is also acceptable. "Chinese economies" written in Chinese characters would be "Chuka economies."

Chinese Economic Community

Kajin economies and Chuka economies would both be "Chinese economies" and Kajin economic community and Chuka economic community would be both "Chinese economic community." However, in Chinese, there is no neutral word that corresponds to the English word Chinese, which can mean both Kajin and Chuka.

It is true that the expressions Kajin economic community and Chuka economic community can be misleading. However, there is no other way but to use the term Chinese economic community (CEC) here. The economic power of CEC is huge. For instance, foreign currency reserves of Mainland China ($168.3 billion or 21.03 trillion yen), Hong Kong ($102.7 billion), Macau ($2.8 billion) and Taiwan ($106.7 billion) put together amount to $380.5 billion. When the economy of Singapore, a Kajin society, is added, the total amount surpasses the foreign currency reserves of Japan, whose amount is the world's largest at $357.1 billion, by $103.6 billion as of May 2001.

Incidentally, the total population of the four areas is 1.3076 billion, 10.3 times that of Japan's at 126.9 million. The four areas made exports worth $592.5 billion (mainland China $240 billion, Hong Kong $202 billion, Macau $2.5 billion and Taiwan $148 billion) in 2000, 1.3 times more than Japan's at $460 billion.

Asian countries, Thailand, the Republic of Korea (South Korea), Indonesia and Malaysia in particular, were strongly hit by the 1997 Asian economic crisis. By contrast, the economies of the four Chinese areas and Singapore were not seriously affected. Although the Taiwan economy has recently begun to show signs of slowing down, these Chinese economies are expected to continue steady growth into the future.

The policy of government intervention on economic affairs in the form of foreign exchange control and regulation on the inflow of short-term capitals in these Kajin and Chinese societies are highly evaluated as effective measures in preventing the spread of the Asian economic crisis.

Complimentary Chinese and Japanese Economies

Asian economies and the Japanese economy are mutually complementary. Asian Kajin businesses are good partners of Japanese businesses in terms of capital, technical and management know-how. Quite a few Kajin business groups in Asian countries grew as a result of cooperation with Japanese companies.

The Malaysia-based Loh Boon Siew business group is known to have advanced, thanks to cooperation with Honda Motor Co. When Loh, a former auto mechanic, rode a taxi during his visit to Tokyo in 1958, it was overtaken by a motorcycle that passed with a roaring engine. Surprised, he asked the taxi driver to speed, caught up with the motorcycle and stopped it. He asked the driver to show the engine and asked him how much the motorcycle cost. Confident that it would sell in Malaysia, Loh immediately acquired the right to be Honda's sales agent in his country and made a fortune.

Other cases of successful tie-ups include, the Singapore Hong Leong Group, which built a cement factory in a joint venture with Mitsui & Co. and the former Onoda Cement Co. and Indonesians Salim Group and Lippo Group, which established Central Sari Metropolitan together with the former Long-Term Credit Bank of Japan and Japan Leasing Corp. The Lippo Group also established Daiwa Lippo Finance jointly with Daiwa Bank.

With the rise of nationalism in Asian countries, Japanese companies also need to be always careful about establishing cooperative relations with local national businesses. However, for Japanese companies to advance into Asia, cooperation with Kajin businesses is indispensable.

At the same time, China's economic development of the last 23 years under its policy of reform and openness also owes largely to technical, capital and management know-how provided by Japan as well as Japan's official development assistance (ODA). A major problem for Japan is how to recover its "lost decade," achieve economic reconstruction and contribute to the recovery of Asian economies after the Asian economic crisis.

Using Japanese ODA for the development of mainland's local companies and small and medium-sized Asian businesses is expected to produce positive results. Japan is also urged to help Asian countries in their effort to reorganize their financial industries and settle bad debts.

Now that we have entered the new century, it has become even more important for Japan to advance economic cooperation with Chinese economies as well as for Japanese companies to cooperate with local Asian businesses. At the same time, they must also make use of the capital of Kajin businesses with which they have developed strong ties over a long time. The use of extensive product distribution networks and Kajin business philosophies of attaching importance to trust and selling large quantities of products at a narrow profit margin is also indispensable. Likewise, Chinese people in Mainland China, Hong Kong, Macau and Taiwan as well as Kakyo and Kajin communities in Southeast Asia also need Japanese capital and technology to develop in the Asia-Pacific region. Open Kajin and Chinese economies that can withstand difficult times are the key to long-term advancement.

Notes

1   Lim Hua Sing, "Chinese living abroad face multiple problems", *Asahi Shimbun*, 5 March 2001.
2   Lim Hua Sing, "Chinese adopt patriotism of their new homes", *Asahi Shimbun*, 6 July 2001.
3   Lim Hua Sing, "What Japan should do with Chinese economies", *Asahi Shimbun*, 25 May 2001.

CHAPTER 14

APEC, ASEAN and China

Challenges in China as APEC Heads to Shanghai Meet[1]

APEC in Progress

Since it was established in 1989, the Asia-Pacific Economic Cooperation (APEC) forum has been holding annual ministerial meetings.

In 1993, leaders of APEC member economies met unofficially for the first time in Seattle to take part in an APEC summit at which the formation of a "Pacific Community" was proposed.

The following year, the leaders met in Indonesia to adopt the Bogor Declaration. In 1995 they met in Osaka, and in 1996 in Manila, each time agreeing on plans of action. Canada, Malaysia, New Zealand and Brunei have also hosted unofficial APEC summits that are held annually on a grand scale.

The number of participating economies has also increased from 12 in 1989 to the current 21. APEC is significant in the sense that it provides an opportunity for leaders of the Asia-Pacific region, including Australia and New Zealand, to meet on a regular basis.

At the eighth unofficial APEC summit held in Brunei in last November, members discussed such problems as economic globalization, the New Economy, the holding of a new round of multilateral trade talks under the World Trade Organization (WTO) framework, regional economic cooperation, the development of human resources, technical cooperation and oil prices. Overall, that unofficial summit led to common understanding being reached in many areas.

It also saw the adoption of the APEC 2000 Leaders' Declaration, and the Action Agenda for the New Economy.

Problems and Shortcomings of APEC

Looking back at the past eight APEC summits, I think it is particularly important to note the following four points.

First, the Association of Southeast Asian Nations (ASEAN) has kept a certain distance from APEC. Malaysian Prime Minister Mahathir Mohamed boycotted the Seattle meeting in 1993 principally because US President Bill Clinton opposed his proposal to establish an East Asian Economic Caucus. In 1998, Clinton did not attend the APEC summit hosted by Malaysia, mainly to protest against the dismissal of former Deputy Prime Minister Anwar Ibrahim by Mahathir.

A Big Challenge for China

Meanwhile, ASEAN has always viewed APEC with scepticism since its conception and took part in its meetings while maintaining a certain distance from it. ASEAN is afraid that APEC could turn ASEAN into a mere name. It appears that ASEAN is always on the watch so that APEC would not be influenced by Japan, the USA and Australia.

Secondly, APEC has not been able to exercise influence as an international organization. It sat back and did nothing to resolve the Asian economic crisis in 1997. Whether it can prove its true worth as an organization established to promote economic cooperation of the Asia-Pacific region is being tested. When Malaysia presented preventive measures and solutions to cope with economic crises at the 1998 APEC forum in Malaysia, members only showed understanding. At this year's Brunei meeting, they failed to even clearly agree on when to hold the new round of WTO trade talks, showing how difficult it is to adjust the clashing interests of developing and industrialized nations.

Thirdly, the North-South problem is an important one for APEC members. The 1994 Bogor Declaration set the target date for liberalization of trade and investment at 2010 for industrialized nations and 2020 for developing nations. However, the Asian economic crisis delayed the timetable and APEC has not been able to clearly settle on new target dates.

The fourth problem is the widening gap between bilateral agreements and multilateral negotiations. While APEC was established to promote economic cooperation of the entire region, bilateral agreements, such as Japan-Republic of Korea (South Korea), Japan-Singapore, Singapore-New Zealand, Australia-New Zealand, and others, precede multilateral dialogue. It would not be a problem if bilateral agreements advanced multilateral negotiations, but in the case of APEC they could work against them. Were that to happen, it would be fatal to APEC.

At the Brunei meeting, developing nations were to the fore in advocating development of human resources and strengthening of economic technical cooperation. Japan is expected to play a prominent role in this area.

Meanwhile, China's move also deserves attention. China is the host of next year's APEC meetings to be held in Shanghai. It will be the first time since the foundation of the People's Republic of China 52 years ago, or indeed in China's 4,000-year history, that the representatives of APEC's 21 members gather in China. Can Chinese President Jiang Zemin, who has attended the last eight APEC summits, overcome the above-mentioned four problems? Can he advance the policy of reform and openness that China has been promoting since 1978, while keeping in step with China's official admission to WTO and the liberalization of investment and trade advocated by APEC? It is a big challenge for China.

ASEAN's Complex Relationship with an Open China[2]

Opportunities and Challenges for ASEAN

China introduced its reform and open-door policy in 1978. The drastic shift from the policy of planned economy that China had continued for nearly three decades since 1949 sent shock waves throughout the world, most notably in the Asia-Pacific region, where it triggered heated debate.

In particular, opinion was divided between those in favour and those against it among political, economic and academic circles of the members of the Association of Southeast Asian Nations (ASEAN). The change triggered mixed reactions of hope and anxiety because ASEAN thought it could open up opportunities and present problems at the same time.

Since ASEAN's establishment in 1967, little effort was made to advance regional economic cooperation in investment, trade and economic assistance. As a result, members were facing a deadlock in economic development, with some in more serious trouble than others. As an important breakthrough, ASEAN looked to newly industrializing economies (NIEs) and strengthened economic ties with them.

Later, however, ASEAN started to feel the limits of economic cooperation with NIEs. At the same time, the opening of the Chinese market and China's advancement into the world economy were welcomed by ASEAN as a good opportunity for economic advancement. The fact that economic cooperation between ASEAN and China steadily advanced in the last 22 years attests to that.

On the other hand, ASEAN has also felt threatened by the advancement of the Chinese economy into the international market for the following reasons.

First, Japanese, European and American capital and business could flow into China instead of ASEAN. Second, Japan, Europe and the United States could expand their trade with China. Consequently, trade with ASEAN could decline. Third, economic assistance of Japan, Europe and the United States as well as international financial institutions directed at developing nations could flow toward China instead of ASEAN.

As it turned out, these fears all became reality. Ironically, as China advanced its reform and open-door policy, ASEAN itself came to attach greater importance to having its capital and business make inroads into the Chinese market and promoting trade with China.

ASEAN's labour-intensive industries looked to the Chinese market as a way of survival. Some 25 million people of Chinese descent who live in ASEAN countries also started to promote economic advancement into China. This is partly because ASEAN started to see the limits of expanding trade with Japan. ASEAN-China economic cooperation thus entered a new stage.

Overall, it can be said that ASEAN is inclined to regard China's policy of reform and openness more as an opportunity than a threat. While China's international advancement brings about many negative aspects, it is a major challenge for ASEAN to expand its positive aspects.

Socialist Market Economy

In the fall of 1992, China further declared that it would plunge into promoting complete market economy under the slogan "socialist market economy." In response, ASEAN actively promoted economic cooperation with China even more than before. The most important thing is for ASEAN economies to develop and advance by strengthening their economic ties with China.

China announced plans for the major development of its western region in 1999. The project is mainly aimed at narrowing the economic gap between the western inland region and the coastal special economic zones. At the same time, China also wants to show people both at home and abroad that "socialist market economy" is indispensable to China as a whole with the promotion of the western region development. The Chinese government is also greatly counting on the advancement of ASEAN capital.

ASEAN capital, in particular that which is linked with ethnic Chinese, has moved into China's coastal region and special economic zones in the last 22 years. In addition to the labour-intensive manufacturing sector, it has mostly advanced to the real estate and service industries. Some has also advanced to the social and industrial infrastructure. Although concrete plans have yet to be made, ASEAN is also eager to take part in the major development of the western region.

Internalization of the China Economy

China is set to join the World Trade Organization (WTO) this year. The move is expected to accelerate China's internationalization. Like Japan and Europe, ASEAN has supported China's membership, which can be interpreted as a natural outcome of China's policy of reform and openness.

WTO membership can trigger China's economic development. At the same time, it could also have a major impact on the Chinese economy as a whole. While membership is expected to promote the reorganization and advancement of Chinese companies, making them more competitive, it may also give rise to a large number of unemployed people as a result of a decline especially in farming. It could also cause weaker businesses in the banking, service, telecommunications and construction industries to be eliminated.

As China's economy becomes more international, advancement of ASEAN capital and business into China is expected to accelerate.

Devaluation of the renminbi is also expected. When that happens, Japan, Europe, the USA and NIEs are expected to rapidly increase their investment in China. As a result, inflow of foreign capital to ASEAN is likely to drastically drop. China's membership in WTO is sure to require ASEAN to reexamine its economic policy, including measures to draw foreign capital, while forcing it to reorganize its industries.

Asians Need to Look After Themselves for the Future[3]

Japan's Poor Economy and the Asian Financial Crisis

While Japan is expected to contribute to the revival and development of the Asian economy, it faces two problems. Firstly, since the asset-inflated economy collapsed in 1991, it has been unable to get back on track. Secondly, the nation's role and initiatives have always been viewed sceptically by its Asian neighbours.

The slowdown of the economy from 1991 to 1996 is considered a serious factor behind the Asian financial crisis. At the time, Japan's direct investments to Asia declined, as did Asian exports to Japan. The strong yen weighed heavily on Asian debtor nations.

These factors had a negative impact on the growth of the Asian economy as a whole and, combined with the influx of short-term capital in Asia and the misguided macroeconomic policies of several countries, they consequently brought about the Asian financial crisis.

During the 1985-1990 asset-inflated economic boom, Japan invested heavily in Asia. At the same time, Asian exports to Japan also reached remarkable levels. However, because Japan extensively expanded its loans to Asia, when Asian countries were struggling with bad debts during the Asian financial crisis, Japan suffered the most among creditor nations. Unless something is done to settle the bad debts of Asian countries, Japan will continue to suffer.

AMF and ASEAN Foreign Currency Swap Agreement

One of the aims of the New Miyazawa Initiative proposed by Finance Minister Kiichi Miyazawa is to help Asian countries settle their bad debts. In Asia, there is a growing trend to strengthen economic cooperation. Under these circumstances, the most important thing is to adopt the initiative and advance the establishment of an Asian Monetary Fund (AMF).

The International Monetary Fund cannot concern itself with Asian affairs alone. International organizations for Asian countries should be established by Asian countries themselves. Even the USA has withdrawn its opposition to an AMF.

Miyazawa got China's agreement to cooperate with the establishment of an East Asian monetary fund (EMF). Like an AMF, the EMF will be made up of the members of the East Asian Economic Caucus (EAEC). What the organization is called is of little significance so long as it prevents the recurrence of a new financial crisis in Asia or, should a crisis occur, it is able to help unaffected countries before the crisis spreads through the region.

In May, Japan, China, the Republic of Korea (South Korea) and the 10 members of ASEAN concluded the ASEAN foreign currency swap agreement. This is a positive step toward the realization of a new organization. Japan has an important role to play through the implementation of the New Miyazawa Initiative.

Notes

1   Lim Hua Sing, "Challenges in China as APEC heads to Shanghai meet", *Asahi Shimbun*, 25 December 2000.
2   Lim Hua Sing, "ASEAN's complex relationship with an open China", *Asahi Shimbun*, 29 January 2001.
3   Lim Hua Sing, "Asians need to look after themselves for the future", *Asahi Shimbun*, 30 October 2000.

CHAPTER 15

Japan and the China Market

Settlement of Japan-China Trade Dispute Vital[1]

Trade Friction between Japan and China

As if the ongoing trade war between Japan and China is not enough, the Japanese history textbook issue, former Taiwanese President Lee Tenghui's visit to Japan and Prime Minister Junichiro Koizumi's visit to Yasukuni Shrine are complicating matters between the two nations, whose relations are rapidly cooling.

The trade dispute this time started April 23, when the Japanese government imposed temporary import curbs, or safeguards, on leeks, fresh "shiitake" (mushrooms) and rush used to make "tatami" (mats) from China. After repeatedly objecting to the safeguards, by way of retaliation, the Chinese government decided June 22 to impose 100 per cent tariffs on imports of Japanese automobiles, mobile phones and air conditioners.

Essence of Trade Friction

The trade friction can be summarized as follows:

(1) While Japanese safeguards are limited to Chinese agricultural products, China's retaliatory measures target leading Japanese industrial products.

(2) The disputed items make up only a very small portion of Japan's total imports and exports in terms of value. According to 2000 statistics, Japan imported 4 billion yen worth of leeks, 10 billion yen worth of mushrooms and 10 billion yen worth of rush from China. The total value of the three imported items, 24 billion

yen, accounts for only 0.05 per cent of Japan's total imports of 40.938 trillion yen. Meanwhile, Japan exported 45.2 billion yen worth of automobiles, 11.1 billion yen worth of mobile phones and 5.6 billion yen worth of air conditioners to China for a total of 61.9 billion yen, accounting for 0.12 per cent of Japan's total exports of 51.654 trillion yen. Incidentally, Japan's automobile exports to China make up only 0.65 per cent of Japan's total automobile exports, worth 6.93 trillion yen.

(3) Although the Japan-China trade dispute is likely to be settled in a short time, there is also a potential danger that it could be prolonged. To China, where approximately 900 million of its population of 1.3 billion relies on farming, restrictions on exports of farm produce have a greater impact on their livelihoods than the economy. Moreover, safeguards could expand to eels, "wakame" (seaweed) and lumber. Such light industry products as towels, neckties and socks could also be affected. Export restrictions of such products are particularly damaging to China, which is a developing nation.

China's Retaliation

At the same time, China must have carefully planned the imposition of heavy tariffs on such leading Japanese industrial products as automobiles, mobile phones and air conditioners. Although the amount of their exports to China is negligible compared with Japan's total exports, the impact it has on Japanese industries is immeasurable. In particular, restrictions on automobiles, a symbolic industrial product of Japan, sent shock waves across Japan. The situation is particularly frightening because it is unpredictable what Japanese industrial products China would target next for the imposition of heavy duties.

Reasons Behind Trade Dispute

Why must the two countries develop a trade dispute? The reasons for Japan, I believe, are as follows: First, the ruling Liberal Democratic

Party had to secure the vote of farmers, on which it heavily relies. Second, import curbs could spread to other Chinese agricultural products and eventually to light and heavy industry products. Third, I dare say, the government is trying to divert public attention from such domestic problems as structural reform and bad debts. If that is the case, the thinking is simplistic.

Japan's Miscalculation

Since China is counting on Japan's official development assistance (ODA) and is set to join the World Trade Organization and host the Olympics, Japan probably thought optimistically that it would not resort to drastic measures.

While Japan insists that it invoked safeguards in accordance with WTO rules, the price it paid was dear. For one thing, as an advocate of free trade, Japan has traditionally resisted import curbs imposed by the USA. This time, though, Japan took the lead in limiting imports and its argument is unconvincing. Moreover, the temporary measures expire on Nov. 8, just before winter, when consumption of leeks and mushrooms soar.

Second, the safeguards have a negative impact on development imports by Japanese businesses. Promoting the advancement of Japanese companies in foreign markets and limiting development imports are contradictory. Moreover, safeguards do not necessarily help weak domestic industries that they are meant to protect get stronger and do not contribute to structural reform.

Third, although the decision to invoke import curbs might have been made in response to pressure by lawmakers representing the interests of farmers, it deprives general consumers of the opportunity to buy cheap Chinese agricultural products.

Amicable Settlement Vital

It appears that the Japan-China trade war is working in favour of China. China is set to join the WTO in November and won the bid to host the 2008 Olympics. China, which has succeeded in attaining high economic growth in the last 23 years, is expected to show a tougher stance toward Japan in trade negotiations from now on.

Of course, I don't think China wants its economic relations with Japan to deteriorate. Japan's capital, technology and ODA are indispensable to China's future economic development. Needless to say, an early amicable settlement of the trade dispute is very important for both countries.

Japan's Entry into China Market Indispensable[2]

Declining Global Economy

The world is facing a global recession, as the economy continues to show a downward trend since the turn of the century. Europe, the USA, Japan, Asia's newly industrializing economies and the countries that make up the Association of Southeast Asian Nations are all being forced to lower their economic growth rates.

Amid such circumstances, the Sept. 11 terrorist attacks on the USA have accelerated the downward trend of the already declining global economy. The US-led offensive against Afghanistan may lead to a major war and a vicious circle of terrorism and retaliation. When that happens, the global economic situation is sure to aggravate even further.

China Gains Steady Growth

Meanwhile, China remains the only country whose economy continues to show steady growth. Of course, China has many problems — a widening gap in income, difficulties in reforming state-run corporations, spreading imbalance of economic development between the coastal and inland regions, environmental destruction resulting from rapid development and widespread corruption, to name a few.

Nevertheless, as it is set to join the World Trade Organization by December and prepares to host the 2008 Olympics, the whole nation is tackling economic construction.

The Chinese economic society is very active and is a striking contrast with the rest of the world where the economy is sluggish. In the 23 years since 1978, when China launched a policy of reform and openness in earnest, it has continued to attain economic growth dealing with the rest of the world and is expected to continue to do so in the next 10 to 20 years.

The Advancement of Western Companies into China

From Japan's standpoint, how to deal with China in the future is an important matter. The US policy toward China has basically been a repetition of engagement and containment. The Clinton administration regarded its relationship with China as "a strategic partnership" and inclined toward engagement. By contrast, the Bush administration sees China as "a strategic competitor" and is leaning toward containment.

However, apart from the US government's fickle policy, US businesses have continued to advance into Chinese markets. For example, in response to the June 4, 1989, Tiananmen incident, the USA took the lead in imposing economic sanctions against China.

However, the development did not stop US companies from advancing into China. Currently, many US companies in the electronics, telecommunications and automobile industries are advancing into China. Since the first McDonald's hamburger shop in China opened next to Beijing's Tiananmen Square, new shops operated by the chain have found their way into street corners of such major cities as Shanghai and Tianjin.

The advancement of European companies into China cannot be overlooked, either. European automakers made inroads into the Chinese market before their Japanese counterparts. Many high-class European and American brands also operate boutiques in the 66 Heng Long Square surrounded by modern high-rise buildings near Shanghai's Huai Hai shopping area. The sight is quite impressive.

The Advancement of Japanese Companies into China

How about the advancement of Japanese companies into China? While Japan is closer to China, both geographically as well as historically, culturally and linguistically, than are Europe and the USA, it is behind them in its advancement to Chinese markets.

Recently, Japan-China trade has expanded and Japanese investment toward China has increased. However, as a whole, Japanese companies are slow to advance to China. Why? I wish to cite the following factors.

Five Reasons Affect Japan's Advancement into the China Market

The first one is political. Such pending issues as the Senkaku islands dispute, the history textbook controversy, Prime Minister Junichiro Koizumi's official visit to Yasukuni Shrine, former Taiwanese President Lee Tenghui's visit to Japan and the legislation of surrounding situations law which strengthens the Japan-US security system are giving rise to distrust between the two countries, undermining their friendship. In other words, Japan's postwar failure to settle its history is the very factor that stands in the way of personnel and economic exchanges between the two countries and the advancement of Japanese companies into China.

The second factor is macroeconomic. While some Japanese companies that advance into China are successful, quite a few fail. The reasons behind their failure, I believe, are poor management on the part of Japanese companies, delay in transferring and adapting Japanese-style management practices (pay scale and promotion based on seniority, for example) to meet the Chinese situation and lateness in dealing with Chinese policies on foreign capitals and failure to catch up with the rapid change in laws.

The third problem is Japan's lack of understanding of China's local situation and its people. Although China and Japan share the use of the same characters and belong to the same race, their business customs, management philosophies and national traits are very different. It is very difficult for businesses that do not understand China to be successful there.

Moreover, China's legal system is inadequate and its laws are said to change frequently. One way for Japanese companies to advance into China is to do so together with companies run by Asians of

Chinese descent. At any rate, they should plan their advancement into China after fostering venturous entrepreneurship and a good understanding of the nation and its people through education.

The fourth problem is the characteristics of Japanese companies and the way decisions are made based on corporate management philosophies. Since the Japanese asset-inflated economy collapsed in 1991, the way Japanese companies are run has come under fire. Japanese-style management that continues to conduct business without settling bad debts is inefficient. In particular, the bottom-up decision-making process of Japanese companies by consensus cannot keep up with the rapidly changing times.

Above all, Japanese companies advancing into China need corporate strategies that allow them to aptly and promptly respond to local conditions and to make appropriate decisions accordingly. As things stand, Japanese companies' slow decision-making is causing them to let business chances slip by. Unless they change it, they will fall further behind their competitors in overseas markets.

The fifth factor is the stability of the Japanese currency. Since the Plaza Accord of the fall of 1985, the exchange rate of the yen has shown violent fluctuations. That must also be a reason behind Japanese companies' hesitation to advance into China. They wanted to avoid the risk of foreign exchange losses. The important thing is to maintain the stability of the yen.

Japan's Advancement into the China Market Indispensable

As I mentioned earlier, the US economic sanctions to China did not stop American companies from advancing into China. At the time, Japan did not completely act in concert with US economic sanctions. It also continued to provide official development assistance to China.

Yet, Japanese companies were more passive about advancing into China than their US counterparts. Currently, while the USA positions China as a strategic competitor, American companies continue to advance into Chinese markets. Japan is showing understanding toward US Chinese policy. However, if it causes Japanese companies to hesitate to advance into China, they could repeat their mistake.

It is natural for Japanese companies to advance into foreign markets at a time of globalization. When Japanese companies actively advanced overseas in the second half of the 1980s, the hollowing out of domestic industries became a serious concern. While the advancement of Japanese companies into China may also give rise to such concern although not as seriously as before, they are urged to do so as part of structural reform of the Japanese economy and reorganization of its industries.

China, with a population of 1.3 billion people, is a huge market into which Western companies as well as those run by Asian Chinese are making inroads. China is also a global production centre.

In addition to securing China as a market, Japanese companies should also make use of it as a production base. The development of international markets is an indispensable international management strategy for the Japanese economy.

Advancing Regional Economic Integration is Key[3]

The World Has Plunged into Recession

The world has plunged into a simultaneous recession. Japan and the USA are suffering from economic contractions. As of December 2001, Britain and France were about the only countries within the European Union whose gross domestic product had achieved a growth rate of around 2 per cent. Most other EU countries recorded lower growth or zero growth.

Of the Asian newly industrializing economies (NIEs), the Republic of Korea (South Korea) had a growth rate of 2 per cent or less, Hong Kong zero, while the economies of Taiwan and Singapore contracted 4.2 per cent and 5.6 per cent, respectively.

Myanmar (Burma) and the three countries of Indochina that recently joined the Association of Southeast Asian Nations (ASEAN) showed temporary growth as their economies got off the ground in the initial phase of development. But Thailand, which continued remarkable growth, had a growth rate of 2 per cent or less, and Malaysia's economy showed a contraction of 1.3 per cent.

The Sept. 11 terrorist attacks on the USA slowed down their already sluggish economy and caused Asian exports to the USA to drop sharply. In 2000, Asian countries that suffered serious damage in the 1997 financial crisis were beginning to show slow signs of recovery, but they have fallen into a recession again.

The economies of Europe and North America are bound by the EU and the North American Free Trade Agreement (NAFTA), respectively. As such, they are making efforts to get through the recession with regional economic integration and cooperation. As of 1996, 62 per cent of EU exports and imports were conducted within the region. In 1997, 49 per cent of NAFTA's exports and 39.9 per cent of imports stayed within it. By comparison, ASEAN economic integration and cooperation are not as advanced.

ASEAN Has Made Little Progress

In 1991, the establishment of the ASEAN Free Trade Area (AFTA) was proposed to make the region a free trade area in the next 15 years. However, the plan has made little progress. Since ASEAN countries have lured capital from Japan, Europe and the USA to advance electronic industries and machinery and equipment production, their products are alike. That is why regional trade has remained inactive. The ratio of ASEAN regional exports, which stood at 19.8 per cent in 1991, for example, only increased to 20.6 per cent in 1998. At the same time, imports showed a slight increase from 17.5 per cent to 21.4 per cent.

Export partners of Indonesia, Malaysia, the Philippines and Thailand in 1996 were concentrated on NIEs (32.7 per cent), the USA (23.1 per cent) and Japan (12.6 per cent). They also depended heavily on Japan (31 per cent), NIEs (22.3 per cent) and the USA (16 per cent) for imports. In the same year, however, exports and imports to and from China remained at 1.5 per cent and 1.9 per cent, respectively.

The Asian financial crisis, the collapse of Japan's asset-inflated economy and the Sept. 11 terrorist attacks all aggravated the already ailing economies of Asia-Pacific nations. In fact, expanding trade with Japan, the USA and NIEs is extremely difficult for ASEAN, which has no choice but to explore new frontiers for economic cooperation. In that respect, cooperation with China becomes particularly important.

Meanwhile, the Chinese economy has been showing rapid growth. However, its exports to the USA have slowed. Trade friction with Japan is also a problem and it is not necessarily to China's advantage to rely solely on Japan and the USA as trade partners. That is why strengthening ties with countries in the Asia-Pacific region, in particular ASEAN, is a pressing issue for China.

China-and-ASEAN FTA

A free trade area comprising China and ASEAN would form a market of 1.7 billion people - larger than the EU or NAFTA. It would have a gross domestic product of $2 trillion (260 trillion yen) with trade worth $1.23 trillion.

On Nov. 5 last year, leaders of ASEAN, Japan, China and South Korea met in Brunei. At the meeting, Chinese Premier Zhu Rongji officially proposed the formation of a China-and-ASEAN free trade area (CAFTA) within the next 10 years.

Malaysian Prime Minister Mahathir Mohamad said he did not want Malaysia to turn into nothing more than an export market for China. A number of other ASEAN leaders also expressed apprehensions that China could overwhelm ASEAN as a trading partner because of its competitiveness.

ASEAN countries are increasingly nervous because Chinese products such as motorcycles, air conditioners, digital video disc players and colour televisions are inundating the global market. In 2000, China made $45 billion - accounting for 70 per cent of direct foreign investment in East Asia.

However, Singapore Prime Minister Goh Chok Tong welcomed the proposal, calling CAFTA an ideal opportunity that ASEAN must not miss. As a whole, no strong objections were raised. It appears ASEAN has recognized the importance of establishing a mutually complementary economic relationship with China.

ASEAN also appears set to promote political and regional security cooperation with China. When the foreign ministers of Thailand, Laos and Myanmar met, Thai Foreign Minister Surakiat Sathirathai referred to China's CAFTA proposal and expressed hope that stronger cooperation with China would prevent drugs produced in the golden triangle from spreading throughout the world by way of China.

At the same summit meeting in Brunei, Japan called on others to join the international fight against terrorism, but their reactions were cool. The lack of cooperation must have been a shock to Japan, but it shows how Japan needs to better understand ASEAN.

"The internal affairs" of Islamic states such as Indonesia (which has the largest Muslim population in the world), Malaysia and Brunei are not as simple as they appear to outsiders. Leaders at the Brunei summit harshly criticized the Sept. 11 terrorist attacks. However, they turned down the resolution proposed by Malaysia and Indonesia to demand the USA to immediately stop attacking Afghanistan. Thus, ASEAN's position concerning international anti-terrorism measures is by no means monolithic.

The gap in understanding between Japan and ASEAN is wide. ASEAN's plan to link Singapore with Kunming, China, by rail is another example. Japan thinks it is better to build a road.

Japan has close ties with ASEAN in terms of trade, direct foreign investment and official development assistance. But China-ASEAN relations are advancing at a faster pace than Japan-ASEAN relations. While Japan stands by free trade, it has opposed the conclusion of bilateral trade agreements. However, American and European economies are moving toward bloc economies and regional integration.

To keep up with the trend, the Asia-Pacific region should also promote the conclusion of multilateral and bilateral free trade agreements and economic regional integration.

Japan signed a free trade agreement with Singapore on Jan. 14, 2002. It went relatively smoothly because Singapore has no farming sector. Since Japan is bent on protecting domestic farmers, I doubt it can sign free trade agreements with Thailand and South Korea just as easily. The same goes for other ASEAN nations. In this regard, CAFTA is easier than a free trade agreement between Japan and ASEAN. Unless Japan seriously considers solving the problems related to the protection of domestic agriculture, it would be difficult to conclude free trade agreements with ASEAN countries.

In the Asia-Pacific region, Japan has yet to present concrete plans for the establishment of a forum of ASEAN plus Japan, China and South Korea, an ASEAN currency swap agreement and an Asian monetary fund.

Unless Japan squarely tackles such important issues to further strengthen economic cooperation with ASEAN, it will be left in the dark in the move to advance regional economic integration.

Koizumi Unclear on Asian Economic Initiative[4]

In January 2002, Prime Minister Junichiro Koizumi toured the Philippines, Malaysia, Thailand, Indonesia and Singapore, which belong to the Association of Southeast Asian Nations (ASEAN), in one week. Although the trip was not as rushed as the day trips he previously made to China and the Republic of Korea (South Korea), it was nevertheless an energetic trip he made in a short time.

In Singapore, his last destination, Koizumi signed a free trade agreement with Singaporean Prime Minister Goh Chok Tong. The following day, Koizumi delivered a speech in which he asked for a frank partnership and presented a proposal for comprehensive economic cooperation for Japan to advance together with the Asia-

Pacific region, including ASEAN. The proposal was reportedly welcomed and praised by ASEAN leaders and US Secretary of State Colin Powell.

I also think the proposal is right for Japan to build an economic partnership with Asian countries centring on ASEAN. At the same time, however, I wish to address the following problems.

ASEAN 10-plus-5-plus-1

First, the scope of the proposed partnership is too broad. In addition to ASEAN countries, Japan hopes to include China, South Korea, Australia and New Zealand as key members of the partnership. Even if Japan concludes a free trade agreement with ASEAN (JAFTA), it is understandable that Japan would not want to form a closed and exclusionary community because it would run counter to Japan's national interests.

However, ASEAN 10-plus-three (Japan, China and South Korea), ASEAN 10-plus-five (Japan, China, South Korea, Australia and New Zealand) and ASEAN 10-plus-five-plus-one (the USA) have many problems ahead.

At the ASEAN summit in November 2000, South Korean President Kim Dae Jung officially proposed the establishment of the ASEAN 10-plus-three framework. But ASEAN rejected the proposal because of complex problems within Japan and South Korea that have to do with protection of domestic agriculture. I expect the ASEAN 10-plus-five plan will also be immediately met by opposition from Malaysia and China.

The reason is simple. From the time Malaysian Prime Minister Mahathir Mohamad proposed the establishment of the East Asian Economic Grouping (EAEG, later renamed East Asian Economic Caucus) in 1990, Australia and New Zealand were excluded from the plan, from the viewpoint of regional unity. China, which supported EAEG, has continued to oppose the inclusion of Australia and New Zealand, both officially and unofficially.

There is no doubt the 10-plus-five concept is more difficult to realize than 10-plus-three. On the other hand, the 10-plus-five-plus-one plan that Prime Minister Koizumi is believed to be contemplating is virtually no different from the Asia-Pacific Economic Cooperation (APEC) forum when it is seen from the viewpoint of its members. What is the actual significance of establishing ASEAN 10-plus-five-plus-one? This is difficult to understand.

Actually, in recent years, the significance and role of APEC itself is being questioned. Under such circumstances, the proposal of ASEAN 10-plus-five-plus-one is completely meaningless. The scope of the proposed comprehensive economic cooperative partnership is too broad and ambiguous.

Second, there are no set target dates and clear objectives. I think Japan's decision to make 2003 the year of Japan-ASEAN exchange and the proposal to hold a meeting to discuss an East Asia development initiative is good. But there is no indication whatsoever how long it will take JAFTA to materialize. I think this is fatal. By contrast, China has reached an agreement with ASEAN to realize a so-called CAFTA within the next 10 years.

I think the most unwise thing to do is to put off the matter indefinitely and set ASEAN's teeth on edge.

The Japan-Singapore free trade agreement finally took shape thanks to the efforts of three Japanese prime ministers — Keizo Obuchi, Yoshiro Mori and Koizumi. How many prime ministers and how many years will it take for JAFTA to come into reality?

Even if Japan clearly specified a target date, ASEAN leaders may worry if it can really be met. Since Japan has avoided setting a target date, it cannot be helped if ASEAN thinks it cannot understand Japan's true intentions.

The third problem is that Japan did not present solutions to its domestic agricultural problems. With the exception of Singapore, ASEAN members are basically farming countries. Unless they can promote exports of agricultural products to Japan, having a free trade agreement with Japan has little appeal to them.

Possible Trade War

Agriculture is a particularly sensitive issue in Japan because it involves domestic politics. Import curbs on Chinese agricultural products that Japan recently implemented triggered a trade war between Japan and China. Although the dispute has subsided, if trade between Japan and ASEAN advances in the future, a similar situation could develop between them over imports of agricultural products.

In 2000, Japan imported 28.88 billion yen worth of foodstuff (meat, fish, shellfish, fruits, vegetables and alcoholic beverages) and 12.45 billion yen worth of raw materials (lumber, pulp, iron ore and nonferrous metal scrap). Of Japan's total imports from Singapore, foodstuff accounted for 4.2 per cent and raw materials accounted for 1.8 per cent. However, in concluding the Japan-Singapore free trade agreement, the Japanese government caved in to Liberal Democratic Party lawmakers representing the interests of domestic farmers and failed to abolish tariffs on nearly 2,000 agricultural and fisheries products. The outcome shows how difficult it is to abolish tariffs on such products in realizing a free trade agreement with Japan.

In 2000, Japan imported 541.9 billion yen worth of food and 412.6 billion yen worth of raw materials from ASEAN. Food accounted for 8.5 per cent and raw materials 6.4 per cent of Japan's total imports from ASEAN. However, once Japan's domestic agricultural and fisheries markets are opened, imports from ASEAN are expected to rise sharply. When that happens, Japan needs to come up with effective measures to deal with the situation. Incidentally, China, which has a farming population of 900 million, announced that it will liberate the farming sector when it proposed CAFTA. If Japan wants to advance JAFTA, it should also show a clear vision.

It has been 25 years since then Prime Minister Takeo Fukuda announced the Fukuda doctrine in Manila in 1977. Since then, Japan and ASEAN have advanced their friendship based on an equal partnership. However, a close international organization has yet to be formed.

While Prime Minister Koizumi stressed that Japan will move forward with ASEAN as a frank partner without concrete proposals and targets, it is unclear what kind of a framework of comprehensive economic cooperation can be realized between them. The prevalent view within the Japanese government is that conclusion of a free trade agreement between Japan and ASEAN is most unlikely since the economic gap between them is too wide. The Asian mass media even let out that ASEAN leaders' commendation of Koizumi's proposal is nothing more than diplomatic language.

Of course, some ASEAN leaders disagree. Philippine Minister of Trade and Industry Manuel Roxas expressed concern that advancing free trade with China would hurt domestic farming and asserted that ASEAN should conclude a free trade agreement with Japan rather than China. Cambodian Commerce Minister Cham Prasith says ASEAN plus-five should form an Asia-Pacific trading bloc within the next 10 years. However, neither view is prevalent in ASEAN.

Indeed, Japan must tackle many problems. The first thing Japan must do to strengthen economic cooperation with ASEAN is to recover the economy of the lost decade. Unless the Japanese economy can get back on a recovery track, ASEAN will be disappointed in Japan. The recent plunge of the yen has brought about confusion in Asian economies, causing Asian leaders to complain and severely criticize Japan.

Unbalanced Relationship

The economic relationship between Japan and ASEAN is also unbalanced. In terms of trade, there is always an excess of imports on the part of ASEAN. The excess, which stood at 897.6 billion yen in 1998, rose to 912.7 billion yen in 1999 and 957.6 billion yen in 2000.

Meanwhile, Japan's direct investment in ASEAN is declining year by year. This is basically due to the decrease in Japan's overseas direct investment resulting from the collapse of the asset-inflated economy and a shift to China. Japan's direct investment in ASEAN decreased from 515.9 billion yen in 1998 to 440.4 billion yen in 1999 and 275.1 billion yen in 2000.

Attracting Japanese capital to ASEAN is a problem that needs to be addressed. Both trade and investment should be improved by strengthening Japan-ASEAN economic cooperation.

Notes

1 Reprinted from *Asahi Shimbun*, 31 August 2001, with kind permission of the publisher.
2 Reprinted from *Asahi Shimbun*, 2 November 2001, with kind permission of the publisher.
3 Reprinted from *Asahi Shimbun*, 11 January 2002, with kind permission of the publisher.
4 Reprinted from *Asahi Shimbun*, 22 February 2002, with kind permission of the publisher.

CHAPTER 16

Japanese and Chinese Economies in Perspective

Utilizing Foreign Talents to Achieve Economic Growth[1]

Asian countries which were trying to develop saw Japan's economy in the 1980s shinning. Appraisals on their economic performances were anywhere in Asia.

But, now what happened to Japan? Asian countries were deeply disappointed at the country which still agonizes over its bad loan problems and has lost its confidence after experiencing what they called "the lost decade".

In order to get out of the economic dead-end, Japan should seek a breath of fresh air all over the world. I think, the fresh air in this context is talented foreigners which Japan should accept systematically and massively.

Among industrialized countries Japan is the most passive one to make use of foreign experts and engineers. Foreign workers in Japan constitutes only one per cent of the total workers or 700,000. Out of the foreign workers, those who are specialists amounts only to 100,000.

There are no comparable developed nations which have such a small number of foreign workers like Japan, not to speak of the United States whose main sources of vitality depends on immigrants and foreign researchers.

Japan is no longer allowed to say: "Wait a minute. We need time to implement a rehabilitation policy." Because the crisis is imminent. Japan will soon enter the stage where the society is occupied by aged population with an extremely low birthrate. The population of those whose life depend on pension will rapidly increase while those who earn bread and butter will decrease.

People who are employable in terms of age recorded 87 million in 1995. The population as such is expected to lower to 57 million in the middle of this century.

Japan not only cannot keep competitiveness but also unable to achieve an economic growth at all.

U.N. Population Division warned at the end of 2000 that Japan needs to accept 610,000 immigrants annually in order to maintain the current level of employable population under the period of the extreme low birthrate.

Business leaders proposed ideas which are positive in accepting foreign engineers. The Ministry of Justice and the Ministry of Health, Labor and Welfare have begun discussing whether to seek human resources abroad for the development of computer software. But the prolonged economic slump have overshadowed this discussion and they won't be able to come up with a conclusion in the near future.

Japan appears to be still under the influence of the closed door policy which took place in 300 years of the Edo period? Going abroad is nothing unusual among Japanese. But, Japan is still a homogenous society and closed toward foreigners whose cultural backgrounds are of variety and heterogynous.

Japan does not make use of talented people in the world and the country's policy is very different from the United States and European counterparts which compete with each other to secure capable foreign experts.

It would take a long time for Japan as a whole to psychologically be ready to accept massive immigrants. But, if Japan wants to sustain and develp itself depending on technology and to achieve economic growth, it is an urgent task for the country to institute a systematic mechanism to accept foreign experts at first. I think, this is a realistic policy which Japan can implement.

Could China's Red-hot Economy Collapse?[2]

Fifteen years have passed since the collapse of Japan's asset-inflated economy.

Finally, though, structural reforms to overhaul the political, economic and social systems have begun to take effect and the economy is showing signs of recovery.

In the Lower House election on Sept. 11 last year, Prime Minister Junichiro Koizumi led his Liberal Democratic Party to a landslide victory by going directly to voters with his postal privatization program, which had been rejected by the Upper House.

Just as the Koizumi government had started using the political capital from its electoral victory to push ahead with its reform agenda, Japan was rocked by a rapid succession of three major news stories.

These included the falsification of earthquake resistance data by a rogue architect, the discovery of animal parts believed to be at high risk for transmitting mad cow disease in a shipment of American beef, and a securities fraud scandal involving Livedoor Co.

These incidents supplied ample ammunition for critics of the Koizumi administration and its reform agenda, putting the ruling coalition in political hot water and hindering the reform process.

Slower Comparative Recovery

The crash of the Japanese economy in 1991 was triggered by sudden drops in land and stock prices. Six years later, in July 1997, similar bubbles popped throughout East Asia, setting off a regional financial crisis.

Real estate and stock prices nosedived in Thailand, South Korea, Indonesia and Malaysia, bringing an abrupt halt to a period of high economic growth that had started in those countries in the 1970s and 1980s.

It took about two years of painful struggle for those economies to start their recovery, but they have since largely regained their health.

The pace of recovery has been much slower in Japan, the world's second largest economy. Yet Japan's economic fundamentals — its trade balance, unemployment rate, foreign currency reserves, et cetera — are in far better shape than most other industrial countries. Why the slow recovery?

There is no simple answer, but some plausible explanations have been offered.

One suggestion is that the structural problems of the Japanese economy that lie behind the formation and collapse of the bubble are more serious than those of other Asian countries.

Another is that, given that it took Japan more than 15 years to get back on the right path, the economic rebound of other Asian countries could be false. In other words, it is possible that these countries' economic reforms, particularly financial, have in fact been far from sufficient in a long-term perspective.

Thirdly, some say that Japan's measures to deal with the post-bubble blues have been lacking, both in efficiency and effectiveness.

Although it is showing signs of life again, the Japanese economy has yet to really get back into stable, sustained growth. It remains unclear whether Japan will be able to sustain its stable economic expansion.

China was not hit by the Asian financial crisis directly. The country embarked on market reforms in late 1978, opening its economy to the outside world, but Beijing keeps careful control over its financial markets, and pushed through various changes under a central planning regime.

When the financial crisis erupted, Chinese authorities further tightened their grip on the financial markets, and were not hesitant about intervening aggressively. As a result, China successfully insulated itself from the financial storm that swept over its neighbors.

Although it protected itself from the fallout of the financial crisis, China has nonetheless allowed some economic excesses to develop at home.

The Chinese economy has been steaming ahead for several years, fueled mainly by a construction boom and rapid growth in the auto industry. A lot of momentum is also coming from strong exports (especially to the United States) and two big upcoming national events: the 2008 Olympics in Beijing and the world exposition in Shanghai in 2010.

Observers have been warning for some time about the overheating of investment in the construction and auto sectors. Many point out that Chinese industry is awash in excess capacity, causing a large output gap between actual and potential production. The Chinese steel industry, for instance, produced 350 million tons of steel in 2005 but has the capacity to produce 470 million tons annually. When new plants currently under construction go online, production capacity will top 600 million tons.

Ordinary Chinese Still Poor

The Chinese auto industry is overcrowded, with more than 120 companies. The domestic auto market grew explosively by 50 per cent between 2002 and 2003.

Again, there is excess capacity: the industry can churn out more than 8.70 million vehicles, but only 5.72 million cars were sold in 2005.

For many Chinese workers, cars remain a luxury beyond their reach. The average annual income of Chinese workers is about 5 per cent that of their Japanese counterparts, yet Japanese cars are sold in China at prices three times higher than in Japan. The big question is how long the Chinese car market can continue to expand.

The current building boom is also troubling. Rare is the vacant lot in Beijing where a new building is not being put up. The construction frenzy seems to be leaving little space for those public facilities essential to a comfortable living environment, such as green zones and parks.

In Shanghai, there are mounting concerns about land subsidence, stemming from a growing forest of high-rise buildings and excessive exploitation of underground water.

Luxury houses and condominiums are sprouting up in many parts of the nation. Sales of high-end condos and mansions with price tags well above 100 million yen are robust.

After a recent international conference in Shanghai, I took a quick post-conference tour around one of the city's upscale neighborhoods. The average house was a two-story, 460-square-meter mansion, built on a 660-square-meter plot, with three garages and a 25-meter swimming pool, going for an eye-popping 38 million yuan (about 540 million yen). There was even one palatial mansion worth 200 million yuan (about 2.85 billion yen).

Assuming that the monthly pay of professors at Beijing or Tsinghua University is about 4,000 yuan, the 38-million yuan price of the average house in this district is equivalent to 800 years' worth of salary.

Professors from Canada and Australia who joined the tour said similar houses in their countries would cost them more like 10 years' worth of annual income, while a professor from Singapore estimated that in his country it would be about 30 years' worth.

Although the buyers of these fancy houses are not necessarily Chinese, their hefty prices inevitably limit the size of the potential customer base. They symbolize the wide and growing income gap between a small number of newly rich urbanites and the rest of China, as well as the growing asset-price bubble.

Like the rapidly deteriorating environment, this is one of the increasingly urgent problems facing a nation whose economy has now grown steadily for the last 27 years.

The Chinese government has been trying hard to curb the expansion of its own bubble economy, one driven by excessive capital investment and industrial production. The government has instituted restrictions on lending by banks and other financial institutions. It has also started taking steps to stem the rise of property prices.

These steps will help ease the red-hot Chinese economy into a sustainable cruising speed. There is still, however, a pretty good chance that the bubble will continue at least until the Beijing Olympics in 2008 and the Shanghai expo in 2010.

U.S. Must Abandon Unilateralism on Beef Issue[3]

Japan's ban on U.S. beef imports is now a major source of trade friction. Japanese consumers enjoy the taste of U.S. beef but want assurances it is safe to eat. The United States should adopt stringent safety measures, comparable to those observed in Japan, if it really wants to resume exporting its product to Japan.

Safety Paramount

Instead of thinking about the protection of ranchers, the U.S. government needs to set up a system that guarantees risky parts are removed before beef is shipped to Japan. Food safety is paramount.

Under the presidency of George W. Bush, the U.S. campaign to export beef can be likened to U.S. beef unilateralism. The aggressive manner in which it has applied pressure to Japan, with hints that it is ready to impose sanctions if its requests are not met, remind me of U.S. Commodore Matthew Perry's 1853 visit that ended Japan's more than two centuries of isolation.

Am I the only one who gets the impression the superpower United States is trying to throw its weight around?

Washington should listen to Japanese consumers. It should invite Japanese consumer groups to U.S. cattle ranches to discuss the problems, and with U.S. officials, if necessary.

The United States is the world's largest producer of beef. It raises about 100 million head of cattle of which about 35 million are processed annually for human consumption. In 2003, Japan was the top importer of U.S. beef at 37 per cent (41,700 tons) of total U.S. exports, followed by Mexico and South Korea both at 23 per cent (267,000 tons), and Canada at 9 per cent (103,000 tons).

On Dec. 23, 2003, a Holstein cow in the United States tested positive for Bovine Spongiform Encephalopathy (BSE), more commonly known as mad cow disease.

The news immediately sent shock waves through the U.S. beef industry. Japan announced a ban on U.S. beef imports the following day. Japan was among more than 10 countries that refused to accept U.S. beef until the problem was cleared up. These nations accounted for 70 per cent of the U.S. beef export market. As a result, exports of what is known as dressed carcass dropped from 1,142 tons in 2003 to 209 tons in 2004. It was a severe blow to the U.S. cattle industry.

Before the ban on U.S. beef imports, Yoshinoya D&C Co. and four other restaurant operators were serving more than 1 million bowls of rice topped with beef each day. U.S. beef was the key ingredient.

With a moderate amount of fat, U.S. beef seems to suit the Japanese palate.

The restaurants now serve dishes made with beef from Australia, New Zealand and China but they are not as popular with customers as those that use U.S. beef.

Japan took very strict measures to ensure that beef available to Japanese consumers is safe. When a calf is born in Japan, its date of birth, breed, the address and name of the producer and the identification number of its mother are registered with the government. A tag with a number assigned to each calf is affixed on its ear. Matsuzaka beef, whose marbled meat is likened to "a work of art," is so expensive that in 2002, a cow named yoshitoyo-go was auctioned for 50 million yen, the highest price ever. Only Japanese black heifer cattle can be called Matsuzaka beef. Each heifer is raised for more than 500 days and given daily massages to activate blood circulation and make it fatty. The animals are also fed beer to increase appetite and massaged with shochu, an alcoholic beverage, to make the fur shiny and beautiful.

Since October 2001, Japan has blanket-tested all cattle slaughtered for human consumption, as well as those that died of illness or accidents. There are four U.S.-approved facilities within Japan that process beef for export to the United States. U.S. inspectors visit them once a year. A manual for U.S. exports lists a strict set of rules that must be observed by processors. For example, they are required to wash their hands each time after processing an individual animal, check each hour the temperature of refrigerators where beef for export is kept and ensure once a day that thermometers are not broken.

In the United States, cattle are put out to pasture for a year and then moved to large production farms where they are kept and raised until they are butchered. There is no strict traceability system as in Japan.

Compared with Japan's strict safety control measures, I am flabbergasted at the slipshod manner in which the United States failed to remove risky animal parts from a beef shipment to Japan.

Resuming U.S. beef imports is an important matter for both Japan and the United States. The Japanese government officially lifted a two-year ban on beef imports from the United States and Canada on Dec. 12, 2005. In doing so, it limited imports to meat from cattle 20 months old or younger. However, on Jan. 20, 2006, Japan reimposed a complete ban on U.S. beef after spinal column, a risky part, was found in a shipment.

The U.S. side strongly opposed this decision. Bush and other U.S. government officials, including Secretary of Agriculture Mike Johanns, Undersecretary of Agriculture J.B. Penn, U.S. Ambassador to Japan Thomas Schieffer and Secretary of State Condoleezza Rice, have been pressing Japan for early lifting of the ban. However, they have yet to explain how the United States intends to strengthen safety measures to win the trust of Japanese consumers.

U.S. Should Concede

To break the deadlock, I urge the United States to develop an extensive campaign to reach out to Japanese consumers. Why not invite Japanese consumer groups to the United States to visit ranches and beef processing plants, let them explain their ideas of food safety directly to U.S. beef producers and processors, have them exchange views with them and sample U.S. beef that is considered safe?

Basically, I think the U.S. side should concede to meet Japanese safety standards. If Japan's ban on U.S. beef imports continues, it could have a serious effect on bilateral trade. The situation should be rectified quickly.

Notes

1   Reprinted from *Asahi Shimbun*, 24 January 2003, with kind permission of the publisher.
2   Reproduced from *Asahi Shimbun*, 11 February 2006, with kind permission of the publisher.
3   Reproduced from *Asahi Shimbun*, 27 April 2006, with kind permission of the publisher.

CHAPTER 17

Japan's Distorted Policies towards Asia

Abe Likely to Follow Koizumi's Lead on East Asia[1]

The trade ministers of Japan and the Association of Southeast Asian Nations (ASEAN) met in Kuala Lumpur on Aug. 23.

At the meeting, trade minister Toshihiro Nikai proposed the idea of signing an East Asia Economic Partnership Agreement (EPA) the following day.

The agreement would include the so-called ASEAN Plus Three (Japan, China and South Korea), plus three (India, Australia and New Zealand).

The idea is very similar to the "comprehensive economic partnership" proposed by Prime Minister Junichiro Koizumi to ASEAN in January 2002.

Practically, the only major difference is that Koizumi's idea included the United States instead of India.

Nikai probably chose India in view of its remarkable growth in the last four to five years. It seems he has no intention of excluding the United States from East Asia. What is more, the proposed members had already been approved at the East Asian summit in Malaysia in Decembe last year.

Where ASEAN Stands

ASEAN members are taking Nikai's proposal seriously. At the same time, however, they insist that they should first advance three ASEAN Plus One frameworks: ASEAN Plus Japan, ASEAN Plus China and ASEAN Plus South Korea.

They believe that unless these three groupings can be made to work, there is no way Nikai's proposal will go further.

The Nikai proposal seems to stem from three things:

- An acknowledgment of India's extraordinary growth, as well as consideration toward Australia and New Zealand, countries with which Japan has long had close ties
- The fact that Japan got a late start on the ASEAN Plus Three initiative, and has found it difficult to strengthen economic cooperation with China and South Korea because of an impasse in political relations
- A desire to weaken China's influence.

ASEAN nations are eager for ASEAN Plus Three, but rivalry between Japan, China and South Korea has become an obstacle. To break the deadlock, it will be necessary to agree on the three ASEAN Plus One initiatives and stay open to ASEAN Plus Six.

As a group, ASEAN has been playing a leading role in the promotion of economic integration in the greater East Asian region. The union is also actively working toward EPAs with India and the United States, and is applying pressure on Japan, China and South Korea to get the three ASEAN Plus One initiatives off the ground. I expect it to play an increasingly central role in East Asian economic integration.

ASEAN maintains a neutral position regarding Japan's political strife with China and South Korea. Certainly it has criticized Koizumi's visits to Yasukuni Shrine, and Singapore and Malaysia are particularly unhappy with the situation. But ASEAN also hopes to strengthen economic cooperation with Japan, thinking the establishment of an East Asian economic community otherwise impossible.

Japan urgently needs to improve its Asian relations.

In general, its relations with ASEAN are not the problem. There are no territorial disputes or major problems between them. Japan signed EPAs with Singapore and Malaysia in 2002 and 2006, and has entered the final phase of negotiations for similar agreements with Thailand and the Philippines. If Japan can compromise on opening up its domestic agricultural market, I think EPAs with ASEAN countries will not be far off.

The real problem is with China and South Korea.

Summit meetings with those two countries have been suspended because of Koizumi's visits to Yasukuni Shrine.

His latest, on Aug. 15, seriously aggravated matters.

It would be no exaggeration to say that things have gotten so bad that the damage may be beyond repair.

And Abe?

What about Chief Cabinet Secretary Shinzo Abe, seen as the most likely candidate to succeed Koizumi?

It appears likely that Abe will follow the policies that the Koizumi administration has advanced over the last five years.

In addition to political, economic and social reform, he is expected to push to revise the pacifist Constitution and turn the Self-Defense Forces into a full-fledged military.

On foreign policy, he is likely to stick with the traditional policy of staying close to the United States and distancing Japan from Asia. He will also probably take a firmer stand against North Korea. It thus appears highly unlikely that he will be able to improve political and diplomatic relations with China and South Korea.

In the unlikely event the ruling Liberal Democratic Party loses next year's Upper House election, I don't think Abe would step down. The Abe administration looks set to be long-lived.

He is probably looking to establish a stable majority in the next Lower House election by strengthening party unity. Although it is hard to predict exactly how long he will stay in power, I think improving relations with China and South Korea will be extremely difficult for some time.

Yet, even if he takes a firmer stand against China and South Korea than Koizumi, on becoming prime minister Abe could conceivably adopt drastic measures to reverse Japan's Asian policy and break the deadlock with China and South Korea.

Prime Ministers Yasuhiro Nakasone and Takeo Fukuda, for example, were both known for their hawkish positions and tough talk toward China. Yet, they worked hard to establish friendly relations with China and South Korea nonetheless.

How the Abe administration reacts to future changes in the domestic and international environment will be closely watched.

Either way, if the new administration takes off under Abe's leadership in September, and depending on how he deals with China and South Korea, there could be a major impact on the ASEAN Plus Three or Plus Six frameworks—and eventually on the formation of any East Asian community.

For now, Abe is expected to follow the Koizumi administration's policy of "comprehensive economic cooperation" and support Nikai's ASEAN Plus Six initiative.

At the same time, the new administration is likely to accelerate negotiations on bilateral EPAs with ASEAN nations, and work toward a Japan-ASEAN EPA and an eventual East Asian community.

In Koizumi's Wake, Abe Must Turn towards Asia[2]

At age 52, Shinzo Abe is postwar Japan's youngest prime minister. His relative youth brings a precious breath of fresh air into Japanese political society, which has traditionally been dominated by older men.

But with the country facing a mountain of problems both at home and abroad, the Abe administration's ability to get things done and the effectiveness of its policies will be put to the test.

What does Asia expect of the Abe administration? For the last five-and a-half years, Abe has been studying and training under the wing of former Prime Minister Junichiro Koizumi. Therefore, he is likely to basically continue Koizumi's policies on structural reform and Asian relations.

It is on the latter that I would like to focus.

Three Asian Problems

First, where does Japan place Asia in its world strategy?

Koizumi always said that the better Japan's relations with the United States, the more it can strengthen ties with China, South Korea and other Asian countries.

From the Asian point of view, that sounds a lot like staying close to the United States and breaking away from Asia—or even following the United States and abandoning Asia entirely.

Since Japan and the United States are allies, it is a matter of course that they maintain close political, economic and diplomatic ties. Most Asian countries have shown a certain level of understanding toward this. Still, they cannot dispel the fear that Japan is trying to curry favor with the United States.

The idea that Japan would be better able to build strong relations with Asia the closer it is to the United States is logically flawed. It is a policy that the Abe administration needs to modify.

The second problem relates to the prime minister's visits to Yasukuni Shrine.

It is extremely unlikely that China and South Korea will give in to Japan over this problem. Still, it would be wiser for both to refrain from saying that they will not hold summit meetings with Abe if he visits Yasukuni. Doing so could provoke Abe into trying to arouse public opinion on the side of not bowing to foreign pressure, and ultimately push him to visit the shrine. He went in April, and it is important to keep a close eye on how he will act in the future.

Third, it is wiser for Japan not to turn the Yasukuni controversy into such a quagmire that it isolates Japan from Asia.

Some politicians maintain that China and South Korea are the only countries in the world that criticize Japan over the visits. Such comments are absurd. There have been official statements criticizing the visits issued by the United States and countries in Europe. Other Asian countries, including Singapore and Malaysia, have also been critical.

On the surface, most Asian countries are calmly standing by the principle of non-interference in Japan's domestic affairs. They do not want to get caught in Japan-China and Japan-South Korea disputes. But the fact remains that they did not approve of Koizumi's visits to Yasukuni.

Abe's administration is seen by Asia as hawkish. Abe and Foreign Minister Taro Aso are both considered hard-liners, as are two new Abe appointees, Liberal Democratic Party Secretary-General Hidenao Nakagawa and LDP Policy Research Council Chairman Shoichi Nakagawa. Asia is worried that these politicians will stick to toeing the hard U.S. line toward China and South Korea.

With his visits to China and South Korea on Oct. 8 and 9, however, Abe was able to resume Japan's long-suspended summit meetings with the leaders of those countries.

The development on Japan's side can be attributed to the following:

- An attempt by the Abe administration to break from Koizumi's influence, and to assert its independent stance;
- Consideration to criticism from the opposition parties and within the LDP itself;
- That the Association of Southeast Asian Nations (ASEAN), the European Union and the United States also want Japan to improve its relations with China and South Korea;
- Strong demand from the business world for better relations;
- The increasing importance of economic relations with South Korea and China; and
- That cooperation with the two countries is indispensable to a range of other problems, such as the abduction issue, North Korea's missile and nuclear tests, and the six-party talks over Pyongyang's nuclear program.

The summit meetings are a start. But Koizumi met repeatedly with his Chinese and South Korean counterparts, and those relationships deteriorated anyway. Summits are only a means to improving relations, not an end.

Ambiguous Policy

In that sense, Abe's meetings with the leaders of China and South Korea are nothing more than a first step toward breaking the deadlock. Diplomatic relations could once again deteriorate, depending on what happens with regards to the Yasukuni problem and the debate over historical recognition.

Which makes the question of how long Abe will continue his ambiguous policy toward China and South Korea all the more important. Should he one day decide to visit Yasukuni, the summit meetings could break off at once.

Japan, China and South Korea should strengthen cooperation and develop closer ties. Abe is expected to meet the leaders again at November's Asia-Pacific Economic Cooperation forum in Vietnam and again in December at the East Asian summit in the Philippines. He should take advantage of those occasions to improve the diplomatic relationship.

Unfortunately, the LDP has no consistent policy on how to deal with Asia. There is also opposition within it to free trade agreements (FTAs) and economic partnership agreements (EPAs) with countries in East Asia.

Some politicians think that since Japan is dependent on trade, it should eliminate trade barriers and actively promote trade with countries around the world.

But although Japan is moving toward economic cooperation and integration with East Asia, quite a few politicians remain skeptical of the concept.

They maintain that since the economic gap between Japan and the rest of East Asia is wide, it would be almost impossible for it to conclude trade agreements with Asian countries.

In the meantime, Japan's reluctance to open up its agricultural, marine and labor markets leaves it no choice but to be passive with regards to concluding EPAs centering on ASEAN.

China-ASEAN free trade is currently more advanced than Japan-ASEAN economic partnership.

Japan should make a greater effort to strengthen its East Asian relations, and that means improving its ties with China and South Korea.

Japan is the most significant economic power in Asia. A Japan-ASEAN EPA, a successful ASEAN-plus-three, and a future East Asian economic community cannot be realized without Japanese participation.

Discord with China and South Korea could have an immeasurably negative impact on Asian regional economic integration. The Abe administration is urged to change Japan's Asian policy accordingly.

India May Play Key Role in East Asian Economy[3]

India has made remarkable economic advances in recent years. There is no doubt such industries as information technology, automotive manufacturing, medicine, steel and electronics will contribute to India's economic growth into the future. While we must refrain from overestimating its economic strength, India may become a key player in the integration of an East Asian economic community.

However, in order for India to become a major economic power, it needs to eliminate many obstacles. They include environmental pollution, bipolar distribution of wealth resulting from the caste system, serious delays in building socio-industrial infrastructure and the language barrier, which is making it difficult for people who speak different languages to communicate.

In economic advancement, India is said to be lagging behind China by about 20 years and is at least 60 years behind Japan, although some analysts have predicted optimistically that India's GDP will exceed Japan in the year of 2030.

Expanding ASEAN

While India is expected to make steady economic growth along with China, it should not be overestimated. Japan, in particular, tends to view India's economic development as a "myth." But India's booming economy is most likely why the nation, together with Australia and New Zealand, was admitted as a regular member of the East Asian summit, which was held for the first time in Malaysia in December 2005. The second meeting took place in the Philippines in January 2007.

In fact, the idea of "ASEAN 10-plus-three-plus-three" (The Association of Southeast Asian Nations plus Japan, China and South Korea plus Australia, New Zealand and India) was mentioned in the "comprehensive economic cooperation" initiative that was announced in January 2002 by then Prime Minister Junichiro Koizumi during his visit to Singapore. It was also included in the "East Asia economic partnership agreement" proposed by then Minister of Economy, Trade and Industry Toshihiro Nikai at a meeting of trade ministers in Malaysia on Aug. 23, 2006. China and Malaysia were less enthusiastic, attempting to limit East Asian economic integration to ASEAN 10-plus-three.

Recently, however, the two countries have begun to soften and show signs of compromise. Why? Let me cite three possible reasons.

1) Japan and ASEAN nations—Indonesia, Singapore and Thailand for example—welcome the participation of India and Oceania. 2) Since China strengthened its economic ties with India and Australia, it may be unwise for China to exclude them. 3) The United States intends to advance ASEAN 10-plus-three to ASEAN 10-plus-three-plus-three-plus-one by strongly backing up India and Australia. (The concept of a free trade area for the Asia-Pacific (FTAAP) proposed by U.S. President George W. Bush just before the meeting of the Asia-Pacific Economic Cooperation (APEC) forum in Vietnam in November 2006 is a typical example.)

Thus, it is likely that plans for East Asian economic integration would from now on advance under the framework of ASEAN 10-plus-three-plus-three.

Moreover, at the APEC forum to be held at the end of the year in Australia, discussions to give shape to the FTAAP initiative are expected to start in earnest. Since the membership of FTAAP proposed by the United States is likely to be the same as that of APEC, how to make the two compatible is a major issue.

Up to now, Japan, China and South Korea have played a leading role in advancing the East Asian economic integration initiative in cooperation with ASEAN. But the United States maintains a distance from East Asia. The Japanese presence is also waning. By incorporating India, Australia and New Zealand into the framework, Japan and the United States are trying to counter the Chinese offensive and weaken its influence, observers say.

Leadership Needed

But the prospects for the East Asian economic integration initiative are by no means rosy. To begin with, ASEAN, which forms the foundation of the initiative, has reached a turning point and is seeking a new direction.

It lacks a competent leader who can display strong leadership over member nations.

The political situation in Myanmar (Burma) remains fluid. Thailand has yet to recover from the aftereffects of the September 2006 coup. Indonesian President Susilo Bambang Yudhoyono skipped the East Asian summit in the Philippines and went home because of domestic political unrest. With a lack of centripetal force, ASEAN appears to be at a loss to present concrete plans to realize East Asian economic integration.

As for China, the balance of its foreign currency reserves for fiscal 2006 stood at $1.0663 trillion thanks mainly to a huge trade surplus and the introduction of foreign capital. At the same time, the inflow of foreign currency before the expected revaluation of the renminbi is also likely to have played a positive role in boosting the reserves.

It is a virtual miracle that China, a developing country that aims to be "a well-off society," surpassed Japan as the world leader in foreign currency reserves.

It is true that China has become economically stronger. This can be seen in its greater role in the second East Asia summit in Cebu, the Philippines, in January. The way Asian media devoted much time on Chinese affairs shows Japan's waning influence. China's growing importance in Asia and the steady advancement of China-ASEAN economic cooperation are attracting global attention.

China hosted a China-ASEAN summit in Nanning, Guangxi province, and a China-Africa summit in Beijing in November 2006. It would be no exaggeration to say that it took advantage of these occasions to establish its position in Asia and on the African continent.

Under such circumstances, perhaps it may be easier to realize East Asian economic integration based on the framework of ASEAN 10-plus-three. But the trend is centered on ASEAN 10-plus-three-plus-three. Economic cooperation between Japan, China and South Korea provides a solid foundation for East Asian economic integration. But political and historical factors continually have a negative effect on Japan-China and Japan-South Korea relations, making them weaker.

This is where India is expected to play an increasingly positive role. Without getting caught in political strife between Japan, China and South Korea, India is urged to maintain close economic ties with China as the world's two major developing nations in order to make a positive contribution to realizing East Asian economic integration.

India's Vast Market is Still a Risky Proposition[4]

India's remarkable economic growth has been attracting international attention for quite a while. But not everything is as rosy as it looks. Instead of focusing only on positive aspects of the Indian economy, I suggest that people look at the situation there in its entirety so as to make a calm assessment of the actual state of affairs. With this in mind, I recently visited New Delhi.

Generally speaking, India is regarded as a growing regional power. But it is still a poor one. I flew from Tokyo to New Delhi in November. Twelve years had passed since my last visit. Although the economy class fare on the Air India flight was half that of Japan Airlines, it still cost about 120,000 yen, which I thought was quite expensive.

I was quite taken aback by the aircraft I boarded. When I tried to put carry-on luggage into the overhead compartment, it was literally patched up with pieces of adhesive tape.

When I took my seat, I also found traces of tape on the armrest. The walls of the toilet were repaired with tape and glue.

Despite the poor interior condition of the aircraft, it took off from Narita and landed safely at New Delhi International Airport. Upon arrival, I was once again surprised at how small and shabby the airport was. I stepped out of the airport and looked for a public telephone. What I found was an old dial phone. Users literally have to ask an operator in front of the booth to dial a number to make a call.

I took a drive on a bumpy expressway and finally made it to Jawaharlal Nehru University. Along the way, I saw a five-star hotel but I was overwhelmed by the slums and heaps of garbage scattered across the city. The water in the rivers on both sides of the expressway was black and foul-smelling. When the car stopped at a traffic signal, children swarmed around the vehicle trying to sell flowers and newspapers. Everywhere I went, cows and dogs were wandering around. Camels were pulling carts and tricycle taxis were threading their way through busy traffic amid cars and pedestrians. People eating outside were busy shooing away flies with their free hand. I also saw people having their hair cut on street corners, while other napped under a scorching sun. It was a common sight to see men urinating in the street.

In the evening, monkeys jumped from tree to tree. Peacocks gave out mournful sounds while they rested in the trees. In the university's guest house, I got bitten by mosquitoes every night.

What I experienced was the opposite of my image of India's modernization and remarkable economic growth. In other words, almost nothing had changed from what I encountered 12 years ago. It was an interesting experience.

The aircraft I used to return to Narita took off 90 minutes behind schedule due to mechanical trouble.

I pondered the reason for the much lower price in airfare compared to Japanese carriers and wondered whether it was partly because the lights above the seats could not be operated individually. Instead, cabin attendants controlled the main switch and passengers could only use them when the main switch was on.

Nevertheless, India is on the Move

But, stories abound of India's bright side. Recently, the presidents of the United States, China and Russia visited India for summit talks one after another. Indian Prime Minister Manmohan Singh, meantime, has been active on the foreign policy front. He visited Japan in December and attended the East Asian summit in the Philippines in January.

India is a country on the move. It is reaching out to world leaders to develop summit diplomacy, especially in the fields of political and economic cooperation, security, energy development, space development and antiterrorism measures. Indeed, just like China, India is attracting global attention as a newly rising Asian power.

From the standpoint of the Association of Southeast Asian Nations (ASEAN), India has always been a regional power whose influence in the Asia-Pacific region could not be ignored. With a population of slightly more than 1.1 billion, India is the world's largest democracy. It is a huge market for investors and a major consumer power at the same time. India, as everybody knows, is also a technical power. It is proficient at developing and manufacturing anything from pencils to satellites. ASEAN believes that a good balance between Japan, the United States, China and India will help to maintain Asian security by filling a regional "military vacuum."

The presence of India on the world stage is becoming increasingly important. It has attained rapid growth since it implemented a series of economic reform policies in 1991. This can be seen from the fact that it maintained an average growth rate of 6.8 per cent from 2001 to 2005.

China and Russia are actively developing diplomatic ties with India, focussing more on political and military relations rather than on the economy. The United States, on the other hand, seems to be approaching India based on the idea that it could serve as a "counterbalance" to China and Russia. Japan regards India as a "presence that weakens China's influence in Asia."

This is the trend that fueled the "India boom" in Japan, prompting the business world to make major inroads in India.

Japan attaches importance to the concept of "China-plus-one"— meaning another country besides China for it to invest in. This is because Japan-China relations remain somewhat shaky. Industry leaders also believe that investing in China is risky.

Previously, Vietnam was regarded as an ideal investment vehicle. But India's rapid rise has made it an attractive alternative to Vietnam. Here are some of India's potentially lucrative strengths: Wages are low. It has a vast "middle class" comprising 300 million people, a large pool of talent in the information technology industry and a huge domestic market of 1.1 billion people.

At the same time, its high ratios of blindness and illiteracy are factors that contribute to the low quality of Indian labor. In the IT business, the brain drain to the United States and Europe remains a serious problem. Although the domestic market is huge, the purchasing power of Indian consumers remains low. In fact, 65 percent of the population live on $2,000 (approximately 240,000 yen) a year. It is also estimated that 386.29 million Indians survive on less than $1 a day. Incidentally, the number of Chinese who live under the poverty line is said to be about 110 million.

Still a Lot of Risk

It is fine for Japanese businesses to advance into India. But the way some of them only see the good points about the Indian market and disregard its flaws is risky. I am worried that they may make a serious mistake by investing too heavily.

The Indian government plans to spend $350 billion in the next five years to improve infrastructure in the form of electric power networks, roads, airports and urban high-speed railways. India's poor infrastructure is a major factor that is hindering its economic advancement and introduction of foreign capital. This is a problem that needs to be steadily addressed.

Notes

1   Reproduced from *Asahi Shimbun*, 8 September 2006, with kind permission of the publisher.
2   Reproduced from *Asahi Shimbun*, 19 October 2006, with kind permission of the publisher.
3   Reproduced from *Asahi Shimbun*, 7 February 2007, with kind permission of the publisher.
4   Reproduced from *Asahi Shimbun*, 7 March 2007, with the kind permission of the publisher.

CHAPTER 18

The Characteristics of East Asian Multi-Lateral Cooperation

Prelude

Despite the territorial and sovereignty disputes among East Asian countries, East Asian multi-lateral cooperation is currently working on promoting political dialogue and economic alliance. These regional disputes, such as those involving the Diaoyutai Islands or Senkaku Islands, Paracel Islands, Spratly Islands, East Sea Islands and the Korean Peninsula, which could potentially erupt into military confrontation have been halted and eased through diplomatic dialogues.

The East Asian economic cooperation includes establishing the Tumenjiang economic circle, the Japan Sea economic circle, the South China economic circle etc. These economic circles have been developing for years. However, with the exception of the South China economic circle (includes Taiwan, Hong Kong and Macau), the rest have not been showing significant progress. At the same time, the concept of an Asian Economic Union is spreading rapidly throughout Asia, thus marginalizing the previously mentioned economic circles.

The East Asian multi-lateral economic cooperation specifically focuses on pushing for the concept of Asian economic integration. A series of activities, such as the FTA (Free Trade Agreement) and the EPA (Economic Partnership Agreement) best reflect the Asian economic integration concept. The CAFTA (China-ASEAN Free Trade Area), JAFTA (Japan-ASEAN Free Trade Agreement), KAFTA

(Korea-ASEAN Free Trade Agreement), IAFTA (India-ASEAN Free Trade Agreement) and EAEC (East Asian Economic Community) also exemplify this concept. These regional economic concepts, except for the East Asian Economic Community, all involve one of the East Asian countries, such as China, Japan, South Korea and India, with the ASEAN10 countries. The relationship between FTA countries involves large-scale compromise and competition. For the ASEAN region, basically every FTA could be signed within the next four to six years. However, which FTA would eventually become successful and simultaneously be efficient in reaching multi-lateral agreements with East Asian countries is a critical issue of paramount importance.

The concept of regional economic alliance in East Asia, through various means, has been expanding rapidly. These means include academic, economic or political means, or a combination of the three. At the same time, the development of the economic alliance concept can either be bi-lateral (country to country) or multi-lateral (one country to multiple countries). Economic alliance does not merely focus on economic cooperation; it also includes technology transfer, educational cooperation and human resource sharing.

Besides East Asian multi-lateral cooperation and the above mentioned FTAs and EPAs, there are also other numerous economic activities, such as the following:

1. The establishment of the AMF (Asian Monetary Fund);
2. ASEAN Currency Swap Agreement;
3. Asian Bonds Agreement.

These new activities serve as pre-emptive measures after the 1997 Asian financial crisis and aim to consolidate the economic alliance that focuses on financial areas. Without a doubt, this concept of regional economic alliance will miss participation from the East Asian countries (such as China, Japan and Korea) and India.

The United States' Leading Role in East Asian Multi-Lateral Cooperation

As a global power, the United States has not only reflected its leadership militarily and politically, but also in the global economy. Even though the United States is the world's largest debtor (fiscal deficit and international trade deficit; Japan, Europe and China are the largest creditors), it is considered the world's largest economy, with over ten trillion US dollars of Gross National Product, and technologically and legally the most advanced country. At the same time, the United States is also the world's largest consumer country; Europe and Asian's economic forecasts are deeply influenced by the United States' internal consumer market.

In December of 1991, after the collapse of the Soviet Union, the stalemate between the East (Soviet Union) and the West (the United States) came to an end. Yet, the end of the Cold War symbolizes the birth of a new Cold War. The United States stages its presence as the world's political, economic, military and diplomatic super power. Even though Russia and China hold some of the power in Asia, and France and Germany in the European Union, the fact is that the United States has surged to become the world's only superpower and the world has become uni-polar and unilateralism cannot be ignored. The attack on Iraq on 20th March 2003 best demonstrates the United States' unilateralism.

Without the consent of the United Nations and objection from France, Germany, Russia and China, the United States jointly agreed with the United Kingdom and Italy to attack Iraq. Thus, the multilateralism that the world powers retain has come to extinction.

The United States also eagerly wants to play a role in the Korean Peninsula and the Taiwan Straits issue. Soon after President George Bush took office, he listed North Korea, Iraq and Iran as the axis of evil. Due to North Korea's nuclear weapons program, it has already become a military threat to Japan, South Korea and the United States. The United States has always wanted to impose sanctions on

North Korea. However, with the war with Iraq and Iran on hand and also the support for North Korea from Russia and China, the United States has not had the opportunity to do so.

Without any other alternatives, the United States hopes to solve the South and North Korea confrontation and ease the military threat, especially to Japan, through six-side negotiations (China, United States, Japan, Russia, South and North Korea). Despite the progress of the six-side meeting, to peacefully resolve the Korean Peninsula issue still seems to be a long way off.

Being the initiating country in the six-side meeting, China has not been viewed as that influential by other member countries. Nevertheless, China plays a significant role in the six-side meeting. However, in order not to sacrifice the national interests of North Korea and at the same time fulfill the requests from the United States, Japan and South Korea, the role China plays in the multilateral dialogue definitely deserves attention.

As for the Taiwan Strait issue, it is more complicated. China has been waiting to reunify with Taiwan for fifty-eight years, however, the longer it takes the closer Taiwan moves toward independence. Right now, the move for independence in Taiwan is reaching a climax. Domestically, the Chinese government has vowed to use military force to reunify Taiwan. Yet, the United States is the primary factor they do not, and Japan being the secondary factor. Would the United States be fully involved, partially or not at all? The first and third possibilities seem minutely small. If the United States chooses to be partially involved, the question is to what degree? Would the involvement lead to the Sino-US war? Or, would it affect the 2008 Beijing Olympics and 2010 Shanghai World Exposition?

The Chinese first, second and third generation leaders have not successfully and peacefully reunited Taiwan and everyone is concerned about how the next leader will solve such a challenging task. When the current leader is pondering about the issue, the "American factor" inevitably becomes the primary concern.

The Competition between China and Japan in the East Asian Multi-Lateral Cooperation

In Asia, China and Japan have always been competing with each other head-to-head. China is a developing country with major political powers, a mediocre military force and a long history. China is considered as a minor player in the global economy (based on GNP per capita), a mediocre military player (based on national defense budget and military force) and a major political player (based on international influence). By comparison, Japan is a country whose traditional culture has been deeply influenced by China and a contemporary culture shaped by the Europeans and Americans. As the world's second largest economy, a minor player in the political arena and a major military force (with its military expenditure and national defense budget, Japan is considered as a major military country). Japan is a major world economic and military power, but relatively weak in politics. Overall, the two countries are considered equal, weighing their political, economic and military powers. Thus, over-reaction and a self-defense mentality inevitably exist in their cooperation.

From a political perspective, Japan and the United States need help from China in solving the Korean Peninsula issue, thus, they actively participate in the six-side talk that China initiated. Japan especially, wants to leverage on China's power to put more pressure on North Korea. On one hand, Japan hopes to see peaceful reunification between South and North Korea. On the other hand, Japan wants North Korea to terminate its nuclear weapon in order to reduce the military threat. Thus, regarding this Korean Peninsula issue, China and Japan do not need to compete against each other.

However, both China and Japan are not willing to compromise on the dispute over the sovereignty of the Diaoyutai Islands and the East Sea resources (crude oil and natural gas). To retain the wholeness of sovereignty as a priority, the dispute between the two countries has never stopped. Fortunately, under the principle of mutual respect, the occurring disputes have never led to a large-scale military confrontation.

On the issues of CAFTA, JAFTA or the ASEAN plus 3, whether it is China or Japan to play the leading role has apparently become a tug of war. Diplomatically, China has more power to negotiate with the ASEAN, however, economically, Japan has an upper hand (though the Chinese economy has been gaining momentum and the relationship between China and the ASEAN has become closer than before). Which country first signs a FTA agreement with the ASEAN or plays a leading role in the ASEAN plus 3 has a long-term effect on Asia-Pacific economic cooperation.

Regarding the establishment of the above-mentioned three Asia-Pacific financial mechanisms, since Japan's economy is larger than China's, Japan seems to have more advantage.

Speaking about Sino-Japan relations, due to the dispute over history textbooks, Mr.Koizumi's visit to the Yasukuni Shrine, the Diaoyutai Islands and the Sheng Yang Japanese embassy incident, the relationship has been deteriorating. Although from an economic perspective for Japan, the China threat theory has transformed into the China dependency theory. The huge Chinese internal market has provided an excellent platform for Japan's economic revival. The trade with China has consolidated Japan's foundation for economic revival. Sino-Japan relations is positioned in the "pro-economy and against politics" status. It is not easy to change such status, but the negativity of politics should not greatly reduce the good economic trade between the two countries. The people in these two countries are expecting that economic trade will effectively change the negative side of the politics.

The Important Role of the ASEAN in the East Asian Multilateral Cooperation

The ASEAN consists of ten member countries, and the East Asian multilateral cooperation would not be possible without the ASEAN.

The relationship between the two is mutually supportive, meaning that whether it is CAFTA, JAFTA, KAFTA, IAFTA or ASEEAN10 plus 3, the ASEAN10 plays a core role in the cooperation. Recently, the Asian countries are focusing on building the "East Asian Economic Community" and the core structure of this community is the ASEAN10 countries.

The ASEAN established in 1967 with five original members (Indonesia, Malaysia, Thailand, the Philippines and Singapore) and later added another five (Brunei, Vietnam, Cambodia, Laos and Myanmar). When first established, the ASEAN was a political-oriented organization that functioned as a barrier to stop the influence from the socialist countries, such as the People's Republic of China, the Soviet Union and Vietnam. Later, when China started its economic reform, practices market economy along with the fall of the Soviet Union and the collapse of the Cambodian government aided by Vietnam; the threat of Socialism to Southeast Asia declared its demise.

Gradually, the ASEAN focused less on politics and emphasizes heavily on regional economic integration. The ratio of intra ASEAN economic cooperation (foreign direct investment and international trade) is significantly low compared to the NIEs (Newly Industrializing Economies) and has not been showing much growth. Therefore, the ASEAN cannot restrict its economic development merely in the ASEAN region and the NIEs, it is imperative to expand to the whole Asia-Pacific region to include China, Japan and South Korea, the major countries in East Asia. Conversely, from China, Japan and South Korea's perspective, the ASEAN is the only powerful country union in the Asia-Pacific region, so it is also imperative for them to strengthen economic ties with the ASEAN10.

From the ASEAN's perspective, CAFTA, JAFTA, KAFTA and IAFTA are all ASEAN plus 1. On one hand, China, Japan, South Korea and India are actively seeking cooperation with individual countries within ASEAN, and on the other hand, they are also seeking to strengthen economic ties with ASEAN as a whole. Earlier, strong opposition and confrontations existed within ASEAN, because ASEAN countries proposed that individual members should not sign FTAs or EPAs with other countries outside the region. However, since Singapore signed an EPA with Japan, most other member countries have followed Singapore's lead and signed agreements with other countries, especially with Japan.

Would the FTA or EPA between two countries promote or interfere with the ASEAN10 plus 1 agreement? In other words, would unilateralism promote multilateralism, would ASEAN as a whole with East Asian countries be more beneficial for ASEAN? The answer is positive. As long as the ASEAN reaches any agreement with one of the East Asian countries, the ASEAN countries must separately and actively seeking FTA or EPA with the East Asian countries, forming ASEAN10 plus 1 or progressively forming ASEAN10 plus 3. The ultimate goal of the East Asian multilateral cooperation is eventually forming the East Asian Economic Community.

Conclusion

The political situation in East Asian countries is considered stable, and the countries are actively signing FTAs and EPAs. Currently, China, Japan, South Korea and India play important roles in East Asian multilateral cooperation. Comparably, even though Russia has major political and military power, its economy is stagnating. Thus, Russia cannot play as an important role as other East Asian countries in this integration process. China has been reforming its economy for the past 29 years and has shown a significant improvement and continues to grow. Japan, the world's major economy, has been showing signs of revival after the bubble burst 16 years ago. Thus, Japan is considered the axis in the East Asian integration. As for South Korea, the impact of the 1997 financial crisis was considered severe. After a series of economic reforms in the financial industry, the economy has been recovering even though there are still problems existing in the country. The economic strength of South Korea cannot be ignored in East Asian multilateral cooperation. As for India, the rapid economic development over the last decade has attracted much attention. India has been actively participating and has played an increasingly important role in East Asian economic cooperation and integration in recent years.

Overall, China and Japan are considered the main propellers pushing for East Asian multilateral cooperation and economic community, and South Korea and Russia function as the cushion. Right now, the economic strength of China cannot be compared with that of Japan. However, in the mid to long term perspective, China will certainly be Japan's major competitor. China and Japan will definitely be fighting for leadership in East Asian multilateral cooperation. How China and Japan will work together to progress is an important subject to study.

Besides East Asian multilateral cooperation, the ASEAN10 will be the one that East Asian countries are after. The role of the ASEAN10 in Asia is significant, and the failure or success of the multilateral cooperation or integration depends on how East Asian countries build relations with the ASEAN10. Conversely, the ASEAN10 will also become more dependent on China, Japan, South Korea and India. Thus, such a mutually supporting relationship is definitely beneficial to the development of the ASEAN economies.

CHAPTER 19

With Great Power Comes Great Responsibility[1]

When Chinese President Hu Jintao made an official visit to the United States in April 2006, he was invited to a reception held in his honor at the home of Microsoft Corp. Chairman Bill Gates. It was most uncommon for the top leader of a major power to visit the residence of an executive of a private company.

According to reports, also present at the party was Howard Schultz, chairman of the U.S.-based international coffee shop chain Starbucks Corp. Perhaps out of courtesy to show his respect to top U.S. business leaders, Hu paid lip service and said: "If I can find the time, I wish to visit a Starbucks in Beijing to have a cup of coffee." His comment drew laughter.

On July 13, Starbucks announced the closing of a coffee shop it has operated inside Beijing's Forbidden City, which is a UNESCO World Heritage site. The coffee shop opened in 2000 at the invitation of the administrators of the Forbidden City. In the seven years since then, it has enjoyed a thriving business.

But an online campaign led by a well-known Chinese television newscaster who wrote in his blog that the presence of the Western shop does not match well with traditional Chinese culture triggered mass protests and virtually forced Starbucks to withdraw from the historic site.

I visited the Forbidden City in late June. The Starbucks there did not have the familiar white and green circular sign hanging outside to lure customers. Rather, it maintained a low profile so as to not stand out. The shop occupied a corner of a section where souvenirs are sold. The day I visited, three attendants were busily serving customers.

There was always a queue of about 10 people waiting to be served amid the aroma of fresh coffee. Outside the shop, more than 10 Americans and a couple of Japanese were chatting holding Starbucks beverages. As the Forbidden City attracts hundreds of thousands of tourists from around the world, there was a constant stream of people lining up to buy Starbucks products. Although it was a small cafe that measured about 3 meters by 1.5 with only a counter, the rent and turnover must have been very high.

The decision to close the coffee shop had nothing to do with its performance since it was doing very well. I have no choice but to deduce that it was forced to go out of business because public opinion reached the conclusion that it does not blend well with traditional Chinese culture.

At the risk of making an overstatement, I think the Chinese public felt uncomfortable with the presence of a Starbucks, a symbol of Western culture, within the grounds of the Forbidden City, which they regard as the symbol of their cultural heritage. While China advocates a socialist market economy, the controversy shows there are cases in which socialism and the market economy are incompatible.

Image Crisis

Meanwhile, the Chinese food culture and eating habits are undergoing drastic changes as stories of countless harmful products are continually exposed. They include vegetables with large amounts of residual pesticides, processed seafood products that contain harmful substances, fake salt and mineral water, watered down wine, cooking oil made from waste oil and soy sauce made from human hair.

There is a restaurant in my neighborhood in Tokyo that serves eel imported from China. I used to go there twice a week but since I heard that banned antibiotic substances were found in Chinese eel products, I stopped going there.

In China, a nation of 1.3 billion people, some dishonest dealers are developing criminal activities driven by greed. They must be severely punished by law for causing great damage to China's international image. Unless the Chinese government takes a firm stand to regulate, control and crack down on such crime over a long period, it cannot expect to recover national honor.

Food is not the only problem. Such Chinese-made products as toothpaste, toys, clothing and earthen pots were also found to contain substances harmful to human health. Furthermore, some brands of dieting products, home appliances, cars and tires were also reported to be defective. With regard to intellectual property, phony brand-name products in the form of watches, bags, wallets and clothes are openly sold on street corners.

Once when I was walking down a street, a vendor stopped me and tried to sell an imitation Louis Vuitton product, saying, "This one looks more authentic than the real thing. We also have originally designed products that Louis Vuitton does not carry."

Meanwhile, plagiarism of a doctor's thesis by a popular professor of a well-known Chinese university also came to light. The unauthorized use of American and Japanese cartoon characters, including Disney characters, by the state-run Shijingshan Amusement Park in suburban Beijing is also an example of serious intellectual property infringement.

While it may also be true to some extent that foreign media organizations are overreacting and making sensational reports with exaggeration, Chinese authorities must seriously deal with the situation to prevent similar occurrences.

China has become the world's third largest trading power after the United States and Germany. Its exports alone amount to about $1 trillion. With a huge trade surplus, it is buying U.S. government bonds, building foreign currency reserves and merging and buying foreign companies by promoting overseas investments in earnest. Through such activities, it has grown from a regional economic power to a major international one. If poor quality Chinese products inundate the market, the situation would greatly undermine international trust toward Chinese products and could cause immeasurable damage to international trade.

International Spotlight

China will be hosting the Beijing Summer Olympics in 2008 and the Shanghai Expo in 2010. Millions of tourists from around the world are expected to visit China for these major international events. If mass food poisoning or fatal accidents occur, it could develop into a serious international problem. If athletes of international sporting events or officials of international projects get injured, the situation would not only have a serious impact on China's international reputation but could put Beijing into an extremely awkward position in global society. China is urged to show international accountability.

In that sense, in addition to enforcing strong legal measures against violators by the central government and policymakers, China is also urged to advance moral education for the entire nation. I have no choice but to say that unless China can instill a sense of social responsibility in citizens, it would not be recognized by international society as a major economic power.

Note
1   Reprinted from *Asahi Shimbun*, 1 August 2007, with kind permission of the publisher.

Select Bibliography

Arthur D. Little Inc., *The Japanese Non-Tariff Barrier Issue: American View and the Implications for Japan-US Trade Relations* (Tokyo: National Institute for Research Advancement, 1979).

Akrasanee, N. and Rieger, H.C., eds., *ASEAN-EEC Economic Relations* (Singapore: Institute of Southeast Asian Studies, 1982).

Ajia Keizai Kenkyuzyo [Institute of Developing Economies], *Ajia Keizai* [Asian Economies] XXIV, nos. 10–11 (October–November 1983).

Asahi Shimbun (various issues).

Asiaweek (various issues).

APIC, issue 54 (Tokyo: Kokusai Kyoryoku Suisin Kyokai [Association for the Promotion of International Co-operation], 25 September 1982).

Cai Can Wen, ed., *Ru He Da Kai Riben Shichang* [How to Penetrate the Japanese Market] (Taiwan: Jing Ji Ri Bao She, 1984).

Chee Peng Lim and Lee Poh Ping, *The Role of Japanese Direct Investment in Malaysia*, Occasional Paper, No. 60 (Singapore: Institute of Southeast Asian Studies, 1979).

Chng Meng Kng, Linda Low and Toh Mun Heng, *Industrial Restructuring in Singapore* (Singapore: Chopmen Publishers, 1988).

Chusho Kigyo-cho [Board of Small and Medium-sized Businesses], *Chusho Kigyo Hakusho* [White Paper on Small and Medium-sized Businesses] (Tokyo, various years).

Daily Yomiuri (Tokyo, 17 May 1982).

Department of Statistics, *Monthly Digest of Statistics* (Singapore, 1991).

Department of Statistics, *Economic and Social Statistics* (1960–1982) (Singapore, 1983).

Economic Development Board, *Yearbook* (Singapore, various years).

Editorial Staff, "Naze Ima Jyapan Fuiba Nanoka" [Why Is It Japan Fever Now?], *Kokusai Kaihatsu Jyanaru* [International Development Journal], no. 311 (Tokyo, May 1982).

Embassy of the US, *American Investment: Singapore* (unpublished paper) (Singapore, June 1985).

Fiscal Bulletin of the International Students Institute (Tokyo, various issues).

Foreign Affairs Malaysia, 16, no. 1 (Kuala Lumpur: Ministry of Foreign Affairs, March 1983).

Galenson, Walter, ed., *Foreign Trade and Investment: Economic Growth in the Newly Industrializing Asian Countries* (University of Wisconsin Press, 1985).

Hanada Mitsuyo, "Mareisha Fudo no Naka no Nikkei Kigyo" [Japanese Enterprises in Malaysia's Climate], *Kokusai Kaihatsu Jyanaru* [International Development Journal], no. 311 (Tokyo, May 1982).

Hayashi Risuke, "Ryoba no Ken-Maleisha no Toho Seisaku" [A Double-edged Sword — Malaysia's Look East Policy], *Toyo Keizai* (Tokyo, 4 June 1993).

Hayashi Risuke, "Tonan-Ajia no Shinjyo-sei to Nihon" [Japan and New Trends in Southeast Asia], *Keizai Kyoryoku*, no. 144 (Tokyo, 25 September 1983).

Hiramatsu Kenji, "Mareisha-Kindai-ka e Maishin" [Malaysia — Towards Modernization], *Nihon Keizai Shimbun* (Tokyo, 8 October 1982).

Huh Kyung-Mo, *Japan's Trade in Asia* (New York, 1966).

Ichimura, Shinichi, ed., *Nihon Kigyo in Ajia* [Japanese Enterprises in Asia] (Tokyo: Toyo Keizai Shimpo-sha, 1980).

Ichimura, Shinichi, "Debt Problems of Developing Countries and the Asian Perspective", Paper presented at the 14th Pacific Trade and Development Conference in Singapore, 18–21 June, 1984.

Institute of Southeast Asian Studies, "Japan in ASEAN: Potential Trade Frictions", *ASEAN Economic Bulletin*, vol. 1, no. 2 (Singapore, November 1984).

International Monetary Fund (IMF), *Directory of Trade Statistics*, various issues.

International Energy Journal, *Petroleum Economist* (London, February 1984).

Japan Trade Centre, *Bulletin*, (Singapore, Feb–Mar 1984).

Japan Times (various issues).

JETRO, *Hakusho Toshi-hen* [JETRO White Paper on Investment] (Tokyo, various years).

JETRO, *White Paper on International Trade*, (Tokyo, various issues).

JETRO, *Shingaporu ni Okeru Nikkei Shinshutsu Kigyo no Gensei* [The Present Situation of Japanese Affiliated Firms in Singapore] (publisher unknown, 1981).

Jomo Kwame Sundaram, ed., *The Sun Also Sets — Lessons in Looking East* (Kuala Lumpur: Institute for Social Analysis, 1983).

Jyukagaku Kogyo Simpo (Tokyo, various issues).

Kawata, T., *Kezai Masatsu* [Economic Frictions] (Tokyo, 1982).

Keizai Koho Centre [Japan Institute of Social and Economic Affairs], *Japan, An International Comparison* (Tokyo, various years).

Kimura Michio, "Sen Kyuhyaku Hachi-Jyu-Ni Nen no Mareisha" [Malaysia in the Year 1982], in *Ajia Chuto Doko Nempo* [An Annual Report on the Trends in Asia and the Middle East] (Tokyo: Institute of Developing Economies, 31 March 1983).

Kojima Kiyoshi, "Non-Tariff Barriers to Japan's Trade", *Hitotsubashi Journal of Economics* (Tokyo, June 1980).

Kojima Kiyoshi and Komiya Ryutaro, *Nihon No Hi-Kanzei-Syoheki* [Japanese NTBs] (Tokyo: Nihon Keizai Shimbun-sha, 1972).

Kokusai Kyoryoku Tokubetsu Jyoho, 8 (Tokyo: Association for Promotion of International Co-operation).

Krause, Lawrence B., et al., *The Singapore Economy Reconsidered* (Singapore: Institute of Southeast Asian Studies, 1987).

Kunio Yoshihara, *Foreign Investment and Domestic Response* (Singapore: Institute of Southeast Asian Studies, 1976).

Lianhe Zaobao (Singapore, various issues).

Lim Chong Yah and Associates, *Policy Options for the Singapore Economy* (Singapore: McGraw-Hill Book Company, 1988).

Lim Hua Sing, "Dongya Jingjiquan" [East Asian Economic Integration] (New Edition) (In Chinese), (Shijie Zhishi Chubanshe, Beijing), June 2007.

Lim Hua Sing, ed., "Pouxi Dongya Jingji" [East Asian Economies Reexamined] (In Chinese), (World Scientific Publishing, Singapore), January 2006.

Lim Hua Sing, ed., "Dongmeng Riben Yu Zhongguoren Diqu Hezuo" [Economic Cooperation Among ASEAN, Japan and Chinese Communities] (In Chinese), (World Scientific Publishing, Singapore), December 2003.

Lim Hua Sing, *Ajia Yongkyoku Keizai* [The Four-Polar Economy of Asia] (In Japanese), (Daimond, Tokyo), July 1995.

Lim Hua Sing, *ASEAN Keizai No Chikaku Hendou* [The Diastrophism of the ASEAN Economies] (In Japanese), (Dobunkan, Tokyo), November 1993.

Look Japan (Tokyo, various years).

Ministry of Foreign Affairs, ASEAN (Tokyo, March 1982).

Ministry of Foreign Affairs, *Statistical Survey of Japan's Economy* (Japan, 1981).

Ministry of Foreign Affairs, *Waga Gaiko no Kinkyo* [The Recent State of Our Foreign Policies] (Japan, November 1980, 1982, 1983).

Ministry of Trade and Industry, *Economic Survey of Singapore* (Singapore, various years).

Motoyama, Y., *Boeki Masatsu wo Miru me* [Trade Frictions], (Tokyo, December 1983).

Muto Ichiyo, "The Sun Also Sets", *Far Eastern Economic Review*, 8 September 1983.

New Straits Times (Malaysia, various issues).

Nihon Kanzei Kyokai [Japan Customs Association], *Keizai Masatsu to Nihon no Tai-o* [Economic Frictions and Japan's Response] (Tokyo, 1982).

Nihon Keizai Shimbun (Tokyo, various issues).

Nihon Shingaporu Kyokai [Japan–Singapore Association], *Shingaporu no Nikkei Kigyo* [Japanese Business Activities in Singapore] (Tokyo, 1986).

Nomura Research Institute, *Nomura Ajia Joho* [Noruma's Information on Asia] (Tokyo, 1987).

Okita, S., *Sekai Keizai Shindan* [To Diagnose the World Economy] (Tokyo, 1983).

Okura-sho [Ministry of Finance], *Zaisei Kinyu Tokei Geppo* [Statistics on Finance–Monthly Bulletin] (Tokyo, various years).

Organization of Petroleum Exporting Countries (OPEC), *Annual Statistical Bulletin of OPEC 1983* (Vienna, Austria, 1993).

Pang Eng Fong, *Education, Manpower and Development in Singapore* (Singapore: Singapore University Press, 1982).

Peat Marwick, *Shingaporu Zeisei, Kaikei Seido, Kaisha-ho no Gaiyo* [Taxation, Accounting and Company Law in Singapore] (Singapore, 1986).

Pohl, M., ed., *Japan 1980/81: Politics and Economy*, (Singapore: Maruzen Asia, 1981).

Sekiguchi, Suco, ed., *ASEAN–Japan Relations: Investment* (Singapore: Institute of Southeast Asian Studies, 1983).

Straits Times, various issues.

Suzuki Yuzi, "Atarashii Kadai to Look East" [A New Task and Look East], in *Tonanajia no Kiki no Kozo* [The Critical Structure of Southeast Asia] (Tokyo: Keiso Shobo, 1982).

Suzuki Yuzi, "Mahatiru Shusho no Kodo no Genten wo Sagura" [In Search of the Basis of Premier Mahathir's Policy], in *Tonanajia no Kiki no Kozo* (Tokyo: Keiso Shobo, 1982).

Toyo Keizai Shimposha, *Kaigai Shinshutsu Soran* [Japanese Overseas Companies-Facts and Figures] (Tokyo, various years).

Tsusho Sangyo-sho [Ministry of International Trade and Industry], *Tsusho Hakusho* [White Paper on International Trade] (Tokyo, July 1983).

Wee Mon-Cheng, *Economic Diplomacy in the Land of the Cherry Blossom* (Singapore: MPH Distributors, 1977).

Yoshihara, K., *Foreign Investment and Domestic Response* (Singapore: Eastern Universities Press, 1976).

You Poh Seng and Lim Chong Yah, eds., *Singapore: Twenty-five Years of Development* (Singapore: Nan Yang Xing Zhou Lianhe Zaobao, 1984).

Index

www.ingramcontent.com/pod-product-compliance
Lightning Source LLC
Chambersburg PA
CBHW021844020426
42334CB00013B/184